D0172324

Pakistan

Pakistan
Eye of the Storm

Second Edition

Owen Bennett Jones

NB Yale Nota Bene
Yale University Press New Haven and London

First published in 2002 by Yale University Press
This Nota Bene edition published in 2003 by Yale Univesity Press

Copyright © 2002 by Owen Bennett Jones
New material to second edition copyright © 2003 by Owen Bennett Jones

For information about this and other Yale University Press publications, please contact:
U.S. Office: sales.press@yale.edu; yalebooks.com
Europe Office: sales@yaleup.co.uk; www.yaleup.co.uk

Set in Columbus by Northern Phototypesetting Co. Ltd, Bolton, UK
Printed in the United States of America

The Library of Congress has catalogued the previous edition as follows:
Jones, Owen Bennett. Pakistan: eye of the storm / Owen Bennett Jones. p. cm. Includes
bibliographical references and index. ISBN 0–300–09760–3 (cloth: alk. paper) 1.
Pakistan—History. I. Title. DS382 .J66 2002   954.91—dc21   2002006944

ISBN 0–300–10147–3 (pbk.)

A catalogue record for this book is available from the British Library.

10 9 8 7 6 5 4 3 2 1

Plate captions: (5) Stanley Wolpert, *Zulfi Bhutto of Pakistan: His Life and Times*, Oxford
University Press, New York, 1993, p. 60; (6) Confidential telegram from the American
consulate in Karachi to the US State Department, July 1971; (7) *Guardian*, 16 May 2001;
(8) Stanley Wolpert, *Zulfi Bhutto of Pakistan: His Life and Times*, Oxford University Press,
New York, 1993, p. 325; (9) Benazir Bhutto's speech to the US Committee for Human
Rights, 30 May 1999; (10) *Guardian*, 16 May 2001; (15) *Hindustan Times*, 19 July 2001.

For my parents

Contents

Illustrations

Plates

Maps

Designed with the help of the Army Press, Rawalpindi

Tables

Figures

Cartoons

Preface

Pakistan is an easy place for a journalist to work. Most Pakistanis, from policemen to politicians, shopkeepers to soldiers, love to talk about politics. Admittedly, the more they know the less willing they are to speak on the record but nevertheless Pakistan remains a very open country. Indeed, Pakistan's willingness to tolerate the scrutiny of local and foreign journalists is one of the reasons it has an image problem. Countries such as Saudi Arabia manage to avoid hostile media coverage simply by refusing to grant journalists sufficient access to do their work.

My first thanks, then, are to the many Pakistanis who were so willing to share their views with a foreign visitor. I should mention in particular the BBC's long-standing Islamabad correspondent Zaffar Abbas, who was remarkably generous with both his time and his unrivalled knowledge of Pakistan. For over a decade now, he has had the unenviable task of explaining the finer points of Pakistani politics to successive BBC correspondents sent from London. Beyond expressing my thanks, all I can say is that I look forward, one day, to reading a book written by him.

I would also like to record my thanks to Shahid Abbasi, Idrees Bakhtiar, Amit Baruah, Jaffar Bilgrami, Admiral (Retd.) Fasih Bokhari, Cecil Chaudhry, Paul Danahar, Karen Davies, Michael and Kim Keating, Ms. Ha, Hussain Haqqani, Mishal Husain, Abida Hussain, Mushahid Hussain, Talat Hussain, Fakhar Imam, Chris and Valerie

Kaye, Saleem Khan, Tanvir Ahmed Khan, Shahid Malik, Farooq Memon, Jugnu Mohsin, Niaz Naik, Abbas Nasir, Bob Nickelsberg, Richard Parrack, Haroon Rashid, Brigadier Saulat Raza, Najam Sethi, Akhter Shah, Sydney Sober, Brigadier (Retd.) Shaukat Qadir, Andrew Whitehead, Ali Faisal Zaidi and S. Akbar Zaidi.

Jaleel Akhtar did a tremendous job in responding to my ceaseless requests for books, figures and various documents.

Last, but by no means least, thanks to my wife Amanda for her support throughout the time I was writing this book. An editor by profession, she not only improved the text but also ensured I had the time necessary to complete the task.

Introduction to the Second Edition

The twelve months that have passed since the hardback edition of this book was published have been as turbulent as ever for Pakistan. In the summer of 2002 as many as a million soldiers massed at the Indo-Pakistani border and the two countries nearly went to war. There was also intense military activity on Pakistan's border with Afghanistan. The American military, fighting in neighbouring Afghanistan, regularly crossed into Pakistan in hot pursuit of suspected members of the Taliban and Al Qaeda. Meanwhile, inside Pakistan, Islamic militants mounted a number of murderous attacks. The parliament had been restored after the general election and General Musharraf held a referendum that gave him five more years in power and also introduced far-reaching constitutional changes.

The referendum, held in April 2002, posed the following, heavily-loaded question: 'For the survival of the local government system, establishment of democracy, continuity of reforms, end to sectarianism and extremism, and to fulfil the vision of Quaid-e-Azam, would you like to elect President General Pervez Musharraf as President of Pakistan for five years?' The outcome of the referendum was never in question. Some public sector workers were threatened with redundancy if they failed to vote and public funds were lavishly distributed for Musharraf's election rallies. The final result gave Musharraf no fewer than 97 per cent of the votes cast. The rigging was so obvious that, afterwards, General

Musharraf felt it necessary to issue a muted apology for the 'over enthusiasm' of some of his election officials.

The poll left no doubt that General Musharraf intended to break his promise to hand power back to the civilians after three years. After the 1999 coup, under considerable international pressure, he had committed himself to holding parliamentary elections in October 2002. His challenge was to work out how to allow the election of a parliament while at the same time remaining in charge. A referendum seemed to be the best answer. He calcualted that should the parliament try to challenge his legitimacy he would be able to argue that he had a direct mandate from the people. Many people have criticised General Musharraf's decision to hold a referendum. But it was not just an exercise in political vanity. If he was to remain in power then the referendum was an attractive and practical option. Opinion polls in the run-up to the vote showed that Musharraf did enjoy widespread popular support with an approval rating of 60 per cent. Even if many people had reservations about his policy of backing the United States' 'war on terrorism', they also realised that Pakistan had little choice and the General did manage to secure significant amounts of aid and debt relief. Furthermore, many Pakistanis supported General Musharraf's statements against Islamic extremists and they thought that his regime was notably less corrupt than the civilian administration of the 1990s.

The problem was not so much the decision to hold a referendum as the way in which it was conducted. The blatant rigging meant that, to a large extent, the exercise backfired. Many Pakistani intellectuals who had been enthusiastic about the 1999 coup began to worry that Musharraf might be no different from Pakistan's previous military rulers. The oft-repeated cycle of Pakistani politics was turning once more. The elation that greeted the coup was changing into a feeling that perhaps the civilian politicians had not been so bad after all. These difficulties stemmed from the military's unwillingness to take any risks. Rather than taking a chance on whether Musharraf could win an honest contest – and he might well have done – the army decided that victory had to be certain.

Having declared victory in the referendum the General went a step further. In August 2002 – by Presidential decree – he introduced a Legal

Framework Order (LFO) consisting of no fewer than twenty-nine constitutional amendments. He argued that the Supreme Court, in validating his coup, had given him the authority to alter the Constitution and that as a result there would be no need to refer his amendments to the new parliament. The LFO had far-reaching consequences. Amongst other things it gave the President the right to appoint Supreme Court judges and military commanders. It also institutionalised the role of the army. The military-dominated National Security Council was given to recommend the government's dismissal.

The army, then, was in control, and the October 2002 elections were only ever intended to provide the regime with a democratic veneer. But managing the election process was not easy. The army wanted a parliament that would not, and indeed could not, mount a significant challenge. While the LFO gave the military legal cover, the army also wanted to ensure that the majority of the members of the new parliament would be relatively pliant. It employed a number of mechanisms to achieve that outcome. It encouraged divisions in the Muslim League, the party led by Nawaz Sharif. Within days of Musharraf's coup some senior members of the Muslim League had shown a willingness to accommodate themselves to what they correctly presumed would be a long period of military rule. Others in the party – a minority – remained loyal to the ousted Prime Minister and demanded a return to full democracy. By the time of the 2002 election, with the army's help, that underlying tension had split the Muslim League in two.

The Muslim League had always been a pro-establishment party and it was not difficult for the army to persuade some of its senior members to start co-operating with the military regime. Those inclined to do so formed the Muslim League (Q) while the Sharif loyalists became members of the Muslim League (N). In the run-up to the National Assembly elections the army concentrated on the task of hindering the Muslim League (N) candidates. By increasing the number of seats in the National Assembly from 207 to 272, for example, the military was able to redraw constituencies to suit favoured candidates. And since many National Assembly candidates were vulnerable to corruption allegations the army was also able to threaten prospective members with exposure and court cases should they step out of line.

The army's plans, however, depended on one other factor: the need to prevent Nawaz Sharif or Benazir Bhutto returning from exile to run an election campaign. General Musharraf feared that either leader might be able to mobilise significant public support for a return to democracy and various obstacles were put in their way. For example, a decree was passed stating that no Prime Minister could have a third term in office even if they had failed to complete their first two terms. The ruling prevented both Sharif and Bhutto (and nobody else) from standing. A whole series of different legal measures with the same objective were forced through but perhaps the most persuasive method was the army's clear warning that if either Bhutto or Sharif did return they would face immediate arrest on corruption charges. In the event, as the army calculated, neither was willing to undergo a period of imprisonment in order to play the role of political martyr in the hope of eventually forcing the military out of power.

From the army's point of view these meticulous preparations paid off. Neither the Pakistan People's Party (PPP) with seats nor the Muslim League (N) with just 14 was able to form a majority. The single largest party, as the army had hoped, was the Muslim League (Q) with 77 seats. The surprise came from a coalition of five religious parties, the Muttahida Majlis-e-Amal (MMA), which won 60 seats (up from two in the previous Assembly), enough to make it the main opposition party in the National Assembly. It was a striking result but most commentators have overstated its importance. While the MMA won 20 per cent of the seats in the National Assembly, across Pakistan as a whole it won only 11.1 per cent of the vote, and mainly in northern Balochistan and North West Frontier Province (NWFP). The location of the MMA's support base was significant. Many of its voters were not so much voting for Islamic government as protesting against the continued US military presence in nearby Afghanistan and, in particular, against US-led operations within Pakistan. Furthermore, the first-past-the-post electoral system gave a false impression of the MMA's backing. It is true that the MMA did attract some support because its five constituent parties had, for once, overcome their sectarian differences. Nevertheless, the vast bulk of the Pakistani people – over 88 per cent – voted for mainstream parties. It is also worth noting that, for the religious parties, the October 2002 result was not as good as the 14 per cent they had won in 1970.

The religious right in Pakistan still has the potential to challenge the army and the secular civilian politicians. The Islamic parties do have a political ideology and they can argue that they are the only political force in Pakistan which has not been given a chance to govern. But for all that the October 2002 elections amounted to minor rather than major progress for them.

Whilst the elections showed that the religious parties remain quite unpopular in Pakistan, the events of 2002 in Kashmir demonstrated once again the centrality of the Kashmir dispute in Pakistani politics. In the summer of 2002 Kashmir was the cause of a major military stand-off between India and Pakistan. For several months there were genuine fears that an all-out war would erupt. The immediate cause of the confrontation was India's ultimatum that it would invade Pakistan, or maybe just Pakistani-held Kashmir, if Islamabad did not stop infiltrating militants across the line of control.

India's timing was astute. It hoped that in the post-September 11th atmosphere its long-standing campaign to get the militants in Kashmir defined as terrorists might bear fruit. With fears of a possible nuclear exchange between India and Pakistan the international community became closely involved in trying to calm the tensions between the two countries. India's steadfast refusal to enter serious negotiations over Kashmir was taken as a given. It was Pakistan that came under pressure.

Many Pakistanis felt this was unfair. As one sardonic Pakistani diplomat put it: 'when we gave the West what it wanted after September 11th, we expected we would be betrayed – but not this quickly'. Under intense US pressure General Musharraf did seal the line of control and prevented militants from crossing it. Some of the militants' training camps in Pakistani-held Kashmir were relocated to areas within Pakistan itself and strict controls were placed on the movement of militants. It was a major reversal of a long-standing Pakistani policy and it caused acute resentment within the army and amongst the militant groups.

In June 2002 the British Foreign Secretary, Jack Straw, told the House of Commons in London that there was a clear link between Pakistan's main intelligence agency and the militant groups sending fighters into Kashmir. The government in London had believed this to be true for some years but had hitherto not said so in public. And Mr Straw went further. He described the militants in Kashmir as terrorists and, for good measure, backed India's line that the dispute between India and Pakistan was a bilateral matter. Mindful of the need for Pakistan's co-operation in their war with Al Qaeda, the Americans took a more nuanced line. Whereas Jack Straw wrote off all Kashmir militants as terrorists, the line from Washington (although never explicitly stated) seemed to be that whilst indigenous Kashmiri militants could continue to fight for their liberation from Indian rule, Pakistanis and Arabs involved in the struggle would be classified as terrorists.

Nonetheless it was clear from the outset that, in domestic political terms, General Musharraf would find it very difficult to sustain the policy of sealing the line of control without some reciprocal concessions from Delhi. In absence of any Indian response, however, by September 2002 the militants were, once again, moving across the line of control. From the Pakistani point of view this return to the *status quo ante* amounted to a significant achievement. India had mobilised hundreds of thousands of men and had threatened war to prevent infiltrations. By the end of the summer it was clear that that strategy had failed: the Indian troops had been withdrawn and the infiltrations continued.

The timing of the renewal of the infiltrations was significant: General Musharraf wanted to disrupt Kashmiri elections due to be held in October. India, by contrast, hoped to secure a high turn-out and claim that Indian rule had been endorsed. Hundreds of people were killed during the election campaign and the result was something of a shock. The National Conference lost over half of its seats and was forced to relinquish its long grip on power. The turn-out, at over 40 per cent, was relatively high but it was hardly fair to conclude that this level of participation indicated an acceptance of Indian rule. Many Kashmiris had become so exhausted by the violence that they voted for parties that offered to restrain the security forces and open some kind of dialogue with militants.

In the final chapter of this book I argue that while General Musharraf has a clear idea of the type of reforms he would like to introduce, he has not had much success in implementing them. The events of the last twelve months have confirmed this. Many of his most important policy initiatives such as the tax-raising drive, de-weaponisation and anti-corruption campaigns have all run into the sand. That may be in part because General Musharraf has been forced to focus on another issue: Islamic militancy. As well as having to cope with the Americans' demands for co-operation in searching for Al Qaeda and Taliban activists hiding in Pakistan, there have been a significant number of militant attacks on Pakistani soil. In January 2002 the American journalist Daniel Pearl was kidnapped and later murdered. In March 2002 there was a grenade attack on a church near the US embassy in Islamabad. In May a bomb outside the Sheraton Hotel in Karachi killed fourteen people including eleven French nationals. In June 2002 a bomb exploded outside the US Consulate in Karachi, and in September the police foiled a plot by an offshoot of Harakat ul-Mujahideen to assassinate General Musharraf. There were also attacks on Christian targets in Sialkot and Murree and Taxila.

Given these events it seems remarkable that towards the end of 2002 General Musharraf decided to release from detention some 1,500 militants from Jaish-e-Mohammed and Lashkar-e-Toiba. Those let out included the organisations' two leaders, Mullah Masood Azhar and Hafiz Seed. Others released included members of the Sipah-e-Sahaba, Tehrik-e-Jafria Pakistan and Harakat ul-Mujahideen and Lashkar-e-Jhangvi. There were two factors at play here. First, many of those in detention were low-level activists and the state had no evidence whatsoever that they had been involved in crimes. Second, General Musharraf was concerned that if the militant organisations had so many members behind bars it would not be possible for them to keep up the pressure on the Indian forces in Kashmir. Once again, the army's obsession with Kashmir risked increasing the levels of militancy within Pakistan itself.

Before closing this introduction I would like to highlight one issue which could come to fore in the years ahead. In a speech in Lahore in January 2003 General Musharraf warned that Pakistan could become the US's next target after Iraq. He is worried that Pakistan's record on nuclear proliferation may not stand up to close scrutiny. In October 2002 the *New York Times* published an article that quoted US intelligence officials as saying that since 1997 Pakistan has been a major supplier of equipment for North Korea's nuclear programme. Pakistan vigorously denied the *New York Times*'s report but Musharraf's January speech indicated his fear that this is an issue which will not go away. It is an open secret that Pakistan's Ghauri missile system is an improved version of the North Korean Nodong system. There has always been a question mark over what Pakistan gave North Korea in return for this missile technology and American officials have become increasingly explicit in suggesting that the answer may be nuclear know-how. Any American campaign to disarm North Korea could have significant implications for Pakistan.

Oxford, April 2003

Introduction

Those Pakistanis old enough to remember the advent of independence in 1947 could be forgiven for thinking that they have been in the eye of a storm all their lives. Ever since its creation, Pakistan's political development has been turbulent and chaotic. The country has been under military rule for nearly half its existence. No elected government has ever completed its term in office. It has had three wars with India and has lost around half of its territory. Its economy has never flourished. Nearly half its vast population is illiterate and 20 per cent is undernourished. The country's largest city, Karachi, has witnessed thousands of politically motivated murders. Religious extremists have been given free reign. Pakistan's proximity to Afghanistan, Iran, India and China; its political volatility; and its need for huge foreign loans; have ensured that the country has always been the subject of considerable international concern. But after May 1998, when Pakistan conducted nuclear tests, those concerns became still more acute. Indeed, South Asia's nuclearisation has rendered it one of the most politically sensitive regions on earth and made the dispute over Kashmir one of the world's most potentially dangerous conflicts.

When Britain's last viceroy of India, Lord Louis Mountbatten, organised the partition of India he approved the incorporation of the state of Kashmir into India. Pakistan's insistence that it should have been given control of the Muslim-majority state has given rise to a bloody and debilitating dispute that remains unresolved half a century later. The fight for Kashmir, which began within months of independence, has cost tens of thousands of lives and, arguably, has been the single most significant reason for Pakistan's chronic instability. The dispute has encouraged the growth of militant Islam, drained scarce economic resources and fuelled Pakistan's sense of insecurity about India.

Visitors to Pakistan sometimes wonder why the country should be so 'paranoid' about its southern neighbour. India's image as the world's largest democracy and its success in creating a polity where, for the most part, different religious and ethnic communities can live side by side, leads many to conclude that Pakistan's concerns are irrational. Yet those fears are genuine.

The Kashmir dispute has helped Indo-Pakistani hostility to thrive. But there have also been other factors at play. Immediately after independence many Indian leaders made no secret of their hope that Pakistan would collapse and that the subcontinent would consequently be reunited. The belief of many Pakistanis that India secretly wished to demolish their country was reinforced by the wars of 1965 and 1971. In 1965 Indian forces struck across the international border between the two countries and came close to occupying one of Pakistan's most important cities, Lahore. Of course, the immediate cause of the 1965 war was Pakistan's decision to send in fighters to renew the fight for Kashmir. But to this day, many Pakistanis tend to overlook their own country's role in triggering the crisis and dwell instead on the subsequent Indian invasion.

The 1971 war was an even bigger blow. When Pakistan came into being it was composed of two geographically separate entities, East and West Pakistan, which lay a thousand miles apart.[1] Even Mountbatten predicted that this arrangement could not last for more than twenty-five years. Events fully justified his pessimism. Almost certainly Bangladesh would have come into existence without India's help. The attitude of Pakistan's first generation of politicians, who tended to treat the Bengalis in East Pakistan as little more than colonial subjects, undoubtledly contributed to the break-up of the country. But for all that, India's decision to invade East Pakistan in support of the Bengali independence movement inflicted on Pakistan a humiliation from which it has still not recovered. India's victory left a wound that festers to this day.

If many outside observers fail to appreciate fully Pakistan's sense of insecurity, some Indian leaders have shown greater understanding. In

February 1999 the nationalist Indian prime minister, Atal Behari Vajpayee, accepted an invitation from his Pakistani counterpart, Nawaz Sharif, to visit Lahore. During his trip Vajpayee made a point of visiting the Minar-e-Pakistan, a monument built to mark the spot where, in 1940, the Indian Muslims had first articulated their demand for a separate state. Vajpayee's advisers made it clear that their prime minister had chosen the site deliberately. The Indian leader wanted to show the Pakistani people that Delhi fully accepted their right to live in a separate country. But Vajpayee's attempt at reassurance made little impact. After all, many Pakistanis pointed out, just nine months earlier it was the very same Vajpayee who ordered Indian scientists to conduct nuclear tests.

Because of its sense of vulnerability, Pakistan has always been on the look-out for big-power friends. When, during the cold war, Delhi tilted towards Moscow, Islamabad was quick to see its chance. Pakistan's first military ruler, Ayub Khan, declared Pakistan to be the United States' 'most allied ally'. Twenty years later, another military ruler, General Zia ul Haq, adopted a similar approach. After the Soviet invasion of Afghanistan he ensured that Pakistan became a frontline state in the battle against communism. In 2001 another military man, General Pervez Musharraf, was ruling Pakistan. Within hours of the 11 September attack on the World Trade Center and the Pentagon he remained true to the policies of his predecessors, abandoned his Taliban allies and aligned Pakistan with Washington.

Pakistan's efforts to ingratiate itself with the United States have never produced long-lasting dividends. One of Pakistan's greatest political thinkers, Dr. Eqbal Ahmed, used to liken the relationship between the United States and Pakistan to that of an errant husband and his mistress. When in the mood, the United States would overwhelm Pakistan with loving attention and generous gifts. But the tempestuous relationship was never steady. And when Washington's ardour cooled it would abandon its South Asian partner without a thought. Many Pakistanis consider the US to have been a disloyal, inconstant friend. General Musharraf hopes that, this time, Washington's declarations can be taken at face value. He will almost certainly be disappointed.

Indian strategists have done their best to undermine Pakistan's somewhat desperate search for foreign friends. For years now Delhi has tried to portray Pakistan as a rogue state filled with Islamic extremists hell-bent on exporting terrorism. While this message has resonated neatly with Western anti-Islamic prejudices, I shall argue in this book that such a depiction of Pakistan is unfair. This is not to deny the indisputable fact that successive Pakistani governments have given a remarkable amount of leeway to Islamic extremists. It is an appalling fact, to give just one example, that in recent years Islamic militants have been able to tour Pakistani mosques displaying the heads of Indian security personnel killed in Kashmir. The state's reluctance to rein in the militants has been, in part, a result of the perceived need to support anyone involved in the struggle for Kashmir. But deeper factors have also been at play.

Ever since its creation, Pakistan has grappled with the issue of what role Islam should play in the state. When he called for the establishment of Pakistan, Mohammed Ali Jinnah advanced the two-nation theory. Muslims and Hindus, he argued, constituted two nations that could never live together. A strict interpretation of the two-nation theory has led some Pakistanis to conclude that the country was always intended to be an Islamic state. But others – and in my opinion the majority – have a different view. They believe that Jinnah was trying to create a country in which Muslims could live in safety, free from Hindu dominance. Most Pakistanis do not want to live in a theocracy: they want their country to be moderate, modern, tolerant and stable.

During the 1980s this vision of Pakistan received a substantial setback. General Zia ul Haq – perhaps the only one of Pakistan's four military rulers to deserve the epithet 'dictator' – consistently advanced the cause of radical Islam. The effects of Zia's Islamisation campaign are still being felt today. The militant groups remain well-organised, well-armed and well-financed. The current military ruler, General Musharraf is trying to dismantle Zia's legacy. His attempt to downplay the role of religion in the state directly challenges the interests of well-entrenched and highly motivated elements of Pakistani society. His success or failure – the likelihood of which are discussed in the final chapter – will have far reaching implications not only for Pakistan but also the region and the international security system as a whole.

The Kashmir dispute, the relationships with India and the United States and the need to define the role of Islam are only some of the issues that confront Pakistan today. There are many other serious challenges. The country's most economically important city, Karachi, has for years been plagued by huge displays of politically motivated violence. In some out-lying rural areas, where feudal landlords rule like kings, many people feel greater loyalty to their province than they do to Pakistan. The army's willingness to overthrow civilian governments has stifled democratic development. The very high levels of corruption have led many Pakista-nis to become deeply disillusioned with their ruling elite.

Countless newspaper articles have been written on these issues. But for those who want to acquire a deeper understanding of Pakistan there are only a handful of books to consult. Two of them are by journalists. Emma Duncan's beautifully written *Breaking the Curfew* and Christina Lamb's *Waiting for Allah* are well worth reading. But both were pub-lished over a decade ago and are inevitably somewhat out of date. More recently, two Western academics have written histories of Pakistan. Lawrence Ziring's *Pakistan in the Twentieth Century* and Ian Talbot's *Pakistan: A Modern History* both cover the period from 1947 until the late 1990s and while both are comprehensive accounts, they are very much works for a scholarly readership.

Although I spent two and half years as a journalist travelling around Pakistan, this is not a journalistic memoir. It is a history of Pakistan. By avoiding political science jargon and a theoretical approach I have tried to bridge the gap between the academic histories of Ziring and Talbot and the journalistic accounts of Duncan and Lamb. Unlike Ziring and Talbot I have not dealt with the subject matter chronologically. Pakistan faces many critical issues which lend themselves neatly to a thematic approach. I hope that readers who want to know about a particular issue, for example, Kashmir or the nuclear programme will find this arrangement convenient.

Any Western, and in particular British, author writing about Pakistan is undertaking a hazardous exercise. With considerable justification many Pakistanis resent the way they have been portrayed by outsiders. I can only hope that those Pakistanis who read this book will think it provides a less biased picture of their country than is generally put for-ward. I should perhaps add that I have always had relatively limited ambitions for this book. I am not trying to offer any 'new theory' of Pakistan and most well-informed Pakistanis will be familiar with much of the subject matter. The real target for this book is non-Pakistanis who want to understand more about an important and underrated country.

Note on Spellings

In transliterating words from Urdu and Pakistan's other languages I have tried to strike a balance between reflecting the local pronunciation and finding a spelling that eases comprehension for a Western reader. To give an example, I favour the simpler spelling 'madrasa' over one possible alternative, 'madrassah'.

Names can be, and often are, spelt in several different ways. I have opted for the spelling preferred by the person being referred to with one exception. In the interests of consistency I have used the standard 'Mohammed' even if the bearer of that name has used a different spelling. I have not, however, standardised the spelling where it refers to an author of a printed book mentioned in my text or listed in the bibliography.

The word Baloch refers to the people, Balochi to the language. In line with official usage in contemporary Pakistan I shall use Baloch and Balochi rather than the British imperial versions Baluch and Baluchi. Similarly, in line with official usage, I prefer Sindh to Sind and Sindhi to Sindi.

Pathan, Pushtoon or Pukhtoon? I favour Pukhtoon on the grounds that it is closer to local pronunciation in North West Frontier Province. Similarly, Pukhto for the language. In line with contemporary usage in Pakistan I refer to the dreamt-of Pukhtoon homeland as Pukhtoonkwa throughout the text.

All other place names are according to the *Times Atlas of the World*. In cases where I quote extracts from passages of text I have kept to the original spelling.

Chronology

1947	Independence of Pakistan
	Start of the first war in Kashmir
1948	Death of the founder of Pakistan, Mohammed Ali Jinnah
1952	Language riots in East Pakistan
1953	Anti-Ahmedi riots lead to the imposition of martial law in Lahore
1955	West Pakistan provinces are amalgamated into 'One Unit'
1956	Pakistan's first constitution is passed
1958	General Ayub Khan takes over in the first military coup
1959	The capital moves from Karachi to Islamabad
1965	Second war with India over Kashmir
1966	Bengali leader Mujibur Rahman publishes his Six Points
1969	General Yayha Khan takes over from General Ayub Khan
1970	First ever national elections are held in East and West Pakistan
1971	War in East Pakistan leads to the creation of Bangladesh
	Zulfikar Ali Bhutto comes to power
1972	Zulfikar Ali Bhutto signs the Simla accord
	Zulfikar Ali Bhutto calls on Pakistani scientists to build a nuclear bomb
1973	Start of Baloch uprising demanding greater autonomy
1974	First Indian nuclear test
1977	General Zia ul Haq takes over in a coup
1979	Zulfikar Ali Bhutto hanged
	Soviet invasion of Afghanistan
1984	Siachin conflict begins
1986	MQM formally registered as a party
1988	General Zia killed in an air crash
	Benazir Bhutto begins first administration
	Start of Kashmir insurgency
	Soviets withdraw from Afghanistan

1990	Benazir Bhutto's first administration is dismissed
	Nawaz Sharif begins first administration
1993	Nawaz Sharif's first administration is dismissed
1994	Benazir Bhutto begins second administration
1996	Benazir Bhutto's second administration is dismissed
	Taliban come to power in Afghanistan
1997	Nawaz Sharif begins second administration
1998	India and Pakistan conduct nuclear tests
1999	Kargil conflict in Kashmir
	General Musharraf takes over from Nawaz Sharif in a coup
2001	General Musharraf abandons Taliban regime in Afghanistan
2002	Musharraf wins referendum allowing him to stay in power for a further five years

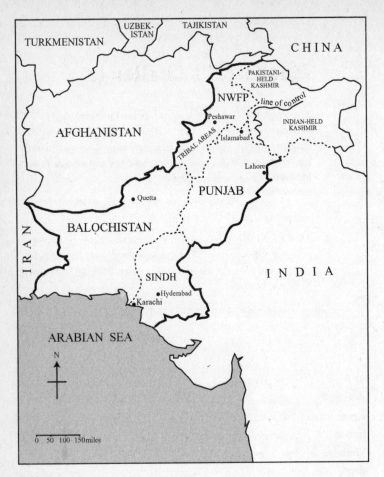

Pakistan, 2001

1 Musharraf's Challenge

Some scholars and religious leaders are inclined towards
making emotional decisions . . . They are poised to create
dissensions and damage the country. There is no reason why
this minority should be allowed to hold the sane majority as a
hostage.

—General Pervez Musharraf, 19 September 2001

If the 1.8 million students of the religious schools come out
onto the streets today for the implementation of the rule of
Sharia law in the country, no power on earth could stop them.
Not even the 0.6 million strong army of Pakistan.

—Islamic activist Ali Bin Mawiya, writing in *Al-Muslim*,
September 2001

At 8.55 a.m. on the morning of 11 September 2001 an American Airlines
Boeing 767 tore into the North Tower of New York's World Trade
Center at 400 miles per hour. Eighteen minutes later another 767 crashed
into the South Tower. And then a third plane was seen approaching
Washington. Just a few miles outside the city it suddenly made a 270-
degree turn and lined up on the Pentagon. At 9.43 a.m. the nose went
down and the plane ploughed through the heart of America's military
industrial complex.

It took just a few hours for the US administration to conclude that the
attacks had probably originated from Afghanistan and that any effective
counter-attack would require the co-operation of Pakistan. On the afternoon of 11 September Pakistan's ambassador to Washington, Maleeha
Lodhi, was in her office watching television coverage of the twin towers
attack. With her was Lt. General Mehmood who, as a reward for his leading role in General Musharraf's 1999 coup, had been made the director
general of Pakistan's main intelligence agency, Inter Service Intelligence,

or ISI. Mehmood had just completed an official visit to Washington but his return to Pakistan had been delayed because, following the attacks, all the airspace around New York had been closed. The State Department called the embassy at 5.00 p.m. Lodhi and Mehmood were asked to attend a meeting with senior US officials the next morning.

At 8.00 a.m. on 12 September the US deputy secretary of state, Richard Armitage, told the two Pakistanis that their country had to make a choice. Islamabad could align itself with the Taliban regime in Afghanistan or with Washington. 'You are either 100 per cent with us or 100 per cent against us,' he said. 'There is no grey area.'[1] Straight after the meeting Mehmood called Islamabad and spoke to General Musharraf. Pakistan's military leader made a snap decision. He told Mehmood that Washington would get what it wanted. At 3.00 p.m. Armitage held a second meeting with Lodhi and Mehmood. This time he had more specific demands. The US would need basic logistical support and a high degree of intelligence co-operation. Mehmood assured Armitage that Pakistan would co-operate.

Musharraf may have taken his decision quickly but he abandoned the Taliban with some reluctance. Before 11 September he had consistently supported Mullah Mohammed Omar's Kandahar regime. This was not because he sympathised with the Taliban's interpretation of Islam (on the contrary, he clearly rejected their obscurantist outlook) but because he believed the Taliban served Pakistan's regional interests. For Musharraf the Taliban had two main advantages. First, since most of the Taliban were ethnic Pukhtoons, they had a natural affinity with Pakistan which also has a significant Pukhtoon community. Islamabad, Musharraf argued, had always backed Pukhtoon regimes in Kabul: the alternative was to have a hostile Afghan administration filled with Tajiks and Uzbeks. Second, since the Taliban had been created largely in and by Pakistan, the leadership in Kandahar was relatively sensitive to Pakistan's interests. With Mullah Omar in charge, Musharraf believed, Pakistan had strategic depth. His army could concentrate on guarding the border with India and had no reason to fear an attack from the northwest.

Musharraf realised that once the US had made up its mind to topple the Taliban there was no point in Pakistan continuing to support them. But he had not yet sold the decision to the rest of the army leadership.

On 14 September, he called a meeting of his corps commanders in the army high command's nuclear bunker in Chaklala where the top brass hoped they could talk without the risk of American surveillance. He told his colleagues that Pakistan faced a choice. It could either align itself with the United States or be isolated as a terrorist state. For Musharraf the issue was never in doubt but many of his senior commanders, such as the deputy chief of army staff Lt. General Usmani, were reluctant to overturn Pakistan's long-standing Afghan policy. They argued that Pakistan should wait to see exactly what Washington would offer in return for Islamabad's co-operation. But Musharraf insisted there could be no delay. It took six hours for Pakistan's president to get his way. He clinched the argument by pointing out that any Pakistani prevarication would present India with an opportunity to curry favour with the US. The corps commanders duly fell into line.

Musharraf's decision brought immediate financial benefits to Pakistan. By January 2002 Pakistan had secured US $3 billion worth of external assistance in the form of debt relief and the rescheduling of interest payments.[2] And while the decision helped Pakistan's balance sheet it also benefited Musharraf's international political standing. Before 11 September he was perceived as a military dictator who should announce, and abide by, a road map for the restoration of democracy. After 11 September his status was transformed: the Western world had a stake in his survival.

General Musharraf may have won friends in the West but within Pakistan he had made enemies. Thousands of Islamic radicals, swearing loyalty to their Islamic brethren in Afghanistan took to the streets in the cities of Quetta, Peshawar, Karachi and Islamabad. One of the demonstrators was a 25-year-old from Peshawar, Mohammed Ali. A student in a local madrasa, or religious school, Ali was typical of those who decided to protest. The attack on the United States, he believed, was a Jewish plot. He had heard that thousands of Jewish employees at the World Trade Center had not reported for work on 11 September. 'It was obviously planned by the Jews,' he said. 'Why else would there have been a camera there, ready to film it all?'[3]

It was hardly surprising that Ali had a somewhat unrealistic view of the world. He had started his religious education when he was six years old. His parents, landless farmers who could not afford to send him to a mainstream school, had handed him over to the madrasa. Since Ali would get free meals and lodging, it meant there was one less mouth to feed. He would also receive an education.

By the time Ali was twenty-five and taking part in the anti-US protests, his mind was not cluttered by worldly concerns. He knew the Quran off by heart and, for as long as he could remember, his life had consisted of prayer and little else. His only possessions were the clothes he stood in: a pair of sandals, a cotton shirt with matching trousers and a small white hat. He had not earned a single rupee in his life. But he did have prospects. The religious training provided by the madrasa opened up the possibility of climbing up the social ladder. He hoped that by the time he graduated at the age of thirty, he could become a respected figure in the community: a mullah.

Ali had left his home city of Peshawar just once in his life – to go on a month-long Islamic study tour in Karachi. His political views were completely in line with the vitriol that the mullahs had been yelling at him since he was six. America and Israel were hell-bent on the destruction of Muslims. Islam was a universal religion that would take over the world. Pakistan's rulers were and always had been power hungry, corrupt traitors to their faith whose venal greed had destroyed the dream of an Islamic state. It was, perhaps, hardly surprising that Ali had become a self-righteous zealot. Like Christian puritans in the West, he disdained those who frittered away their days on worldly pleasures. Watching television, playing cricket, drinking alcohol, listening to music, dancing and even flying kites were all wrong. So, too, was wearing a tie. A tie, Ali pointed out, resembled the Christian cross and was therefore un-Islamic.

General Musharraf was always aware that his decision to back America would provoke a furious reaction from the likes of Mohammed Ali. The question was just how many Pakistanis would join the protests. On the face of it there were some good reasons for Musharraf to be concerned. He was well aware that in many respects Pakistan had become a more religiously conservative society than it was when it was created in 1947. Although there are no reliable statistics to prove the point, it is widely accepted that increasing numbers of people, especially in the cities, regularly attend prayers at the mosques. Although millions of Pakistani women still choose not to wear the all-enveloping burqa, many do now take greater care to cover their heads than did their mothers and grandmothers. Men are also changing their habits. A beard – a badge of the Islamic faith — is still by no means *de rigueur* in Pakistan but more men wear one now than was the case in the past.

Successive Pakistani leaders had feared the Islamic clerics' capacity to arouse public opinion. Yet, as he weighed his options, Musharraf was also well aware that throughout Pakistan's history no religious leader had been able to translate the possibility of a mass-based Islamic revolutionary movement into reality. Although some religious parties have participated in elections they have never done well. It is often said that they have never won more than 5 per cent of the vote. In fact they once did much better than that. In 1970 – one of the few occasions when all the three main religious parties contested an election – together they won the support of over 14 per cent of the electorate in the areas that now make up Pakistan and in Punjab they won no less than 20.5 per cent of the vote.[4] In subsequent elections, though, the religious parties have never come close to those figures and have indeed consistently secured less than 5 per cent. There are various explanations for their lack of success, of which the most obvious is their unpopularity. But while some of the electorate do perceive the religious parties as a bunch of interfering killjoys there are reasons to believe that the number of votes the religious parties have received has not fully reflected the degree of support they have.

In his analysis of voting patterns in Punjab, Andrew Wilder concluded that the top priority of many Pakistani voters is to back the likely winner in the hope of benefiting from that candidate's patronage.[5] Given that the religious parties rarely look like winning, many people are reluctant to waste their vote on them. The religious parties themselves support this conclusion saying that in election campaigns they are repeatedly told that people would like to vote for them but do not see the point in doing so.

Despite that qualification, the point stands that the religious parties have never come close to winning power in Pakistan and, in terms of their influence on national politics, they have consistently punched above their electoral weight. The two most significant parties are Jamiat

Ulema-e-Islami (JUI) and Jamaat-e-Islami. The JUI's political heartland is in the Pukhtoon areas of Balochistan and North West Frontier Province (NWFP) where the party has control of a large number of radical madrasas. It is a grass-roots party that not only promotes Islam but also campaigns against social injustice. The JUI has won seats at the national and provincial level and has joined coalition governments in NWFP and Balochistan. Unlike the highly disciplined Jamaat-e-Islami, the JUI has long suffered from factional splits. The JUI's most prominent leader, Fazlur Rehman, is known for his strong anti-American statements and, in the late 1990s, the party offered moral and material support to the Taliban regime in Afghanistan.

While the JUI is a largely rural party, Jamaat-e-Islami draws its strength from the urban middle classes. It is an ideological party and advocates nothing less than Islamic revolution. Its specific policy objectives include the imposition of Sharia law, (divine law based on the Quran and the words and deeds of the Prophet) the redistribution of wealth, the banning of interest payments and the establishment of common Muslim defence arrangements so that occupied lands such as Palestine and Kashmir can be liberated.[6] The party was founded in 1941 by a leading Muslim intellectual Abul Al Maududi.[7] The best way to put Islam into practice, he believed, was to create a Leninist style, highly disciplined party that would act as a vanguard for the Islamic revolution. True to that tradition, some elements of Jamaat argue that the party should not participate in parliamentary elections but, rather, press exclusively for revolutionary change. Jamaat's party discipline is tight. Party decisions are subject to internal consultation (and compared to most Pakistani political parties the process of consultation is genuine) but once a party line is agreed, every member must follow it. Jamaat is the only Pakistani party to have computerised membership lists, a daily newspaper and its own academic journal. Jamaat's message may be backward-looking but its methods are more advanced and contemporary than any other political party in the country.

Despite being well-organised, Jamaat has always remained on the margins of Pakistani electoral politics and has posed little threat to the ruling establishment. Its credibility has always suffered from the fact that its founder, Maududi, was a strong opponent of the Muslim League's campaign for Pakistan. He viewed the Muslim League leadership in general, and Mohammed Ali Jinnah, the founder of Pakistan, in particular, as westernised elitists with no legitimate claim to represent the Muslims of the subcontinent. Ever since that major miscalculation, Jamaat leaders have consistently shown a remarkable lack of political acumen. The current leader Qazi Hussain Ahmed still talks of an Islamic revolution but has, at various points, sought short-term political advantage by allying himself to other political parties according to his reading of public opinion. Sixty years after the party was created, Jamaat's revolutionary credentials are in tatters.

The third significant Islamic party is the Jamiat Ulema-e-Pakistan (JUP). The JUP has proved to be a far less resilient organisation than either the JUI or Jamaat-e-Islami. Repeated electoral failures have persuaded many in the JUP leadership that their organisation should become a pressure group rather than an electoral party. Indeed, by the late 1990s, the JUP had even given up standing in elections although some of its leaders did manage to secure seats by forming local level alliances with mainstream parties such as the Muslim League.

The religious parties, especially Jamaat-e-Islami, have always had a reputation for being able to organise impressive displays of street power. But their repeated electoral failures led Musharraf to conclude that his opponents were not strong enough to destabilise his regime. He believed that most Pakistanis did not share the Taliban's austere interpretation of Islam. And even if many of his compatriots did have a grudging respect for Osama Bin Laden's willingness to stand up to the West, they would not want to jeopardise their way of life by trying to defend him. On 19 September 2001, in a televised address to the nation, Musharraf stated his case and insisted that those opposing him were only a minority who represented no more than 10 to 15 per cent of the Pakistani population. 'There is no reason', he said, 'why this minority should be allowed to hold the sane majority as a hostage. I appeal to all Pakistanis to display unity and solidarity and foil the nefarious designs of such elements who intend to harm the interests of the country.'[8]

Mohammed Ali and General Musharraf represented two ends of a debate that has existed as long as Pakistan itself. The general, and his

While a globally minded sprinter prepares to run into the future, a bearded mullah looks in the opposite direction, back through time. *The Muslim*, 19 January 1992.

'sane majority', can best be described as modernists. That by no means makes them atheists: the vast majority of Pakistanis would consider themselves devout Muslims. Nor can all the modernists be described as secularists: many relatively liberal Pakistanis believe that Islam should inform public policies in the country. Indeed, they believe that Islamic principles can make a positive contribution to contemporary democratic theory and practice. The modernists believe Pakistan should play a leading role not only in the Muslim world but also the international community as a whole and they are open to Western scientific advances. The modernists, in short, believe that time-honoured tenets of Islam sit easily with a progressive political outlook.

On the other side of the debate stand the Islamic radicals. They are often described as fundamentalists. It is an unsatisfactory label. For many in the West, 'fundamentalism' has become a term of abuse aimed at any Muslim who challenges any aspect of the Western way of life. Pan-Arab nationalists, Palestinian activists, Islamic extremists and even religious moderates are all written off as fundamentalists. The defining characteristic of the Islamic radicals is their view that the political systems that existed in the cities of Mecca and Medina 1,400 years ago should be emulated today in every detail. Their attitudes are backward-looking and regressive: they shun modern scientific knowledge and favour a return to a medieval-style theocracy of the type attempted by the Taliban regime in Afghanistan.

An Islamic State

The conflicting views of the modernists and the radicals are reflected in the different schools of Islamic thought on the sub-continent. While some 75 per cent of the Pakistani population are Sunni Muslims, there are significant fissures within the Sunni community. Some Sunnis in Pakistan describe themselves as Barelvis; others say they are Deobandis. It is an important distinction.

Deoband is a town a hundred miles north of Delhi and a madrasa was established there in 1867. It brought together many Muslims who were not only fiercely hostile to British rule but also committed to a literal and austere interpretation of Islam. The founders of the madrasa saw modern technology as nothing more than a method by which the people of the West kept Muslims in subjugation. They argued that the Quran and Sunnah (the words and deeds of the Prophet) provided a complete guide for life that needed no improvement by man. Despite the fact that most leading Deobandi clerics were strongly opposed to Jinnah's call for the creation of Pakistan, many Deobandi teachers moved to the new country in 1947. They have been a vocal, and often militant, element of Pakistani society ever since.

Talibs (religious students) from Deobandi madrasas formed the backbone of the Taliban movement that swept to power in Afghanistan in 1996. Some leading Deobandi clerics, such as Sami ul Haq from the famous Haqqaniya madrasa at Akhora Khattak in NWFP, have freely admitted that whenever the Taliban put out a call for fighters they closed down their schools and sent their students to Afghanistan.[9] The Deobandi talibs have also tried to impose their views within Pakistan. In December 1998, for example, just before the onset of Ramadan, some Deobandis began a campaign to purge the Baloch capital Quetta of video rental shops, video recorders and televisions. The campaign has continued periodically ever since. In late 2000 young religious students encouraged by madrasa teachers and local mullahs ordered the burning of television sets, video players and satellite dishes in a number of villages in NWFP. 'This is an ongoing process,' said one mullah who helped organise a TV bonfire. 'We will continue to burn TV sets, VCRs and other similar things to spread the message that their misuse is threatening our religion, society and family life.'[10]

General Musharraf has never shown any sympathy for the Deobandi mindset. His claim that only around 10 to 15 per cent of the Pakistani people opposed his decision to align Pakistan with the US rested on the fact that some 15 per cent of Pakistan's Sunni Muslims would consider themselves part of the Deobandi tradition. A far greater number, some 60 per cent, are in the Barelvi tradition. Compared to the Deobandis, the Barelvis have a moderate and tolerant interpretation of Islam. They trace their origins to pre-partition northern India. There, in the town of Bareilly, a leading Muslim scholar, Mullah Ahmad Raza Khan Barelvi, developed a large following. Barelvi and his followers felt there was no contradiction between practising Islam and drawing on the subcontinent's ancient religious practices. The Barelvis regularly offer prayers to holy men or pirs, both dead and alive. To this day, many Pakistanis believe that pirs and their direct descendants have supernatural powers and, each year, millions visit shrines to the pirs so that they can participate in ceremonies replete with lavish supplies of cannabis and music. The Deobandis shun such practices as pagan, ungodly distractions.

Ever since Pakistan was created, the Barelvis have been the Islamic radicals' most effective obstacle. In a fascinating study,[11] an American academic, Richard Kurin, has illustrated why that is the case. Kurin went to live in a small Punjabi village so that he could assess attitudes to Islam in a typical Barelvi community. He found that two men in the village were trying to propagate Islam: the local syed (descendant of the prophet) and the mullah. The syed's chosen method was to commandeer the loudspeaker of the village mosque at dawn and deliver a lecture on the merits of following the ways of the Quran and the Prophet. He would speak for several hours at a time. Much to his frustration, however, the villagers failed to show much interest in his exhortations and he regarded most of them as uneducated cheats. In private, the villagers would talk about the syed as a man who took life too seriously and who got worked up about issues that didn't really matter.

The second Islamic figure in the village, the mullah, was expected to preside over the daily prayers, teach the Quran to young boys and generally, as the villagers put it, 'do all the Allah stuff'. Like the syed, the mullah felt he had to put up with a somewhat wayward flock. Only a handful of the villagers would say their prayers five times a day and in the month of Ramadan most only managed to fast for five to ten days rather than for the whole month. Worse still, around a dozen villagers were having adulterous affairs that were the subject of much idle gossip. The villagers did, however, show considerable enthusiasm for attending the many shrines in the area. Virtually every man in the village had a pir who would offer him spiritual guidance.

The picture presented by Kurin is true of many villages throughout Pakistan. Clearly there are important cultural distinctions that affect attitudes in different parts of the country. In many Barelvi communities in Sindh, for example, any hint of adultery would be taken far more seriously and could well lead to the murder of those involved. Such conduct, however, is more a reflection of cultural as opposed to religious conservatism. The situation is complicated by the fact that in many parts of the country a Deobandi-style interpretation of Islam is used as an excuse to justify regressive cultural practices. Separating Deobandi orthodoxy from traditional practice is not easy not least because, to some extent, the two feed off each other. It is nonetheless important to remember that most Pakistanis are loyal to the Barelvi tradition. That fact has had an important bearing on the nature of the Pakistani state.

The dispute between the modernists and the radicals predates Pakistan's creation. As he advanced the arguments for a separate Muslim state, Mohammed Ali Jinnah relied in part on an appeal to Islam. Indeed, religious identity provided the basis for his demand. The argument that Jinnah presented to the British was that the Muslims and the Hindus of the subcontinent constituted two separate nations that could not live together. In 1947 his arguments prevailed and Pakistan was created as a Muslim homeland. But what did that mean? Was it simply a country for Muslims to live in or was it, in fact, a Muslim country? Was Jinnah the founding father of an Islamic state or merely a state in which Islam could be practised without fear of discrimination? Ever since 1947 the modernists and the Islamic radicals have fiercely contested these questions.

Many of the men who led the Muslim League, Mohammed Ali Jinnah included, never envisaged the creation of a state in which Islam would provide the framework for all political activity. Like most of his followers, Mohammed Ali Jinnah was a modernist. His educational background owed more to Oxbridge than Deoband. And his demand for Pakistan was opposed not only by Britain and the Congress leadership in India but also by many Islamic radical scholars. In pre-partition India the vast majority of the Ulema (religious scholars) saw Mohammed Ali Jinnah as a Western-trained lawyer who had lost his religion. Jinnah meanwhile viewed most of the Ulema as ignorant, power hungry, and often corrupt, theocrats. In 1946, for example, he dismissed their demand for the imposition of Sharia law as laid down by the Quran and Sunnah. 'Whose Sharia?' Jinnah asked. 'I don't want to get involved. The moment I enter his field the Ulema will take over for they claim to be the experts. I certainly don't propose to hand over the field to the Ulema.'[12] Many of Jinnah's speeches clearly indicated his progressive attitude to Islam. The most famous passage of all was delivered to the Constituent Assembly of Pakistan on 11 August 1947:

> You are free; you are free to go to your temples, you are free to go to your mosques or to any other place of worship in this state of Pakistan. You may belong to any religion or caste and creed – that has nothing to do with the business of the State . . . We are starting with this fundamental principle that we are all citizens and equal citizens of one State.[13]

The case for Jinnah as a modernist is compelling. But the Islamic radicals can also produce some evidence to back up their claim that Jinnah was on their side. When one leading cleric, Mullah Shabbir Ahmed Osmani, addressed the Constituent Assembly in 1949 he tried to counter the claim that Jinnah was a secularist:

> Islam has never accepted the view that religion is a private matter between man and his creator and as such has no bearing on the social or political relations of human beings . . . The late Quaid-e-Azam [Great Leader, i.e. Jinnah] made the following observations in the letter he wrote to Gandhiji in August 1944: 'The Quran is a complete code of life. It provides for all matters, religious or social, civil or criminal, military or penal, economic or commercial.'[14]

Any fair-minded assessment of Jinnah would have to recognise that he did make some comments about the all-encompassing nature of the Quran. But it would also have to acknowledge that such remarks were few and far between and that anyone studying Jinnah's speeches has to go through them with a toothcomb to find many examples. Furthermore, when he did make such comments Jinnah often had a pragmatic, short-term political reason for doing so. His views, it is true, did change over time and towards the end of his life he became increasingly religious and placed greater emphasis on the need to respect Islamic values. But one thing is clear: at no stage of his life would Mohammed Ali Jinnah have had any time whatsoever for the regressive prejudices of the Taliban regime in Afghanistan and their Islamic radical supporters in Pakistan.

After Jinnah's death the arguments between the radicals and the modernists became more intense. As the politicians debated the content of the Pakistani constitution the Islamic-based parties pressed for a document that would establish Pakistan as an ideological state committed to Islam. Some even asked whether a constitution was necessary. The Quran and Sunnah, they maintained, lay down all the rules necessary for life and there was no need for mere men to create political institutions that could only distort Allah's word. Throughout the 1950s the politicians charged with writing the first Pakistani constitution grappled with these issues. And when they produced the 1956 constitution they came down firmly on the side of the modernists. As a sop to the radicals, the constitution's preamble did include a clause that recognised the sovereignty of Allah over the entire universe. But read as a whole, the document made it clear that, in practice, the people of Pakistan would be sovereign. As Prime Minister Liaquat Ali Khan had said when proposing the Objectives Resolution that formed the basis of the constitution:

> All authority is a sacred trust, entrusted to us by God for the purpose of being exercised in the service of man, so that it does not become an agency for tyranny or selfishness. I would, however, point out that this is not a resuscitation of the dead theory of divine right of kings or rulers because in accordance with the spirit of Islam the preamble fully recognises the truth that authority has been delegated to the people . . . this naturally eliminates any danger of the establishment of a theocracy.[15]

Even if the vast majority of Pakistan's first generation of politicians were firmly in the modernist camp it is significant that they tried to avoid a direct confrontation with the Islamic radicals. Faced with growing challenges from Baloch, Sindhi, Pukhtoon and Bengali nationalists, even the most secular leaders found it was expedient to appeal to Islam so as to foster a sense of Pakistani unity. In doing so, the politicians established a trend which has been a feature of Pakistani politics ever since. Pakistani politicians have never wanted to share power with the Ulema but they have also been reluctant to offend them. Few have wanted an Islamic state but they have been hesitant to say so with any clarity.

Pakistan's first military ruler, General Ayub Khan, was an exception to this rule. From the moment he took power in 1958 he brought the dispute between the modernists and the Islamic radicals into the open. In his autobiography *Friends Not Masters* he complained about the 'obscurantists who frustrate all progress under the cover of religion'.[16] He recognised that Pakistan had witnessed a conflict between the Ulema and the educated classes, and he left no doubt as to whose side he was on. Many of the Ulema, Ayub pointed out, had opposed Jinnah and the creation of Pakistan. And once Pakistan was established they tried to carve out a niche for themselves by denouncing the political leadership and calling for a more orthodox Islamic state. As Ayub put it, the Ulema 'spread throughout the length and breadth of the country to convince the people of the misery of their existence and the failings of their government. They succeeded in converting an optimistic and enthusiastic people into a cynical and frustrated community.'[17]

Ayub clearly opposed those who wanted to put Islam at the heart of the Pakistani state. When he proposed a new constitution in 1962 he tried to change the name of the country from 'The Islamic Republic of Pakistan' to 'Republic of Pakistan'. His Muslim Family Laws Ordinance of 1961 was in much the same vein. Amongst other things, the measure was intended to make it more difficult for Pakistani men to take more than one wife. Under the Ordinance no man could enter a second marriage without the consent of his first wife. 'A Muslim', Ayub later wrote,

is allowed by Islam to have more than one wife, under certain conditions. This permission has been used to practise indiscriminate polygamy causing immense misery to innumerable tongue-tied women and innocent children. Thousands of families have been ruined because of the degenerate manner in which men have misused this permission to suit their convenience.[18]

In the event, for all his military strength, Ayub was unable to make his reforms stick. His Family Laws Ordinance, like his encouragement of family planning and his distaste for the burqa, all ran into deep-seated traditional cultural, as well as religious, objections. Ayub Khan, though, could at least say that he had tried to confront the radicals. The next strong leader to emerge in Pakistan, Zulfikar Ali Bhutto, didn't even try.

Although he was one of the most modernist leaders Pakistan has ever had, Bhutto consistently gave in to radical demands. He was cynical in his exploitation of religion. A man of broad intellectual horizons, he repeatedly pandered to the Islamic radicals in the hope of securing short-term political advantage. This characteristic was apparent early in Bhutto's period of office. The first major religious issue to confront him concerned the Ahmedis or Qadianis – a sect that followed the teachings of a nineteenth-century Punjabi cleric, Mirza Ghulam Ahmed. Ahmed said he had revelations direct from Allah: he maintained, in other words, that he was a prophet. Even though Ahmed considered himself subservient to Mohammed, his claim clashed with the basic Islamic tenet that Mohammed was the last and final Prophet. In 1953, long before Bhutto came to power, radical Islamists had demanded that the Ahmedis be declared non-Muslims. The issue had led to rioting throughout Punjab. Many Ahmedis had had their properties looted and burnt and some of the riots had become so violent that Ahmedis had been murdered. Faced with this outburst, the central government, after some prevarication, had decided to resist the rioters' demands and had called out the army to restore law and order in Lahore.

Twenty years later, faced with renewed anti-Ahmedi demands, Bhutto caved in and gave the radicals what they wanted: the Ahmedis were declared non-Muslims. Bhutto followed a similar approach three years later when he was desperately trying to cling on to power after the 1977 elections. In the face of sustained opposition protests, he again tried to appease the religious parties. He imposed a ban on drinking, gambling and nightclubs and declared that Friday, not Sunday, would be the weekly holiday. It was a futile effort. Few of the religious leaders, who all knew that Bhutto himself was a regular drinker, were prepared to side with him. Bhutto's tilt to Islam convinced nobody.

For the first three decades of its history, then, no Pakistani leader had any sympathy with the Islamic radicals. But after Bhutto was ousted in a coup, came General Zia ul Haq. He was to rule for twelve years and throughout that period he consistently promoted the role of Islam in the state. Indeed, the moment he grasped power, Zia made Islam the centrepiece of his administration: in his first address to the nation he clearly stated that he would try to create an Islamic state. In December 1979 a decision taken thousands of miles away, in Moscow, gave Zia the chance to advance his programme. The ailing secretary general of the Soviet Communist Party, Leonid Brezhnev, approved the invasion of Afghanistan. Brezhnev and his colleagues were chiefly motivated by their concern that instability in Afghanistan could spread across the Soviet Union's southern border. But their decision to move their tanks into Kabul had profound consequences for Pakistan. For General Zia, the invasion seemed like a gift from Allah. At a stroke he became a key cold war ally of the United States. Zia's support for America's anti-Soviet campaign not only provided him with enough foreign exchange to sustain his regime but also gave him a free hand to ignore internationally accepted human rights norms. As Zia pressed on with his Islamicisation campaign, Washington turned a blind eye.

Zia's campaign affected every aspect of the Pakistani state. His first measures concerned the legal system. In July 1977 he declared that theft could be punished by 'amputation from the wrist of the left hand of a right-handed person and vice versa'. Some other crimes, he decreed, could be punished by public whippings.[19] The Hudood Ordinance of 1979 stated that punishments laid down in the Quran and Sunnah were now operative in Pakistan. Under the Zina Ordinance, rape was to be punished by the public flogging of the woman as well as the man. Zia also created a Federal Sharia Court. Its task was to: 'examine and decide the question whether or not any law or provision of the law is repugnant to the provisions of Islam'.[20] Any law found to be repugnant would immediately become void. Potentially, this was one of the most far-reaching of all Zia's reforms. Interestingly, though, he was quick to see its dangers and in a move that clearly demonstrated the limits to Zia's Islamic radicalism, he declared that the Sharia Court could not challenge any martial law regulation or order. The military, it seemed, was above Islamic law.

Zia also tried to Islamicise the economy. In 1981 interest payments, explicitly banned in the Quran, were replaced by so-called 'profit and loss' accounts. In reality the profit accruing to a bank account was interest by another name but Zia insisted that he had at least taken a first step towards an Islamic banking system. Zia also introduced Islamic fiscal measures in the form of a Zakat tax. The measure provided for a 2.5 per cent annual deduction from the money resting in someone's bank account on the first day of Ramadan. Zia justified Zakat on the grounds that the Quran and Sunnah specifically mentioned it as one of the five pillars of Islam and he decreed that the Zakat revenues were to be used for poverty relief.

Zia also wanted Islam to be given greater status in the education system. Textbooks were overhauled to ensure their ideological purity and un-Islamic reading matter was removed from libraries and schools. Government officials were given the task of persuading people to pray five times a day and government offices were required to allow for prayer time in drawing up their schedules. Zia also insisted that the confidential annual assessments of civil servants should include a section in which staff were given marks for regularly attending prayers and for having a good knowledge of Islam.

Throughout his period in office Zia rewarded the only political party to offer him consistent support, Jamaat-e-Islami. Tens of thousands of Jamaat activists and sympathisers were given jobs in the judiciary, the civil service and other state institutions. These appointments meant Zia's Islamic agenda lived on long after he died. The campaigns for women to cover their heads, for shutting down restaurants during Ramadan and for enforcing the Hudood and Zina ordinances can all be ascribed to the fact that, after Zia, Islamic radicals held positions of authority.

General Zia's impact on Pakistan was so enduring in part because his civilian successors in the 1990s, Benazir Bhutto and Nawaz Sharif, did little to dismantle his legacy. Benazir Bhutto followed much the same policy as her father. While she had little sympathy for the Islamic radicals, she consistently failed to confront them. Privately, she made little secret of her modernist outlook. In public she repeatedly stressed the role of Islam in the state. To some extent, Benazir Bhutto was motivated by a desire to meet the criticism that as a Western-educated woman she was an inappropriate choice to lead Pakistan. Determined to prove the Islamists wrong, she felt the need to present herself as a prime minister who could be trusted to protect and even advance the role of Islam in the Pakistani state.

Her rival, Nawaz Sharif, had a different approach. As Zia's protégé, and coming from a religiously conservative family, he always felt more comfortable with the Islamic radicals. In October 1998 Sharif began a process that could have handed the radicals a massive victory. He managed to secure the passage of the 15th Constitutional Amendment through the National Assembly. The measure had huge implications: it stated that Sharia law would become the supreme law in Pakistan. At a stroke the prime minister would have won the power to interpret the Quran and Sunnah in any way he pleased and to act accordingly.

Despite being prime minister, Sharif was never particularly interested in politics. He had only stood for the National Assembly in the first place because his father, seeking political influence to protect his business interests, had told him to do so. Sharif was an appalling administrator who consistently favoured making grand announcements rather than seriously attempting to implement policies. It is quite possible that he never fully understood that the Sharia Bill would have fundamentally altered the nature of the Pakistani state. As far as he was concerned it would improve law and order in the country and remove irritating constraints on his power, such as parliament and the constitution.

By the time of the 1999 coup Sharif was unsure that he could muster the necessary two-thirds majority to force the Sharia Bill through the Senate. It is quite possible that, had he done so, the army would have felt it had to intervene to save Pakistan's political institutions. In the event, Musharraf removed Sharif before the issue came to a head and once Sharif had gone the Sharia Bill was forgotten.

Sharif's successor, General Musharraf, has never made any secret of his modernist views. After his coup Islamabad's formidable rumour machine relayed stories about his penchant for whisky and the general himself freely recounted how he had gambled in casinos. He said that while most people favoured a 'double or quit' strategy in roulette he had found 'treble or quit' to be a better approach.[21] His relatives, too, made little effort to conceal their attitude to religion. Shortly after the 1999 coup, a BBC interviewer asked the general's father: 'Does your son pray five times a day?' 'If the father doesn't', came the deadpan reply, 'I don't see why the son should.'

Musharraf himself gave an early indication of his thinking when he described the Turkish secularist Mustafa Kemal Ataturk as his hero. And in his first major policy speech Musharraf included a passage on Islam:

> And now for a few words on exploitation of religion. Islam teaches tolerance not hatred; universal brotherhood and not enmity; peace and not violence; progress and not bigotry. I have great respect for the Ulema and expect them to come forth and present Islam in its true light. I urge them to curb elements which are exploiting religion for vested interests and bring bad name to our faith . . .[22]

Even if he chose his words carefully, in the context of Pakistani political discourse, the general's meaning was clear: he was distancing himself from the Islamic radicals. While Zia had used his military might to try to Islamicise Pakistan, Musharraf was indicating that he wanted to modernise the Pakistani state.

In April 2000, Musharraf began to act. He backed a proposal to reform Pakistan's notorious blasphemy law. Under the law anyone can be imprisoned simply on the basis of an accusation from a member of the public. Should someone be accused, for example, of taking the Prophet's name in vain or desecrating a copy of the Quran, then that person has to be detained immediately, before an investigation. The law, which carries the death sentence, is clearly open to abuse. There is no simpler way of getting rid of a business rival or an irritating neighbour than accusing him or her of blasphemy. Minority groups had long complained that the law was used to discriminate against them and in May 1998 a Catholic bishop, John Joseph, became so incensed by the blasphemy law that he shot himself dead as a protest against it.

Under Musharraf's amendment to the blasphemy law, a case could be registered only if the district administration had first investigated the veracity of an accusation. The measure was modest. It in no way lessened the punishment for proven cases of blasphemy. The Islamic parties, however, strongly opposed the change and on 16 May 2000, Musharraf backed down: 'As it was the unanimous demand of the Ulema and the people, therefore, I have decided to do away with the procedural change . . . [of] . . . the blasphemy law.'[23] Even a military ruler, it seemed, was unable to introduce a modest administrative reform if the Islamic radicals opposed him. Intriguingly, Musharraf announced his U-turn on the blasphemy law on the tarmac of Chaklala airport in Rawalpindi immediately after stepping off a plane, having concluded an official visit to Turkmenistan. The decision to back down, it seemed, had been taken in his absence – presumably by senior military colleagues.

Despite his failure to change the blasphemy law, Musharraf continued to express opposition to religious extremism. In June 2001, well before the attacks on the twin towers in New York, he gave a keynote speech to leading Pakistani Islamic scholars and clerics whom the government had transported to Islamabad for the purpose. His comments, which struck many of his audience dumb, comprised one of the clearest statements of Islamic modernism ever made by a Pakistani leader. 'How does the world look at us?' he asked,

> The world sees us as backward and constantly going under. Is there any doubt that we have been left behind although we claim Islam will carry us forward in every age, every circumstance and every land . . .? How does the world judge our claim? It looks upon us as terrorists. We have been killing each other. And now we want to spread violence and terror abroad. Naturally the world regards us as terrorists. Our claim of tolerance is phoney . . . We never tire of talking about the status that Islam accords to women. We only pay lip-service to its teachings. We do not act upon it. This is hypocrisy.[24]

The June speech was a major political event in Pakistan. Since the 1950s no Pakistani leader had dared to speak to the clerics in this way. But there were still strict limits on how far Musharraf was prepared to go. He feared that Pakistan's state institutions could not survive a confrontation with the militant elements of Pakistani society. The fate of the army's much vaunted de-weaponisation drive provides a good example of Musharraf's reluctance to provoke a showdown with the radicals who, ever since the anti-Soviet struggle, had held large stockpiles of weaponry. In February 2001 Musharraf announced a ban on the public display of weapons, but the initiative soon ran into the ground. When religious leaders addressed rallies they were still flanked by kalashnikov-toting bodyguards and the army did not even attempt to disarm them. Once again, the state was unwilling to provoke a confrontation with the radicals. But there was one issue about which Musharraf felt so strongly that he was prepared to act with greater determination. From the moment he took power, General Musharraf had made it clear that he considered sectarian violence to be an abhorrence that had to be eliminated. And he knew that many millions of Pakistanis agreed with him.

Sectarianism

To non-Muslims, the dispute between the Shias (who make up around 15 per cent of the Pakistani population) and the Sunnis is arcane. After the death of the Prophet in 632 the question arose as to who should succeed him. To this day, the Shias believe that the job should have been given to Mohammed's son-in-law Ali ibn Abi Talib. Ali did eventually take over as caliph but only after three other men had had a stint at the job. The Shias' support for Ali is the basis of the Shia-Sunni dispute. For the first three decades of Pakistan's history, the Shia-Sunni divide was not a significant issue, though that is not to say there was no conflict between the two communities. Even in the early years, there were occasional spontaneous sectarian riots especially at the time of Muharram when the Shias paraded through the streets demonstrating the depth of their faith by using small blades to slash their skin to a bloody pulp.

Although such tensions had always existed, the sectarian issue did not become acute until the 1980s. The immediate cause of this development was General Zia's attempt, in 1980, to raise Zakat tax. As soon as the tax was announced the Shias argued that the government's proposals were not in line with their traditions. For centuries the Shias had maintained that Zakat should be donated on a voluntary basis and that no government had the right to collect it. The Shias also disputed the

Sunni's methods of calculating and distributing it. General Zia soon found himself faced with massive Shia protests. In July 1980, emboldened by the Shia-led revolution in Iran, tens of thousands of Pakistani Shias stormed the Federal Secretariat building in Islamabad. And when Zia backed down, accepting the Shia demand to be exempt from Zakat, he provoked a furious response from the Sunni community.

Relations between the Sunnis and Shias deteriorated rapidly and, by the end of the 1980s, well-armed extremists from both sides were murdering each other on a regular basis. Initially, the Shia's most powerful militant organisation was Tehrik-e-Jafria Pakistan (TJP). When the TJP moved towards the pursuit of constitutional politics, Sipah-e-Mohammed Pakistan (SMP) took its place. In the early and mid-1990s the SMP won a reputation as one of the most violent organisations in all of Pakistan and it has been blamed for a whole series of attacks on Sunni militant activists.

Sunnis militants also began to organise themselves. In 1985 Sipah-e-Sahaba Pakistan (SSP) was established in the Punjabi city of Jhang and it demanded that the Shias be declared non-Muslims. The organisation grew with remarkable speed. This was in part because it drew on the discontent of Sunni peasants who felt exploited by the Shia landlords who have traditionally owned large estates near Jhang. The SSP's direct challenge to these landlords enabled them to attract support not only from landless farm workers but also from the urban lower middle classes which also resented the power of the local aristocracy. By 1994 the SSP had become one of the largest religious parties in Punjab. As well as being an exceptionally violent organisation, it also moved into electoral politics and managed to win seats in the National Assembly.

The SSP had become a formidable force in sectarian politics. But in 1995 a group of Sunni militants led by a senior SSP activist, Riaz Basra, split away from the SSP to form Lashkar-e-Jhangvi. The relationship between the SSP and Lashkar-e-Jhangvi was ambiguous and it was never clear to what extent the two organisations were working in tandem. It was surely significant, however, that whenever an SSP activist was killed or arrested, Lashkar-e-Jhangvi vowed to exact revenge. Lashkar-e-Jhangvi always had an explicitly military structure – Basra was its commander-in-chief – and, unlike most other sectarian groups in Pakistan, it did not hesitate to admit responsibility for the assassinations that it carried out, including attacks on many Iranian nationals in Pakistan.

In January 1999 Lashkar-e-Jhangvi stepped up its military campaign by attempting to assassinate the then Pakistani prime minster, Nawaz Sharif. The plot failed because a passer-by accidentally detonated a bomb that had been placed under a bridge that Sharif was due to drive over an hour later. Two months later, a Lashkar-e-Jhangvi activist was arrested near an area where Sharif's helicopter was due to land. Police became suspicious because he was carrying a rocket-propelled grenade.[25] The battle-lines between the Sunni sectarian groups and the government were now drawn and throughout 1999 there were thirty-six extra judicial killings of activists from the SSP and Lashkar-e-Jhangvi.[26] The police were told that anyone who managed to arrest or kill Basra would be given a 5 million-rupee reward.

Despite this, the security forces proved incapable of controlling the militants' activities. Riaz Basra showed his contempt for the police's capabilities when he turned up at one of Nawaz Sharif's political surgeries. Having slipped in with the petitioners who wanted to see the prime minister, Basra positioned himself directly behind Nawaz Sharif and got one of his accomplices to take a picture. Three days later staff at the prime minster's house received a print of the photograph. The faces of Sharif and Basra, within a few feet of each other, had been circled and underneath there was an inscription: 'It's that easy.'[27]

The nature of the sectarian violence in Pakistan has changed over time. Most of the killings have occurred in Punjab although by the end of the 1990s there were an increased number of incidents in Karachi and NWFP. At first the gunmen from both sides concentrated on killing each other's hit-men. In the mid- to late 1990s the emphasis changed: the Sunni groups began targeting high profile Shias such as doctors, businessmen and intellectuals. That in turn was followed by a third phase of sectarian violence in which civilians were targeted indiscriminately. In one attack in April 2000, for example, grenades and gunfire were directed at worshippers attending a Shia mosque in Rawalpindi. Nineteen people were killed in the incident and thirty-seven were injured. Shia activists have been responsible for similar attacks.

Sectarian violence. Number of deaths, 1989–2001

	Punjab	Pakistan
1989	10	10
1990	32	32
1991	47	47
1992	44	58
1993	38	39
1994	73	73
1995	58	59
1996	86	86
1997	90	193
1998	75	157
1999	53	86
2000	29	149
2001	65	261

Punjab figures: 1989–93: Muhammad Qasim Zaman, 'Sectarianism in Pakistan: The Radicalisation of Shi'e and Sunni Identities', *Modern Asian Studies* 32: 3, 1998, pp. 689–716. These are based on official figures and are likely to be low estimates. **1994:** *Schinan Times*, an anti-sectarian website, www.schinan.com. **1995 and 2000:** Interview with senior police official, Lahore, February 2002. **1996:** Institute of Conflict Management, www.satp.org/satporgtp/countries/pakistan/database/sect-killing.htm. **1997:** Human Rights Commission of Pakistan, *State of Human Rights in 1997*, Lahore, 1998. **1998:** Human Rights Commission of Pakistan, *State of Human Rights in 1998*, Lahore, 1999. **1999 and 2001:** I. A. Rehman of the Human Rights Commission of Pakistan, February 2002.

Pakistan figures: 1989–2001: Institute of Conflict Management, www.satp.org/satporgtp/countries/pakistan/database/sect-killing.htm.

From the moment he took power, General Musharraf made it clear that he considered those involved in sectarian violence to be terrorists. In August 2001, he felt strong enough to ban Lashkar-e-Jhangvi and Sipah-e-Mohammed Pakistan. Furthermore, he announced that the SSP and TJP were being put on a terrorist watch list. The bans marked a significant development which indicated that Musharraf was prepared to take some risks in confronting the Islamic radicals. But once again there were questions about implementation. The killing rate did diminish after the ban – but only for a few weeks. In practical terms, the ban made little difference since many activists from the two organisations, already wanted for murder, were keeping a low profile. Nevertheless, Musharraf had laid down the foundations of his policy towards religious extremism and, after 11 September, he was to build on it.

Musharraf's Project

Before 11 September Musharraf's most significant moves against Islamic extremism were his June 2001 speech and the bans on Lashkar-e-Jhangvi and Sipah-e-Mohammed. Other initiatives, such as the reform of the blasphemy law and the de-weaponisation programme had failed to make much impact because the military was reluctant to implement them. After 11 September Musharraf discovered he had greater room for manoeuvre than he had previously thought.

When the US bombing of Afghanistan began in October 2001, Western media organisations poured into Pakistan and broadcast endless stories about the 'Islamic backlash' against Musharraf. The images were striking. Each Friday the West's TV news bulletins were filled with pictures of furious, bearded men burning effigies of President Bush and General Musharraf. But while Western journalists were making dire predictions about a civil war in Pakistan, General Musharraf was drawing precisely the opposite conclusion. The demonstrations that followed the bombing soon petered out. By November 2001 the best the radical clerics could do was to muster a few hundred anti-US protestors after Friday prayers each week. For years the radicals' trump card had been their ability to organise 'street power' but now they stood exposed: their trump card was a bluff. As Musharraf later said: 'I thought ten times about putting my hand in the beehive of religious extremism. But I realised that this was the maximum they could do and the vast majority of people were with me.'[28]

Now he had greater confidence in his ability to implement his agenda, Musharraf decided to consolidate his grip on power. In October 2001 he sacked two of the generals who had helped him to power in the first place: Lt. Generals Mehmood and Usmani were forced into early retirement. Musharraf offered no explanation for the sackings merely saying that he had planned them for some time. Inevitably, there were many theories. Following the 11 September attacks Mehmood had headed two delegations to the Taliban leadership in Kandahar. Musharraf had ordered him to try to persuade the Taliban's leader, Mullah Mohammed Omar, to hand over Osama Bin Laden to the Americans. According to one widely believed version, Mehmood ignored the instruction and instead assured Mullah Omar that the Taliban could count on the continued support of Pakistan's powerful intelligence agency, the ISI.

Whatever the precise reason for the sackings, one fact stood out. Both Mehmood and Usmani were known as very devout Muslims. When, for example, Usmani attended wedding parties he would turn his back if music was played. At the same time as they were sacked, a third senior general, Mohammed Aziz Khan, was 'promoted' to the largely ceremonial post of chairman of the joint chiefs of staff. Aziz was also known to have strong religious views. At a stroke, Musharraf had removed three of his most religiously minded colleagues from decision-making posts in the army's senior leadership and replaced them with officers who shared his modernist outlook.[29]

General Musharraf had now paved the way for a strike against the radicals. Before 11 September he had concentrated his attack on those responsible for sectarian violence. In the immediate aftermath of 11 September he had seen off the pro-Taliban clerics who tried to organise street protests against him. But he still faced one major obstacle that stood in the way of a full-blown assault on the radicals: Kashmir.

The Kashmir Connection

Ever since 1988, when the insurgency against the Indian security forces in Kashmir had begun, Pakistan had officially provided diplomatic, moral and political support to the Kashmiri militants. The militants' ability to find shelter in Pakistani-held Kashmir, and in Pakistan itself, was a source of constant frustration to Delhi. For years the Indian government had described the movement of militants across the line of control in Kashmir as Pakistani-sponsored 'cross border terrorism'. But Delhi's attempts to portray the militants as terrorists met only limited success. The international community, reluctant to get bogged down in the diplomatic quagmire of Kashmir, remained aloof and largely refrained from describing the militants either as terrorists (as India would have it) or freedom fighters (as Pakistan preferred). Successive American administrations were quite tolerant of the militant groups in Kashmir and the only group to be listed formally as a terrorist organisation was Harakat ul-Mujahideen or, as it used to be called, Harakat ul-Ansar, which, in 1995, was held responsible for the kidnapping of five Western tourists in Kashmir. When Harakat ul-Ansar tried to evade the designation by changing its name to Harakat ul-Mujahideen, the US responded by listing that name as well.[30] Washington's message was clear. If the militants restricted their fight to India's security forces in Kashmir they would be left alone. If they tried to attack Western targets they would be treated as terrorists.

After 11 September US policy changed. The fundamental problem for Pakistan was that the United States was no longer prepared to accept Islamabad's claims that there was no connection between Afghanistan and Kashmir. Washington had a point. Links clearly did exist. For a start, the Taliban and the Pakistani-based Kashmiri militant groups had the same origins. Both had emerged from the anti-Soviet struggle in Afghanistan. In the course of their campaign to remove the Soviets, the US had spent huge amounts of money – over US $7 billion according to one estimate[31] – to create an effective Mujahideen force. The most significant group to emerge from the CIA training camps was the Taliban. Once the Soviets had withdrawn, the Taliban concentrated on bringing an Islamic system to Afghanistan but many other Mujahideen focussed on Kashmir. Pakistan's ISI, hopeful of increasing India's discomfort in Kashmir, encouraged this process and provided the militants with support. The agency not only monitored all activities at the camps, it also supplied military equipment and even kept registers of those who volunteered for training.

The ISI's close association with, and material support for, the Taliban further strengthened the Kashmiri militants' ties with Afghanistan. Take, as an example, the Harakat ul-Mujahideen. During the anti-Soviet struggle, many of the organisation's members had fought alongside the people who went on to run the Taliban regime. After the Taliban victory, Mullah Omar provided Harakat ul-Mujahideen with training camps in Afghanistan. This became abundantly clear when, in August 1988, several Harakat ul-Mujahideen activists were killed when the US responded to the Africa embassy bombings by firing cruise missiles into a training camp in eastern Afghanistan. And again, when America launched its attack on Afghanistan in October 2001, twenty-two Harakat activists, including two senior commanders, were killed when the US bombed a building in Kabul.[32]

Throughout the 1990s Pakistan's military establishment felt it was in a strong position. Its close ties to the Taliban allowed the ISI to produce a cadre of well-trained militants who could fight in Kashmir. But after 11 September the policy unravelled. The US was no longer prepared to turn a blind eye to the Afghan–Kashmir nexus. Having decided to back the US-led coalition Musharraf had nowhere to turn. In November 2001, under strong US pressure, he tacitly accepted that the links between Afghanistan and Kashmir did exist. He ordered the closure of Harakat ul-Mujahideen's office in Muzzafrabad. In itself the decision did not make much difference. All that happened was that Harakat's phone line was cut off and the organisation's officials were told to move to another office and to keep a low profile. Nevertheless the incident was significant: for the first time, Islamabad was conceding that the Pakistani-based militants could be perceived not as freedom fighters but as terrorists.

Even though Musharraf was now beginning to face up to the phenomenon of Islamic militancy in all its manifestations, it took one more event to force his hand still further. On 13 December 2001 five men armed with AK-47s, plastic explosives and grenades drove towards the Indian parliament. Their car, an Ambassador, was of the kind used by many Indian ministers. Since it was painted with official markings and had a red light on its roof the guards at the parliament assumed that it was on legitimate business. As the car drew up to the parliament building itself the occupants were finally challenged. The five men then seemed to panic. They jumped out of the vehicle and started firing. During a thirty-minute gun battle the attackers killed six Indian security personnel and a gardener before they too were shot down.[33] Nobody claimed responsibility for the attack but Indian leaders immediately blamed Pakistan-backed Islamic militants. Many Indians believed that their government should respond with just as much force as the Americans had deployed after the 11 September attacks on the World Trade Center. The government seemed to agree. It recalled the Indian High Commissioner from Islamabad, cut rail and other transport links with Pakistan and moved missiles, fighter aircraft and tens of thousands of troops to the Pakistani border. The prospect of yet another military conflict, possibly full-scale war, between two nuclear powers put Musharraf under still more pressure.

The general now realised that he had little choice but to reverse Pakistan's long-standing policy of backing the Kashmiri insurgency. On 12 January 2002 he delivered a landmark speech in which he announced a ban of two of the most prominent Pakistan-based militant groups, Jaish e-Mohammed and Lashkar-e-Toiba. Jaish had not existed for long. It had been founded by Mullah Masood, a former Harakat ul-Ansar member, after he was released from an Indian prison in December 1999 in exchange for 155 hostages who were on board a hijacked Indian airlines plane forced to land in Afghanistan. Within weeks Mullah Masood was recruiting new members for his organisation at a series of public rallies in Pakistan. Musharraf's decision to target Jaish was partly motivated by the fact that, on 1 October 2001, a Jaish suicide bomber had killed himself and thirty-eight others by driving a truck full of explosives into the Legislative Assembly building in Srinagar. Coming so soon after the 11 September attacks it was perhaps inevitable that the operation was perceived as a terrorist activity. Washington had immediately put Jaish on the US State Department's terrorist watch list: now Musharraf had followed suit.

The second group to be banned, Lashkar-e-Toiba, was based on a 190-acre site in the town of Muridke just outside Lahore. The organisation had always put Islam at the heart of its ideology. It wasn't just fighting for Kashmir's liberation but also for its Islamisation. In fact the extreme Islamic radicalism of Lashkar's members – manifested, for example, in throwing acid in the faces of Kashmiri women who did not wear a burqa – managed to alienate many of the people it was supposed to be liberating in Kashmir. Lashkar had also demonstrated the extent of its extremism by proclaiming a strategy of mounting operations not only in Indian-held Kashmir but also in India itself. In December 2000 it claimed responsibility for a suicidal attack on an Indian army installation inside the Red Fort in Delhi. And while Lashkar denied involvement in the 13 December attack on the Indian parliament, the authorities in Delhi were quick to accuse the organisation of being responsible. While many Pakistanis believed the attack in the parliament to have been carried out by Indian agents provocateurs, few doubted that Lashkar was perfectly capable of mounting such an operation.

While he banned Lashkar and Jaish, Musharraf did not abandon the insurgency altogether. He made no move against the most prominent of all the militant groups active in Kashmir, Hizb ul-Mujahideen. Like Jaish and Lashkar, Hizb ul-Mujahideen had many close links with Pakistan. Its leader Syed Salahuddin based himself in Pakistani-controlled Kashmir and the group is tied to the Pakistani political party Jamaat-e-Islami. Despite that, Hizb ul-Mujahideen has managed to sustain its image as a predominantly indigenous group, not least because some 80 per cent of its members are of Kashmiri origin. In sparing Hizb ul-Mujahideen from a ban, Musharraf may also have taken into account that the group is motivated not only by Islamic ideology but also Kashmiri nationalism. Unlike Lashkar and Jaish, Hizb ul-Mujahideen had never required its new recruits to be strongly religious.[34] Musharraf was also able to argue that Hizb ul-Mujahideen had few links with Afghanistan. While it was true that before the Taliban came to power Hizb ul-Mujahideen had a number of training camps in Afghanistan, they had all been closed down. The Taliban was hostile to Hizb ul-Mujahideen because of its close links with Jamaat-e-Islami, that in turn had supported one of the Taliban's most powerful adversaries, Gulbuddin Hekmatyar.

The 12 January speech had a huge impact in Pakistan. For the first time in decades a Pakistani leader seemed to be charting a genuinely new course. 'The majority of religious scholars', Musharraf said,

> are very enlightened people. But the extremists carrying out these protests [against the US bombing of Afghanistan] think they are the sole custodians of Islam. They looked at the Taliban as if they were the renaissance of Islam and at those who were against the Taliban as, God forbid, not Muslims. But these people have no respect for human rights and the Pakistani people were let down by these so-called religious scholars.

Musharraf then went on to announce the banning of the militant organisations. From now on, he said, 'No organisation will be able to carry out terrorism on the pretext of Kashmir.'[35]

And having done the difficult thing – banning groups involved in the Kashmiri insurgency – Musharraf did not hesitate to announce a whole series of other modernist reforms and launch a number of other broadsides against the radicals. In the week after the January speech he arrested thousands of Islamic activists. He banned the two remaining powerful sectarian groups, the SSP and the TJP. He announced measures to control the construction of mosques and introduced limits on their use of loudspeakers. Musharraf no longer felt constrained. If he was strong enough to ban Lashkar-e-Toiba and Jaish-e-Mohammed he believed he could go much further in other areas. One of the reforms announced after the January speech – the decision to abolish separate electorates – provides a good illustration of the change in Musharraf's attitudes before and after 11 September.

In 1985 Pakistan's previous military ruler, General Zia ul Haq, had introduced separate electorates for Pakistan's minorities. Under the measure, Muslims voted for Muslims, Christians for Christians and Hindus for Hindus. Zia defended the system on the grounds that it ensured that the minorities had more representation in parliament than they would otherwise have been able to achieve. Christian and Hindu leaders, however, complained that they could not participate in elections on the same basis as the majority of Pakistani citizens and that they felt excluded from the mainstream of the nation's political process. Whatever the merits of the arguments for and against separate electorates, the issue came to acquire symbolic importance: the Christian community in particular resented it and the Islamists argued for its retention.

In August 2000 General Musharraf had announced the arrangements for the first local elections after his coup. Many in the minority communities hoped he would take the opportunity to do away with the separate electorates system. In the event, though, his fear of angering the conservative Islamic lobby led him to decide to leave the existing arrangements in place. After 11 September Musharraf felt strong enough to reverse that policy. In January 2002 he announced that the forthcoming national elections would be held on the basis of one universal electorate. The radicals were appalled but, as Musharraf predicted, they felt too weak to oppose him.

Musharraf also expressed determination to control the madrasas which had played an important role in fostering Islamic militancy. At the time of Pakistan's independence there were an estimated 250 madrasas in the country. The Soviet invasion of Afghanistan transformed the situation. The madrasas won a well-deserved reputation for producing highly motivated anti-Soviet fighters. As a result, foreign funds, chiefly from the US and Saudi Arabia, flowed into the madrasa system. By 1987 there were 2,862 madrasas producing around 30,000 graduates each year.[36] Having received this boost, the madrasa movement went from strength to strength. A survey carried out in Punjab in 1995 revealed that there were 2,512 madrasas in that province alone.[37] In 2001 General Musharraf said that there were 7,000 or 8,000 madrasas in Pakistan, and between 600,000 and 700,000 students attending them.[38] What started as an alternative system for a small number of conservative religious families on the periphery of Pakistani society had been transformed into a countrywide parallel education system, catering for a substantial proportion of Pakistani children.

The education offered by the madrasas was, and remains, woefully inadequate. Even those that do teach some non-religious subjects rely on ancient sources. In some Pakistani madrasas, for example, medicine is taught through a text written in the eleventh century[39] and geometry teachers use material written by Euclid in 300 BC. Many of the madrasa students have received such a limited education that they have no prospect of finding a job in the mainstream economy. For men like these, the militant outfits offer a purpose; a way of winning respect in the community and more than just a touch of glamour. They also offer money. For many recruits the promise of a small regular salary can be a significant factor in their decision to become a Jihadi or holy warrior. And there is another consideration: if a Jihadi dies in a 'military' operation their families will be provided for. One charitable foundation in Pakistan has dispensed hundreds of thousands of dollars to martyrs' families since 1995.[40]

Before 11 September General Musharraf had expressed his concern about the madrasas and had taken some limited steps to control them. The government sent a four-page form to all the country's madrasas asking them to give details of their syllabi and sources of their funding. Few bothered to reply and once again it looked as if a government initiative would wither away. After 11 September Musharraf had greater confidence and he announced sweeping measures to control the madrasas. Clerics running the schools were told they had to turn away any foreign students who did not have a letter of approval from their own governments and to start teaching science, English and Pakistan studies alongside religious subjects. Musharraf also ordered the creation of a registration system for all those attending the madrasas. The US provided US $10 million dollars to purchase the necessary computer equipment.[41]

Two years after he grasped power Musharraf was, for the first time, demonstrating real resolve to reverse Zia's legacy. Ironically both men were presented with the opportunity to pursue their diametrically-opposed agendas because Washington needed to secure Pakistan's support to determine the course of events in Afghanistan. Musharraf, like Zia before him, can pursue his programme in the knowledge that billions of dollars of aid are flowing into the country. And, like Zia, he can be confident that the US will not be pressing for the restoration of democracy. Even so he faces an enormous challenge.

Only one of his predecessors, Ayub Khan, attempted to confront the radicals. He failed. It is not yet clear whether Musharraf will succeed. Pakistani leaders have always been better at declaring their policies than implementing them. In many ways, Musharraf faces even greater problems than Ayub Khan. The Islamic radicals, both internationally and withinPakistan, are stronger now than they were in the 1960s. Furthermore by the start of the twenty-first century Pakistan had become a heavily indebted country with a 40 per cent illiteracy rate, no democratic tradition worth speaking of and endemic corruption. Musharraf also has to face the fact that the Islamic radicals are not the only ones pressing for change in Pakistan. Nationalists in Sindh, Balochistan and NWFP are also calling for an overhaul of the country's political institutions. The strength and nature of Islamic sentiment in the armed forces will also be a critical factor as will the future of the Kashmir conflict. These themes are the subject of this book. And only after understanding the depth of Pakistan's problems can we reach an assessment of whether General Musharraf will be able to achieve his goals. Let us see how he got into power in the first place.

2 The 1999 Coup

> I advised Karachi Air Traffic Control that I had 198 souls on board, a limited amount of fuel and that if we were not allowed to land we would lose the aircraft and that would be the end of the story.
>
> —Pilot of PK 805, Captain Sayed Sarwat Hussain

On the morning of 12 October 1999, Nawaz Sharif finally made up his mind. His army chief would have to go. Like many Pakistani leaders before him, Sharif had surrounded himself with a tightly woven cocoon of sycophants. Family relatives and business cronies filled the key posts of his administration. The chief of army staff, General Pervez Musharraf, did not fit in.

Sharif had appointed Musharraf in October 1998 and quickly came to regret the decision. He regarded his army chief with distaste. The origin of the antagonism, which was mutual, lay in the snow-clad, Himalayan peaks of Kashmir. In the spring of 1999 Musharraf gave the final order for Pakistani troops to cross the line of control that separates the Indian and Pakistani armies in Kashmir. The soldiers, posing as divinely-inspired Islamic militants, clambered up the snowy passes that led to one of Kashmir's most strategic locations: the dusty, run-down town of Kargil. Having caught the Indians off guard, the Pakistani troops made significant territorial gains. Tactically, the operation was a success. Politically, it was a disaster. As India cried foul, Sharif found himself in the midst of a major international crisis. And while General Musharraf had sent the troops in, Prime Minister Sharif was left with the unenviable task of getting them out. For three decades the Pakistani people had absorbed a steady flow of vitriolic propaganda about the Kashmir issue: Sharif's decision to withdraw seemed incomprehensible and humiliating. As the man who had defied world opinion and tested Pakistan's nuclear bomb, Sharif had been acclaimed as a national hero. As the man who pulled out from Kargil, he was denounced as a supine coward. Sharif's sense of resentment was acute. General Musharraf, he complained, had marched his men to the top of the hill without considering how he would get them down again.

The generals, though, were also unhappy. By deciding to pull out of Kargil without negotiating any Indian concessions in return, they argued, Sharif had squandered a militarily advantageous position and caused a crisis of confidence within the Pakistan army. After the Kargil withdrawal Musharraf faced a surge of discontent within the army. As he toured a series of garrisons he repeatedly faced the same question: 'If Kargil was a victory then why did we pull back?' Musharraf told his men that it was the prime minister's fault and that the army had had no choice but to obey his order. It was a disingenuous response. Musharraf had been fully consulted on the withdrawal order and had raised no serious objection to it.

Sharif was never in any doubt that removing Musharraf would be a high-risk exercise. In 1993 Sharif's first government had been forced out of office in part because the military high command lost confidence in him. He was determined to avoid a repeat performance. Indeed, from the moment he took over as prime minister again in 1997, Sharif had devoted himself to making his political position impregnable.

He began by tackling the press. Newspaper editors were bullied into submission. The government distributed bribes to its media allies and ordered tax investigations into those editors who continued to print critical articles. Parliament, too, was emasculated. Sharif forced through a constitutional amendment that required all members of the National Assembly to vote according to party lines. The judiciary posed a more formidable challenge. In 1997 the Supreme Court summoned Sharif to appear before it in a contempt of court case. Twice he submitted to the court's will. On the third occasion his patience ran out. A mob of his supporters, led by some cabinet members and close advisers, ransacked the Supreme Court, disrupting proceedings and smashing furniture. The terrified judges caved in and the contempt of court case was dropped.

Within weeks it was the turn of the president, Farooq Leghari.
Initially appointed by Benazir Bhutto, Leghari had abandoned his patron
and switched sides, installing Nawaz Sharif as prime minister. But even
if he owed his premiership to Leghari, Sharif still didn't entirely trust the
president. As soon as Leghari voiced support for the embattled judiciary,
Sharif had him replaced by an old family friend from Lahore, Rafiq Tarar.
A former Supreme Court judge, Tarar had a reputation as both a pious
Muslim and a man who had a huge repertoire of dirty jokes. He was not,
however, known for his ability to stand up to authority. As soon as he
became president, Tarar readily agreed to Sharif's proposal that the
presidency be stripped of its power to remove a sitting government.

Nawaz Sharif went on to target Benazir Bhutto, the only Pakistani
politician who rivalled his national appeal. After a no-expense-barred,
two-year-long investigation, Sharif secured her conviction on corruption charges. The prime minister, though, did not imprison Bhutto.
Aware of her unrivalled capacity to play the role of political martyr, he
calculated that she would be more dangerous inside prison than out.
Consequently he brokered a deal that allowed her to flee to London
where she posed no political threat.

Sharif also made efforts to tame the most resilient Pakistani institution of all: the army. On 6 October 1998, General Musharraf's widely
respected predecessor General Jehangir Karamat, despairing of the
sustained corruption and incompetence of the Sharif administration,
had voiced the frustration felt by countless officers. In a speech to
Lahore Naval College, he called for the establishment of a National
Security Council that would give the military a formal role in the political decision-making process: 'A National Security Council', he said, 'or
similar committee at the apex would institutionalise decision-making.'[1]
Sharif responded ruthlessly: within two days Karamat was forced to
resign and General Musharraf appointed chief of army staff in his place.

Musharraf was not Sharif's first choice. He had wanted to appoint
another family friend, the soft-spoken and highly ambitious Lt. General
Khwaja Ziauddin. Ziauddin, however, had risen through the Engineer's
Corps and, by tradition, the army chief had to have an infantry or
armoured background. Advised that any breach of this tradition would
be unacceptable to the army, Sharif opted for Musharraf instead. But he

also took care to ensure that should another opportunity arise in the future, Ziauddin would be better placed to take over. The prime minister appointed him as director general of the ISI. Normally such a decision would have been taken in consultation with the army chief but, much to General Musharraf's annoyance, Sharif pushed Ziauddin's promotion through just hours after Musharraf himself was appointed.

Even though Sharif did not consider Musharraf to be an ideal choice, the prime minister initially felt comfortable with him. In August 1998 (two months before Karamat's dismissal) Musharraf had used some of his political contacts to secure a meeting with Sharif so that he could put himself forward as a possible successor. It was an astute move. Sharif started perceiving Musharraf as a potentially loyal and subservient army chief. Furthermore, since Musharraf was an Urdu-speaking officer whose family had come to Pakistan at the time of partition, Sharif hoped he would be unable to build a secure power base in the Punjabi dominated army. Not for the first time (or the last) Sharif's judgement was faulty. Although ethnic ties in the Pakistan army are strong, loyalty to the institution itself is generally even stronger. Furthermore, Musharraf was a former commando who had shown scant respect for his senior officers throughout his career. The sacked Karamat had repeatedly stated both in public and in private that he would never mount a coup. He meant it. Musharraf, however, was an unknown quantity.

For his part, Musharraf neither respected nor admired Sharif. Like many of his senior military colleagues, he saw the prime minister as an incapable, power-crazed paranoiac who was failing to produce the economic growth that Pakistan so badly needed. As he settled down to his new job, however, Musharraf put such thoughts aside and concentrated on military matters in which he advocated a more proactive policy. One of his early decisions was to explore the possibility of moving on to the offensive in Kashmir. The result was the Kargil campaign.

After Kargil, the relationship between the prime minister and army chief was severely damaged and, by early September, General Head Quarters (GHQ) was buzzing with rumours that Sharif would sack Musharraf. It was clear that a crisis was imminent. Recalling that time, the former navy chief Admiral (Retd.) Fasih Bokhari has said: 'The two men could not work together and both were preparing to take some

action. I could see that there were now two centres of power on a collision course.'² Bokhari's view was not based on hearsay. In the first
week of September Musharraf, somewhat guardedly, declared his hand.
At an informal meeting with the navy chief, Musharraf described Sharif
as incompetent and incapable of running the country. Bokhari, who was
an ex officio member of the joint chiefs of staff, got the firm impression that Musharraf was sounding out whether he could rely on the
navy's support in the event of a coup.

Bokhari was not the only one to notice the tension between the two
men. On 8 and 9 September 1999 Sharif and Musharraf travelled
together to the Northern Areas. They were to preside over a ceremony
to reward the Northern Light Infantry (NLI) for its role in the Kargil
campaign. Previously a paramilitary force answerable to the Ministry
of Interior, the NLI was to be inducted into the regular army. The trip
got off to a bad start when Sharif noticed the absence of the commander of the 10th corps, Lt. General Mehmood Ahmed. In the previous few weeks Sharif and Musharraf had undertaken two other trips
to the Northern Areas and on both occasions Mehmood had been present. On this third occasion his absence was especially striking as the
Northern Light Infantry was to be transferred to his command. Sharif
knew that Mehmood would be a key figure in any coup against his
government. Clearly, he should have attended the induction ceremony.
As far as Sharif was concerned, there was only one explanation for
Mehmood not being present: Musharraf was afraid he might be
arrested by Sharif and wanted Mehmood away from the scene so that
he could organise a response if the need arose.

On the evening of 8 September Sharif revealed his anxiety. General
Musharraf was in the lobby of the Hotel Shangri-La outside Skardu
showing off a new Italian laser-guided pistol to the information minister, Mushahid Hussain. As Musharraf was explaining how the pistol
could never miss its target, the prime minister walked into the lobby.
Aware of his fondness for high tech gadgets, Mushahid Hussain called
Sharif over. 'Have you seen this new pistol?' he asked Sharif. 'It's
remarkable.' Uncharacteristically, Sharif did not ask how the pistol
worked, but he did put one question to the army chief. 'General', he
asked, 'who are you aiming it at?'³

As he considered the possibility of mounting a coup, Musharraf realised he would not be able to move without the support of all his corps commanders. He called them together in mid-September and raised the question of Sharif's competence. Although there was wide agreement that Sharif was not performing well, the generals decided that the army could not move without clear justification. But if Sharif tried to sack Musharraf, the corps commanders agreed, then they would act: to lose two army chiefs in the space of a year would be unacceptable. With this qualified backing Musharraf went back to Sharif and said he wanted to be given the full chairmanship of the joint chiefs of staff (at the time he was only acting chairman) and, to demonstrate his seriousness, he put the 111 Brigade on standby. It was an unmistakeable signal. 111 Brigade had been used for carrying out every previous coup in Pakistan. Three hundred troops, with a squadron of tanks, were posted at the army's GHQ in Rawalpindi, just 10 miles from Islamabad. The troops were outside the normal chain of command and answerable only to General Musharraf himself.

Sharif's fears were confirmed by one of his few allies in the army leadership, the corps commander from the Baloch capital Quetta, General Tariq Pervez. The two men knew each other well: the general's cousin, Raja Nadir Pervez, was Sharif's communications minister. A few days after the corps commander's meeting, General Tariq Pervez warned Sharif that if he moved against Musharraf, the army would strike. Thoroughly unnerved, Sharif sought the help of his most trusted political ally, Senator Saif ur Rehman. The energetic senator had organised the triumphant corruption investigation into Benazir Bhutto and had blackmailed and bullied countless other government opponents. He now concentrated his efforts on Musharraf, putting a tap on his phones and monitoring his movements.

Sharif next turned his attention to Washington. He wanted to warn the Americans that Pakistan's democratic regime was at risk. The prime minister knew that if he conveyed such a message through official Foreign Office channels it would be leaked back to the military in a matter of minutes. He consequently decided to send a more trustworthy and convincing envoy: his brother, Shahbaz. It was a good choice. With his studied English accent, immaculate three-piece suits and fluent patter about democracy and accountability, Shahbaz knew how to charm Western officials. Indeed, many US diplomats in Islamabad were so impressed with Shahbaz that they openly voiced their opinion that he would make a better prime minister than his brother.

Shahbaz reached Washington on 17 September and briefed the State Department about the risk of a coup. He reminded the Americans that on 4 July 1999 Nawaz Sharif had responded to President Clinton's appeal to withdraw Pakistani troops from Kargil. The prime minister, Shahbaz argued, was paying a high political price for that decision. And who, Shahbaz asked, was responsible for Kargil? None other than the volatile chief of army staff, General Musharraf. Not only had he led the subcontinent into a small war; he was now threatening the democratically elected government.

As well as suggesting that Washington had a moral obligation to help his brother, Shahbaz Sharif also made a significant offer. He told the Americans that the Pakistani government was about to take a tougher line on the Taliban regime in Afghanistan. This was exactly what Washington wanted to hear. The US had long been deeply frustrated by Islamabad's support for the Taliban. The issue became acute after the July 1998 bombing of the US embassies in Kenya and Tanzania in which over 250 people, including twelve Americans, were killed. Washington blamed the attacks on the Afghan-based Saudi dissident Osama Bin Laden and in August 1998 even launched a cruise missile attack on Bin Laden's militant training camps in eastern Afghanistan. Sharif offered to help America kill Bin Laden. He agreed that US troops could visit Pakistan and brief a team of Pakistani troops from the Special Services Group (SSG), who would then go to Afghanistan and try to either capture or kill Bin Laden. Nawaz Sharif was determined to ensure that Washington had a stake in the survival of his government. (The plan to capture or kill Bin Laden never came to fruition. After the coup General Musharraf ditched the plan as unrealistic.)[4]

Shahbaz's visit to the States produced immediate results. On 20 September an unnamed US official in Washington said: 'We hope there will be no return to the days of interrupted democracy in Pakistan.'[5] US officials in Islamabad reinforced the message. While insistent that they were backing not Sharif, but rather the Pakistani constitution, they said

Washington would oppose 'any extra-constitutional actions' in Pakistan.[6] While making these highly unusual public statements, US officials privately urged Sharif to patch up his differences with Musharraf.

Musharraf, however, was pressing ahead with his preparations for a possible coup and the 111 Brigade were reviewing their procedures for taking over. On 21 September staff at the prime minister's official residence noticed that troops were walking around the building's perimeter with headphones and walkie-talkies. Sharif demanded an explanation but when it came it hardly put his mind at rest. The army claimed it had intelligence that the prime minister could be the target of a terrorist attack and had consequently decided to review its procedures for protecting him. Sharif believed that the military were tapping his phones and bugging his offices. Before discussing sensitive issues with close colleagues he would switch up the volume of his television set.[7]

By the end of September Sharif was making detailed plans for Musharraf's removal. Realising that secrecy would be vital, Sharif telephoned his son, Hussain Nawaz, who was doing a business deal in London, and told him to return to Pakistan as soon as possible. He also gave Musharraf some reassuring signals that his three-year term as army chief was not in doubt. To further demonstrate his good faith Sharif promoted Musharraf to chairman of the joint chiefs of staff on a permanent basis. Aware that American support could be crucial, Sharif also delivered on his promise regarding the Taliban. On 7 October, the prime minister told a press conference in Islamabad that his government was demanding the closure of militant training camps in Afghanistan.[8]

If Sharif was trying to lull Musharraf into a false sense of security it did not work. As soon as the army chief heard that General Tariq Pervez had been meeting Sharif he relieved him of his duties. (On 13 October, one day after the coup, Musharraf went one stage further and had the general arrested. The charge sheet said he 'had divulged sensitive information to certain outside quarters which posed a threat to the interests of the Pakistan Armed Forces'.[9]) Musharraf also made a second significant personnel change. Another corps commander, General Saleem Hyder, known to have close links with Sharif, was demoted to the post of master general of ordnance.

Sharif was furious that his few allies in the military were being sacked and demoted. It was now just a question of timing. The prime minister knew that Musharraf was due to be out of Pakistan in October to attend the fiftieth anniversary celebrations of Sri Lanka's army. The army chief was due to return on 12 October; since he would be airborne for four hours, Sharif calculated, the army would be caught off-balance and left unsure how to react to his sacking. By the time Musharraf touched down, his removal would be a fait accompli and a new army chief would have taken his place. Sharif was relying on the element of surprise and felt constrained by his fear that he was being bugged. On 10 October he arranged a flight to Abu Dhabi ostensibly for a meeting with Sheikh Zayed Bin Sultan Nahyan. He took a very limited group consisting of his son Hussain Nawaz, his speechwriter Nazir Naji and the man he wanted to succeed Musharraf, the ISI chief General Ziauddin. Confident that any conversation on the plane could not be overheard, Sharif spent the entire flight talking to Ziauddin: the final plot was being hatched.

On the fateful day, Sharif knew he had to give the appearance of conducting business as usual. At 10.00 a.m. on 12 October he left Islamabad to make a routine political speech in the town of Shujaabad, near Multan. Before leaving, Sharif gave instructions that he wanted his defence secretary, Lt. General (Retd.) Iftikhar Ali Khan, to meet him on his return. He also scheduled an appointment with President Rafiq Tarar for that afternoon, giving instructions that the meeting should not be reflected in his official programme for the day. The prime minister again took a small group with him: Hussain Nawaz, Nazir Naji and the chairman of Pakistan Television (PTV), Pervez Rashid. When the plane landed in Multan, Sharif told Nazir Naji that he should remain on board for a discussion with his son and Pervez Rashid. All the crew, Sharif said, had been told to leave the plane and they could talk in confidence. Once the aircraft door was closed the three men sat down and Pervez Rashid asked Nazir Naji for his mobile phone. Sharif, he explained, could not afford any of the information he was about to divulge to be leaked. Naji was then shown a speech written in Hussain Sharif's handwriting that his father planned to give on television that evening. Although the punch line – the dismissal of Musharraf – was not included in the draft, it was clear that the speech would announce that decision. Naji then worked on the draft, translating it into Urdu.

Two hours later the prime minister's plane was heading back towards Islamabad and when he touched down at the military airbase at Chaklala his defence secretary, as arranged, was there to meet him. As the two men were driven to the prime minister's residence, Sharif declared his hand. The sacking of Lt. General Tariq Pervez, he said, 'has started creating the impression that there is a gap between the government and the army which is not good for the security of Pakistan . . . I have decided to appoint a new army chief.' The defence secretary was shocked: he could guess the army's likely reaction. He suggested that the prime minister might want to discuss the issue with Musharraf but Sharif was adamant. 'The time for this discussion', he said, 'is over.'[10]

As the prime minister's car drew up outside his official residence in Islamabad his principal secretary Saeed Mehdi was, as ever, on hand to greet him. Mehdi was already aware of the prime minster's plans and Sharif now told him to prepare the official papers for the handover of military power. As he walked into his office, the prime minister confirmed that the new army chief was to be none other than the man he had wanted to appoint twelve months before, Lt. General Ziauddin.

As Sharif's officials got to work, General Musharraf had already completed his official programme in Sri Lanka and was preparing to board flight PK 805 which would take him back to Karachi, along with 197 other passengers and crew, including the pilot, Captain Sarwat Hussain. Because the army chief was on board there were extra security checks and the plane took off forty minutes late at 4.00 p.m. At the very moment Musharraf's plane was climbing into the sky, the man who confidently expected to replace him was reaching the prime minster's residence. By the time Sharif went to see him at 4.20 p.m., Saeed Mehdi had completed drafting the official notification. It stated that:

It has been decided to retire General Pervez Musharraf, Acting Chairman, Joint Chiefs of Staff Committee and Chief of the Army Staff with immediate effect. Lt. Gen. Ziauddin has been appointed as the

Chief of Army Staff with immediate effect and promoted to the rank of General.

Before orders to this effect are issued, President may kindly see.

By 4.30 p.m. Sharif had signed the document. The deed was done. He told Ziauddin to assume his command and went to the president's residence to show him the notification. Perhaps aware that the army might not accept the change, and that Sharif's days might be numbered, Tarar displayed some of the political cunning that had enabled him to achieve high office. Rather than writing the word 'approved' on the notification, he employed the more neutral term 'seen' and signed it. With the formalities completed Sharif told Pakistan Television (PTV) to broadcast the news of Musharraf's sacking. It did so on the 5.00 p.m. bulletin. PTV was also told to take pictures of Ziauddin receiving his badges of rank.

Ziauddin was now the de jure army chief, but he knew that to become the de facto leader as well he would have to move fast. Rather than waste time by driving back to the ISI headquarters, he stayed in the prime minister's residence and started making phone calls from there. He thought two men, the chief of general staff Lt. General Aziz Khan and the commander of the 10th corps Lt. General Mehmood Ahmed, were likely to offer him the stiffest resistance. Both were Musharraf loyalists who, within army circles, had been outspoken in their criticism of Sharif. Ziauddin decided to remove both of them. He called an old engineering corps friend, the quarter-master general Lt. General Akram, and offered him the job of chief of the general staff. Excited by his promotion, Akram said he would come straight round to the prime minister's house. Ziauddin then called the man who had recently been removed by Musharraf, General Saleem Hyder. Hyder was playing golf and was not immediately available. Eventually the two men spoke and Hyder was offered General Mehmood's job: 10th corps commander. Having sorted out the two key posts, Ziauddin called round other corps commanders. Most were non-committal. They were in an awkward position: they did not want to repudiate the new army chief but were also aware that Musharraf loyalists might resist him.

While Ziauddin was trying to shore up his new position, the two men best placed to stop him, Lt. Generals Aziz and Mehmood, were playing not golf but tennis. They realised that there was a problem when both their mobile phones started ringing on the side of the court. The man who called them was the Peshawar-based Lt. General Syed uz Zafar. As the longest-standing corps commander, he was serving as the acting chief of army staff in Musharraf's absence. Consequently, Ziauddin had called him to tell him about his own elevation and Musharraf's sacking. But rather than simply accept Ziauddin's statement as a fait accompli General Syed uz Zafar called Aziz and Mehmood in Rawalpindi. The second they were told what was happening Aziz and Mehmood held a brief conversation and decided to act. As one eyewitness put it, 'I have never seen two senior officers move so fast.' They sped to GHQ and, as they changed out of their sports kit, considered their options. One thing, they decided, was beyond doubt: they could not permit a change of army chief while Musharraf was out of the country. The first priority, then, was to get the news off PTV. The two generals despatched Major Nisar of the Punjab Regiment, together with fifteen armed men, to the PTV building in Islamabad. He was ordered to block any further announcement about Musharraf's sacking. As the major set off, Aziz called a meeting of all available corps commanders and other senior officers at army headquarters in Rawalpindi. Some already knew what was up: they had received the telephone calls from Ziauddin. And with Mehmood and Aziz determined to resist Ziauddin's appointment, the corps commanders decided to implement the decision they had taken in principle in September: Sharif had to go. Within minutes, the infamous III Brigade was ordered to do its job.

Unaware of the growing crisis, PTV continued to put out the news of Ziauddin's appointment. The station's managers first became aware of a problem when Major Nisar and his men rushed past the guards on the gate and stormed into the control room. The major ordered the PTV staff to block the news of Musharraf's dismissal. 'Take it off! Take it off!' he yelled. Faced with fifteen armed men and a screaming major, the staff complied.

At 6.00 p.m. Nawaz Sharif was sitting in the TV lounge of his official residence waiting for the news bulletin. But when it came on, he was dismayed that there was no mention of Musharraf's sacking. He told his military secretary, Brigadier Javed Iqbal, to go straight to the

TV headquarters and find out what was going on. Sharif was now convinced that he had to prevent General Musharraf's plane from landing. Ziauddin agreed. He advised Sharif that if Musharraf were kept out of the country the army would have to accept his removal.

The prime minister picked up the phone and made a desperate attempt to save his administration. First he spoke to Aminullah Choudhry, the Karachi-based director general of the Civil Aviation Authority. A classic civil servant, Choudhry could be relied upon to execute the prime minister's orders without hesitation. Sharif told Choudhry that flight PK 805 should not be allowed to land in Pakistan. Choudhry immediately called the air traffic control tower at Karachi: 'Which international flights do you have coming in at this time? Is there any coming in from Colombo?' he asked.[11] Having learnt that PK 805 was due to land within an hour, he ordered the closure of Karachi airport. Minutes later, the runway lights were switched off and three fire engines were parked on the landing strip – one at each end and a third in the middle. Choudhry also ordered the closure of PK 805's alternate destination, a small rural airport in Nawabshah, 200 miles east of Karachi.

Back in Islamabad, Sharif's military secretary, Brigadier Javed Iqbal, an excitable man at the best of times, was manically preparing for his mission to the TV station. As he left the prime minister's residence, he noticed a group of men from the Punjabi Elite Police at the gate. They were Shahbaz Sharif's personal bodyguards. He took the men with him and made the short journey to PTV headquarters. He arrived at 6.15 p.m. and went straight to the control room where he found Major Nisar with his fifteen men. 'Disarm yourself immediately!' the brigadier yelled.[12] Major Nisar refused. The brigadier then drew a pistol and pointed it at Nisar's chest. The Punjabi Elite Police and the Punjabi Regiment were moments away from a shoot-out. Nisar blinked first. He handed his gun to the brigadier and told his men to lay down their weapons. Within minutes the major and his men were locked in a room with an armed guard at the door. The jubilant military secretary ordered the Elite Police to shoot anyone who offered resistance and headed back to report his success to the prime minster. (Later, Brigadier Iqbal was to rue his actions. On 13 October he was arrested and charged with drawing a pistol on a fellow officer.)[13]

With the TV station back under civilian control, the news about Musharraf's retirement was rebroadcast at the end of the 6.00 p.m. bulletin. Encouraged by this turn of events, Sharif renewed his efforts to keep Musharraf out of the country. He called a long-time political ally, the chairman of Pakistan International Airlines (PIA), Shahid Abbasi, and repeated his order that PK 805 should not land in Pakistan but be sent to Muscat or anywhere else in the Middle East. He did not give a reason but, having just seen the news bulletin, Abbasi wasn't in much doubt about the prime minister's motivation.

Both Choudhry and Abbasi, though, soon realised that a disaster was in the making. Officials at PIA's operations department told Abbasi that the plane was 50 miles away from Karachi and lacked sufficient fuel to reach the Middle East. Choudhry's staff at the Civil Aviation Authority had already reached the same conclusion. The plane would have to land in Pakistan. Aminullah Choudhry called the prime minster and told him. But, Choudhry subsequently claimed, Sharif was adamant: the plane must not land in Pakistan.

Back at PTV headquarters, Major Nisar and his men were still being held under armed guard. When army officers at GHQ saw the news of Musharraf's sacking being replayed at the end of the 6.00 p.m. news bulletin, they realised something had gone wrong. A second army unit was despatched to PTV. At 6.45 p.m. another major, this time with five armed soldiers, asked the guards at the gate if they could enter the building. With the Punjabi Elite Police breathing down their necks, the guards refused to let the major through. Half an hour later, the major returned with a truckload of troops. Again he was refused entry, but this time he would not be denied. With a flick of his wrist the major ordered his men to clamber over the PTV gate. Journalists who had gathered at PTV filmed the pictures that within hours were leading news bulletins all over the world. The Elite Police, realising they were outnumbered and outgunned, offered no resistance; some even put their weapons on the ground and sat on them. By 7.15 p.m. PTV was off-air.

By then the coup was well underway. The first soldiers to reach the prime minister's residence had arrived at around 6.30 p.m. Having secured the gatehouse, a major took fifteen men over the extensive lawns and headed for the building's main entrance. As the porch came into view, the major saw General Ziauddin on the steps with six plain clothes ISI officers. The major ordered the ISI men to lay down their weapons. They refused and General Ziauddin tried to persuade the major to back down. The major started trembling. He was, after all, disobeying an order from the duly appointed army chief. Beads of sweat poured down his forehead. 'Sir', he threatened Ziauddin, 'it would take me just one second.' Ziauddin, recognising that resistance was futile, told his men to lay down their weapons.

Once inside the prime minster's residence, the soldiers soon found all the key figures of Sharif's administration. The prime minister, realising that he was about to be ousted, had gone to his private quarters to shred some documents. That done, he gathered with his brother Shahbaz and his son Hussain Nawaz to await their fate. General Ziauddin, his new chief of staff Lt. General Akram and other Sharif allies were also there. Having heard about Musharraf's sacking, Sharif's trusted ally Saif ur Rehman had gone to the residence. So had his brother, Mujib ur Rehman, the chairman of the Pakistan Cricket Board, who had turned up with his young son to congratulate Sharif on getting rid of Musharraf. Mujib had never been an important political figure and, but for his naivety, he would have been able to leave the residence a free man. An army officer asked for Mujib's child to be removed. Rather than just taking his son away, a terrified Mujib ur Rehman asked if that meant he could fly to Dubai. The officer immediately became suspicious and told Mujib to stay put. With the residence secured, Lt. General Mehmood himself arrived and confronted Nawaz. 'I was praying and hoping', the general said, 'that it wouldn't come to this.'

But if developments on the ground were reaching a conclusion, the same could not be said for the events in the air. The pilot of PK 805, Captain Sarwat Hussain, was becoming increasingly agitated. Despite his misgivings, Aminullah Choudhry was still trying to implement the prime minister's order to prevent the plane from landing in Pakistan. As the recordings from the air traffic control tower reveal, Choudhry's staff knew that there could be a disaster. 'If it crashes, then?' asked one. 'We cannot take the blame if it crashes,' responded another. To add to their woes, the air traffic controllers now had the military coming on the line. GHQ in Rawalpindi had already ordered troops in Karachi to take over the airport so that Musharraf could land. The chief of Pakistan's air defence, Lt. General Iftikhar Hussain Shah, called the air traffic controller in person. He took a paternalistic but uncompromising approach: 'Son, do this', he told the hapless controller, 'it must not be diverted.' This admonition came just five minutes after Aminullah Choudhry had repeated his order to redirect the flight. The tape-recorder in the air traffic control tower captured the controller's reply. It is best transcribed as 'Uuuuhn!'

These were critical minutes. The air traffic controllers were caught between two authorities. They decided to obey their immediate boss, Aminullah Choudhry.

18.43:
Air Traffic Control Tower (ATC): 'PK 805. If your alternate is Nawab-shah, the Nawabshah airfield is also closed.'
PK 805: 'OK, sir. We understand the situation very very clearly now.'

For all his sardonic calm, the pilot's situation was now desperate. He could not land in Pakistan but he did not have enough fuel to reach the Middle East. The air traffic controllers, however, would not back down.

18.59:
ATC: 'PK 805. It's up to you. You have to decide what you have to do. Proceed as per your decision.'
PK 805: 'We understand that Karachi very well. The point is we have limited fuel. Either we run out of fuel and that's the end of the story or you allow us to land . . .'
ATC: 'PK 805. You cannot land at any airport in Pakistan and you can proceed outside Pakistan.'

While these anguished conversations were going on, Aminullah Choudhry was trying to reach the prime minister to restate the point that the plane did not have enough fuel to reach the Middle East. By this stage, troops had already entered Sharif's official residence and, in the confusion, Choudhry could not get through to the prime minister. Eventually he managed to speak to Sharif's military secretary, Brigadier Javed Iqbal, and explained the problem once again. After some minutes, the brigadier called back. He said the aircraft should be allowed to land at Nawabshah, isolated at the end of the runway, refuelled and sent on to the Middle East. No one, he said, should be allowed to disembark. Air traffic control relayed the new instructions and told the plane it could land at Nawabshah. With immense relief the crew of PK 805 turned the plane around and headed for their alternate destination.

The tapes recorded in the air traffic control tower give a good indication of what was happening on board PK 805, but they do not tell the whole story. The control tower could not hear all the conversations between Captain Sarwat and General Musharraf. The general, however, gave his account of what happened in the cockpit.[14]

As soon as he had learnt that all the airports in Pakistan were closed to him, Captain Sarwat had concluded that his unenviable predicament had something to do with General Musharraf's presence on board his plane. He called Musharraf to the cockpit and told him that air traffic control had denied permission to land. The pilot said the plane had just enough fuel to land in Ahmedabad in India. 'We are actually now left with forty-five minutes of fuel', the pilot said, 'and we can only go to India.' 'Over my dead body,' replied Musharraf. 'We are not going to India. Tell that to the air traffic control.' The air traffic control tower, however, was adamant that the Pakistani airports remained closed.

'By this time', Musharraf recalled,

> the pilot said we did not even have the fuel to go to India. We had maybe thirty-five minutes to land. So I said 'OK Hell with everything, land at Karachi'. The pilot, however, said that the landing lights at the runway must have been switched off. There must be something across the runway which would not allow us to land. In fact it would be a total disaster. I had to accept but I said: 'Paint this picture immediately to the air traffic control tower because we can't go anywhere.'

Musharraf gave a very similar version of these events to the news magazine *Newsline*.[15] In that interview he added one detail. Having eventually received permission to land in Nawabshah, Musharraf recalled the following conversation: 'I asked the pilot whether we could reach Nawabshah and he said: "Yes. We can." So I said: "OK. Let's go."' The pilot did just that.

A couple of minutes after PK 805 set off for Nawabshah, the army arrived at Karachi airport and took it over. The first soldier to reach the air traffic control tower was Brigadier Jabbar Sahib who demanded that the plane be brought back to Karachi. The air traffic controllers decided to check with their boss, Aminullah Choudhry:

19.14:
ATC: 'Brigadier Jabbar Sahib and his team are here.'
Choudhry: 'Yes.'
ATC: 'And they have said to bring it back to Karachi.'
Choudhry: 'Uh. OK.'
ATC: 'Yes sir.'
Choudhry: 'I see. If they are saying this. And I am going to say that he has to be off-loaded also, that man.' [Musharraf]
ATC: 'So far they have asked for its landing.'
Choudhry: 'OK. OK. I see. Then you let it land. Yes.'
ATC: 'OK sir. OK sir.'

Choudhry realised that if a brigadier was in the control tower, a coup was underway and he would have to submit to the army's will. The air traffic control called PK 805 back to Karachi. The plane was now midway between Karachi and Nawabshah and running ever shorter of fuel. The pilot, however, ignored the instruction to return to Karachi and instead climbed to a higher altitude where the plane would use less fuel. This was a strange decision and Brigadier Jabbar could not understand what was going on. He told the traffic controllers that they had to get the plane to Karachi. 'Our men have reached everywhere now,' he said. 'We will blow you up. You have to get that plane to land. Send a direct message. Do whatever. It must not be diverted anywhere else.' Staff at the control tower assured the brigadier they were trying to do just that. PK 805, though, still refused to come down. Eventually, Lt. General Iftikhar went to the air traffic control tower in person:

19.26:
ATC (Iftikhar): 'PK 805. This is Karachi ATC. Over.'
PK 805 (CREW): 'Go ahead. Over.'
ATC (Iftikhar): 'This is General Iftikhar. You are hereby directed to

land at Karachi airport. The Karachi control tower will guide you. There is no need to divert anywhere. Is that clear? Over.'

The message was relayed to Musharraf who still refused to comply. He told Captain Sarwat that he wanted to hear from one man and one man alone, his friend and trusted colleague, the Karachi corps commander, General Usmani.

19.30:
PK 805 (crew): 'I have been directed by the chief that the Corps Commander should come on the line.'
ATC (Iftikhar): 'Please convey to the Chief: this is General Iftikhar. I would like to speak to him.'
PK 805 (crew) 'Standby, we will get the General.'
(Musharraf): 'Iftikhar this is Pervez. Where is Usmani?'
ATC (Iftikhar): 'PK 805, go ahead.'
PK 805 (Musharraf) 'This is Pervez. Message for Iftikhar. General Iftikhar where is Usmani?'
ATC (Iftikhar): 'Sir, this is Iftikhar on the set. General Usmani is in the VIP lounge. He is waiting at the gate for you. I am in the control tower.'
PK 805 (Musharraf): 'Where is Iftikhar now? Is that Iftikhar speaking?'
ATC (Iftikhar): 'Affirmative.'
PK 805 (Musharraf): 'Iftikhar, what is the problem?'
ATC (Iftikhar): 'I am sure you would not know. About two hours back your retirement was announced and you were to be replaced by Zia. The army has taken over and they were trying to divert your plane, so that it does not land here. We have taken over the airport and you are coming in now.'
PK 805 (Musharraf): 'Iftikhar thank you. Tell Mehmood and Aziz nobody will leave the country.'

Musharraf knew he was running out of time. But the fact that he had still not spoken to the one man in Karachi in whom he had complete trust, General Usmani, made him nervous. Accordingly, his aides on the plane prepared for the possibility that General Iftikhar was tricking them and that there had been an internal army putsch that would result in Musharraf being arrested at Karachi airport.

For some years Pakistan International Airlines had had a policy of deploying armed air marshals on three of its routes: to and from Delhi, Kathmandu and Colombo. Consequently, three marshals were, like General Musharraf and his entourage, sitting in the first class seats of PK 805. The chief of army staff now wanted their guns. Having identified the air marshals, Musharraf's military secretary, Brigadier Nadeem Taj, made the request. After a few minutes' deliberation, the air marshals decided they could not hand over their weapons. But they did offer to help Musharraf. If anyone tried to storm the plane, they said, they would resist and fire back even at the cost of their lives. Slightly reassured, but nonetheless sweating profusely, General Musharraf decided the time had come to descend. As he later recalled, he ordered the pilot to go to Karachi: 'I told him: "Return to Karachi".'[16] Even when he landed, Musharraf was unsure whether or not he would need the air marshals' help. He refused to get off the plane until General Usmani had come on board to reassure him that the army was indeed united and that the coup had been on his behalf.

Nawaz Sharif later came to trial for his role in diverting the plane and was convicted of hijacking. The state's prosecution lawyers argued that the positioning of fire engines on the runway at Karachi meant that the prime minister had used force to take control of an aeroplane. Sharif's defence lawyers, however, maintained that if anyone was guilty of hijacking, it was General Musharraf himself. The army chief, they said, had taken control of the plane. When Captain Sarwat gave his evidence, Sharif's defence lawyers repeatedly tried to establish why the pilot had initially refused to return to Karachi. They argued that it was in fact General Musharraf who had refused and that the pilot had submitted to his will. Captain Sarwat steadfastly denied this. He said that he ignored the instruction to return to Karachi because he had lost confidence in the air traffic control tower. Since there had been so many contradictory orders, he argued, he wanted time to consider his options and await developments. He had calculated that he still had a little fuel to spare and that he could afford to wait a few minutes before finally committing himself to either Nawabshah or Karachi.

But the defence lawyers were right. Musharraf's own account of the events on PK 805 clearly indicates that he had taken control of the flight (although he had not used any force – a necessary element to prove hijacking). Conclusive evidence of General Musharraf's active role in the decision-making on board the plane was readily available. The Cockpit Voice Recorder (CVR) or black box records every sound made in the cockpit. The CVR has a looped, thirty-minute tape which allows investigators to hear everything said during the half hour before the plane comes to standstill. It would consequently have contained material that was not available on the air traffic control tower tapes. The court that tried Nawaz Sharif, however, never heard the black box recording. The military subsequently claimed that the CVR was left on the plane and that the recording of Musharraf's conversations with the pilot were erased. The police did eventually get hold of the black box but apparently did not listen to it. That may have been true: Pakistan does not possess the specialised equipment required to listen to a Cockpit Voice Recorder and obtaining a transcript of its contents would have meant sending the black box abroad. Precisely what happened to the black box is not clear. All that can be said with certainty is that it would have contained material embarrassing to General Musharraf and that the material never came into the public domain.

In assessing the role of the principal players in the PK 805 drama it is important to remember that it was Nawaz Sharif who first ordered the plane's diversion. It was, at the very least, an unethical decision. PK 805 was a commercial flight. For plainly political objectives Sharif put the passengers' lives at risk. He not only redirected the plane but did so without making any effort to apprise himself of the fuel situation. Even when informed about the lack of fuel on board he repeated his order that the plane should be sent outside of Pakistan. But General Musharraf also took a significant gamble. After he was told the plane could return to land at Karachi he waited for seventeen minutes until he was reasonably sure that General Usmani was waiting for him at the airport. Needless to say, General Musharraf was one of the last men who wanted the plane to crash: he was, after all, on board. He also had the benefit of precise information about the fuel situation, which was supplied to him by the crew members. Nevertheless, Musharraf's conduct, at best, fully justified his reputation as a risk-taker and, at worst, was reckless. When the plane landed at 7.47 p.m. Musharraf said it had just seven minutes' worth of fuel to spare. The flight log shows that 1,200 kilograms of fuel were left. That would last around five minutes if the plane was climbing and between ten to fifteen minutes if it was cruising.

By then the coup was all but over. Sharif and his key colleagues were in the army's hands, as were the airports, PTV stations and the telephone exchanges. By 8.00 p.m. the army had reached Ministers' Colony in Islamabad (a house in the colony is a perk of ministerial office). Some members of the cabinet were trying to make a run for it. Seeing the army approach, one minister dashed into his garden, scaled the back wall and then tried to hail a taxi. Another put on the scruffiest clothes he could find, gathered his possessions in a bundle and set off on foot. The army's action in Islamabad was replicated throughout the country. The military detained all Sharif's key supporters in Lahore, Peshawar and Karachi. Mindful of Musharraf's order that no one should leave the country, the army blocked all international flight departures and troops tried to seal Pakistan's notoriously porous border with Afghanistan.

At 10.15 p.m. PTV came back on air to announce the dismissal of Nawaz Sharif's government. Thousands of people, supporting the army action, had gathered outside the TV building. General Musharraf, PTV said, would address the nation shortly. He did so the next day at 2.50 a.m.:

> I was in Sri Lanka on an official visit. On my way back the PIA commercial flight was not allowed to land at Karachi but was ordered to be diverted to anywhere outside Pakistan. Despite acute shortages of fuel, imperilling the lives of all the passengers, thanks be to Allah, this evil design was thwarted through speedy army action ... My dear countrymen, having briefly explained the background, I wish to inform you that the armed forces have moved in as a last resort to prevent any further destabilisation.[17]

Another period of military rule had begun.

3 Kashmir

Kashmir will fall into our lap like a ripe fruit.

—Mohammed Ali Jinnah, August 1947

In August 1947, Kashmir's autocratic ruler, His Highness Maharaja Sir Hari Singh Indar Mahindar Bahadur Sir Hari Singh, was faced with a momentous decision. The imperial government in London had always allowed some major landholders on the subcontinent a degree of autonomy and, technically, Kashmir had never been part of British India. The maharaja's antecedents had secured the right to govern some of their own affairs by recognising the paramountcy of the British Crown. The compact between the British and the maharaja's family was symbolised by the payment of a tribute: each year Hari Singh had to provide the British government with a horse, twelve goats and six of Kashmir's famous shawls or pashminas.

When the British left, the maharaja had three options: Kashmir could become independent or join either India or Pakistan. The rulers of over 550 Princely State rulers faced the same decision but in the case of Kashmir the issue was especially sensitive. Its large population and proximity to both China and Russia gave the state considerable strategic importance. The matter was further complicated by religion: Kashmir was one of a handful of Princely States in which the ruler did not practise the same religion as most of his people. While the maharaja was a Hindu, over three-quarters of his subjects were Muslims. The fact that Kashmir was not only predominantly Muslim but also congruous with Pakistan convinced Mohammed Ali Jinnah that the maharaja's decision would go in his favour. 'Kashmir', he said at the time of partition, 'will fall into our lap like a ripe fruit.'[1] It was a naive misjudgement of Himalayan proportions.

The maharaja had most of the foibles associated with India's decadent aristocracy. He was a hedonist and a reactionary whose main interests were food, hunting, sex and, above all else, horse racing. As his own son put it: 'Quite clearly, my father was much happier racing than administering the State . . .'[2] On one occasion, he had been tricked by a prostitute in London's Savoy Hotel who proceeded to blackmail him.[3] He showed a similar lack of judgement in matters of state. In July 1947, with the transfer of power just weeks away, he took the view that 'the British are never really going to leave India'.[4]

The maharaja's ancestors had been blessed with greater political acumen. The State of Jammu and Kashmir had been established in the first half of the nineteenth century by a relatively minor Jammu chieftain, Gulab Singh. A combination of adept military conquests and astute financial deals enabled him to create one of the largest Princely States on the subcontinent. By 1850 he had moved on from Jammu (with its Hindu majority population) and had added Ladakh (Buddhist majority), Baltistan (Muslim majority) and the Kashmir Valley (Muslim majority). In the latter half of the nineteenth century, Gulab Singh's successors extended their control to another Muslim majority area, Gilgit.

Gulab Singh's successors, then, were Hindus ruling over a multiethnic state and their Muslim subjects were especially hard pressed. In 1929, one of Maharaja Hari Singh's officials, Sir Albion Bannerji, resigned his post declaring that the Muslims were illiterate, povertystricken and 'governed like dumb driven cattle'.[5] Elsewhere in India, Gandhi and his colleagues were campaigning against the British. In Kashmir the Muslims focussed most of their discontent on the maharaja. He responded with force. The first significant crisis came in July 1931 during the trial of a radical Muslim activist, Abdul Qadeer, who advocated a violent uprising against Hari Singh's royal household. When protestors gathered outside the prison in which he was held, the police killed over twenty demonstrators.

By 1941 the Muslims' situation had not improved. A Hindu writer, Premnath Bazaz, reported that most Muslims in Kashmir were serfs working for absentee landlords: 'The poverty of the Muslim masses is appalling. Dressed in rags and barefoot, a Muslim peasant presents the appearance of a starving beggar.'⁶ The maharaja himself hardly ever met his Muslim subjects. As his son later recalled: 'As for the Kashmiri Muslims, our contacts were mostly limited to the gardeners and the shooting and fishing guards.'⁷

As the British prepared to leave, it was clear that the maharaja wanted independence. He faced the opposition not only of Jinnah and Nehru (who both hoped to incorporate Kashmir into their new countries) but also the British. Lord Louis Mountbatten, who had been appointed viceroy of India so as to oversee and manage the process of Indian independence, considered the future of the Princely States, which covered no less than 45 per cent of the subcontinent's landmass, to be an important issue. In July 1947 many of the Princely State rulers gathered in their favoured forum, the Chamber of Princes, to hear Mountbatten speak. He urged them to opt either for Pakistan or India: 'You are about to face a revolution', he said. 'In a very brief moment you'll lose for ever your sovereignty. It is inevitable.'⁸ Mountbatten's success in persuading the vast majority of the Princely States to accept the new post-imperial dispensation and to abandon their hopes of retaining some autonomy was a remarkable achievement. But some of the more powerful rulers, including Maharaja Hari Singh, held out. This was despite the fact that Mountbatten had made special efforts with regard to Kashmir: his heavy workload in the run-up to the transfer of power notwithstanding, Mountbatten set aside six days for a visit to the maharaja's summer capital, Srinagar.

Mountbatten's talks in Srinagar have given rise to many controversies. Pakistani historians have argued that he improperly used his influence to steer the maharaja away from Karachi and towards Delhi. A typical Pakistani account can be found in the memoirs of the former Pakistani prime minister, Chaudri Muhammad Ali, who maintains that Mountbatten failed to give proper advice to Hari Singh. 'At no stage did he tell the maharaja, that, in view of the geographical and strategic factors and the overwhelmingly Muslim population of the State, it was his plain duty to accede to Pakistan.' In this, Ali maintains, Mountbatten was behaving inconsistently. When discussing similar issues with the Muslim leaders of Hindu majority Princely States he urged immediate accession to India.⁹

While Pakistani authors complain about Mountbatten's conduct in Srinagar, their Indian counterparts take the diametrically opposed view arguing that the viceroy behaved quite properly. Mountbatten, they insist, went to great lengths to advise the maharaja not only that the final decision was his alone but also that the Indian government would not consider it an unfriendly act if Kashmir did accede to Pakistan.[10]

Exactly what was said in Srinagar will never be known and, in any event, the issue is of limited significance. There are more serious charges made about Mountbatten's role in creating the conditions for enduring conflict in Kashmir, not least his alleged role in trying to influence the findings of the Boundary Commission, which was responsible for implementing the partition of the subcontinent by demarcating the new international borders that would run through Punjab.[11] The terms of reference of Sir Cyril's commission stated that: 'the Boundary Commission is instructed to demarcate the boundaries of the two parts of Punjab on the basis of ascertaining the contiguous majority areas of Muslims and non-Muslims. In doing so it will also take into account other factors.'[12] The man charged with drawing this highly important line was an austere and widely respected barrister Sir Cyril Radcliffe. Since he had never even set foot on the subcontinent Sir Cyril could hardly be accused of prejudice. And to further secure the Commission's image as an impartial body, Mountbatten said he wanted to isolate Sir Cyril from political pressures. He gave his staff explicit instructions to have no contact with him.

Two of Sir Cyril's decisions have given rise to prolonged, angry debate. The first concerned a Muslim majority area called Ferozepur. Ferozepur was of strategic importance not only because it was home to an irrigation head-works but also because it had the only arsenal which Pakistan could hope to have on its territory. There is now little doubt that Radcliffe intended to award Ferozepur to Pakistan and that Mountbatten persuaded him to change his mind. The most damning piece of evidence is a map that Radcliffe sent to the last governor of Punjab, Sir Evan Jenkins, on 8 August 1947. Jenkins received advance notice of all Radcliffe's awards so that he could get security personnel in place ahead of partition. The map showed that Ferozepur had been allocated to Pakistan. By the evening of 12 August, however, Jenkins had been instructed to change

the map and to note that Ferozepur was now to be part of India. The
matter came to light in 1948 when Pakistan managed to get hold of a
copy of the original map that had been left in Sir Evan Jenkins's safe.

In 1989, Christopher Beaumont, the man who had worked in Delhi
as Radcliffe's private secretary, published his account of what had happened. Having heard that Ferozepur was going to Pakistan, Mountbatten arranged a private lunch with Radcliffe. There is no record of exactly
what was said but by that evening Radcliffe had changed his mind.
'Mountbatten interfered', Beaumont concluded, 'and Radcliffe allowed
himself to be overborne: grave discredit to both.'[13]

Indian historians[14] now accept that Mountbatten probably did influence the Ferozepur award. The area, though, was of limited importance
in relation to Kashmir. Of far greater significance was another Muslim
majority district, Gurdaspur, which provided the only practicable land
link between India and Kashmir. If it were to be awarded to Pakistan it
would be difficult to see how the maharaja could realistically opt for
India. Mountbatten was certainly aware of Gurdaspur's strategic importance. In June he publicly raised the possibility that, despite its Muslim
majority, Gurdaspur could be awarded to India[15] and in early August he
stated that if that happened, then the maharaja's options regarding the
future status of Kashmir would be kept open.[16]

While Mountbatten's meddling in the Ferozepur award is now well-
established there is less evidence concerning his role in the decision about
Gurdaspur. While Pakistani historians claim that Mountbatten ensured it
went to India, their Indian counterparts insist he did no such thing.
Mountbatten's biographers, Larry Collins and Dominique Lapierre, have
also argued that there was no foul play in the Gurdaspur award: 'Unin-
tentionally, almost inadvertently', they assert, 'Radcliffe's scalpel had
offered India the hope of claiming Kashmir.'[17] It is interesting to note
that while Christopher Beaumont was convinced that the Ferozepur
award was fixed he did not believe the same was true of Gurdaspur. In
his 1989 testimony he wrote: 'No change, as has been subsequently
rumoured was made in the northern [Gurdaspur] part of the line.'[18]

The motives behind the Gurdaspur award remain disputed. But even
if Mountbatten's role in relation to the Boundary Commission was less
neutral than he claimed, his many critics tend to overlook an important

aspect of his views: he consistently supported a referendum to determine Kashmir's future status. Since it was a Princely State Mountbatten could not insist on a referendum but he did recommend one. When he met Hari Singh in June 1947 in Srinagar, he advised him to 'consult the will of the people and do what the majority thought best'.[19] Later, in October 1947, when India's first prime minister, Jawaharlal Nehru was deploying troops in Kashmir, Mountbatten insisted that any decision by the maharaja to accede to India would only be temporary prior to a referendum, plebiscite or, at the least, representative public meetings. When Mountbatten accepted the maharaja's decision to accede to India he told him:

> . . . my Government have decided to accept the accession of Kashmir State to the Dominion of India. Consistently with their policy that, in the case of any State where the issue of accession has been the subject of dispute, the question of accession should be decided in accordance with the wishes of the people of the State, it is my Government's wish that as soon as law and order have been restored in Kashmir and its soil cleared of the invaders, the question of the State's accession should be settled by a reference to the people.[20]

Pakistani historians have never given Mountbatten credit for this: their feelings towards him have been best captured by Jinnah's biographer, Akbar S. Ahmed, who describes the viceroy as the 'first Paki-basher'.[21] The acrimonious debate about his role has perhaps taken on an exaggerated importance, as the man who made the final decision about Kashmir was not Mountbatten but the maharaja. Too close a focus on Mountbatten's role also obscures the performance of another key player: Mohammed Ali Jinnah. Pakistan was to pay a heavy price for his complacent view that that the 'ripe fruit' of Kashmir would fall into his lap. Throughout 1947 Jinnah's approach to Kashmir was inept and at every stage his Indian counterparts outmanoeuvred him.

Jinnah's failure over Kashmir is all the more striking in view of the maharaja's dislike (or 'hate' as Mountbatten put it) of Nehru. Since his family originally came from the Kashmir Valley, Nehru had always taken a close interest in the state. As early as 1934 he identified the man who would become his main political ally there: the secular, nationalist

intellectual Sheikh Mohammed Abdullah. To the considerable irritation
of Hari Singh, Nehru and Abdullah became close friends. Abdullah was
the son of a merchant in the Kashmir Valley and had opponents within
the Muslim community. In 1939 some Kashmiris started to oppose
Abdullah's alignment with Congress. The most significant was Ghulam
Abbas who increasingly looked to Jinnah's Muslim League. In 1942,
when Abbas came out in favour of Pakistan, the battle lines were drawn.
Nehru backed Abdullah and Jinnah backed Ghulam Abbas. The
maharaja was on his own. Jinnah's visit to Kashmir in May 1944, when
he declared his support for Abbas, was the only time he ever went there.
Even more remarkably, no other senior Muslim League leaders visited
the state in the run-up to partition. The Congress leadership had a completely different attitude towards the Kashmir issue. Nehru visited Kashmir in July 1945 when he addressed a massive National Conference rally.
In July 1946 when Sheikh Abdullah was spending one of his many
spells in prison, Nehru immediately headed for Kashmir to show his
solidarity. He ended up being arrested at the border himself but eventually reached Srinagar and met the imprisoned Abdullah. By these
visits – and a series of representations to the British on Abdullah's
behalf – Nehru established his interest in Kashmir. It was to stand him
in good stead. As the Pakistani historian Hasan Zaheer has written: 'The
Muslim League leadership, overwhelmed by the issues arising from the
creation of the new state, did not apply itself seriously to the Kashmir
situation in the period preceding independence day, while India was sys-
tematically working at securing the accession of the state by any
means.'[22] By the time that the British transferred power the maharaja
still favoured independence. But the Congress leadership's lobbying
effort meant that in the event of that option being ruled out, Hari Singh
was at least giving serious consideration to the possibility of acceding
to India not Pakistan. The Muslim League was paying the price for
its passivity.

The maharaja's room for manoeuvre, however, was limited. Even
before the transfer of power, the political situation in Kashmir had been
deteriorating. Once the British left the subcontinent, the state started
disintegrating. In Jammu, the maharaja's political heartland, the partition of Punjab sparked an outbreak of communal violence. Massacres

forced hundreds of thousands of Kashmiri Muslims to flee their homes: many headed for the safety of Pakistan. From the maharaja's point of view, however, the situation was especially acute in Poonch where the violence was aimed directly at his rule. He had long considered the impoverished Muslims of Poonch to be amongst his least loyal and potentially most troublesome subjects and now ordered them to hand over their weapons. Feeling distinctly vulnerable, the Poonchis looked for another source of arms and found they were readily available from NWFP. The tensions reached a climax in the second week of September 1947 by which time an armed revolt had spread to the whole of Poonch. The uprising caused considerable interest in Pakistan where Jinnah and his colleagues hoped that it might force the maharaja to opt for Pakistan. On 12 September the country's prime minster Liaquat Ali Khan himself became involved in drawing up plans to help the rebels. He insisted, however, that Pakistan (unlike India which later showed no such inhibitions regarding difficult Princely States) should not become associated with an invasion of Kashmir. Liaquat Ali Khan thereby formulated a policy that has continued for fifty years: that Pakistan fights for Kashmir by proxy.

In truth, Liaquat Ali Khan had little choice. The division of the Indian army meant that Pakistan's armed forces were virtually non-existent. British officers held most of the senior jobs and the prime minister (quite correctly as it turned out) feared that they would be unwilling to act in Kashmir. But having said that, Liaquat Ali Khan did not make the most of the resources at his disposal. When he convened a high level meeting to discuss Kashmir on 12 September only one professional soldier, Brigadier Akbar Khan, was present. (The brigadier later went on to launch a coup attempt in Pakistan known as the Rawalpindi conspiracy and cited the government policy failures over Kashmir as one of his main justifications.) Many other Pakistani officers were available to the prime minster but he apparently saw no need to consult them.

Pakistan's effort to support the Poonchi rebels was small-scale and uncoordinated, and the country's diplomatic campaign was equally unimpressive. In mid-October Liaquat Ali Khan sent a Foreign Office official, A. S. B. Shah, to Srinagar to urge accession to Pakistan.[23] It was too little, too late and Shah could not hope to reverse in a few days all

the work that had been put in by Congress leaders over several months
and years. Indeed, given the fact that the maharaja felt he was facing a
Pakistani-backed rebellion in Poonch, he didn't even want to meet the
envoy from Karachi. While Pakistan was becoming the maharaja's
enemy, the Indians continued their efforts to be seen as his friends.

In October a new factor came into the equation: tribesmen from
NWFP started making their way to Kashmir to fight alongside their
Muslim brethren. While it is not clear what role the central Pakistani
government played in organising the invasion, there is no doubt that
some officials in NWFP helped with logistics and supplies. Liaquat Ali
Khan certainly knew about the operation and the British officials who
had stayed in Pakistan after partition advised him to block the tribesmen's advance: advice which he rejected.[24] Some say Jinnah also knew
about it and others insist he did not. Perhaps the most plausible account
comes from the governor of NWFP, George Cunningham, who
recorded that, when Jinnah first heard about the tribesmen's move, he
said 'Don't tell me anything about it. My conscience must be clear.'[25]
The upright, constitutionally-minded Jinnah could easily have made
such a remark. Kashmir, however, was never going to be secured by
such ambivalent leadership.

Whatever the level of Jinnah's involvement, several thousand tribesmen crossed into Kashmir on the night of 21 October. At first they
enjoyed considerable success defeating, or just as often dodging, the
maharaja's forces. Muslim soldiers in the maharaja's army deserted their
posts and joined the tribesmen and, by the end of October, the Poonchi
rebels and their Pukhtoon allies were within striking distance of Srinagar. Their most spectacular achievement was to sabotage Srinagar's
power supply. As the city plunged into darkness the maharaja concluded
that he was in serious trouble. His son has recalled what happened:

> On that fateful day I was left virtually alone in the palace while my
> father and members of the staff were attending the Darbar in the
> beautiful hall at the city palace on the Jhelum with its richly deco-
> rated papier mâché ceiling. Suddenly the lights went out – the
> invaders had captured and destroyed the only power house . . . After
> a few minutes the eerie silence was broken by the sudden, blood-

chilling howl of jackals. Weirdly the cacophony rose and fell, then rose again into a mad crescendo. Death and destruction were fast approaching Srinagar; our smug world had collapsed around us.[26]

At this crucial juncture, when Kashmir was ready for the taking, Pakistan paid the price of the haphazard nature of its operations in Kashmir. Rather than striking forward, the tribesmen became distracted by the opportunities for plunder. Their increasingly lawless conduct had a disastrous consequence. The local Muslim population, rather than seeing them as liberators, began to fear them and, far from providing help to the tribesmen, turned against them. These developments and the bad international press Pakistan was receiving as a result of the invasion dismayed the government in Karachi. Officials not only disowned the tribesmen but also obstructed them. Sherbaz Khan Mazari, a seventeen-year-old tribal leader from Balochistan who tried to take some men to join in the fighting, later recounted that when he tried to enter Kashmir, 'I was stopped by Pakistani officials who told me in clear cut terms that I would not be allowed to cross into Kashmir. It became clear that they thought we were intent on partaking in the plunder that was taking place.'[27]

From the maharaja's point of view, however, the tribal invaders were still very much a threat. But he knew full well that any help from Delhi would come with a price: accession. Eventually he did sign an accession document and the precise timing of that act is one of the most keenly disputed aspects of the Kashmir issue. The basic question is whether he signed before or after Delhi despatched troops to Kashmir. No one disputes that Indian troops were deployed at dawn on 27 October. The question is whether the maharaja signed the accession document on the 25th, 26th or 27th. Pakistani commentators argue that if the act of accession took place after the Indian deployment then India's move into Kashmir, and the subsequent occupation of parts of the state, was, and remains, illegal.

The historian Prem Shankar Jha has provided the most recent Indian version of these events. He relies on the evidence of Colonel (later Field Marshal) Sam Manekshaw who has said that he and one of the Congress party's most senior politicians, V. P. Menon, went to Srinagar on

25 October. According to Manekshaw, Menon told the maharaja that if he did not sign the Instrument of Accession there and then Delhi would be unable to send Indian troops to help him. Faced with this ultimatum the maharaja signed the document on the evening of the 25th and on the 26th Menon took it back to Delhi. Manekshaw does not claim to have actually seen the maharaja sign the document but he recalled that Menon came out of the maharaja's offices saying, 'Sam, we have got it!' According to Manekshaw, the Defence Committee of the Indian cabinet was handed the signed document on the 26th and sent troops to Kashmir that day.[28] There are, however, a number of problems with Manekshaw's account. To name just one, his claim that Indian troops were sent to Kashmir on 26 October is false. The airlift of Indian troops began on 27 October.

Prem Shankar Jha's reliance on Manekshaw's account in fact amounts to something of a tactical retreat in the Indian position on the signing of the Instrument of Accession. Previously, Indian historians had relied on V. P. Menon's memoirs. According to Menon, the maharaja signed the Instrument not on the 25th but during the afternoon of the 26th and the deployment of Indian troops followed the next day. There is also, however, a serious flaw with Menon's account: he was not in Kashmir on the afternoon of the 26th. He was, in fact, at Delhi airport trying to get to Srinagar. Staff at the airport turned him back because, they said, it was too late to take off since the airport at Srinagar had no night-time landing facilities.[29]

The fact that Menon could not have secured the accession on the 26th, because he was not even in Kashmir, has led some to conclude that the Instrument was in fact signed on the 27th October. By that time, the maharaja had fled from Srinagar to Jammu. According to this version, V. P. Menon, having missed his flight from Delhi on the 26th, travelled to Jammu on the 27th and it was there and then – after the deployment of Indian troops – that the Instrument was signed.[30]

The debate over when the Instrument was signed has gone on for fifty years and a complete perusal of all the evidence could, in itself, fill a book. But, as even Jha has acknowledged, the conflicting Indian accounts 'could not fail to create the impression that the Indian government had something to hide'.[31] And, considered from Pakistan's perspective, the question of whether the maharaja did sign before the deployment of Indian troops remains, at the very least, unproven. But having said that, no one can dispute that the maharaja wanted Indian help and accepted that, to obtain it, he would have to accede. Whatever the precise timing, that is exactly what happened.

Far from plucking the ripe fruit of Kashmir, Jinnah watched it fall into Delhi's lap. Pakistani writers have tended to blame this outcome on Nehru, Mountbatten and the maharaja but their own leader, Mohammed Ali Jinnah, also played a significant role. The peculiar circumstances on the subcontinent before the transfer of power had played to Jinnah's strengths. He had managed to pull off a feat unprecedented in modern history: he created a new state entirely legally. He neither lifted a gun nor even ordered anyone else to do so; and it is hard to think of anyone else who created a nation without spending even a single day in prison. In his whole life Jinnah was arrested just once – for disorderly behaviour at the 1893 Oxford–Cambridge boat race.[32] Jinnah's monumental achievement rested on a combination of talents that constantly frustrated the British: a refusal to compromise and a brilliant ability to grasp and articulate the most complex legal issues. But while these attributes helped Jinnah create Pakistan they became a handicap when it came to consolidating the new country. Jinnah's apologists argue that his failure to secure Kashmir should be forgiven. His administration was weak and overwhelmed by the arrival of refugees; he was sick and he was hampered by his British military commanders. These factors undoubtedly played a part but they cannot conceal the extent of Jinnah's failure – especially in the period before partition. In terms of hard-nosed realpolitik the Indian leaders in Delhi were leagues ahead.

By the end of October there were thousands of Indian troops in the Kashmir Valley. The speed of the deployment bore testament to the extent of the planning that Indian leaders had put into Kashmir. Pakistan, by contrast, was only beginning to realise that reliance on a few thousand tribesmen to liberate the state was insufficient. On the 27 October Jinnah ordered Pakistani troops to go to Jammu and Kashmir. It did not happen. The acting commander-in-chief of the Pakistan army, Lt. General Sir Douglas Gracey, said he could not obey the order. The Indian army, like that of Pakistan, still included a number of British officers and the general was not prepared to let them fight each other.

From Pakistan's point of view, the situation was bleak but not entirely lost. Some parts of Kashmir were under its control. The Poonch rebellion and the tribal invasion had secured significant amounts of territory. Furthermore, in Gilgit the Muslim-dominated Gilgit Scouts declared their desire to join Pakistan. The British commander of the Scouts, Major William Brown, wrote a telegram to the chief minister of NWFP, Khan Abdul Qayum Khan: 'Revolution night 31st to 1st Gilgit Province. Entire pro-Pakistan populace has overthrown [the maharaja's] Dogra regime. Owing imminent chaos and bloodshed Scouts and Muslim State Forces taken over law and order.'[33] Some areas under Indian control, such as Jammu, were of relatively little interest to Pakistan. The real problem for Jinnah and his new state lay in the most densely populated part of the state: the Kashmir Valley. Pakistan believed they should have it but the Indians were already there.

Once again, however, Jinnah failed to explore all the options open to him. One possibility was to make compromises over another Princely State, Hyderabad. The Muslim ruler or nizam of Hyderabad faced the same dilemma as Maharaja Hari Singh. He wanted independence but was far from sure he could achieve it. Jinnah understood that it was never realistic to expect the nizam to accede to Pakistan: Hyderabad was entirely surrounded by Indian territory. But he always hoped that the nizam could pull off independence. He considered Hyderabad to be the 'oldest Muslim dynasty in India'[34] and hoped that its continued existence as an independent state right in the heart of India would provide a sense of security for those Muslims who didn't move to Pakistan. Once again, however, Jinnah was thinking in terms of legally possible options rather than political realities. In the long term the independence of Hyderabad, while constitutionally proper, was never going to happen. The new Indian leadership saw the issue clearly enough and when the nizam tried to strike a deal which would allow him to hang on to some degree of autonomy, Delhi flatly refused to consider the idea.

In retrospect most Pakistanis would agree that it would have been worth abandoning the aspiration for an independent Hyderabad if it had meant securing Kashmir's accession to Pakistan. Furthermore,

Jinnah had good reason to believe that such a deal could have been struck. In late November 1947 Nehru and Liaquat Ali Khan met to discuss the situation in Kashmir. To understand their conversation it is first necessary to consider briefly what had happened in yet another Princely State, Junagadh.

The Muslim nawab of Junagadh ruled over a million people, 80 per cent of them Hindus. Junagadh was located in western India and, even though it was not strictly contiguous with Pakistan, its coastline offered the possibility of sea links to the Muslim state that was just 200 miles away. The nawab of Junagadh, guided by his pro-Pakistani chief minister Sir Shah Nawaz Bhutto (the father of Zulfikar Ali Bhutto), decided to ignore the feelings of his Hindu population and acceded to Pakistan. It was the mirror image of the situation in Kashmir. The Indian government did not accept the decision, blockaded Junagadh and then invaded it. Delhi then imposed a plebiscite and secured the result it desired: Junagadh became part of India.

When Liaquat Ali Khan met Nehru at the end of November he exposed the illogicality of India's position. If Junagadh, despite its Muslim rulers' accession to Pakistan, belonged to India because of its Hindu majority, then Kashmir surely belonged to Pakistan. When Liaquat Ali Kahn made this incontrovertible point his Indian interlocutor, Sardar Patel, could not contain himself and burst out: 'Why do you compare Junagadh with Kashmir? Talk of Hyderabad and Kashmir and we could reach agreement.'[35] Patel was not alone in this view. On 29 October 1947 officials at the American embassy in Delhi had told the US State Department: 'the obvious solution is for the government leaders in Pakistan and India to agree . . . [to the] accession of Kashmir to Pakistan and the accession of Hyderabad and Junagadh to India'. British officials in London concurred.[36]

Jinnah, however, never did the deal and the fighting in Kashmir carried on throughout 1948. The Pakistani leadership, fearing that they could lose control of those parts of Kashmir they already occupied, again asked the British commanders to deploy troops there. This time General Gracey had become more willing to fight for the Pakistani interest and, with India looking ever stronger in Kashmir, he advised the government in Karachi that:

if India is not to be allowed to sit on the doorsteps of Pakistan to the
rear and on the flank at liberty to enter at its will and pleasure; if the
civilian and military morale is not to be affected to a dangerous
extent; and if subversive political forces are not to be encouraged and
let loose within Pakistan itself, it is imperative that the Indian army
is not allowed to advance . . .[37]

Gracey was concerned that Pakistan's very existence was in jeopardy.
Not only might India react to events in Kashmir by crossing the international boundary but, in addition, there was the risk that defeat in
Kashmir could lead the Pukhtoon tribesmen to turn their anger on Pakistan itself, causing insurmountable law and order problems. The presence of the Pakistan army in Kashmir made a difference. By the end of
the year, Delhi controlled about two-thirds of Kashmir and Karachi one-
third. Pakistan then planned a major counter-offensive in western Kashmir despite the clear risk that in doing so it might tempt India to invade
Pakistan itself and strike for Lahore. The fear of an all-out war between
the two countries was real and persuaded the British, who still had officers commanding both armies, that the fighting had to stop. The Indian
and Pakistan governments agreed and one minute before midnight on
the 1 January 1949 a ceasefire came into effect.

1949–1965

As the ceasefire took hold, the politicians on both sides considered their
options. Liaquat Ali Khan decided that two areas under Pakistani control, Gilgit and Baltistan (which became known as the Northern Areas),
should not be fully incorporated into Pakistan's democratic structures.
Instead, the area was kept constitutionally separate from the rest of
Pakistan and ruled directly by the Ministry of Kashmir Affairs in
Karachi. Liaquat calculated that if a Kashmiri referendum were ever
held, Pakistan might need the votes of the Muslims there. (To this day
Pakistan's Foreign Office advises governments that any move to incorporate the Northern Areas into Pakistan would undermine Islamabad's
case that the whole issue of Kashmir should be resolved on the basis of

UN resolutions.) Pakistan also let things remain largely as they were in Azad (or Free) Kashmir. This was an area in which the local Muslim populace had declared independence and started establishing rudimentary governmental structures.

India had to pursue a much more proactive policy. Its overall objective was to consolidate the maharaja's accession. To do this, the leadership in Delhi looked to their old ally Sheikh Abdullah. In March 1948 the maharaja had reluctantly recognised the popularity of the 'Lion of Kashmir' as Abdullah was universally known and made him prime minister. Predictably enough, the two men disagreed about almost everything and not least Abdullah's plans to take land from the (predominantly Hindu) elite and give it to the (predominantly Muslim) peasantry. The two men's relationship was unsustainable. Delhi sealed the maharaja's fate in June 1949. Having persuaded him to take a holiday outside of Kashmir, the Indian government advised him to stay out of the state indefinitely and his son Karan was appointed as regent. Hari Singh never returned to Kashmir: he died thirteen years later in Bombay.

There was now no one in Kashmir to rival the popularity and authority of Sheikh Abdullah. But to Delhi's dismay, when it came to the big questions of Kashmir's constitutional status, he pursued a remarkably similar line to his old royal adversary. In public Abdullah stated his commitment to a secular India; in private he made no secret of his desire for independence or at least a considerable degree of autonomy. In September 1950, for example, he told the US ambassador to India, Loy Henderson, that he favoured Kashmiri independence.[38] But as Abdullah was to discover, Kashmir was already locked in a vice. From the moment the maharaja signed the document of accession the voice of the Kashmiris was drowned out by those of the politicians in Pakistan and India.

Abdullah was not working in isolation. The United Nations was also involved in seeking an outcome that would bring stability to the mountain state. Ever since the issue had been referred to it by India in January 1948, the UN had made great efforts to broker a solution. In general terms the various UN proposals can be summarised thus: there should be some form of plebiscite in Kashmir. Initially both India and Pakistan said they agreed with this. Nehru repeatedly pledged that he

would consult the wishes of the Kashmiri people and in October 1947
had written to Liaquat Ali Khan saying:

> Our assurance that we shall withdraw our troops from Kashmir as
> soon as peace and order are restored and leave the decision regard-
> ing the future of this state to the people of the state is not merely a
> pledge to your government but also to the people of Kashmir and to
> the world.[39]

The devil, though, was in the detail: India insisted that the first
priority was to withdraw the tribesmen and any Pakistani forces in
Kashmir. Pakistan meanwhile argued that no referendum would be fair
if the Indian troops remained in place. With both sides afraid of losing
whatever territory they held, the issue ran into interminable deadlock.
The Kashmir dispute was one of the first to expose the United Nations'
weakness: it could, and did, launch a whole series of initiatives but the
parties to the conflict resisted a compromise and the UN was powerless
to impose one. The situation was complicated by the influence of the
cold war. While Pakistan increasingly looked to the United States for
big power support, India sought to improve its relations with the Soviet
Union which, in return, liberally used its veto power on the Security
Council in Delhi's favour.

China also got involved. In 1957 a Chinese magazine published
a map showing the location of a road that Beijing had constructed
in Aksai Chin, a desolate and largely uninhabited area in eastern
Kashmir. Ever since the 1920s the Chinese and the British had wran-
gled over border demarcation issues: one of them concerned Aksai
Chin. Following the transfer of power, the Chinese had occupied Aksai
Chin and built a road across it without India even noticing. The publication of the Chinese map rang alarm bells in Delhi and the
relationship between Delhi and Beijing rapidly deteriorated. By 1962
the two countries were fighting. China's overwhelming defeat of the
Indians sent shock waves through the Western world. The significance
of the conflict lay not in Aksai Chin itself but in its impact on the
regional strategic balance. Concerned about Chinese expansionism, the
US and some West European powers offered significant supplies of
weapons to Delhi.

Pakistan, which had long hoped that US pressure might force a settlement in Kashmir, was left as a frustrated bystander. The only initiative that it could make was to recognise the Chinese claim to Aksai Chin. The recognition was qualified. Pakistan said that if the Chinese-occupied area should ever be granted to Pakistan then it would not challenge the Chinese presence there. For its part, China pledged that if an international settlement resulted in Aksai Chin being granted to India then Beijing would be willing to renegotiate the issue. Predictably enough, India complained bitterly that Pakistan had given up territory to which it had no right and which it did not even control.

Despite the reverse in Aksai Chin, India felt it was making progress elsewhere in Kashmir. Throughout the 1950s it consolidated its rule on the state. In 1952 the Congress leadership had decided that Abdullah had become too much of a loose cannon and engineered his dismissal. The decision was welcomed by both the Hindus in Jammu and the Buddhists in Ladakh who feared that Abdullah was creating a Muslim one-party state in which they had little stake. Abdullah was succeeded by one of his closest advisers, Bakshi Ghulam Mohammed, who proceeded to order the arrest of his long-time friend and master. For Abdullah it was the start of a long stretch in prison – he was to remain in detention for most of the next fifteen years. Bakshi, who fully appreciated that he owed his position to Delhi, acted accordingly. His ten-year administration was marked by one policy above all others: increasing India's influence and authority in Kashmir. As far as Delhi was concerned, Kashmir had become an integral part of its territory and there would be no more talk of a plebiscite. The demand for a referendum, however, did not go away. In one of his brief periods out of prison, Abdullah, who by this stage had become perceived as a hero in Pakistan, insisted that the Kashmiri people themselves must decide on their future. Within a matter of days he was back behind bars.

The Indians believed that the internal political situation in Kashmir was stabilising but in 1963 Delhi received a brutal reminder that, in fact, the state remained highly volatile. In December of that year a devastating rumour, later confirmed as true, spread through the Kashmir Valley. A religious relic, a hair from the Prophet's beard, had been stolen from a shrine near Srinagar. The hair was eventually returned but the incident produced an intense outburst of Muslim feeling and provoked a wave of social unrest in Kashmir. The incident made Pakistanis wonder whether the time was ripe to push the Indians a little harder.

The 1965 War

The 1965 war between Pakistan and India was a particularly futile conflict. At the end of it the two sides agreed a ceasefire line identical to the one with which they had started. So, why did the two countries join battle in the first place?

The conflict of 1965 was waiting to happen. Both India and Pakistan were suffering from a sense of insecurity. Ever since partition Pakistan had distrusted Indian intentions. Senior politicians and military officers feared that their counterparts in Delhi secretly hoped and, in many cases, believed that the whole Pakistan project would fail and that the subcontinent would be reunited. India also had genuine concerns: after its defeat at the hands of China in 1962, the country faced a major crisis of confidence. One contemporary American observer who tried to catch the mood of the two young nations described the volatile mix of distrust and disdain that marked public opinion on both sides of the border:

> Again and again I have heard Pakistanis say that India does not accept Pakistan and is determined to destroy it; that Indians can't fight and won't fight . . . again and again I have heard Indians say that Pakistan is a ruthless dictatorship and theocracy; that Pakistan is bent on destroying India and determined to destroy the large Hindu minority in Pakistan.[40]

Regional politics also played a part in galvanising the conflict. Pakistan's improving relationship with China affected its perceptions of its strength vis-à-vis India. Ayub Khan visited China in March 1965. He was given a rapturous reception and secured China's firm support for a plebiscite in Kashmir. Ayub also visited Moscow. Even though the results of the Soviet trip were less striking, the fact that a Pakistani leader was cordially received in Moscow inevitably caused concern in Delhi. Moscow, an important Indian ally, seemed to be wavering.

Ayub Khan and his young foreign minister Zulfikar Ali Bhutto were further encouraged by their perception of the state of opinion in Kashmir itself. The riots that followed the disappearance of the hair of the prophet's beard encouraged them to believe that the people of Kashmir were ready for a fight. Speaking immediately after the incident, Zulfikar Ali Bhutto said the people of Kashmir were 'in revolt. Unmistakably in revolt.'[41] Pakistani intelligence reports seemed to confirm that the levels of discontent in Kashmir had reached new heights. If Pakistan could show the Kashmiris that removing the Indians was a real possibility, Bhutto believed they would readily join an anti-Indian uprising. There were also signs that Sheikh Abdullah was pursuing an increasingly independent line and that he might even side with Pakistan. In March 1965, much to India's annoyance, Abdullah met the Chinese prime minister, Chou En-Lai. A few days before the encounter Abdullah had said that 'we did not make those sacrifices all these years for our rights in vain, and we will not leave it now because of fear of India's might. It is wrong to say that Pakistan is instigating us.'[42]

Ayub was also increasingly confident about Pakistan's military capability. Immediately after independence, Pakistan's armed forces had been hopelessly weak and had proved incapable of playing a decisive role in the war of 1947–48. Ayub had subsequently given high priority to creating an effective military machine and, by the early 1960s, it was widely believed that he had succeeded. Pakistan may have had less manpower than India but the close Pakistani–US relationship ensured that its personnel were better trained and better equipped. Pakistan was increasingly prepared to test its strength and Bhutto in particular itched for an opportunity to do so. Ever since he became Ayub's foreign minister in 1963, Bhutto had focussed on the Kashmir dispute. He had also taken care to foster good relations with senior military officers and was well aware that the generals in Rawalpindi were also devoting considerable time to the issue. By late 1964 they had developed a strategy that would become known to the world as Operations GIBRALTAR and GRANDSLAM. In Operation GIBRALTAR armed militants would cross into Indian-held Kashmir and instigate a general revolt. They could be backed up, if necessary, by Operation GRANDSLAM in which Pakistani troops would be deployed with the same objective. The idea was to restrict any fighting to Kashmir itself and avoid an escalation into full-scale war.

Excited by the prospect of decisive action in Kashmir, Bhutto advised Ayub that the time had come to fight. Both UN resolutions and bilateral talks, he argued, had failed. He spoke of the possibility that China would intervene on Pakistan's side. India, he said, was too weak to engage in a major war and would never dare invade Pakistan itself. Furthermore, he told Ayub, the opportunity might slip away. Ever since Delhi's defeat in 1962, the Western powers had been pouring arms into India so as to contain Chinese expansionism and, in the long run, the military balance was bound to tilt in Delhi's favour. Ayub, he argued, had already missed one opportunity by failing to move troops into Kashmir in 1962 when the Indians were in disarray. He must not, he urged, make the same mistake twice.

As he considered his options, Ayub took heart from the outcome of a recent military clash between India and Pakistan on a tract of marshland off southern Sindh, the Rann of Kutch. The area had been disputed territory ever since 1947. As an imperial power, the British had stated that the Rann of Kutch, as its name implies, was part of Kutch State. Since Kutch went to India, so too did the Rann. Pakistan, however, argued that since the Rann was flooded each monsoon it was really a sea. Consequently, Pakistan maintained the boundary line should be drawn halfway through the Rann between, as it were, the two shores. The dispute had far more symbolic than strategic importance: the area had no economic significance whatsoever. As one Pakistani military historian put it: 'A minor border dispute was escalated to a point where restraint by either side would be contrived by the other as chickening out.'[43] Fighting in the Rann began in early 1965 with a series of small-scale exchanges in which the two sides attacked each other's posts.

As the monsoon approached, both India and Pakistan recognised the inevitable: the forces deployed in the Rann would have to stop fighting because the area would become flooded. They agreed to a British-sponsored ceasefire that also allowed for a UN tribunal of three members to resolve the basic dispute in the Rann. The international diplomacy eventually took both sides to Geneva where a three-man panel (with representatives from Yugoslavia, Iran and Sweden) considered the issue and searched for a settlement. India had apparently conceded the principle that it would, after all, accept international mediation to resolve a bilateral dispute with its Muslim neighbour. But, far from contributing to stability on the subcontinent, the international arbitration created new resentments in India and fresh hopes in Pakistan.

In July 1965 Ayub finally made up his mind: he would take Bhutto's advice. The infiltration of Kashmir outlined in Operation GIBRALTAR began and, on 10 August, a body no Kashmiri had previously heard of, the Revolutionary Council, called on the people to rise up against their Indian occupiers. The Council declared that, having formed a National Government of Jammu and Kashmir, it would henceforth be 'the sole lawful authority in our land'.[44] The anticipated Kashmiri revolt, however, never occurred. Pakistan had not put the necessary preparations in place. Kashmiri leaders had not been consulted about Operation GIBRALTAR and some even suspected that the infiltrators were Indian provocateurs. When the militants contacted supposedly sympathetic mullahs they found that most were reluctant to help.[45]

From Pakistan's point of view the results of Operation GIBRALTAR were disappointing. For India, though, the situation was alarming. Having learnt from the Rann of Kutch that agreeing to negotiations would be seen by his domestic opponents as a sign of weakness, the Indian prime minister, Lal Bahadur Shastri, opted for an all-out military campaign. In mid-August the Indians launched a major offensive and, in doing so, they crossed the 1947 ceasefire line so as to prevent further infiltration. The Indians were soon able to cut off the militants' supply lines, leaving the infiltrators short of material and completely isolated.

Some Pakistani generals could see the writing on the wall but Bhutto urged Ayub to carry on. He said he would not 'even consider allowing this movement to die out . . . such a course would amount to a debacle which could threaten the existence of Pakistan'.[46] On 29 August Ayub once again accepted his minister's advice and opted for war. He sent a top secret order to his army chief General Mohammed Musa:

1. . . . to take such action as will defreeze Kashmir problem [*sic*], weaken India's resolve and bring her to the conference table without provoking a general war. However, the element of escalation

is always present in such struggles. So, whilst confining our actions to the Kashmir area we must not be unmindful that India may in desperation involve us in a general war or violate Pakistani territory where we are weak. We must therefore be prepared for such contingency.

2. To expect quick results in this struggle, when India has much larger forces than us, would be unrealistic. Therefore our action should be such that can be sustained over a long period.

3. As a general rule Hindu morale would not stand for more than a couple of hard blows delivered at the right time and the right place. Such opportunities should therefore be sought and exploited.[47]

Two days later Pakistan's armed forces launched Operation GRAND-SLAM with a major offensive in western Kashmir. Initially the Pakistanis enjoyed considerable success. Within five days they were just 20 miles from Jammu and threatening India's only all-weather land route to Kashmir. But the Pakistani plans contained a fatal flaw. The strategists in Rawalpindi were relying on their extraordinarily complacent assumption that India would not extend the fighting beyond Kashmir. India saw no reason to show such restraint. On 6 September Delhi opened up a 50-mile-wide front near Lahore, launched an offensive in Sindh and made a drive for the Pakistani city of Sialkot. Despite the predictability of the Indian action, the Pakistani planners were taken by surprise.

In a matter of hours Pakistan's strategy was turned on its head. All thoughts of offence were abandoned. The priority now was to save Lahore. Ayub Khan himself conceded privately that the situation was dire. 'It is catastrophic,' he told the American ambassador on 7 September. 'We are getting ready for a desperate fight.'[48] He knew that Lahore was extremely vulnerable: the commander in charge of the city's defence, Major General Sarfraz Khan, had been specifically ordered to put no defensive measures in place. When a junior officer implored him to deploy troops in defensive positions he had replied: 'Sorry, GHQ has ordered no move, no provocative actions.'[49]

Despite being unprepared, the Pakistanis did manage to halt the Indian advances on Lahore and Sialkot. Ayub Khan realised that if he was to achieve his original war objectives in relation to Kashmir he would need outside help and he looked to China. There were some indications that Beijing might play a decisive role. While the fighting in Kashmir was underway, China had resuscitated a long-standing territorial dispute concerning some Indian military installations that, Beijing maintained, were on Chinese territory. After some opening diplomatic exchanges, China declared on 16 September that India would face 'grave consequences'[50] if it did not dismantle its military installations within three days. For good measure, Beijing also demanded the return of 800 sheep and 59 yaks which it claimed India had kidnapped.

Ayub and Bhutto visited Beijing on 20 September to see if China was prepared to back up these statements by launching an offensive on India. Their hosts offered plenty of moral support but not much more. Beijing realised that attacking India could provoke a devastating Western response and suggested instead that Ayub could abandon some major cities near the border and conduct a 'people's war' against India. On 21 September China de-escalated the crisis in its relations with Delhi by announcing that India had dismantled its military installations. The sheep and yaks were forgotten. Ayub's last card had been played. By the time he returned to Pakistan he was determined to agree a ceasefire. India, which had achieved its objective of preventing the loss of Kashmir, was like-minded. With both parties to the conflict in search of a settlement, the UN's peace brokers were, for once, able to achieve something. The fighting stopped on 23 September 1965.

As the situation in Kashmir stabilised, India and Pakistan came under increasing pressure to talk. In January 1966 they did so in Tashkent and the two sides agreed to go back to their pre-war positions. For the Pakistani public it was a shocking and disappointing outcome. Even after the ceasefire the official media in Pakistan had given the impression that India had suffered a humiliating defeat: it was now perfectly clear to everyone that the true result was closer to a draw. The joint statement made at Tashkent merely noted the existence of the Kashmir dispute. This amounted to a significant climb-down by Ayub Khan. When Pakistan had agreed to a ceasefire in 1949 it had not only secured control of the one-third of Kashmir that was under Pakistani control but also won an Indian pledge to a referendum. The exaggerated hopes that Ayub's regime had encouraged and the subsequent let-down at

Tashkent began the process that eventually forced the field marshal to relinquish power.

The greatest beneficiary of Tashkent was Zulfikar Ali Bhutto. Despite the leading role he had played in instigating the 1965 war he successfully disassociated himself from the Ayub regime and relentlessly pursued his drive for power. He achieved it six years later, after Pakistan had fought and lost another battle against India. In 1971, with Indian military help, the eastern wing of Pakistan broke away to become Bangladesh and it fell to Bhutto to re-establish a modus vivendi with India. In June and July 1972 Bhutto met his Indian counterpart Indira Gandhi at Simla. The talks concentrated on issues such as the return of the Pakistani prisoners of war captured in 1971 but Simla is best remembered for its impact on the Kashmir dispute. In the first place Bhutto agreed to the use of the term 'line of control' rather than 'ceasefire line'. It may have seemed like a semantically insignificant point but, after Simla, Bhutto was repeatedly accused of having sold out Pakistan's interests. His critics maintained that the change in terminology signalled Bhutto's willingness, at some stage in the future, to transform the ceasefire line into an international border. Some Indian participants at Simla have said this was their impression too.[51] Bhutto himself always rejected this interpretation of Simla and insisted that he gave no secret undertakings. The second important development at Simla was the agreement that the two sides would 'settle their differences by peaceful means through bilateral negotiations or by any other peaceful means mutually agreed between them'.[52] Ever since, successive Indian governments have relied on Simla to deny Pakistani demands that the Kashmir dispute should be the subject of international mediation.

For the Muslims of Indian-held Kashmir, the 1965 war was a disaster. It was not a conflict of their own making and yet they paid the price. After 1965 India tightened its grip. A plebiscite was out of the question but Indira Gandhi could see that a political rather than military solution gave India the best prospect of long-term success in Kashmir. By 1974, like Nehru before her, she had come to the view that Sheikh Abdullah held the key. Persuading Abdullah to work with the Indian government was not easy. Not only had he spent a good proportion of his life in Indian jails but he had also refused to give up on the idea that the Kashmir people, and not the politicians in India (or, for that matter, Pakistan), should determine the future of the state. Despite these apparently significant obstacles the Indian government and Abdullah did reach an agreement. Under the Kashmir Accord of February 1975, Abdullah accepted that Kashmir was 'a constituent unit of the Union of India' albeit with special status.[53] In return he became chief minister.

Abdullah's Kashmiri opponents and the Pakistani government denounced the accord as a sell-out and there was no escaping the fact that it represented a great achievement for Indira Gandhi. In October 1975 she celebrated her political breakthrough by paying a state visit to Srinagar. Sheikh Abdullah laid on a traditional boat procession. When thirty-two turbaned oarsmen carried the Indian leader across the Dal Lake, the banks were lined by thousands of people. Given what has happened in Kashmir since 1975 it is a remarkable fact that they cheered her on her way.

If the Indian government was making some limited moves to find an accommodation with the Kashmiri people, it remained determined to ensure that Pakistan be kept at bay. The latent hostility between Islamabad and Delhi found violent expression in 1984 when the country's two armies clashed once again, this time fighting on the Siachin Glacier in the east of Kashmir. Despite all the attention paid to ceasefire lines in 1948, at Tashkent and at Simla, no one had seen any point in demarcating the glacial wasteland that lay at the eastern end of the line of control. In any event, the territory was so hostile that independent survey teams were unable to access it. Consequently, the line of control stopped short of the glacier and there was no internationally recognised line that clarified which parts of it belonged to which side. The crisis over the Siachin Glacier had been developing for some years. In the late 1970s, India was concerned to note that some mountain-climbing expeditions were seeking Pakistani, rather than Indian, permission to climb on the glacier. In 1984 Delhi became even more worried: some recently published Pakistani maps showed the glacier as part of Pakistani-held Kashmir. Delhi responded to this 'cartographic aggression' by deploying troops on the glacier, capturing the high ground that they have never subsequently relinquished. The two sides have fought for the glacier ever since, although the severity of the climate means that more people die as a result of the cold than through military actions.

The Insurgency

As she glided across the Dal Lake in 1975, Mrs Gandhi may have thought she was well on the way to solving India's Kashmir problem. But even as she was fêted, new forces were developing in the state. For as long as he lived, Sheikh Abdullah, with his immense popularity and increasingly authoritarian habits, was able to keep a lid on the pressure building up but after he died, in 1982, a new generation of activists, many inspired by Islam, found their voice. True to South Asian tradition, Abdullah's son, Farooq, took over the reigns of power but he was never as strong as his father. For all his political manoeuvring, Sheikh Abdullah's long years in prison had made him the symbol of Kashmiri defiance in the face of Indian authority. Farooq, by contrast, was seen as a lightweight political dilettante and he found it difficult to walk the impossibly fine line of keeping both Delhi and the Kashmiri people content.

During the 1980s anti-Indian opinion steadily hardened and Kashmir's Jamaat-e-Islami, an offshoot of the Pakistani party of the same name, emerged as a force to be reckoned with. While Jamaat favoured union with Pakistan another group, the Jammu and Kashmir Liberation Front (JKLF), advocated independence. The organisation had its roots in England's large Kashmiri population and first came to prominence in 1984 for its alleged role in the kidnapping and subsequent murder of an Indian diplomat in the British city of Birmingham. By the late 1980s the JKLF was becoming active in Kashmir itself. And it found many people in the state were ready to respond.

On 31 July 1988 Srinagar rocked to a series of explosions. They were claimed by the JKLF although in reality their provenance was rather more complicated. The JKLF, it was true, had laid the bombs but the materials had been provided by the Pakistani state, more precisely, the ISI. In 1987 the ISI and the JKLF had, with General Zia's approval, struck a deal. The JKLF agreed to recruit would-be militants in Indian-held Kashmir, bring them across the line of control and deliver them to

ISI trainers. The ISI in turn agreed to provide the JKLF fighters with weapons and military instruction. The young men were then sent back across the line so that they could mount attacks.[54]

The 31 July explosions marked the start of the 'insurgency'; Kashmir's version of the Palestinian intifada. The insurgency has continued ever since and, according to the Pakistani government, has cost over 60,000 lives. India claims the figure is closer to 20,000 but on any account far more people have died as a result of the insurgency than in the wars of 1947 and 1965 put together.

When the insurgency began the JKLF, with its ISI backers, was clearly the dominant force. But there was a problem: the ISI became increasingly concerned about the JKLF's pro-independence position. It was perhaps inevitable that the ISI would look for more politically amenable clients in Kashmir and it turned to Jamaat-e-Islami's armed wing Hizb ul-Mujahideen. The organisation, which supported the union of Kashmir and Pakistan, duly received considerable logistical and financial support from Islamabad and the JKLF found itself eclipsed. The new awkwardness in the relationship between the Pakistani government and the JKLF was fully exposed in 1992 when the JKLF leader, Amanullah Khan, tried to demonstrate his opposition to the division of Kashmir by leading a peaceful march across the line of control. The Pakistani authorities stopped the march by force, killing seven JKLF activists in the process. Pakistan's hostility to the JKLF was soon reflected on the ground in Kashmir itself where JKLF and Hizb ul-Mujahideen militants started targeting each other.

There are many other groups now active in Kashmir. Throughout the 1990s Hizb ul-Mujahideen remained the most influential group although by the end of the decade it faced significant competition for the hearts and minds of radical Kashmiri youth. Lashkar-e-Toiba and Jaish-e-Mohammed both demonstrated the capacity to recruit activists and mount devastating suicide attacks. The two organisations clearly benefited from the support of Pakistan's state institutions, especially the ISI. Indeed, before Musharraf's decision, in January 2002, to ban Jaish-e-Mohammed and Lashkar-e-Toiba, backing the insurgency was a major element of Pakistani state policy. Even after January 2002, Musharraf did not completely abandon the Kashmiri uprising. He made no move against Hizb ul-Mujahideen and he did not act against the plethora of smaller groups. They include Al Badr which has a history dating back to the war of 1971 in East Pakistan. It subsequently fought in Afghanistan before switching its focus to Kashmir. Other militant organisations that continue to operate in Indian-held Kashmir include Tehrik-e-Jihad which has especially close links to the Pakistan army – many of its members are Kashmiris who used to serve in the military. While Tehrik-e-Jihad is almost exclusively focussed on Kashmir, yet another group, Harakat-e-Jihad-e-Islami, conducts wide-ranging operations not only in Kashmir but also in Myanmar and Chechnya. It claims to have members from Turkey, Saudi Arabia, Iran, Britain and Bangladesh. In November 2001 eighty-five of its fighters who were supporting the Taliban's attempts to defend the northern Afghan city of Mazar-i-Sharif were killed by US bombing.[55] Harakat-e-Jihad-e-Islami is closely related to Harakat ul-Mujahideen. Both were factions within Harakat ul-Ansar before it disbanded and recreated itself when the US put it on its list of banned organisations in 1985. The list of militant groups goes on and on: every political position and religious affiliation is catered for. Shias, for example, who want to fight in Kashmir, can join Hizb ul-Momineen whilst Kashmiris with a pro-Pakistani political position will feel at home with Jamiat-ul-Mujahideen.

The militants' struggle has provoked a terrible response. India's atrocious human rights record in Kashmir is an established fact: Amnesty International, Human Rights Watch and India's own National Human Rights Commission have produced copious reports documenting the repressive conduct of the Indian security forces. Year after year, the US State Department's human rights reports have spoken of extra-judicial killings on an almost daily basis, the systematic use of rape as a weapon of terror and the routine recourse to torture to extract information from suspected militants. Methods used by the Indian army, the border security force and the police have included beating, sexual abuse, burning with cigarettes and hot rods, suspension by the feet, the crushing of limbs by heavy rollers and electric shocks. The security force personnel have carried out those activities with virtual impunity and only a tiny proportion has faced prosecution.[56]

Throughout the 1990s this brutal display of state power failed to break the insurgency. But the militants, too, have been responsible for gross human rights violations. In addition to targeted killings of security force personnel and anyone who dared speak out against their campaign of violence, the militants have also carried out several random mass murders of civilians. In 1998, for example, there was a series of six attacks on Hindu villages in which nearly a hundred men, women and children were killed. The militants have also carried out numerous kidnappings. In November 1997 the Indian government claimed that since 1989 there had been 1,900 kidnappings and that in 700 of those cases the captives were killed.[57]

The relationship between Pakistan and the Kashmiri people is an awkward one. As Pakistan's support for the insurgency grew in scale many Kashmiris came to resent the way in which their conflict with the Indian security forces was being overshadowed by the dispute between the Indian and Pakistani governments. And many in Kashmir were also disturbed by the way in which the insurgency was becoming coloured by communal considerations. Kashmir had always been home to a mix of different religious and ethnic communities and at a local level there had always been high levels of tolerance. Under the pressure of the insurgency some of those long-established relationships started breaking down.

The single most important event in this process was the exodus of a large proportion of the Hindu population from the Kashmir Valley in 1990. The Hindus there claimed that the Islamic groups were singling them out for targeted assassinations. The scale of their migration has been disputed. Officially-inspired Indian versions claim that as many as a quarter of a million Hindus left the valley. More considered Indian accounts put the figure at around 100,000.[58] The Hindus came from the minority Pandit community (of which Jawaharlal Nehru had been a member) and most moved to refugee camps in Jammu and Delhi. Their departure was used by the propagandists in Delhi to assert that Hindus, too, were the subject of human rights abuses in the Kashmir Valley.

The number of groups operating in Kashmir has weakened the insurgency and at times there has been fierce and deadly rivalry between different organisations. The anti-Indian politicians in Kashmir have made some efforts to present a united front. In 1993 they founded the All Parties Hurriyat Conference (APHC), an umbrella group for Kashmiri political parties including Jamaat-e-Islami of Indian-held Kashmir and the Muslim Conference. The APHC claims to represent Kashmiri opinion and some of its leading members have tried to increase their political strength by creating militant groups. The APHC, however, has faced many challenges not least from hardline groups that have disagreed with its strategy of holding occasional rounds of covert talks with the Indian authorities. Inevitably, the splits between the militant groups worked to the advantage of the Indian security forces. The rifts also undermined the standing of the liberation struggle in Kashmiri popular opinion. Although the militants still enjoyed a wide platform of support, a significant number of Kashmiris began to have their doubts. Far from seeing the fighters as liberators, some perceived them as a disruptive element waging a communal, internecine and possibly futile struggle. The militants' practice of turning up unannounced at people's houses and demanding sanctuary left many householders scared and resentful. Families also objected to the pressure to provide not only funds but also their young men for the struggle and many did not appreciate the efforts of some militants to force the Kashmiris to adopt a more Islamic lifestyle. Shortly before Musharraf banned it, for example, Lashkar-e-Toiba put up some notices in Srinagar saying that women should wear the burqa or face the consequences. The next month, in two separate incidents, women who were not wearing burqas had acid thrown at them. Five women were severely disfigured in the attacks. As a result, many women did start wearing the burqa although a significant number refused to accept that a foreign-based organisation should dictate their lifestyle and resisted the edict.

The figures given below of the number of killings in Kashmir between 1995 and 2000 come from official Indian sources and should not be taken at face value: many in Pakistan and Kashmir believe them to be an underestimate. They do, nonetheless, demonstrate a trend: that in the late 1990s the militant campaign – and the Indian response to it – became ever more intense. The steady fall in the number of civilians killed in the insurgency is partly explained by the fact that, after ten years' experience, the Indian security forces have become more adept at ensuring that when they engage militant forces civilians are not caught in the cross fire.

Kashmir killings, 1995–2000

	Civilians	Security forces personnel	Militants
1995	1,050	202	1,308
1996	1,214	94	1,271
1997	918	189	1,114
1998	867	232	999
1999	821	356	1,082
2000	762	397	1,520

Source: US Department of State, Human Rights Reports 1995 to 2000. The figures for 1995 and 1996 are based on Indian press reports. The figures for 1997, 1998, 1999 and 2000 are official Indian government figures. See www.state.gov/www/global/human_rights/hrp_reports_mainhp.html.

By the time Musharraf banned Lashkar-e-Toiba and Jaish-e-Mohammed the insurgency had been underway for over thirteen years. And for all the loss of life it had achieved remarkably little. But the militants were not alone in failing to force a breakthrough in Kashmir. In 1999 they had been joined by a more formidable force: the Pakistan army.

Kargil

Karnal Sher Khan was always destined for a military career. The name Karnal, selected by his grandfather, was a corruption of 'colonel' and it revealed his family's ambitions. By the summer of 1999 Karnal had made it to the rank of captain in Pakistan's Northern Light Infantry. He never did become a colonel. He died in the Kargil campaign. In one way, though, the captain exceeded his family's expectations. He fought with such courage that he was posthumously awarded Pakistan's highest military honour, the Nishan-e-Haider and became a national hero. His picture, repeatedly published in the Pakistani press, became a symbol of Pakistani pride. He was recommended for the award by an Indian

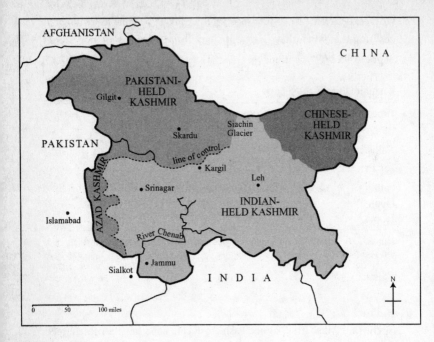

Kashmir, 2001

officer, who had seen Captain Karnal Sher Khan's valour at first hand and who insisted that the captain's memory should be treated with due respect. 'We are a professional army', the Indian officer said, 'and respect another professional soldier, even when he is from the enemy side. And we would feel happy if a soldier like Karnal Sher gets recognition for his bravery.'

Captain Karnal Sher Khan's last moments were spent in a hopeless attempt to hold on to a post high in the Himalayas in Kashmir. Having been shelled and strafed for three days and nights, the captain and the men under his command were surrounded by Indian troops. After repelling two Indian attacks they were exhausted, outnumbered and outgunned: surrender was their only realistic option. But the captain would not give up. Instead he ordered a counter-attack. His final battle lasted just a few minutes. By the end of it Karnal Sher Khan was out of ammunition and surrounded by Indian soldiers. Undaunted, he tried to carry on fighting with his rifle butt. The Indians shot him dead. 'It was suicidal for Sher to launch the attack in broad daylight because we could see his movements,' the Indian officer recalled. 'Yet in the highest military traditions he launched the attack.'[59]

That much both India and Pakistan can agree on. But virtually every other aspect of Captain Sher Khan's last hours is controversial. At the time, the Pakistanis claimed the captain had died at a post on the line of control. The Indians, by contrast, insisted he, and hundreds more Pakistani troops, were well inside Indian-held territory. The difficulty for Pakistani officials was that the captain's body was in Indian hands – indeed it had been flown to Delhi. Pressed to explain how the Indians had managed to get the body from the Pakistani side of the line of control, Pakistani spokesmen suggested that the Indians had dragged the corpse across the line so as to mount a propaganda offensive.

The fate of the captain's remains became an international issue. The Indian authorities, which released television pictures of the body, said they would not hand it over unless Pakistan admitted that the captain had been a member of the army deployed on the Indian side of the line of control. Delhi suggested Pakistan could send some officials and relatives of the captain to identify the corpse but Pakistan demanded that the body be sent to Islamabad for verification.[60] Eventually the two sides reached a compromise. Pakistan did not send anyone to Delhi but it did accept that the captain was a member of its army. Two weeks after his death, the Indian government handed over the body to the International Committee of the Red Cross and his coffin, draped in a Pakistani flag, was flown to Karachi.

Three months later, General Musharraf implicitly conceded that Captain Sher Khan had indeed been on the Indian side of the line when he died. At a ceremony to pay tribute to the Pakistani soldiers who had died in Kargil, he said that Captain Karnal Sher Khan had killed fifteen enemy personnel while carrying out 'offensive defence'.[61] Despite Musharraf's use of the phrase 'offensive defence' and, on another occasion, 'aggressive patrolling', Pakistani officials still insist, at least in public, that none of their troops were involved in the Kargil campaign. The whole operation, they maintain, was carried out by Kashmiri militants who, on their own initiative, decided to step up their campaign against the Indian forces in Kashmir.

To this day, General Musharraf refuses to admit that one of his first acts as army chief was to order his men into Indian-held territory in Kashmir and thereby launch the Kargil campaign. His denials are partly explained by his need to be consistent. From the outset, he maintained that Kargil was the work not of his soldiers but of militants intent on liberating their homeland and he has stuck to that story ever since. The international community has helped sustain the myth. In private, foreign governments made it clear to Islamabad from the beginning that they simply did not believe the claim that no Pakistani regular troops were involved in the offensive. To mount a large-scale operation in such harsh terrain, they pointed out, was clearly beyond the capability of the militant groups. But, throughout the Kargil campaign, politicians in Washington and Europe assiduously avoided making any public accusation about Pakistan's official involvement in Kargil. The furthest they went was to talk about 'Pakistani-backed forces'. The Western diplomats were reticent for a simple reason: they wanted to make it easier for Pakistan to de-escalate the crisis by withdrawing. After all, if Pakistani troops had never crossed the line of control then it was far easier for the Pakistani Prime Minister, Nawaz Sharif, to withdraw them without losing face.

The refusal to acknowledge what happened at Kargil has permeated the Pakistan military itself. Even within the army – which is, of course, well aware of the role it played in Kargil – the issue is off-limits. Pakistani officers attending courses at the Military Academy, the Staff College and the National Defence College routinely analyse and discuss every war, battle and skirmish in the history of the Pakistani army, but they still don't talk about Kargil. Instructors usually claim that this is because 'not all the details have yet been collected'. The truth is far simpler: Kargil was a piece of adventurism that totally backfired because Pakistan's high command had not thought through the consequences. And the man who must take most of the responsibility for the debacle is none other than the army chief at the time the operation took place – General Pervez Musharraf. To this day, the Pakistani press has, for the most part, kept quiet about this and only a handful of journalists have made a muted mention of the army's role in Kargil.[62] For as long as Musharraf stays in power, open discussion of Kargil will remain taboo.

When they speak 'off the record', however, Pakistani politicians and army officers tell a very different story, freely conceding that the denials about Kargil were nothing more than barefaced lies. The Northern Light Infantry, they admit, did cross the line of control. The truth is that, just as in 1947 and 1965, Pakistan tried to fudge its offensive by saying it was carried out by volunteers and not regular troops. In reality, the Islamic militants probably accounted for no more than 10 per cent of the total force and were given only portering duties.

For the Pakistani generals who organised the Kargil campaign, it all seemed to start so well. In the spring of 1999 their troops occupied over 40 square miles of Indian-held territory without firing a single shot. The operation relied on stealth. Between 1,000 and 2,000 men crossed the line of control (supposedly one of the most heavily guarded frontlines on earth) and moved 6 miles into Indian territory before they were even identified. To the considerable embarrassment of India's massive intelligence apparatus, the Pakistani intruders were first spotted by a couple of shepherds. When the Kargil conflict was over, the failure to notice, let alone predict, the incursion was closely examined by an official committee of enquiry in India. The committee's report suggested that the intelligence agencies could perhaps be forgiven: no one could have thought that Pakistan would deploy troops in an area which was so high and so cold that surviving, not to mention fighting, was a major challenge. The report pointed out that over the years, the Indian military had undertaken various war-gaming exercises in which the possibility of a Pakistani offensive around Kargil had been considered. Each time it had been ruled out as totally impractical. 'Pakistan's action at Kargil', the report concluded, 'was not rational.'[63]

India's tactics for controlling the territory around Kargil were largely determined by the area's hostile climate. In view of the fact that the winter temperatures regularly drop to as low as minus 20 degrees Celsius, the Indian army had developed the practice of vacating some of its posts around Kargil each October and then reoccupying them the following March. Pakistan's military planners calculated that if they took advantage of the spring weather a few weeks before the Indians, they could move into the territory unopposed – which is exactly what they did.

It is not clear precisely when the operation began but some Pakistanis, presumably on reconnaissance missions, crossed the line of control as early as October 1998. On the 13th of that month, the body of a Northern Light Infantry soldier, Haider Khan, was returned to his village in Pakistan's Northern Areas by four of his NLI comrades, who were ordered not to divulge how or where he had died. Haider Khan's family were given no information. Later it emerged that he was probably the first victim of the Kargil campaign. In June 2000, when the Pakistani government decided to honour the NLI for its role in Kargil, Haider Khan's name was included in the list of those who had died during the campaign.[64]

Many more Pakistanis crossed the line of control in the first six weeks of 1999 and established a series of logistics bases on the Indian side. In March their work was held up by heavy snow: an avalanche claimed the lives of some Pakistani troops and the operation had to wait for the weather to clear. By April the conditions had improved and a far larger group of men crossed the line. Not all of them were from the NLI: some were commandos from the Special Services Group and others were civilians recruited from Islamic militant groups. As they advanced, the Pakistani troops and their civilian counterparts moved surreptitiously. The Indians did have regular flights patrolling the area but every time the intruders heard a helicopter coming they simply ducked for cover. By the end of April they were both delighted and somewhat amazed that they were still undetected.

The high command in Rawalpindi could not have asked for more. The operation to infiltrate and then dig into Indian-held territory had exceeded their expectations. But, as so often with Pakistani military operations, the objectives were somewhat unclear. At a tactical level the plan was simple enough. The preparations for Kargil had begun in 1994 when the Indians managed to cut the Neelum Valley road that lay just inside Pakistani-controlled Kashmir. The Indian action was highly disruptive: the Pakistan army was forced to move supplies to the local population by mules until it was able to construct a bypass protected from Indian artillery positions.

As it took stock of what had happened in the Neelum Valley the Pakistani army considered various possible responses. By 1996 it had drawn up a detailed plan that concentrated on a road in Indian-held

Kashmir from Srinagar to Leh, the only land route available for supplying the Indian troops at the Siachin glacier. The road had long frustrated Pakistan's military strategists. For several years artillery emplacements on the Pakistani side of the line had tried to target the road but since they were unsighted, hitting it was more a matter of luck than judgement. The planners concluded that if they could hold the high ground above Kargil, they would be not only able to direct artillery fire towards the Srinagar–Leh road with greater accuracy, but also close enough to use small arms against Indian targets. And if the road was cut, then the Indians would have to move in all their supplies to Siachin by air: a hugely expensive proposition.

Attacking the road, then, was the immediate objective but the Pakistani strategists had other goals in mind as well. Many senior officers feared that the anti-Indian insurgency was on the wane. They worried that many Kashmiris, tiring of the violence, might settle for a compromise favourable to Delhi and hoped that a major operation in Kargil would provide the insurgency with a shot in the arm, thereby keeping up the pressure on India. There were also broader objectives. The army hoped that the Kargil incursion would increase the level of international diplomatic involvement in Kashmir. Once the Pakistani move became known, the thinking went, the international community would become concerned about a possible nuclear exchange and exert strong pressure for a ceasefire. Pakistan would have not only increased the amount of territory under its control but also drawn international attention to the Kashmir dispute.

The Pakistanis had considered India's likely response to the Kargil incursion. The crucial question was whether India's high command would order a repeat of 1965 and extend the conflict beyond Kashmir by launching an attack on Pakistan itself. The various war-gaming scenarios played out by the Pakistani planners suggested that this would not happen. The Indian army still enjoyed a considerable numerical superiority over Pakistan but the Pakistanis predicted – correctly – that Delhi would move some divisions from the border with China to Kashmir and would then find that it did not have enough strength to guarantee a victory over Pakistan itself. It was also thought that the nuclear dimension would act as a constraint on Delhi.

India, in short, would find itself in a very awkward position. The Pakistani troops, the plan went, would be occupying posts so high that they were impregnable. According to a late addition to the plan, Pakistani-backed militants would then up the ante by launching attacks on military installations throughout Indian-held Kashmir. This would serve a number of objectives: the insurgents would be encouraged; the pressure on the Pakistani troops occupying the heights would be relieved and, because more Indian troops would have to be deployed throughout Kashmir, the risk of an attack on Pakistan would be further reduced. The Pakistan army also calculated that if the plan went wrong for any reason they could deny involvement and say that militants, over whom they had no control, carried out the whole operation. As exit strategies go this was woefully inadequate. One Pakistani cabinet minister later put it that, 'the army had climbed up a pole without considering how it would get down'.[65]

The incursion was eventually discovered in the first week of May. Having been tipped off by the local shepherds, Indian army patrols confirmed that a significant number of infiltrators had crossed the line. Delhi, however, still did not appreciate the scale of the Pakistani operation and the Indian prime minister, Atal Behari Vajpayee, was not informed until 9 May.[66] As late as 16 May the Defence Minister George Fernandes was predicting that the intruders would be evicted in 48 hours. It was a hopelessly optimistic assessment. The Pakistanis had dug in on high, very defensible, positions. On 21 May the Indian air force conducted an air survey of the Kargil sector. It was only then that Delhi realised what they were up against: the photographs revealed that as many as eight helipads were in place on the Indian side of the line of control.

Atal Behari Vajpayee had a lot to worry about. He was faced with a major political and military challenge. To complicate matters further his coalition government, led by the Bharatiya Janata Party (BJP), had suffered a parliamentary defeat in March and was consequently in the midst of an election campaign. The opinion polls indicated that Vajpayee was in a precarious position: the outcome of the election was far from certain and anything that could be interpreted as defeat in Kashmir would clearly reduce his chances of winning another term. Vajpayee also felt betrayed. Just three months before, in February 1999, he had gone to Lahore for peace talks with his Pakistani counterpart, Nawaz Sharif.

Although the formal text that came out of the summit, the Lahore Declaration, contained only one reference to Kashmir, the two leaders had discussed the issue in some depth. Sharif and Vajpayee had a one-hour session at which no one else was present and during which they reached a private understanding. They agreed that they should try to find a solution to the Kashmir problem by the next millennium, in other words, by the end of the year. The two prime ministers knew that if they asked their respective foreign ministries to conduct the negotiations then the officials would adopt rigid positions and the talks would be doomed before they had even begun. Instead the two leaders decided to set up a diplomatic back channel: each would appoint an expert who would be charged with conducting the secret talks. Since the process would be entirely deniable it was hoped that the two sides could discuss fresh approaches to the Kashmir dispute. Vajpayee appointed the prominent Bombay newspaper publisher, R. K. Mishra, and Sharif opted for a retired diplomat, Niaz Naik.

And so began a series of extraordinary meetings. On 27 May Naik and Mishra met in a luxury suite in Delhi's Imperial Hotel. Having unobtrusively slipped into India on a PIA flight, Naik was determined to keep a very low profile and barely left his room. For four days, between endless rounds of room service, he and Mishra discussed possible solutions to Kashmir. Both agreed that they would have to go beyond their governments' public positions on the issue. Delhi would have to stop talking about Kashmir as being an integral part of India and Islamabad would have to stop asking for the implementation of UN resolutions and, in particular, give up the demand for a plebiscite. The two men also agreed that any solution had to be balanced: it must take into account the requirements of Pakistan, India and the Kashmiri people. Having established these initial rules of the game, the two men informed Vajpayee about their discussions. The Indian prime minister added one new element: any solution, he said, must be final and not partial.

Naik and Mishra then started discussing possible solutions. This was in itself remarkable. Two men, directly appointed by the Indian and Pakistani prime ministers, were seriously debating how to solve the Kashmir dispute. As they did so, the scale of their task became ever clearer. Many proposals were rejected as being unacceptable to one side or the other. Naik immediately ruled out the idea of converting the line of control into a border: 'It's the status quo,' he said. 'If we accept that then why did we fight two wars?' Mishra was equally dismissive of the idea of Kashmiri independence. India, he argued, could not allow such a precedent for fear that other Indian states would also try to break away. They also rejected other possibilities such as greater autonomy, and a division of Kashmir on the basis of the religious affiliation with Muslim majority areas going to Pakistan and Hindu majority areas to India. Mishra thought the result would be the same as it was fifty years before during partition: 'It will result in a blood bath,' he said.[67]

Naik and Mishra in fact knocked down every possibility they could think of. They considered regional plebiscites and models for joint sovereignty. They discussed how the city of Trieste was governed after the Second World War and they considered the model of the British and Irish governments' arrangements for Northern Ireland. As the discussions continued, the two men gradually came to the point where they shared some ground. If a solution were to endure it would have to be based on a new verifiable, clearly defined international border. Kashmir would have to be carved up between Delhi and Islamabad. But where would that border be?

Naik suggested that India should keep everything south and east of the Chenab River. Since Mishra did not know exactly where the river was Naik went to the hotel bookshop to buy a tourist map. As he looked at the map, Mishra wondered whether the proposal could work. He neither accepted nor rejected the idea. It was progress, and on 1 April Naik and Mishra decided they needed to pause and report back to their prime ministers before meeting again. But it was never to be. The peace initiative was shattered by the Kargil offensive. As soon as the Indians became aware of the Pakistani infiltration, the back channel was diverted from long-term thinking into immediate crisis management. It is difficult to believe that the Chenab River proposal would have been acceptable to the Indian government; nevertheless, a great opportunity for genuine dialogue had been missed.

Instead of seeking a solution to the Kashmir dispute, Vajpayee was now focussed on the immediate task of expelling the Pakistani intruders. On

25 May he approved the use of air power. The next morning the airfield at Srinagar was used to launch over forty sorties of MiG-21, MiG-23 and MiG-27 fighter aircraft. Mi-17 helicopters were also used for air strikes. The aircraft, however, made little impact. Since many of the targets were located at between 13,000 and 17,000 feet, the planes had to fly in at over 25,000 feet to avoid the Pakistani's anti-aircraft fire. The Indian pilots descended to around 20,000 feet at the last moment before firing and making good their escape. At these heights the planes and their missiles were pushed beyond their technical limits. The thin mountain air affected the bombs' performance and the Indians found themselves having to recalculate predicted trajectories. Even if they could work out the direction the bombs would take, locating the tiny Pakistani positions in the mountainous terrain was virtually impossible. This was, in part, because the air force could not use its laser-guided bomb systems, supposedly due to cost considerations.[68] The real reason was that the Indian forces did not have a direct line of sight to most of the Pakistani positions: it was impossible for Indian ground troops to fix laser beams on the majority of the targets.

The Indian aircraft faced another problem. Many of the targets were very close to the line of control and the pilots found it difficult to remain inside Indian-controlled air space. On 27 May the Pakistanis shot down a MiG-27 and a MiG-21, claiming that both had strayed across the line of control. The next day, Pakistani troops on the Indian side of the line shot down a Mi-17 helicopter. Concerned by the extent of the losses after just four days of the air campaign, the Indian air force decided to deploy some French-built Mirage 2000 fighter-bombers. The new planes not only had better defensive equipment but also gave the Indians the possibility of flying at night. Indian officials subsequently claimed that the Mirage planes were far more accurate and enjoyed a far higher success rate than the MiGs.[69] If the Mirages did perform better that was partly because the air force switched its emphasis from searching for the Pakistani positions on the peaks and instead concentrated on rearward camps and logistics bases. It was a longer-term strategy but it worked: the Pakistani supply lines were successfully disrupted.

The air force may have been improving its performance but the Indian ground troops still faced a daunting task. The Pakistanis had occupied over 130 separate positions. To reach them the Indian soldiers had to climb thousands of feet. As they approached the peaks, they then entered a killing zone. The Pakistanis could fire at will, picking off the Indians one by one. Furthermore, the craggy nature of the terrain meant that, on most of the summits, the Indians could deploy no more than ten to twenty men in any single attack. If there were more than that they would end up forming queues vulnerable to Pakistani fire.

As the Indian army considered its options it concluded that two Pakistani positions – at Tololung and Tiger Hill – were the most vulnerable. Both had a direct line of sight to the Leh–Srinagar road and to the Indian military cantonment at Dras. From the Pakistani point of view that made the positions invaluable – they could direct accurate fire at the Indians. But the direct line of sight also offered India an opportunity to aim artillery fire back at the Pakistani soldiers. And once a battery of Bofors guns was moved into position that is exactly what happened. The artillery onslaught was unrelenting and forced the Pakistanis to shelter behind the crest of the peaks. That, in turn, enabled Indian troops to climb up towards the peaks unopposed.

Tololung was the first to fall but taking the second, Tiger Hill, was still a monumental task. An Indian journalist's account of the battle for Tiger Hill gives an impression of the difficulties the Indians faced:

> Soldiers of three crack infantry units have been at it since mid-May in a vain attempt to dislodge Pakistani troops at the crucial peak. The scenario is near hopeless: hauling yourselves up on ropes at 15,000-odd feet, over a killing 80 degree gradient mountain face, weighed down by 40 kg backpacks, braving icy winds and sub-zero temperatures. Forget enemy guns, even boulders flung from the top take lives.[70]

The decisive battle for Tiger Hill took place on the night of 3 July and lasted eleven hours. The Indian infantry made its move, planning to reach the 16,000-foot peak around midnight. They attacked from three sides. By that time, over 30,000 rounds had been fired into the mountain. As the Indian troops neared the summit the artillery stopped. For the Pakistanis on the summit it might have seemed like a blessed relief, but this didn't last long.

The first Indian soldiers to reach the peak ascended an almost vertical cliff. One of them, nineteen-year-old Yogendra Singh Yadav, later described what happened. 'It was a near-90 degree incline and we had to climb with the help of ropes,' he recalled. Yadav was one of the first to reach the summit and when he got there he could see that the Pakistanis were taken by surprise; they had not expected anyone to make it up the cliff-face and consequently had left it undefended. Yadav then saw a bunker in which some Pakistanis were sheltering: 'There were four men inside. I hurled my grenade inside and saw two of them die.' By the time Yadav was joined by the other two assault teams, many of the fifty or so Pakistani defenders had decided to slip away and in the end, the Indians said, they found only seven Pakistani bodies on the top.[71]

The recapture of Tololung and Tiger Hill was a significant victory for the Indian forces. The Indian defence minister, George Fernandes, caught the mood: 'We will now be able to dictate terms to the intruders. Our army is in a position to do anything,' he said.[72] The truth was very different. The peaks above Dras had only fallen because the Indians had a clear line of sight that enabled them to use artillery fire. Most of the Pakistani positions were not visible to the Indians and it was much more difficult to ensure that artillery shells found their mark. Despite this crucial distinction, the battles above Dras did have a decisive impact. While Indian morale soared, the Pakistani politicians and even some in the military began to wonder whether they had overextended themselves.

When Tiger Hill fell, Nawaz Sharif concluded that the military position was becoming untenable. His military commanders had assured him that all of the positions they had occupied were impregnable. Sharif now believed they had been overconfident. Two important posts, after all, had just been taken. The military top brass insisted – with considerable justification – that they could still hold on to large tracts of Indian territory but Sharif no longer trusted their judgement. With the supply lines cut and no chance of sending in reinforcements, he believed it was only a question of time before the Indians secured a complete victory.

Sharif wanted a way out but it was far from clear how he could extricate himself from Kargil. He knew that any order to withdraw would be deeply unpopular and seen by many Pakistani voters as a cowardly abandonment of the Kashmiri cause. But withdrawal, he believed, it had to be. Eventually he decided to go to the United States in search of some political cover. To an extent President Clinton obliged. In return for Sharif's commitment to issue an order for withdrawal Clinton agreed to two things. First, he would make no statement about the fact that Pakistani regular troops had been involved in the conflict and, second, he would make a public statement about his personal commitment to finding a solution to the Kashmir dispute. It wasn't much but it was all Sharif could get.

Indian sources have claimed that by the time Sharif met President Clinton over 80 per cent of the Pakistani intruders had been dislodged from their positions.[73] Neutral observers, probably relying on Pakistani sources, have suggested that the Pakistani troops had been dislodged from only twelve of 134 defended positions.[74] Another estimate suggests that India had overrun only four out of 132 positions.[75] Whatever the precise figure the important point is that Pakistan was still in control of a large area and would, in all likelihood, have been able to hang on to it for the remaining weeks of the summer. They could then have dug in, maintained a light presence and waited to see whether there would be any diplomatic movement before fighting could resume the next spring. The planned militant attacks on Indian installations in the rest of Kashmir would add to Delhi's discomfort.

The Pakistanis' strength on the ground helps explain why so many in the military establishment resented the order to pull back. The former director general of the ISI, General (Retd.) Hamid Gul, for example, claimed after the conflict that Sharif: 'lost a war in Washington that had already been won in Kargil'. Hamid Gul is known for the extremity of his views but on this occasion a significant number in the Pakistan military agreed with him. In the days immediately before Sharif's visit to Washington the army had no intention of a rapid pullout. On the contrary, some senior officers were still drawing up plans to establish permanent posts on those positions that remained under Pakistani control. The views of the army chief, General Musharraf, remain unclear. Most insiders, though, say that he was in full agreement with Sharif's decision to go to Washington.

Even if Musharraf and Sharif were able to present a united front over Washington, the Kargil campaign did create a deep and lasting rift between the military and civilian leaderships that eventually manifested itself in the October 1999 coup. During his trial, after Musharraf's take-over, Sharif made a remarkable claim that exposed the extent of that divide. He said he had had no advance knowledge of what the army was planning to do in Kargil: 'This ill-planned and ill-conceived operation was kept so secret', Sharif complained, 'that the Prime Minister, some Corps Commanders and the Chief of Navy and the Air Force were kept in the dark.'[76]

His comments echoed claims made during the Kargil campaign. On 11 June the Indian government had released two tapes of conversations between General Musharraf and his chief of general staff, Lt. General Mohammed Aziz. At the time of the second conversation on 26 May, General Musharraf was on a trip to China and although it was never clear which intelligence agency had recorded the tapes, no one seriously doubted their authenticity. One remark made by Lt. General Aziz sug-gested that the prime minister may indeed have been uninformed about Kargil. Aziz had had a meeting with Nawaz Sharif and he informed General Musharraf what had happened: 'We told him [Sharif] there is no reason for alarm and panic. Then he [Sharif] said that: "I came to know seven days back, when the Corps Commanders were told".' Aziz then told Musharraf how he had explained to Sharif that: 'the entire reason for the success of the operation was total secrecy. Our earlier efforts failed because of lack of secrecy. So the top priority is to accord confidential-ity to ensure our success.'[77]

When Indian ministers heard this tape some concluded that Nawaz Sharif had not been told about Kargil in advance. The suggestion fitted in with a remark made by Sharif on 10 May. When Vajpayee had called him that day to complain about the incursion at Kargil, Sharif had claimed he knew nothing about it.[78] The Pakistani army has consistently denied this claim. During the Kargil campaign Musharraf pointedly told a television interviewer that 'everyone was on board' the Kargil opera-tion. Sharif's and Musharraf's versions contradict each other. But there is considerable evidence that the military did hold back a significant amount of crucial information from the prime minister.

Army officers claim that the Kargil operation was first mentioned to Sharif in a meeting that took place in the ISI office in Lahore in February 1999. The meeting was routine and took the form of a regular quarterly briefing on Kashmir in which the ISI briefed the civilian leadership about latest developments. As usual, the ISI invited the prime minister, the chief of army staff and some of their senior colleagues. According to the military version, Sharif was told about Kargil at this meeting. Army officers point out that the prime minster had a famously short attention span and may not have fully understood everything that he was told. They claim that Sharif seemed bored by the briefing and asked for it to be shortened.

Sharif and two other participants at the meeting have a different version.[79] They say that although there was talk about the need to bolster the insurgency, no one ever mentioned the possibility of the Northern Light Infantry being deployed in Kashmir. Indeed, it would have been unusual for such an issue to be raised at the ISI briefing. For many years the military operations in Kashmir had been the preserve of the army while the ISI had responsibility for supporting the insurgency. If the army were planning an initiative in Kashmir it would have been more customary for it to organise a separate briefing for the prime minister, either at his office or at army headquarters in Rawalpindi.

The February meeting is of interest because it took place prior to the Lahore summit and raises the possibility that Nawaz Sharif knew about the plan to deploy troops in Indian-held Kashmir when he invited Atal Behari Vajpayee for talks. But no one suggests that any final decisions were taken in February. As far as the army is concerned, the prime minster granted his formal approval of the Kargil plan in the second week of March at a meeting held at ISI headquarters in Islamabad. The meeting was attended by the ISI chief General Ziauddin, the chief of army staff General Musharraf and his two most powerful colleagues, Generals Mehmood and Aziz. The air force and navy chiefs and other corps commanders were excluded. On the political side Sharif was joined by his religious affairs minister Raja Zafar ul Haq, his foreign minister Sartaj Aziz and the minister for Kashmir affairs, Lt. General (Retd.) Majid Malik.

Two eyewitnesses at this meeting have claimed that even at this stage (when the military intervention was already well underway) there was no mention of troops crossing the line of control. According to their version, while there was talk of increasing the level of militant activity in Kashmir, the discussion was framed entirely in terms of the insurgency. The army stated its fear that the resistance movement could die out. It argued that if the Lahore process was to bear fruit then the Indians must be made to believe that the pressure in Kashmir would not go away. The army failed to disclose the role of the Northern Light Infantry and did not identify Kargil as a military objective.[80] It is widely agreed, however, that at this meeting the army secured Sharif's agreement to 'increase the heat' in Kashmir. The intriguing question is whether the army wilfully misinterpreted an endorsement of increased militant activity as an order to go ahead with the full-blown Kargil campaign. According to the Sharif version of events that is exactly what happened and he was not told about the role of the NLI until after the Indians had discovered the intrusion in early May. In a meeting in the second week of that month, one participant recalled, 'Sharif heard it for the first time'. It is an incredible claim that, if accurate, would lend weight to the Indian allegation that Pakistan has a rogue army.

It is difficult to draw firm conclusions about what happened in the run-up to Kargil. The two versions are utterly contradictory. The most likely explanation is that the army did tell Sharif what was happening but, for a number of reasons, a full discussion did not develop. First, the army did not believe that Kargil would become such a big issue. The planners thought they were mounting a relatively limited operation that would amount to little more than a skirmish near the line of control. Had the Pakistani intrusion been discovered and stopped earlier this is precisely what would have happened. Second, Sharif never took much interest in detailed military matters. If the army wanted to scrap for a few posts near the line of control he was not the man to stop them. Third, the army would not have wanted Sharif to get too closely involved in the decision-making process. Senior officers not only resented civilian intervention in such issues but also wanted to keep the whole matter secret: it is widely accepted that those corps commanders who were not directly involved in Kargil were not told until after it had happened.

Yet even if one takes the army's version at face value it indicates a hopelessly inadequate approach to decision-making. The army's claim that Sharif was told about Kargil in advance but failed to take it in suggests that nothing was put down on paper. It indicates that, at the very least, there was no thoroughgoing debate about the implications of the Kargil operation. The Foreign Office was not asked for its opinion and little thought was given to what would happen if India responded with a major counter-attack. Just as in 1965, no one seemed to scrutinise the prediction (this time accurate) that India would not extend the war beyond Kashmir and launch an attack across the international boundary. It was a remarkably casual way for a nuclear power to run a war.

Kargil was a disaster for Pakistan. Afterwards the international community insisted with even greater vehemence than hitherto that the line of control was inviolable and that Pakistan should respect its sanctity. For all its efforts to concentrate world opinion on India's human rights abuses in Kashmir, Pakistan had instead managed to enhance its image as an aggressive and unpredictable state.

The fight for Kashmir has been extremely costly and not only in terms of human life. The sustained conflict between the two biggest powers in South Asia has held back the region's economic development. For Pakistan the conflict has carried an especially high price. Not only has the Kashmir issue diverted attention from more important national objectives, such as reducing poverty, but it has also contributed to a destabilising radicalisation of youth opinion in Pakistan. India, too, has suffered because of Kashmir: the dream of Gandhian principles governing the world's largest democracy has been shattered by the Indian security forces' brutal suppression of Kashmiri opinion.

Despite this, it is often said that the Kashmir dispute will not be solved because significant power centres in India and Pakistan have an interest in sustaining the conflict. There is some truth in this argument. The armed forces in both countries use the Kashmir issue to justify their huge shares of public expenditure. The conflict also provides a rallying cry for extremists in Pakistan's Islamic groups and India's nationalist parties. Politicians on both sides know that continuing to pour out a steady stream of vitriolic rhetoric about Kashmir is the safe option. Any move from established positions (a necessary pre-condition of a settlement) would inevitably be denounced as a sell-out.

The positions of Islamabad and Delhi have become deeply entrenched. Officials from both capitals can, at a moment's notice, deploy a whole series of legal arguments to justify their attitudes towards Kashmir. India relies on one point above all others: that the maharaja acceded to India. But the timing of that act; the Indian promises to hold a plebiscite; the Indian invasions of Hyderabad and Junagardh; the various UN resolutions; the agreements at Tashkent and Simla, have added layer upon layer of complexity to the issue. Ultimately, however, those who rely on the legal arguments miss the point. Kashmir is a political rather than a legal problem.

The conflict has defied many would-be peacemakers. No obvious solution is in sight. But in considering the future it is worth making some points. Although India maintains its claim over the areas occupied by the tribesmen in 1947, it is quite clear that Azad Kashmir, Gilgit and Baltistan are lost to India forever. Any attempt to establish Delhi's control there would lead to a popular revolt. True, there are some people in all three areas who resent Pakistan but that does not mean they would prefer be governed by India. Equally, a majority of the Hindus of Jammu and the Buddhists of Ladakh would be content to become a regular part of the Indian state. The real problem lies in the Kashmir Valley. India's huge military presence there and the militants' unceasing insurgency demonstrate the scale of the impasse.

For many in the international community, the Kargil dispute added weight to the view that the line of control should become an international border. There are two standard objections to this proposal. First, it is maintained that many Muslims in the Kashmir Valley will never accept direct Indian rule and, in the unlikely event of Pakistan recognising Indian control over the valley, the insurgency would continue albeit in a weakened form. Second, it is argued that the Pakistan army, the ISI and a significant proportion of the Pakistani people could never accept that so many lives have been sacrificed for no gain whatsoever. To accept the line of control would be to concede that the 1965 war and the insurgency have been for nothing.

The repeated and consistent demand of most Kashmiris has been for self-determination through the mechanism of a plebiscite. As far as the UN resolutions are concerned, any plebiscite would offer two choices: accession to India or to Pakistan. A vote on this basis would be counterproductive because the losing side would not accept the result. If, for example, a majority voted for accession to Pakistan then some communities such as the Pandits, the Hindus of Jammu and the Buddhists would feel so vulnerable that they would probably flee to India.

A plebiscite, then, raises difficult issues. One way of getting around some of them would be to hold regional plebiscites in Kashmir. These would satisfy the Kashmiris' basic demand for self-determination. Jammu and Ladakh would probably vote for accession to India; Azad Kashmir and the Northern Areas could be incorporated into Pakistan. The difficulty, as ever, is in the Valley. On the face of it, independence for the Valley, and the Valley alone, would seem to circumvent some of these difficulties even if it would be opposed by those militants who favour the independence of Kashmir as a whole.[81] If India remains unwilling to accept independence for the Valley (as it probably would) then it might be prepared to settle for greater autonomy in the valley with Islamabad and Delhi agreeing to some form of joint sovereignty over the area. For the moment though, India rejects this proposal as totally unacceptable.

Musharraf's speech on 12 January 2002 had clear implications for Kashmir. By announcing bans on Lashkar-e-Toiba and Jaish-e-Mohammed, he increased the chance that the insurgency in Kashmir would be weakened. If it faced a less intense battle in Kashmir, it is likely that the Indians would want to put the issue on the back burner. But it is worth bearing in mind two developments. First, the Kashmiri people are tiring of the struggle. Most informed Pakistanis now accept that, given the chance, most Kashmiris would opt for independence rather than a merger with Pakistan. But above all else the people of Kashmir want peace. That is not to say they will accept any settlement but it does raise the possibility that most would accept a compromise. The second new element is that many Pakistanis are also tiring of the conflict. Before Musharraf's January speech it was conventional wisdom that no Pakistani leader could confront the religious extremists and remain in office. The lack of any backlash to Musharraf's speech helped dispel that myth.

Might the same be true of Kashmir? Proponents of the view that no Pakistani leader can afford to back down in Kashmir rely on a number of arguments. First, the Pakistani people, informed by decades of intensive propaganda, are highly mobilised on the issue. Second, the army has made so many sacrifices in Kashmir that a significant climb-down would be seen as unacceptable. Not even an army chief, it is suggested, could compromise on Kashmir and expect to survive. That may be true, but there are counter arguments. Despite all the propaganda, many people in India and Pakistan are not particularly concerned about the Kashmir dispute. Many of those living, for example, in Sindh or Tamil Nadu would be quite happy to see any settlement of a dispute that is quite clearly holding back the subcontinent's social and economic development. After a decade of insurgency, there is a growing feeling in Pakistan that India will never pull out. Pakistan's size and economic weakness means it is not in a position to force the hand of a country with a billion people and great power aspirations. If General Musharraf or any subsequent Pakistani leader did make a compromise on Kashmir he or she might receive more support than is generally predicted.

In his account of the Kashmir dispute, the Indian author Sumantra Bose has rejected the idea of splitting up Kashmir because, he argues, none of the political districts are either ethnically or religiously homogeneous. In the Jammu region, for example, one third of the population is Muslim. Indeed, some of its districts have strong Muslim majorities. In Ladakh, meanwhile, the Buddhists may have a clear majority in Leh but the adjoining Ladakhi district of Kargil has a predominantly Shia Muslim population.[82] Whilst Bose undoubtedly has a point, the history of the late twentieth century, for better or for worse, suggests that his objections to the possible partition of Kashmir are far from overwhelming. In the Baltic States and former Yugoslavia, to give just two examples, international boundaries were redrawn without regard to the fact that, in the process, new minority populations were created.

The difficulty of finding a solution to the Kashmir dispute has been enhanced by the never-ending arguments about the merits of bilateralism versus international mediation. Ever since the Simla Agreement, India has rejected any suggestion of international involvement. Pakistan meanwhile has (unsuccessfully) concentrated its diplomatic effort on internationalising the dispute. The focus on the mechanism by which a solution might be found rather than on the compromises needed to find that solution has worked to no one's advantage. The process of reconciliation in two other apparently insoluble disputes in the Middle East and Northern Ireland was helped by the intervention of outside mediators from Norway and the United States respectively. The issue of third party involvement, however, has become such a prominent part of the diplomatic tussle over Kashmir that it is difficult to foresee any Indian government accepting any such mediation even if it were conducted under conditions of tight secrecy.

Ever since 1947 the views of the Kashmiris have been obscured by the dispute between India and Pakistan. With the insurgency over a decade old most Kashmiris are sick of the conflict and are desperate for a peaceful settlement. But for both India and Pakistan the symbolic importance of the Kashmir dispute means that they will inevitably follow their own perceived national interests rather than those of the Kashmiri people. If the Kashmiris had been conducting a straightforward fight for independence in the same way as the Chechens or East Timorese they would have had a greater chance of success. The tragedy of Kashmir is that the voices of the Kashmiri people themselves have been drowned out by the Islamists, nationalists and ideologues in Islamabad and Delhi.

4   Nationalism

> My description of the partition as the greatest blunder in the
> history of mankind is an objective assessment based on the
> bitter experience of the masses . . . Had the subcontinent not
> been divided, the 180 million Muslims of Bangladesh, 150
> million of Pakistan and about 200 million in India would
> together have made 530 million people and, as such, they
> would have been a very powerful force in undivided India.
>
> —Muttahida Qaumi Movement (MQM) leader Altaf Hussain,
> October 2000[1]

'I have been a Baloch for several centuries. I have been a Muslim for
1,400 years. I have been a Pakistani for just over fifty.'[2] The tribal chief
Nawab Akbar Bugti Khan has little love for Pakistan. Secure in his
heavily guarded, mud-walled fort deep in the Baloch desert, he runs a
state within a state. Pakistan may have been in existence for over half a
century but he still considers any Pakistani troops in his vicinity as part
of an occupation army. Other tribal chiefs, feudal leaders and politicians
in Balochistan, rural Sindh, NWFP and even some in southern Punjab
share his attitude towards Pakistan. Islam was meant to be the binding
force – but, for many, ethnic ties have proved to be stronger.

Like Israel, Pakistan was created in the name of religion. In 1948
there were just a few hundred thousand Jews living in their new country's territory; most Israelis came from elsewhere. When Pakistan was
created, by contrast, there were already over 70 million Muslims living
in the 'land of the pure' and they were by no means united. As well as
the Bengalis in East Pakistan, the new state had to integrate five major
groups: the Sindhis, the Baloch, the Pukhtoons, the Punjabis and the
incoming Mohajirs.[3]

Successive Pakistani leaders have shown little interest in Pakistan's
cultural diversity. Mohammed Ali Jinnah insisted on loyalty and alle-
giance to Pakistan, and Pakistan alone. Speaking in Dhaka in March
1948, he said:

What we want is not talk about Bengali, Punjabi, Sindhi, Baluchi, Pathan and so on. They are of course units. But I ask you: have you forgotten the lesson that was taught us thirteen hundred years ago? You belong to a nation now. You have carved out a territory, a vast territory. It is all yours: it does not belong to a Punjabi or a Sindhi or a Pathan or a Bengali. It is all yours. You have got your Central Government where several units are represented. Therefore, if you want to build yourself up into a nation, for God's sake give up this provincialism.[4]

Subsequent Pakistani leaders have consistently echoed that line. In 1954 the first Pakistani commander-in-chief, Ayub Khan, wrote: 'The ultimate aim must be to become a sound, solid and cohesive nation . . .'[5] When he made his final address to the nation eleven years later Ayub's view had not changed. Warning that some people wanted to destroy the country established by Jinnah, he said: 'I have always told you that Pakistan's salvation lay in a strong centre.'[6]

In 1971 Pakistan faced the most significant nationalist challenge of its short history when the Bengalis split away and formed Bangladesh. There are some in Pakistan today, such as the advocates of Sindudesh, for example, who would like to follow suit. One might think that the loss of East Pakistan in 1971 would have alerted Pakistani leaders to the dangers of ignoring local nationalist sentiment. It did not. In 1974 Zulfikar Ali Bhutto was quite adamant on the matter. Speaking about Baloch demands for greater autonomy, he said the idea of a confederation (rather than a more centralised federation) was 'a ridiculous one for a country that wants to count for something in the world. It will never work.'[7] General Zia saw it the same way. Asked in 1978 about the possibility of introducing a multinational Pakistan in which the Baloch, Pukhtoons, Sindhis and Punjabis would be entitled to local self-rule, he replied: 'I simply cannot understand this type of thinking. We want to build a strong country, a unified country. Why should we talk in these small-minded terms? We should talk in terms of Pakistan, one united Pakistan.' He went on to say that, ideally, he would like to break up the existing four provinces of West Pakistan and replace them with fifty-three small provinces, erasing ethnic identities altogether.[8] Whatever their background, Pakistani leaders have consistently seen expressions of provincial feeling as a threat to the Pakistani state. Nationalist leaders in the provinces have tended to associate such centralist attitudes with Punjabi arrogance. In reality, it has never been as simple as that. After all, Jinnah was born in Karachi, Ayub Khan was a Pukhtoon and Zulfikar Ali Bhutto came from Sindh.

It is ironic that the nationalists in Pakistan's provinces have repeatedly cited, as a source of legitimacy, the very document that provided the basis for Pakistan itself: the Lahore Resolution. Although the resolution did not include the word 'federation' it did say that the independent states it called for should have 'constituent units' which would be 'autonomous and sovereign'. The terms autonomous and sovereign are notoriously difficult to define but national groups such as the Sindhis and the Baloch can certainly argue that, by any definition, sovereignty must include the power of a constituent unit to decide whether or not to remain in a larger entity.

Provincial breakdown by population, 1951

Province	Percentage of West Pakistan	Percentage of East and West Pakistan
Punjab	62.1	27.7
Sindh	17.1	7.6
Balochistan	3.4	1.5
NWFP	17.4	7.8
Bengal	0.0	55.4
Total	100	100

Source: Keith Callard, *Pakistan: A Political Study*, George Allen & Unwin, Oxford, 1957, p. 156.

This chapter will analyse the various nationalist challenges to Pakistan (apart from that of the Bengalis which is discussed in chapter 5). The most sustained campaign has come from the most unlikely source: the refugees or Mohajirs who moved to Pakistan in 1947. Over the course of thirty years the attitude of those Mohajirs who ended up in Sindh has gone through an extraordinary transformation: Pakistan's keenest advocates became the country's most bitter critics. The difficulty in explaining the turnaround in Mohajir attitudes, and the fact that the emergence of Mohajir nationalism was so closely intertwined with that of the Sindhis, means that most of this chapter must be devoted to developments in Sindh. There are also briefer discussions of Baloch and Pukhtoon nationalism and the increasingly strident stance taken by the Seraiki speakers in southern Punjab. There is no separate discussion of Punjab. As the dominant province in Pakistan, Punjab has never seen the need to press for greater autonomy.

When independence was attained, millions of people in northern India gave up their jobs, homes and communities and began a terrifying journey. Most travelled on foot or by train and, in doing so, they risked their lives. An untold number never made it: they became victims of the frenzied violence triggered by partition. For those who crossed the rivers of blood that separated the two new nations, the feeling of relief was intense. Not only were they participating in the birth of a new Muslim nation; they had survived.

There are no reliable figures for the number of people who fled to Pakistan in the wake of partition. Ayub Khan estimated that there were 9 million.[9] Whatever the total, it is widely accepted that a majority of the incomers were Punjabis from the Indian side of the border who settled into Pakistan with relative ease. That is not to say there were no tensions. The incoming East Punjabis tended to be better educated than the West Punjabis and their need for suitable properties to live in did cause some resentment amongst the host population. To this day, the difference between Punjab's traditional population and the post-partition incomers is reflected in voting patterns.[10] Nevertheless cultural, linguistic and, in some cases, familial links meant that the assimilation process was relatively smooth. Compared to the refugees who headed for Sindh, the East Punjabis tended to have lower expectations of Pakistan. They suffered dreadfully during partition and many of those who survived the journey to Pakistan saw horrific acts of violence, including the murder of family members before their eyes. They did not arrive with a long list of demands: they were glad to be alive.

Most of the non-Punjabi migrants came from the United Provinces, Rajastan and other Hindu majority parts of northern India and the majority headed for Sindh where they hoped they could find work in the new capital, Karachi. Despite the Mohajirs' repeated claims that they made huge sacrifices for Pakistan it is clear that the East Punjabis suffered more during partition. While the East Punjabis had to move to save their lives, the Mohajirs chose to move to build a new future. The Mojahirs had campaigned for Pakistan only to find that, to live in the new country, they had to relocate because their own home areas did not become part of Pakistan. And the impact of the Urdu-speaking Mohajirs on Sindhi cities such as Karachi and Hyderabad was enormous. By 1951 the native Sindhi community in Karachi, for example, had been completely outnumbered; just 14 per cent of the city's population spoke Sindhi as opposed to 58 per cent who spoke Urdu. In other Sindhi cities the figures were even more striking. In Hyderabad over 66 per cent of the population was Mohajir.[11] It was quite possible for Mohajirs to live in these cities and seldom meet a Sindhi, never mind interact with one.

Many of the Mohajirs were well-educated: in line with the imperial policy of divide and rule, the British had ensured that the Muslims who lived in Hindu-dominated provinces were well represented in the imperial bureaucracy and the professions. These were people with aspirations, if not to rule, then at least to govern. With some justification, the Mohajirs, especially those from the United Provinces, saw themselves as having been the driving force behind the creation of Pakistan. The Muslims living in the Hindu-dominated areas of British India had always had the most to fear from the end of the empire and had consequently been the most enthusiastic promoters of Pakistan. This gets to the heart of the Mohajir issue. Their subsequent frustrations were a product of their earlier hopes and expectations.

Sindh: The Early Years

The Mohajirs presumed that their sacrifices for Pakistan would be rewarded and, at first, their expectations were largely met. Many fared relatively well in their new country. Since the Mohajirs did not fit into traditional power structures in Pakistan, they turned their attention to areas such as business and the bureaucracy, in which success could be achieved on merit. The Pakistani government guaranteed that members of the British-run India civil service who moved to Pakistan would be given equivalent jobs in the new state. The local Sindhi population, with no middle class to speak of, was no match for the ideologically driven and highly motivated Mohajirs who took over businesses and homes abandoned by the many middle-class Hindus who had abruptly left Sindh for India.

In July 1948 the Mohajirs consolidated their pre-eminence by securing a significant symbolic gain: Karachi, despite the vehement opposition of the Sindhi chief minister Ayub Khuhro, became the Federal Capital Area under the control of the central government. While there are many international precedents for a nation's capital being administered in this way, for the native Sindhis it was a major blow. Sindh's leading nationalist politician G. M. Syed later described the decision in the most vivid terms: 'Mr Jinnah dismembered Sindh by cutting off Karachi, its leading city, from it and handed it over to the central administration of Liaquat Ali Khan as its head, for colonisation of the city by Mohajirs.'[12] In 1948 the Sindhis were not sufficiently politically organised to block the move but many still resented it and began to wonder whether their national identity was under threat. Insensitive to such concerns, the Mohajirs pressed on with their demands, not least that Urdu should be Pakistan's national language. Urdu had become a symbol of Muslim identity and for the Mohajirs it was natural, even wonderful, that the language should acquire national status in Pakistan. It was unfortunate, then, that few Pakistanis spoke it.

The death of Jinnah in 1948 and the assassination of Liaquat Ali Khan in 1951 were setbacks for the Mohajirs. So, too, was the 1955 decision to declare West Pakistan as One Unit which amalgamated the provinces of Sindh, Balochistan, NWFP and Punjab into one administrative structure. The measure was meant to balance the power of East and West Pakistan and, superficially, it seemed to suit the Mohajirs well. It appeared that the provincial power bases, dominated by traditional leaders, would lose out to the new, Mohajir-dominated, Pakistani elite. In the event, though, One Unit exposed just how unrealistic the Mohajirs' hopes of continuing to dominate Pakistani politics were. In 1951 Urdu speakers accounted for fewer than 5 per cent of West Pakistan's population. Inevitably, the Punjabis, who accounted for close to 40 per cent, started to assert themselves. One Unit helped them take jobs from the

Mohajirs not only at the federal level but also in Sindh itself.[13] Furthermore, provincial objections to One Unit tended to strengthen rather than weaken the national movements in Balochistan, NWFP and, crucially for the Mohajirs, in Sindh.

The differences between the Mohajirs and the native Sindhis ran deep. From the Sindhi point of view, a wave of self-important, land-grabbing outsiders had turned up with colonial attitudes to match those of the departed British. The situation was hardly helped by the fact that many Mohajirs viewed the Sindhis as medieval peasants who needed to be dragged into the twentieth century. Some of the Mohajirs' policy initiatives were highly provocative. In 1957, for example, the University of Karachi forbade students from answering questions in Sindhi.[14] In the face of such discrimination it is hardly surprising that the Sindhis' sense of resentment was acute. They had been demanding greater provincial autonomy ever since 1917. For some, the decision to support the Pakistan project was based on a hope that a Muslim state would offer the best opportunity for pursuing Sindh's national interests.

In 1975 G. M. Syed tried to explain away the support he, and other Sindhi politicians, had given to the creation of Pakistan:

> Some of us who all the time remained conscious of the national distinctness of the people of Sind and of their significant past history, participated in the movement for Pakistan solely for the purpose of ensuring thereby political independence, economic prosperity and the cultural advancement of Sind. We remained convinced throughout of the validity of the teaching of our great political thinkers who considered the Sindhi people a separate nation.

The two nation theory he said had been a 'trap' designed to establish: 'Mohajir-Punjabi exploitative hegemony over the Muslim majority provinces'. The Sindhi nationalists had joined the Pakistan movement, he maintained, because they believed the Lahore Resolution would result in Sindhi independence and not 'the accident of history and freak of nature' that became Pakistan.[15]

G. M. Syed's role in first promoting Pakistan and later denouncing it has long been controversial. The record shows, however, that even before the transfer of power he was focusing on Sindhi as opposed to Muslim nationalism. In 1947 he wrote 'The prospect of a unitary Pakistan looms ahead as a terrible nightmare in which the people of Sind will be trampled on as mere serfs by the more numerous and agressive outsiders.'[16] In May 1948 the Sindhi nationalists joined forces with Bengalis, Pukhtoons and the Baloch to form the People's Organisation. Like its successor, the Pakistan Oppressed Nations Movement (PONM), the People's Organisation stopped short of explicitly demanding the break-up of Pakistan and was to make little impact. Nevertheless, the Sindhi nationalists did manage to send a message to the Mohajirs: many in Sindh did not welcome them.

In Pakistan's early years the Mohajirs were too confident to worry about the Sindhis. Even in 1958 when Ayub Khan, a Pukhtoon, took over many Mohajirs remained optimistic. In line with their thinking Ayub Khan wanted to create a strong central government, although he perhaps had a more secular vision than many Mohajirs would have been comfortable with at the time. Furthermore, the Mohajirs were well-disposed towards the military seeing it as not only a source of protection from India but also a non-feudal meritocracy and the embodiment of Pakistani unity. But the Mohajirs' faith in the military was misplaced.

The Pakistani army was always, and remains, Punjabi-dominated: periods of military rule have generally seen a growth of Punjabi influence. Although there are no official figures, it is estimated that 65 per cent of officers and 70 per cent of the other ranks are Punjabis. That compares with the province's 56 per cent share of the population. Pukhtoons from NWFP, with 16 per cent of the population, constitute an estimated 22 per cent of officers and 25 per cent of other ranks. The Mohajirs have generally been over-represented in the officer corps and under-represented in the lower ranks. Despite some somewhat half-hearted efforts to correct these imbalances, the Sindhis and the Baloch have always been severely under-represented.[17]

Under Ayub Khan, Punjabis also took civilian jobs from the Mohajirs. Indeed, the situation was so acute that, on a few occasions, Mohajirs wanting to secure promotion tried to establish that they had Pukhtoon or Punjabi ancestry.[18] The Mohajirs' grip on the bureaucracy was further undermined when, in 1959, Ayub moved the capital from Karachi to Islamabad. It was a clear indication of the Mohajirs' diminishing influence and a significant blow in itself as it further limited their access to government jobs. The Mohajirs became increasingly disillusioned with Ayub Khan. It is no accident that in the 1965 presidential election the general's heaviest defeat in West Pakistan was in Karachi. Most Mohajirs voted for Fatima Jinnah, the sister of their beloved late leader, Mohammed Ali Jinnah.

Ayub Khan's successor, General Yahya Khan did not suit the Mohajirs much better. True, he did reverse the policy of One Unit. The main beneficiaries of this, however, were not the Mohajirs but their provincial rivals who were able to reclaim power that had been taken over by Punjabis. The city of Karachi was returned to Sindh. This time it was the Mohajirs' turn to complain – some said they were surrendering a homeland for a second time. And, by holding Pakistan's first ever national elections, Yayha heightened the Mohajirs' fears that their numerical inferiority would count against them. But Yahya's greatest contribution to the deterioration of ethnic harmony in urban Sindh was the failure of his policy over a thousand miles away in East Pakistan.

The loss of Bangladesh in 1971 added significantly to the Mohajirs' sense of vulnerability. Ever since, their leaders have pointed to the loss of East Pakistan as evidence that the two nation theory was dead and that the Pakistan project, for which they had made so many sacrifices, had failed. The Mohajirs' concerns went beyond the abstract: they were highly aware of the predicament of the Biharis. The Biharis were Indian Muslims who had moved to East Pakistan at the time of partition. Loyal to Pakistan, they were politically isolated in the new Bangladesh where the vast majority of the population was ethnically Bengali. Those who survived the 1971 war ended up in cramped 'refugee' camps where many families were to remain for decades. The Mohajirs have consistently argued the Biharis' case – but to no avail. And many Mohajirs saw the Biharis' plight as a warning: if the Bengalis could pull off independence then might not the Sindhis do the same? And might not the Mohajirs end up in the same situation as the Biharis?

But, if 1971 raised unwelcome questions for the Mohajirs, worse was to come. Under Zulfikar Ali Bhutto their disillusionment became complete. A Sindhi had, for the first time, achieved high office in Pakistan and Bhutto blatantly favoured his traditional constituency at the expense

of the Mohajirs not least by the use of a quota system. To the outrage
of the Mohajirs it applied in Sindh but in no other province. Under the
scheme, 40 per cent of government jobs and educational places were
allocated to people living in urban areas but 60 per cent went to rural
areas where the native Sindhis tended to live. Much to the Mohajirs'
discomfort, Sindhis started to take significant numbers of jobs in the
lower and middle levels of the provincial bureaucracy. The MQM leader,
Altaf Hussain, later complained: 'if you were a Sindhi you got everything. If you weren't, you got nothing.'[19] The MQM's sense of unjust
treatment was added to by the effect of Bhutto's nationalisation programme: it hit many Mohajir businessmen hard.

The Mohajirs' discontent found violent expression in 1972 when, on
7 July, Bhutto passed a Sindh Language Bill in the Sindh National
Assembly. Again, the Mohajirs thought they were being singled out for
discriminatory treatment: there were no similar bills in other provinces.
While making it clear that Urdu's status as a national language remained
in place, the measure gave Sindhi the status of the sole provincial language and had a direct impact on the employability of Urdu speakers.
Under the law, provincial government officials had to learn Sindhi, a
language that many Mohajirs considered beneath them, if they were to
keep their jobs.

Bhutto could be excused for thinking that he could push the Language Bill through without too much difficulty. Throughout Pakistan's
early years Sindhi had been a compulsory language and many Mohajirs
had learnt it. The requirement to learn Sindhi was dropped during Ayub
Khan's martial law because many officers stationed in Sindh said they
did not see the point of studying the language when they would be in
Sindh only for the duration of their posting. Bhutto, then, was restoring a practice that had existed before martial law. Nevertheless, the
reaction to the Language Bill was swift and a warning of what was to
come in later years. The day the bill was passed there were massive pro-
Urdu demonstrations in Karachi. The police tear-gassed the protestors
and announced a dusk to dawn curfew. The next morning's newspapers
hardly helped calm the situation. The Urdu daily *Jang* bordered the
whole of its front page with thick black lines. The banner headline ran:
'This is the funeral procession for Urdu: let it go out with a fanfare.'

That day, 8 July, the Mohajirs returned to the streets. This time the police fired directly into the demonstrators killing twelve people, including a ten-year-old boy. The Mohajir movement had its first martyrs and the protestors responded with fury, burning down buildings throughout Karachi. Students from Karachi University targeted the Sindh department setting all its records alight. On 9 July, with Bhutto insisting that the status of Urdu had not been undermined, ten more people were killed. Calm was restored only when Bhutto eventually passed an ordinance under which, for the next twelve years, no one could lose their job on the grounds that they did not speak Sindhi.[20]

By his overt support for his political heartland in rural Sindh Bhutto had split the province in two. The importance of ethnicity was now plain for all to see. Increasingly, the Mohajirs began to identify themselves not as Pakistan's natural governors but rather as an embattled minority fighting for its rights. The Sindhis, by contrast, were emboldened. Bhutto's blatant bias in their favour gave hope and confidence to the Sindhi nationalists. At last the tide was turning to their advantage. The idea that the Sindhis and the Mohajirs were compatriots together building a new state was lost: the two communities were in enemy camps. G. M. Syed was talking in apocalyptic terms: 'You have already left India,' he warned the Mohajirs. 'The only other place of refuge for you may be the Arabian Sea.'[21]

Given Bhutto's record it is not surprising that many Mohajirs welcomed General Zia's coup. They found his family background encouraging: born in East Punjab, he had attended a school in Delhi and spoke Urdu. Already in the Indian army at the time of partition, he had opted for Pakistan. Better still, he had risen through the ranks on the basis of merit rather than family standing – his father was no great landowner but a junior Raj official.[22] The Mohajirs also appreciated his Islamic outlook which was in line with their conception of why Pakistan had been created in the first place. And they were highly satisfied when he declared that the Mohajirs, having made special sacrifices for Pakistan, deserved special treatment. But Zia's cordial relations with the Mohajirs did not last. In the first place, the Mohajirs wanted Bhutto's quota system reversed. Zia did not grant their wish. In rural Sindh many resented the execution of their leader and champion

Zulfikar Ali Bhutto and, unwilling to alienate the Sindhis further, Zia extended the quota system in Sindh for a further ten years.[23]

If the Mohajirs were to become increasingly suspicious of Zia, many Sindhis were to develop outright opposition to his regime: they wanted to avenge Bhutto's death. The tensions came to a head in 1983. As Zia's unpopularity grew throughout Pakistan, a broad range of politicians from all over the country formed the Movement for the Restoration of Democracy (MRD), which demanded free and fair elections. The Pakistan People's Party (PPP), now led by Zulfikar Ali Bhutto's daughter Benazir, dominated the MRD although ten other parties were also members. In 1981 it launched a campaign of agitation. Rather to the surprise of the salon politicians in Lahore and Islamabad, the MRD found its strongest support in rural Sindh. By August 1983 the PPP supporters and nationalists in Sindh (often the same people) rose up and mounted a sustained rebellion. Even if the uprising in Sindh was, for the most part, motivated by simmering resentment of General Zia's treatment of the Bhutto family, some in Zia's regime worried that it could develop into a full-blown nationalist struggle.

Zia's interior secretary, Roedad Khan, has recorded how the military regime was, in fact, able to turn this perception to its advantage.

> Ironically, it was the intensity of the agitation in the interior of Sindh which aroused the suspicion of the people in the three other provinces, especially in Punjab. The MRD began to be viewed as a Sindhi movement for the redressal of Sindhi grievances and removal of their sense of deprivation and therefore lost its national appeal.[24]

The old British policy of divide and rule was alive and well and, for as long as the unrest remained localised, the military always felt confident they could crush it. Nevertheless, the Sindhi rebels put up a determined fight. For four months they participated in running battles with the security forces, and the army had to deploy thousands of men and even helicopter gun ships to quell the uprising. An estimated 400 people died in the violence.[25]

The MQM

The Mohajir Qaumi Movement (MQM) or Mohajir National Movement as it is also known, has its roots in Karachi University. In 1978 Altaf Hussain and a group of like-minded students founded the All Pakistan Mohajir Student Organisation (APMSO). It was, in large part, a reaction to the existence of other student groups such as the Punjab Students Organisation, the Pukhtoon Students Federation, the Baloch Students Organisation and the Sindhis' hardline Jiye Sindh Students Federation. Altaf Hussain, who was a student in the pharmacy department, argued that if these students' organisations would not accept the Mohajirs as members, then the Mohajirs should create an organisation of their own. Initially, the APMSO campaigned on minor issues, complaining with some justification that Mohajirs faced discrimination in university admissions and the allotment of rooms in the student hostels. But, by 1981, the group was looking beyond the university campus.

Altaf Hussain could see that the Mohajirs had fears and that, as a political leader, he could exploit them. Law and order in Karachi were deteriorating. In addition, new migrants were arriving in Karachi providing unwelcome competition for jobs. After the Soviet invasion of Afghanistan in 1979, Pukhtoons had fled to Pakistan in their millions. Many remained in the border area near Peshawar but a significant number headed for Karachi where they started to work in their traditional activities of running transport networks, dealing in arms and selling narcotics. Many Mohajirs now wanted an organisation that could protect them and a leader who could articulate their fears.

Unlike many Pakistani politicians, Altaf Hussain has never enjoyed the benefits of a private income and a traditionally powerful family. He volunteered for military service but it was not a happy experience:

The 1971 war started and I longed to go to East Pakistan and join in the fighting ... I began to notice that some people received special treatment while others were discriminated against ... One night there was an argument with the Havildar [Sergeant] and he started abusing me. He said 'You Hindustorva [which roughly translates as 'bloody Indian'], what sort of a war will you city dwellers fight? ...'

After that I saw that the Havildar kept the Punjabis and Pathans in his own camp. I talked to the Mohajir boys there and pointed out how unfair all this was. The Pathans and Punjabis then turned against us, and there were fights, and we were punished again.[26]

It was with those experiences in mind that Hussain founded the APMSO and, after a brief spell as a taxi driver in Chicago, he set about the task of building a power base in earnest. He began by creating the MQM.[27] The young leader brooked no opposition. While membership of the party was open, Altaf Hussain devised a system whereby taking an oath of loyalty to the organisation gave a member special status. And with urban Sindh's ethnic tensions steadily increasing there was no shortage of rebellious young Mohajirs, many of them second generation, unemployed graduates, willing to pledge themselves to the only organisation committed to advancing their interests.

In 1985 a minor incident – a traffic accident – demonstrated just how volatile Karachi had become. A student, Bushra Zaidi, was knocked down by a private transport wagon. Bushra Zaidi was a Mohajir. The reckless driver was a Pukhtoon. Karachi exploded. Throughout the city Mohajirs attacked Pukhtoon transport workers and their vehicles. The Pukhtoons retaliated in kind and by the end of the month over fifty-three people had died.

By the summer of 1986 Hussain was ready to flex his political muscles. On 8 August, despite heavy rain, tens of thousands of people gathered in Karachi's Nishter Park to hear him set out his political programme. To the rest of Pakistan, the meeting was a revelation. Overnight, it seemed, a new political force had emerged. Crucially, Hussain called for the recognition of a Mohajir nationality. The size of the crowd – and the heavily-armed bodyguards who surrounded the young leader – gave the Mohajirs confidence that they were now a force to be reckoned with. As the MQM's popularity grew, the biggest losers were the religious parties such as Jamaat-e-Islami and Jamiat Ulema-e-Pakistan which had traditionally attracted Mohajir support. The Pakistan People's Party was also hit hard. Whilst the bulk of their votes in Sindh came from rural areas, the party had also enjoyed substantial support in Karachi and Hyderabad and other Urdu pockets in interior

Sindh. Altaf Hussain threatened to take those votes away. For an organisation that just a few years before had been arguing about room allocations in halls of residence, it was an impressive start.

Increasingly, ethnic rivalry drove the politics of Sindh. And as communal politics took hold, street violence in urban areas became so common that many parts of Karachi were under almost permanent curfew. The MQM proved to be an extremely well-organised and effective outfit. This was partly because the central government could never summon up the political will to take it on. Given a free run, the MQM became ever more confident, fighting with all of urban Sindh's ethnic groups. While its most formidable political opponent in the province was the PPP, various nationalist parties, such as Jiye Sindh, the Sindhi Baloch Pukhtoon Front and the Punjab Pukhtoon Ittehad (PPI), started to gain support. Punjabi settlers in Sindh, many of whom had arrived in the area before partition, and who were relatively non-political, started organising themselves. The trend was clear. Pakistan-wide parties, especially those rooted in Islam, were losing out to smaller nationalist parties that represented specific groups or communities.

Karachi had grown too rapidly. In 1947 there were 400,000 residents in the city: by the late 1980s that number had increased to 6 million. Many Mohajirs were living in fetid slums and competing with the Pukhtoons, Punjabis and Sindhis in a desperate battle for Karachi's limited resources. No one collected the rubbish, the traffic lights did not work and the sewers overflowed. Few homes had water or sanitation facilities and most were subject to extortionate demands from corrupt landlords.

Karachi was ready to explode and, on 14 December 1986, all hell broke loose. At 10 a.m. the loudspeaker of the Pirabad mosque on the outskirts of Karachi broadcast a pre-arranged signal. It was not a call to prayer but a call to arms. Minutes later, under cover of heavy machine-gun fire, several hundred Pukhtoons swept down from the Pirabad hills. The Pukhtoons attacked Biharis and Mohajirs. Pukhtoon and non-Pukhtoon neighbours, who for years had lived in peace, began to slaughter each other without mercy. In some cases, young Mohajirs tied the hands of Pukhtoons behind their backs and burnt them alive. The next morning the rioting spread. Rival mobs were on the streets and the death toll climbed – at least seventy people died on the 15th. There was so much arson that a pall of thick black smoke covered Karachi. On the 16th exhaustion set in, but still twenty-eight people were to die. The railway stations filled with people desperate to flee the city.[28]

It is worth pausing at this point to consider the nature of the MQM's attitudes and demands by the late 1980s. The Mohajirs' dreams of forging a new Islamic nation were long gone. Many had even given up hope of achieving more mundane objectives such as a steady job in the bureaucracy. In 1959 the Mohajirs had 30 per cent of the top jobs in the civil service. By 1989 that figure was down to 7.1 per cent.[29] The idealists who had sacrificed their homes and security to reach Pakistan despaired of their future in a land they considered irreparably damaged by the events of 1971. Many Mohajirs felt that the traditional inhabitants of Pakistan were not just unsympathetic to their plight but even hostile to their presence in the country. When, in February 1987, Altaf Hussain asked a rally in Hyderabad whether they would rise to defend Pakistan in the event of an attack by India they responded in the negative.[30] It was the answer he wanted: the Mohajirs were sending out a message that their loyalty could not be relied upon unless the rest of Pakistan did more to reach out to them.

In terms of specific demands, the crucial question was whether the Mohajirs wanted a separate province. By Altaf Hussain's own admission, such a demand was fleetingly made when the MQM was formed in March 1984: 'When everyone else had a province, we said the Mohajirs should have one too.'[31] But it did not take the MQM leaders long to see that such a bid would set the new party on a collision course with every institution in Pakistan, not least the army. A different formulation was agreed – the Mohajirs should be recognised as the country's fifth nationality.

The MQM also wanted an end to the quota system and more government action to help the Biharis in Bangladesh. This was both a matter of principle and a pragmatic objective: the Biharis would increase the MQM's vote bank, a factor which made the MQM's political opponents reluctant to allow Biharis into Pakistan. In January 1993 an attempt to resettle some Biharis in southern Punjab ran into the vehement opposition of local Seraiki speakers who were themselves trying to transform their long-standing linguistic demands into a full-blown national movement.[32] Some Sindhis also opposed the Biharis' arrival and, to the disgust of the MQM, the Prime Minister Nawaz Sharif bowed to the pressure and shelved the plan.

One of the most remarkable aspects of the MQM story is the total failure of successive central governments to address any of the Mohajirs' concerns. The Mohajirs believed that they should not have to ask any favours from Pakistan – they had earned their place in Pakistani society by virtue of their contribution to Jinnah's campaign. The failure of their indigenous compatriots to recognise their sense of insecurity was, and remains, one of the state's most costly oversights.

The late 1980s and early 1990s marked the MQM's high point. The 1988 National Assembly elections provided solid proof that the party was a force to be reckoned with. It achieved a remarkable electoral breakthrough. While the PPP remained dominant in interior Sindh, the MQM secured no fewer than thirteen of Karachi's fifteen seats. It had become the third largest political party in Pakistan. A party that could genuinely claim to have arisen from the people swept the religious parties and feudal leaders in Sindh out of office. The result gave the Mohajirs new hope. Benazir Bhutto, who was trying to form the first post-Zia administration, now needed the MQM's support in the National Assembly. Consequently, on 2 December she signed a PPP–MQM pact known as the Karachi Declaration. It covered no fewer than fifty-nine points ranging from a promise to reform the quota to a pledge that new road flyovers would be constructed in Karachi. The MQM's acceptance of the deal was enough to convince President Ghulam Ishaq that Benazir Bhutto could command a majority in the National Assembly.

The Karachi Declaration, however, was never implemented: Bhutto did not want to alienate her traditional power base in interior Sindh. Within a month of the signing of the declaration, the PPP and MQM students at Karachi University were denouncing each other as terrorists. The killing rate, which had dipped immediately after the signing, picked up again. The MQM's frustrations at the national level were echoed in the Provincial Assembly. The party had one-third of the seats but that was not enough to push through its programme. Disillusioned MQM activists argued that the ballot box would never deliver any real gains but the party's leaders were enjoying their new found ability to wheel and deal with Pakistan's national political leaders. Frustrated with Benazir Bhutto, they entered into secret talks with her opponents and by October 1989 reached a seventeen-point agreement with Nawaz Sharif's opposition coalition, the Islami Jamhoori Ittehad (IJI). In some respects, the MQM–IJI agreement went further than the Karachi Declaration. Rather than making a rather vague statement regarding the Biharis, for example, the pact included a specific commitment: 'all stranded Pakistanis in Bangladesh shall be issued Pakistani passports and in the meantime arrangements shall be made to repatriate them to Pakistan immediately'. There was also a clear condemnation of the quota system as 'unjust, biased and discriminatory'.[33]

But the MQM was about to discover for the second time that Pakistan-wide parties would promise the earth when they were trying to form an administration only to renege on their commitments once in power. It was a process that encouraged the MQM's extremists to step up their campaign of violence. Furthermore, by throwing in their lot with a quintessentially Punjabi leader, Nawaz Sharif, they further alienated the Sindhis. The gulf between the Sindhis and the Mohajirs became wider and found ever more violent expression.

MQM politicians routinely deny any involvement in violence whatsoever. It is a remarkable fact that journalists who have covered the MQM day in and day out ever since its creation have never heard any of the party's leaders admit direct involvement in the violence. Despite this, there has been no shortage of people willing to accuse the MQM of sponsoring violence. Detained MQM activists have repeatedly admitted carrying out killings on party orders. For all the MQM claims that such confessions were obtained by force, most people in Karachi and Hyderabad believe they were genuine. Those accused include Altaf Hussain who faces charges of murder, extortion, kidnapping and sedition. International human rights organisations have generally focussed on cases in which the MQM has been the victim of state power. Nevertheless, in 1996, Amnesty International reported that:

> Most of the political groupings and parties in Karachi appear to maintain their own militia . . . Despite protestations by MQM leader Altaf Hussain that the MQM does not subscribe to violence, there is over-

whelming evidence and a consensus among observers in Karachi that some MQM party members have used violent means to further their political ends.[34]

It was a fair assessment. Each time Altaf Hussain called a strike, people in the city would die, and many of the city's businessmen were visited by MQM thugs demanding protection money. There was also the uncanny fact that whenever someone from the MQM was killed, a reprisal killing would follow in a matter of days. The MQM has never been just an electoral party: it is also a militant organisation. And its leaders know they cannot escape their party's bloodthirsty reputation. MQM senator Nasreen Jaleel neatly summarised the problem when she attended a diplomatic reception at the British High Commission in Islamabad in 1999. 'When I walk into a room like this', she said, 'all these people see the word terrorist written all over my forehead.' Even if she has had no personal involvement in the campaign of violence, the reasons for such a perception are plain enough.

Despite this, Pakistan's central government took a long time to summon up the courage to tackle the MQM. The first serious attempt to break the organisation's street power came in 1992. Nawaz Sharif's IJI, like its PPP predecessor, had failed to honour its agreement with the MQM and his relations with the party soured. That alone, though, would not have led to a crackdown. The new factor in the equation was provided by the army which was increasingly concerned that the MQM was undermining national development. In May 1992 the military declared its intention to bring peace to Karachi. The army operation began on 19 June and for all the talk of evenhandedness there was no doubting that the MQM militants were the primary targets.

The army's strategy included a plan to open up the MQM's internal divisions. These had been apparent ever since Altaf Hussain declared his intention in 1990 to broaden his party's electoral appeal not least by changing the name of the Mohajir Qaumi Movement to the Muttahida Qaumi Movement or United National Movement. His rhetoric now included passages about the problems faced not only by the Mohajirs but also by the underprivileged throughout Pakistan. He concentrated his political attacks not on other ethnic groups but rather on the landowners in the ruling classes. The strategy, however, did not work:

ethnic affiliations proved to be a stronger bond than class. The MQM continues to reign supreme in urban Sindh but its message has never resonated elsewhere in Pakistan.

But this was the least of Altaf Hussain's problems. Whilst he was looking beyond Sindh, the MQM's militant wing remained focussed on the grievances of the Mohajirs and, as ever, expressed its point of view with violence. With this ideological split in the MQM becoming ever more apparent, the military saw its chance and backed a new, armed rival faction: MQM Haqiqi (The Real MQM). The Haqiqis set about their work with relish, ransacking and occupying MQM offices and creating a mini civil war in Karachi. For months, as the army crackdown continued, the city echoed with gunfire as the army, the MQM and MQM Haqiqi fought pitched battles in the streets. The military revealed the existence of MQM torture cells: the party's favoured method of extracting information from its opponents, it seemed, was to use an electric drill on the victims' knees and elbows. Altaf Hussain, meanwhile, afraid for his personal security, left for London for 'medical treatment'.[35]

The torture chambers were a sign of just how far the MQM had gone in its campaign to be the sole representative of the Mohajirs. But in the midst of the struggle to survive, the MQM had lost its way. Rather than pressing for its basic demands, such as an end to the quota system, the leadership focussed on more immediate issues, such as the release of detained activists. Lacking clear direction, some MQM members became ever more extreme. Some argued that they needed to have an independent homeland, often referred to as Jinnahpur. The military claimed that in the midst of their clean-up operation they found maps of 'Jinnahpur' or 'Urdu desh' which showed how the Mohajirs wanted to carve Karachi, Hyderabad and some other areas out of Sindh.

The MQM insisted that the maps were not authentic. But by September 1994 it seemed that Altaf Hussain, still stuck in London, had decided to make an explicit demand for the geographical division of Sindh. Certainly, he laid the groundwork by distributing a 'questionnaire' on the issue to all MQM members. He claimed to have received hundreds of thousands of letters in response. All but five or six, he said, had called for the establishment of a fifth, Mohajir, province.[36] But once again, he stopped short of making the demand a component of the party's official programme. The furthest he went was to talk of the *possibility* of 'changing geography' if the Mohajirs were not given their rights.

The violence, meanwhile, went on and on. But, time and again, the central government proved unwilling to make genuine, lasting political compromises. Some incidents of sectarian violence added to the confusion. Inevitably, there was another crackdown, this time managed by Benazir Bhutto's second government. Her interior minister, General Nasrullah Baber, did not pull his punches. Unable to rely on the slow, intimidated and corrupt courts, his security forces resorted to extrajudicial killings: some 10 per cent of those who died in politically related violence in 1995 were the victims of so-called 'police encounters'. In most cases, the police would claim they had to open fire to prevent a detainee escaping. 'Peace has been restored in Karachi,' Baber said.[37] There was some truth in his boast. Whilst 1,586 people were murdered in Karachi in 1995, the figure slumped to 524 in 1996. It has never since exceeded 1,000 in a year.[38]

The now familiar political cycle started to turn once more. The 1997 elections gave Nawaz Sharif's Muslim League just 14 of the 109 seats in the Sindh Provincial Assembly. Determined to keep out the better represented PPP, he once more needed MQM support. The 1992 crackdown, Sharif now assured Altaf Hussain, had been a mistake forced on him by the army. He would resign rather than oversee another attempt to quash the MQM by force. He promised prisoner releases, the opening up of Haqiqi-held 'no-go' areas and compensation for families who had suffered as a result of extra-judicial killings.

But once restored to power, Sharif again ran out of patience with the MQM. The trigger this time was the assassination on 17 October 1998 of the widely respected philanthropist and former governor of Sindh, Hakim Said. Apart from adding to the climate of fear in Karachi, the killing had no clear motive and it shocked the Pakistani nation. When Prime Minister Nawaz Sharif openly accused his MQM ally of organising the murder it was inevitable that the MQM–Muslim League alliance would end. Sharif extended the quota system for a further twenty years, introduced Governor's Rule and established military courts which, he promised, would dispense 'speedy justice'. Remarkably, in all the years of politically inspired violence in Sindh, not one person had been given capital punishment. Nawaz Sharif now promised that that would change. Within weeks, though, the military courts ran into a series of constitutional challenges that were ultimately successful.

When he took over in 1999 it was General Musharraf's turn to promise he would address Mohajir grievances but there was little sign that he would actually do so. Musharraf came from a family that had migrated to Pakistan from India. But once he settled into power he showed little sympathy for the MQM and did not open any dialogue with the organisation. This was partly because the MQM responded to his coup with caution and, for several months after October 1999, Karachi was relatively quiet. The MQM were once again made to realise that they lacked the power to get what they wanted.

The Sindhi nationalists are in a not dissimilar position: they remain too weak to threaten the Pakistani state. They have not, though, given up their struggle and they continue to express simmering resentment about Punjab's role in their affairs. In May 1999, for example, at an International Sindh Conference in Washington (such a meeting in Pakistan would have provoked an immediate, massive backlash), leaders such as Mumtaz Bhutto (a cousin of Zulfikar Ali Bhutto) and G. M. Syed's son Imdad Shah rejected the 'ideology of Pakistan' which, the conference declared, was a 'concoction of ill-conceived interpretations of Islam and socio-economic constructs designed to support a heavily militarised fascistic state'. Some speakers called for a referendum on Sindhi independence.[39]

The Sindh's nationalist parties, though, have consistently failed to make a significant electoral breakthrough. They have never attracted the support of more than 5 or 6 per cent of the electorate nor have they ever won any directly elected National Assembly seats. These hard facts, however, are somewhat misleading. Sindh's nationalist parties have always had to compete with the PPP which, ever since it was created, has remained unassailable in rural Sindh. Many nationalist politicians, reckoning that the PPP could not be beaten, decided to join it and many PPP candidates in Sindh are just as nationalistic as their counterparts in the parties devoted to Sindhi issues.

The case of Sindhi nationalists is plain enough: they maintain Sindh is theirs and that they should be governed by Sindhis. Mohajir nationalism is much more difficult to explain. When the Mohajirs came to Pakistan they were not a homogeneous ethnic group: they came from different parts of northern India. They did, though, share some attitudes. Many had been urbanised for two generations, they were relatively well-educated and believed they had something to offer the new country. They looked forward to participating in, and providing leadership for, the construction of a new Islamic nation.

But the Mohajirs were always too small in number to govern Pakistan. Compared to Pakistan's longer established inhabitants, they also lacked a political power base and have never been strong enough to take on all of Pakistan's ethnic groups at once. At first they fought the Pukhtoons and then the Punjabis. Inevitably their early attempts to cultivate good relations with the Sindhis failed and by 1988, after the massacre on 30 September of over 200 Mohajirs in Hyderabad, the two communities were fighting. Finally, with the creation of MQM Haqiqi, the Mohajirs started targeting each other. Even though the Mohajirs were not an ethnic group, their peculiar situation in Pakistan forced them into becoming a homogeneous and politicised community. But once Mohajir unity broke down, it became inescapably clear that religion and Pakistani nationalism no longer provided the glue that bound them together. The Mojahirs became a confused community and, as a result, the MQM's raison d'être is now utterly unclear. The party has no religious or territorial demands. Its members are Urdu speakers but the MQM is clearly more than a linguistic pressure group. On the one hand, the MQM has been a vehicle for demanding Mohajir rights. On the other, it has simply expressed the Mohajirs' frustration and bitterness about their experience in Pakistan. By the turn of the century, Altaf Hussain had no vision of the future whatsoever: his speeches and media interviews simply contained a long series of complaints about how partition had been a mistake. The scope of his ambition, it seemed, had been reduced: he looked far less like an energetic campaigner for Mohajir rights and far more like a would-be mafia boss determined to hang on to control of Karachi.

Successive leaders in Pakistan have failed to recognise the strength of Mohajir opinion or the depth of Mohajir disillusionment. The ethnic divisions in Sindh present a daunting problem. But one thing is clear. The grievances of both the Sindhis and the Mohajirs are not merely law and order problems. Any genuine attempt to resolve them will have to include an attempt to reach out to the various ethnic groups in Sindh rather than trying to subjugate them to the will of the central government.

Balochistan

The politics of Sindh have presented successive Pakistani leaders with a highly complex problem that they have consistently failed to resolve. The recent history of Balochistan, by contrast, has been relatively uncomplicated. With varying degrees of assertiveness, some Baloch leaders have pressed for greater autonomy and, at times, for independence and the Pakistani state has, when necessary, employed all the force at its disposal to suppress such demands.

Many Baloch never wanted to join Pakistan in the first place. In the 1930s some Baloch leaders, foreseeing the eventual departure of the British, started to advance claims for independence. Such demands were most strongly advanced in Kalat, the largest, and by far the most powerful, of four Princely States located in Balochistan. The other three, Makran, Kharan and Las Bela had, at various points of history, been part of the Kalat state. Indeed, in the second half of the eighteenth century the Khan of Kalat, Naseer Khan, had managed to more or less unify the Baloch people.

By the time the British were preparing to leave South Asia, Kalat had lost much of its strength. Nevertheless, Naseer Khan's descendant, Mir Ahmed Yar Khan, argued that, once the British had left, Kalat should be restored as a fully sovereign and independent nation. So as to advance his cause better in Delhi and Whitehall, he even appointed a Briton, Douglas Fell, as his foreign minister.[40] In July 1947 the Khan was given his chance. The British prime minister, Clement Atlee, declared that after partition all the Princely States on the subcontinent would have three options: independence, accession to India or accession to Pakistan. In August 1947, straight after the creation of Pakistan, Mir Ahmed Yar Khan declared Kalat's independence.

Kalat may not have represented all the peoples in Balochistan, but there is no doubt that other Baloch leaders sympathised with the Khan and wanted to see whether the new Pakistani government had the will and the strength to frustrate his bid for independence. Pakistani historians now portray Mir Ahmed Yar Khan as an isolated and recalcitrant individual who ungraciously failed to bow to the inevitable.[41] But for the new Pakistani government, incorporating Kalat into the country was far from easy: almost a year passed before this was achieved – and then only with the use of force. In April 1948 the Pakistan army marched on Kalat and, eventually, the Khan signed an agreement of accession. After 225 days of independence, Kalat became part of Pakistan. The Khan's brother, Prince Abdul Karim, however, responded violently. Having based himself across the border in Afghanistan, he organised a guerrilla campaign and, for some months, harried the Pakistani forces. By June 1948, though, the army prevailed and both Kalat and the rest of Balochistan were secured as parts of Pakistan.

By no means can the fighting in 1948 be characterised as a Baloch-wide rebellion. But it is nonetheless of considerable significance that while other parts of Pakistan were fervently celebrating the creation of the new country, in Balochistan there was armed conflict. Ten years later, Baloch objections to One Unit, which they saw as a centralist measure that undermined their provincial rights, led to another violent confrontation. On 10 October 1958 the Pakistan army emerged victorious over a rebel force of around 1,000 men. Still the Baloch didn't give up. In the early 1960s Pakistani troops in Balochistan were subjected to a series of ambushes, raids and sniper attacks. There were large-scale confrontations involving hundreds of men on both sides in 1964 and 1965. The fighting continued sporadically until One Unit was abolished in 1970.

The major Baloch challenge came in 1973. The trigger was Zulfikar Ali Bhutto's decision to dismiss Balochistan's provincial government in which the PPP had no representation. To help justify the move, Bhutto revealed a cache of 350 Soviet submachine guns and 100,000 rounds of ammunition in the house of the Iraqi political attaché in Islamabad. Bhutto claimed that the weapons were destined for either Pakistani or

Iranian Balochistan. Writing to President Nixon, Zulfikar Ali Bhutto claimed that the discovery showed that 'powers inimical to us are not content with the severance of Pakistan's eastern part; their aim is the dismemberment of Pakistan itself'.[42]

Whether the arms were destined for Balochistan or not was never established but there was no doubt that the Baloch were enraged by Bhutto's decision to remove their government. In response they mounted actions against the Pakistan army which, in turn, responded with force. With Bhutto describing the Baloch rebels as 'miscreants' (causing many to draw parallels with what had happened in Bangladesh), the army was given a free hand to restore Pakistani control. The fighting was to last for four years and the central government had to deploy no fewer than 80,000 troops to suppress an insurgency joined by 55,000 rebels.[43]

By 1974 the insurgents had cut most of the main roads in the province. Their targeted attacks on survey teams forced Western oil companies to abandon their exploration projects in the area. In the largest single confrontation during the insurgency, in September 1974, 15,000 Baloch tribesmen fought a pitched battle with the Pakistan army. The military had vastly superior equipment including Mirage fighter planes and Iranian-supplied (and piloted) helicopters. After three days of fighting, the Baloch ran out of ammunition and withdrew.[44]

The battle was the most intense moment of the conflict. Afterwards, the Baloch increasingly took to the hills and avoided pitched battles. As the pressure from the Pakistani troops increased, some Baloch rebels followed Prince Abdul Karim's example and set up camps in Afghanistan where they could re-group after bouts of fighting. As well as allowing the camps to exist, the Afghans provided the rebels with modest amounts of financial support. Limited assistance also came in the form of a small number of leftist Punjabi intellectuals who went to the Baloch mountains to join the rebels.

What the rebels really wanted, though, was the support of the Soviet Union. They never got it. The Soviets never backed the demands for an independent Balochistan but instead called for greater Baloch autonomy within Pakistan. The Soviet Union's somewhat hesitant approach found echoes in Balochistan itself. From the very beginning of the uprising the Baloch were uncertain of their objective. While some favoured a straightforward push for independence, others, notably in the Baloch People's Liberation Front, argued that secession was unrealistic and that the Baloch should settle for greater autonomy.

The army operation ended only after the 1977 coup when General Zia declared victory and ordered a withdrawal. Some have described the Baloch insurgency as a 'comparatively minor' affair.[45] This is an underestimation of what amounted to a serious and sustained challenge to Pakistan's very existence. Coming so soon after the loss of Bangladesh, this was a battle the Pakistan army had to win. And suppressing the rebellion was no easy matter – the conflict claimed an estimated 9,000 lives.[46]

The reasons for the eventual failure of the Baloch uprising contain important lessons for nationalist groups in Pakistan. In the first place, the Baloch never secured the international support they needed. Secondly, the Baloch were split. Rather than acting as a unified military outfit, the tribal leaders tended to mount their own unco-ordinated attacks on the Pakistani forces. In addition to this, there was a more fundamental division in the province: one third of the people in Balochistan were ethnic Pukhtoons who were more interested in union with the NWFP than Baloch independence. There were also ideological splits amongst the Baloch. While some favoured an old-fashioned nationalist struggle, others (with their eye on possible help from Moscow) pointed to the potential of communist theory as a liberating force. Even among the communists there were differences between adherents of the Chinese and Soviet models. Ultimately, though, the Pakistani forces were simply too determined and too strong.

The military's victory in Balochistan left a situation not unlike that in Sindh where nationalists continue to press the case for self-determination despite having little conviction that it can be achieved in the short term. By the time of Musharraf's military coup in 1999, half of the members of the Provincial Assembly in Quetta represented nationalist parties, all of which complained of Punjabi 'colonisation'. Many of their specific grievances related to the exploitation of Balochistan's natural resources. The Sui gas field, which provides 60 per cent of Pakistan's total needs, lies in territory controlled by Nawab Akbar Bugti. Although he maintains that 'his' gas is being stolen, the nawab's acquiescence has been secured by a mixture of force and the liberal use of government 'grants', including the provision of a fleet of Toyota land-cruisers for his personal use. Other tribal leaders, however, continue to put up a fight. In August 2000 Marri tribesmen took direct action to stop coal-mining on their land. They used rocket-propelled grenades and landmines to prevent coal-laden trucks leaving Balochistan. And when, in 2000, Musharraf's regime tried to explore for oil in the Marri area of Kohlu, fighting led to the death of ten people.[47] Such actions, however, amount to little more than an irritant to Pakistan's central government which now feels no serious threat in Balochistan.

Pukhtoon Nationalism

The nationalists in Sindh and Balochistan are by no means the only Pakistanis to harbour dreams of greater autonomy or full independence. Even if the Pukhtoons have never mounted a challenge to match that of the Baloch in 1973, there has been a consistent demand for a Pukhtoon homeland – Pukhtoonkhwa.[48] The claim is not without historical justification. When the British started taking over Pukhtoon areas in the nineteenth century, the Pukhtoon people were living as one Afghan nation. Their consistent and violent resistance against the British presence forced the imperial government in Delhi to devote tens of thousands of troops to maintain control of them. In 1893 the British tried to stabilise the situation by creating the Durand Line which today constitutes the border between Afghanistan and Pakistan. The line cut the Pukhtoon people in two: roughly one half remained in Afghanistan but the other half now came under the British empire. The situation was further complicated by the British decision to divide those Pukhtoons under their control. While the bulk found themselves in the North West Frontier Province, some ended up in the area that became Balochistan.

The British policies gave rise to Pukhtoon nationalist demands. The first, advanced by the Pukhtoons in NWFP, was that all Pukhtoon people should be reunited in the Pukhtoonkhwa homeland that existed before the British arrived. Pukhtoonkhwa would include all of NWFP and those parts of Afghanistan and Balochistan that had Pukhtoon populations. The second demand, championed by successive governments in Kabul, was for a Greater Afghanistan. Ever since partition, Kabul has argued that the Durand Line was never meant to be an international boundary and has complained that it deprived Afghanistan of territory that historically had been under its control.

As the British prepared to leave the subcontinent, the most effective champion of Pukhtoon nationalism was the 'Frontier Ghandi', Abdul Ghaffar Khan. He argued that the creation of Pakistan would be a disaster because Muslims from Hindu majority provinces in India would come and take over the Pukhtoons. Ghaffar Khan's acumen and anti-imperialist rhetoric, backed by a quasi-military organisation known as the Red Shirts, resonated throughout NWFP. Of all the provinces that were to become part of Pakistan, it was NWFP that had the strongest nationalist movement: Mohammed Ali Jinnah's Muslim League was no match for Ghaffar Khan.

As partition approached, the British announced there would be a referendum in NWFP. The decision brought matters to a head and Ghaffar Khan insisted that as well as offering a choice between India and Pakistan, the British should allow the Pukhtoon voters a third option: Pukhtoonkhwa. The government in Kabul was thinking along similar lines. It also wanted the inclusion of another option: union with Afghanistan.[49]

Jinnah knew that he had to resist all such proposals. To achieve Pakistan he had to secure the Pukhtoons' support. Without NWFP his demand for a Muslim state would be fatally weakened. The crucial moment came on 15 August 1947 when the referendum took place. Mountbatten had rejected the advice of both Ghaffar Khan and the Afghan government and declared that there would be just two choices: union with India or Pakistan. Since he wanted neither outcome Ghaffar Khan boycotted the vote and the devout Pukhtoon Muslims really had no choice. Of those that voted, 99 per cent opted for Pakistan.

Pukhtoon nationalist sentiment did not disappear after the 1947 referendum, however, and Abdul Ghaffar Khan continued to campaign for Pukhtoonkhwa. Indeed, in 1948, Jinnah travelled to Peshawar in an attempt to win him over and disband the Red Shirts. His mission failed and, although the nationalists were reluctant to make their demands explicit, Jinnah left with the impression that the Red Shirts were still committed to some form of independent state.[50] Setting a trend that characterises Pakistani politics to the present day, the Pakistani government responded to Ghaffar Khan's increasingly muted challenge by imprisoning him.

Both in Afghanistan and Pakistan, Pukhtoon nationalists have continued to dream of Pukhtoonkhwa or a Greater Afghanistan. In 1950 the Afghans mounted cross-border raids and in 1956 an Afghan government spokesman said that the Durand Line had no legitimacy and divided the Pukhtoon people artificially. The response from Pakistan was sharp. The foreign minister, Hamidul Haq Chaudhri, insisted that the line: 'has been, is and will continue to be the international boundary between Afghanistan and Pakistan'.[51] But the Afghans have never given up their emotional attachment to the Pukhtoons in Pakistan. In 1955 Afghan objections to Pakistan's plans for One Unit were so strong that public demonstrations led to the ransacking of the Pakistani embassy in Kabul and the consulate in Jalalabad. The two countries withdrew their ambassadors from each other's capitals. And again, in 1979, the Afghan prime minister Hafizullah Amin explicitly stated Kabul's desire for a Greater Afghanistan. The Durand Line, he said, 'tore us apart'. He even suggested that a Greater Afghanistan would incorporate Balochistan:

> Our sincere and honest brotherhood with the Pukhtoons and Baloch has been sanctified by history. They have been one body in the course of history and have lived together like one brother. Now the waves of their love and brotherhood extend from the Oxus to Attock and they want to live side by side, embrace each other and demonstrate this great love to the world at large.[52]

The period since 1979, however, has seen the force of Afghan demands diminish. The Soviet invasion of Afghanistan produced a shift in Kabul's attitude as the Soviet-backed regime echoed Moscow's view that Pakistan should not be dismembered. Kabul now indicated that it was up to the Pukhtoons, Baloch and, for that matter, Sindhis to struggle for greater autonomy if they wanted it. The two decades of fighting in Afghanistan that have followed the Soviet intervention has meant that successive

Kabul governments have been too preoccupied with internal concerns to advance serious claims for a Greater Afghanistan.

India has periodically shown some interest in the Pukhtoon issue as one that could potentially destabilise Pakistan. In 1965 the Indian foreign minister Swaran Singh told the Indian parliament that 'we are fully aware that the fundamental freedoms and natural aspirations of the brave Pushtoons have been consistently denied to them, and their struggle has got our greatest sympathy and we will certainly support the efforts that Khan Abdul Ghaffar Khan might undertake in that direction'.[53] To some extent such proclamations were counterproductive. Few Pukhtoons wanted to be associated with an Indian-backed movement and, for their part, the Indians have never followed such statements with sustained actions. Indeed, India's support for Pakistan's various national movements has never been strong enough to determine the course of events.

Following the lead of Mohammed Ali Jinnah, successive governments in Karachi and Islamabad have been suspicious of the Pukhtoon nationalism advanced by Ghaffar Khan and his son Wali Khan. Wali Khan has, in fact, pursued a pragmatic line and, although some of his statements contain deliberate ambiguities, he has generally presented his demands in the most moderate form possible: a change in the name of NWFP to Pukhtoonkhwa. In comparison to the nationalists' struggles in Sindh and Balochistan, the Pukhtoons' campaign has been conciliatory and unspectacular.

The comparative quiescence of NWFP is partly a result of the Pukhtoons' relatively good representation in Pakistan's central state institutions, especially the army. Whilst Balochistan and Sindh have very little representation in the army, the Pukhtoons have consistently provided between 30 and 40 per cent of the senior officer corps. Two of Pakistan's military leaders, Ayub Khan and Yayha Khan, came from NWFP. The Pukhtoons' share of the top bureaucratic jobs – around 10 per cent – has been less striking but it is more or less in line with NWFP's share of the total Pakistani population.[54] In addition, the Pukhtoons have been particularly active migrants within Pakistan. The large Pukhtoon community in Karachi, for example, means that many Pukhtoon families receive remittances from Karachi and have a direct interest in the stability and continued existence of the Pakistani state. Pukhtoon business interests extend throughout the country and give their owners and employees a stake in the success of Pakistan as a whole. In fact, for those at the centre of power in Pakistan, North West Frontier Province has shown the way. Despite the fact that it had the strongest national movement in 1947, the Pukhtoons have never presented a significant challenge to Pakistan's central institutions. The reasons are clear. The Pukhtoons have been given a considerable share in the country.

Seraikis

The heartland of Seraiki culture is the former Princely State of Bahawalpur in southern Punjab. At the time of Pakistan's independence, it was one of the wealthiest Princely States on the subcontinent. The vast majority of the people of Bahawalpur speak Seraiki, and there are also Seraiki speakers in neighbouring parts of Sindh, Balochistan and NWFP. The Seraiki national movement is a relatively recent phenomenon with demands first appearing in the 1960s. Like the Sindhis and the Baloch, the Seraikis argue that their cultural rights are being surpressed and that they are being economically exploited by Punjab. Many Punjabis, however, refuse to accept that the Seraikis are a distinct cultural, never mind national, group and dismiss their language as nothing more than a dialect of Punjabi.

At first the Seraikis restricted themselves to a demand for language rights. Seraiki and Punjabi are to a large extent mutually intelligible but the Seraikis insisted that they had a separate linguistic tradition. By the 1970s their demands were becoming increasingly political and activists even produced maps of Seraikistan.[55] This area included not only the Bahawalpur Princely State but also the whole of the southern half of Punjab and the district of Dera Ismail Khan in NWFP. The Seraikis, it seemed, wanted to avoid a clash with nationalists in Sindh and Balochistan and tailored their map accordingly. Although their leadership has always been highly fragmented, this decision to limit the extent of Seraiki claims has attracted broad support amongst Seraiki speakers.

Under Zia ul Haq's strongly centralist regime, the fledgling Seraiki movement was forced into hiding. But with the restoration of democracy, it re-emerged. The Seraikis' primary demands were for: recognition as a separate nationality; official documents to be written in Seraiki; more Seraiki language programmes on radio and television; increased employment quotas for Seraikis; and the formation of a Seraiki regiment in the army. Seraiki leaders continue to articulate a series of grievances. Many of these rest on the fact that Seraiki areas are highly fertile and provide a substantial proportion of Pakistan's two most important crops: cotton and wheat. Seraiki speakers complain that their contribution to the Pakistani economy has never been rewarded with any industrial investment, and that, as a result, Seraiki areas remain impoverished and underdeveloped. The Seraikis, in short, argue that the rest of Pakistan exploits them and add that successive governments have given their land to others.

Like other national groups in Pakistan, the Seraikis have stopped short of demanding an independent homeland. For its part the central government has never made any serious effort to address the Seraikis' demands. Indeed, the fact that the Seraikis live in Punjab means that their campaign has always run into the implacable opposition of not only the army but also the Pakistani establishment more generally. The Seraikis argue that this reflects their under-representation in the Pakistani bureaucracy: the army's tendency to recruit in northern Punjab means that the Seraikis have never been a force to reckon with within the military.

In his 1983 book *Can Pakistan Survive? The Death of a State*, Tariq Ali wrote that: 'The national question is the time bomb threatening the very structures of the post-1971 state. The hour of the explosion cannot be far away.'[56] Nearly twenty years later the explosion has not happened.

There is, though, a steady rumble of discontent. It is now commonplace for nationalists from Balochistan, Sindh, NWFP, the Seraiki belt and the Mohajirs to complain of Punjabi domination. Like the Bengalis before 1971, Pakistan's various national communities argue that they are economically deprived because the bureaucracy and the army are both Punjabi-controlled. The claim is difficult to refute. The armed forces and the civil service are the largest employers in Pakistan and many Punjabi families clearly benefit from their province's dominance of these institutions. The national movements may be mainly political in character but they are underpinned by genuine economic grievances.

For the most part though, the nationalists have held back from advancing demands for full independence and the key question is this: do the nationalists pose a threat to Pakistan's existence? The case of Bangladesh certainly provides a clear warning: a national movement has already led to territorial changes in Pakistan.

The first half century of Pakistan's existence has proved that neither Islam nor Urdu has acted as an effective national cement. While many Pakistanis are devout Muslims, most are not Muslim nationalists. The 1981 national census showed that fewer than 8 per cent of the people spoke Urdu as a first language.[57] In April 2000 most urban Pakistanis – 56 per cent – wanted to send their children to English medium schools. Support for Urdu medium schools stood at just 34 per cent compared to 65 per cent fifteen years earlier.[58]

The failure of Pakistani leaders ever since 1947 to foster Pakistani, as opposed to provincial, nationalism has undermined Musharraf's efforts to modernise the country. If the Islamic radicals are indeed about to face their day of reckoning then Pakistan will need an ideology to replace Islam. After long careers in the army Musharraf, and many of his military colleagues, do have such an ideology: they are Pakistani nationalists. But outside Punjab, few share their enthusiasm for, or loyalty to, Pakistan. Despite all Musharraf's talk of decentralisation he has shown no more willingness than his predecessors to give power and authority to the provinces. He fears that doing so would weaken the Pakistani nation. In truth, it would strengthen it.

For good reasons, discontent with the central institutions is growing. Pakistan's government is weak and, fifty years after its creation, does not deliver the most basic services to its people. Nor has it been able to break down the local power bases of traditional tribal, feudal and religious leaders. In many outlying areas of Pakistan, people pay no taxes and have virtually nothing to do with state institutions. Local feudal landlords and tribal chiefs live like kings in their own areas. As the population increases, there is growing competition for scarce resources and it is already well established that rivalry is fought out on largely ethnic lines. The strength of ethnic feeling is plain for all to see. Consider the make-up of the National Assembly before the 1999 coup. Nawaz Sharif's Muslim League drew virtually all its support from Punjab. Its main opponent, the PPP, had eighteen Members of the National Assembly (MNAs), all from rural Sindh. Any further slide in PPP popularity in the future would almost certainly see those MNAs replaced by Sindhi nationalists. Meanwhile, most of the MNAs from Balochistan and NWFP were nationalists calling for greater or lesser degrees of autonomy. The Punjabis, however, remain insensitive to the nationalists' demands and show no sign of making any meaningful political accommodation.

These bleak facts, however, tell only one side of the story. The nationalist groups are as yet no match for the central institutions. Pakistan is now a geographically united country. Arguably, the idea of having a country with two wings over 1,000 miles apart was always unsustainable. Certainly when the 1971 crisis came, the Pakistan army's logistical problems were so daunting that it was never in a position to win. That handicap no longer applies and the Baloch, the Sindhis and the Mohajirs have all learnt that, if and when the need arises, the centre can find the determination and the strength to crush separatist forces. The various national movements are weak in part because they are divided and their demands contradict each other. If Altaf Hussain, for example, were to make a direct appeal for a separate province, he would face the opposition of not only the Pakistani army but also the Sindhis. Organisations trying to unite the different national groups, such as the Pakistan Oppressed Nations Movement, have so far failed to make significant headway.

To be successful, a nationalist movement in Pakistan would probably need committed, sustained external support. To date, only one nationalist movement in Pakistan has received such backing. The Indians directly intervened in favour of the Bengalis and the result was the loss of East Pakistan. The Baloch uprising did show that the tribesman could give the central government a good fight but, without external aid, a Baloch victory was always implausible.

The various regional alignments in South Asia currently pose little threat to Pakistan. Iran, however, is a growing force. Between 1973 and 1977 the Iranian government, fearful that any Baloch uprising could spread into its own Baloch communities, provided Islamabad with direct military support. If the Baloch tried to mount another challenge to Pakistan, Iran would probably respond in exactly the same way. India might be thought to pose a greater threat, but whilst some hawks in Delhi think in terms of Pakistan's ultimate collapse, theirs is a minority view. Ever since the nuclear tests, the prospect of India sponsoring an attempt to dismantle Pakistan has diminished: for all the bellicose rhetoric, Delhi now has an interest in a stable Pakistan. As for Afghanistan in the post-Taliban period, it looks set to be a fractured country with a weak central government in no position to assert its refusal to accept the legitimacy of the Durand Line.

Pakistani leaders have consistently shown great insensitivity to the nationalities question. Many in the non-Punjabi provinces believe there should be a different division of power between the centre and the provinces. There are, however, drawbacks to this proposal. Giving greater autonomy to Sindh, for example, would probably exacerbate the tensions between the Sindhis and the MQM. Whilst some genuine decentralisation would help win the confidence of many non-Punjabi Pakistanis, the most convincing answer to the national question lies in making the country a more genuinely multi-national entity, in which all the peoples have elected representatives who can argue their case in the federal capital and secure resources for their home areas. Of course, Pakistan's economic cake is so meagre that even if it was distributed more widely, it would be difficult to persuade all those in the outlying areas that they were receiving fair treatment. Nevertheless, any attempt to counter the perception that Punjab is exploiting the other provinces would have a positive effect.

Even if the immediate prospects for any of the national groups forcing the further dismemberment of Pakistan seem remote, there is no doubt that they can continue to inflict real damage on the country. The MQM phenomenon, in particular, has already had devastating results.

Beyond the death toll, it is impossible to quantify what the conflict in Karachi, Pakistan's commercial capital, has cost the country in terms of lost investment. Few could argue with the contention that if Pakistan is to thrive, then the central institutions in general, and the Punjabis in particular, must do more to reach out and accommodate the hopes and aspirations of their Pakistani compatriots.

5   Bangladesh

> This was a war in which everything went wrong for the
> Pakistan Armed Forces. They were not only out-manned but
> also out-gunned and out-Generaled. Our planning was
> unrealistic, strategy unsuited, decisions untimely and
> execution faulty.
>
> —Hamoodur Rehman Commission Report[1]

The order went out at 11.30 p.m. on 25 March 1971. Operation
SEARCHLIGHT was underway and all over the East Pakistani capital,
Dhaka, Pakistani troops fanned out to secure key objectives. After months
of talks, the junta in Pakistan had decided on military action to bring the
East Pakistani leadership into line. Pakistan's military planners realised
from the outset that Operation SEARCHLIGHT could alienate Bengali
personnel inside the police and armed forces and that many Bengalis
would disobey orders to suppress their fellow people. Worse still, they
could take their weapons and use them in a fight for an independent
Bangladesh. Consequently, one of Operation SEARCHLIGHT's first objectives was to disarm any Bengali soldiers or police officers. In many places,
the plans went awry.

In Chittagong, home to the Eighth East Bengal Regiment, most of
the soldiers were East Pakistani Bengalis but some of the officers came
from West Pakistan. As soon as the disarming operation began the
Bengalis resisted. Hundreds of Bengalis in the Chittagong cantonment
were killed before Major Zia ur Rehman (who later became president
of Bangladesh) took the initiative. When he found out what was happening he did not hesitate. 'We mutiny!' he said. At midnight he went
with a group of Bengali soldiers to the house of his commanding officer, Lt. Colonel A. R. Janjua and called him to the door. 'I am
taking over and you are under arrest,' he said. Within minutes, Janjua

and six other officers from West Pakistan were locked in an office. The Bengali soldiers wanted blood. At half past midnight the arrested officers, all from Punjab, were shot dead in the office. Addressing Bengali soldiers shortly afterwards Major Zia proclaimed, 'We have mutinied. From this moment on we are in independent Bangladesh. Pakistan is no more.'[2]

In another incident in Jessore on 29 March the most senior Bengali officer in the First East Bengal regiment, Lt. Colonel R. Jalil, was woken at midnight. He was told that he, and all the other Bengalis in his battalion, were going to be disarmed. 'This is an insult,' he retorted. 'It means we are not being trusted.' Eventually, though, he yielded and agreed that he and his Bengali men would gather their weapons and hand them over the next morning. But when the moment came and the hand-over was about to take place, the Bengali battalion commander took off his Pakistani badges of rank and threw them on the ground. 'This means we don't belong to this army,' he said. It was a pre-arranged signal: the Bengali soldiers opened fire on Pakistani officers and men who, twelve hours before, had been their comrades-in-arms. The action was a suicidal gesture. The Bengalis were outnumbered and, by the end of the day, sixty-nine of them had been killed.[3]

In the year 1971 the future of East Pakistan depended on a struggle between three men: a habitual drunk, General Yahya Khan; a professional agitator, Sheikh Mujibur Rahman; and a political operator par excellence, Zulfikar Ali Bhutto. Relying respectively on military force, street power and pure guile, this volatile trio pursued their incompatible objectives. Yahya, Pakistan's military ruler, repeatedly claimed that he had one, and only one, objective: to keep the east and west wings of Pakistan united. If unity was assured then he was prepared to offer East Pakistan substantial autonomy. In fact, Yahya did go further than any other Pakistani leader in trying to make the necessary compromises to find a solution for East Pakistan. A durable settlement, though, eluded him. Ever since the defeat of 1971, many Pakistanis had complained about Yahya's drinking and womanising. But those were the least of his problems. Yahya was simply outclassed. Politically, intellectually and in terms of sheer drive, he was never in the same league as either Zulfikar Ali Bhutto or Mujibur Rahman.

Yahya viewed politicians with disdain and Mujibur Rahman was a politician to the core. Starting out as an angry activist addressing groups of ten to twenty students, he ended up as the founder of Bangladesh, speaking to the hearts of many millions. His creed never altered: he believed in Bengali nationalism. When Mohammed Ali Jinnah struggled for Pakistan he relied on legal arguments. Mujibur Rahman had to engage in a far rougher, dirtier fight for Bangladesh and, unlike Jinnah, he spent long periods in jail. From the moment he became interested in politics at Dhaka University he was never afraid of defying the authorities: on the contrary, he relished it. No one doubts that Mujibur Rahman deserves the title 'founder of the nation' but there are sharp differences of opinion as to when exactly Mujib became irrevocably committed to Bengali independence. Many believe this was his goal from the outset. Speaking after independence, Mujib himself claimed that he had been planning to divide Pakistan ever since 1947. As we shall see, however, there is good evidence that even as late as December 1970 or February or March 1971 he was still thinking in terms of a united Pakistan and did not foresee a complete rupture.

The third contestant in the struggle for East Pakistan had no particular interest in the place. Zulfikar Ali Bhutto may have preferred to keep Pakistan united but he shed few tears when Bangladesh broke away. Bhutto's role in the 1971 crisis has been fiercely debated. He has argued that he did his best to save the country from splitting up but many believe he played a sophisticated, cynical game to fulfil his personal ambitions, even if that meant the Pakistani nation was broken in the process. Bhutto was a man in a hurry. After the 1970 elections, one senior minister told Yahya that if Bhutto did not become prime minister within a year he would literally go mad.[4] Bhutto himself made little secret of his lust for power and, at the start of 1971, General Yahya and Mujibur Rahman were standing in the way of his becoming prime minister. By the end of 1971, having lost a war with India, Yahya was in disgrace and Mujibur Rahman was ruling Bangladesh. The path was clear for Bhutto to take over in the west.

The complicated interplay between Yahya, Mujib and Bhutto had a decisive role in the break-up of Pakistan and the creation of Bangladesh. But Bengali nationalism was alive and well before any of them were even born. The British had always considered Bengal to be a troublesome province: the Muslims there had been the most vociferous champions of Muslim rights and a Muslim homeland on the subcontinent. In 1906 the All India Muslim League was inaugurated in Dhaka and thirty-four years later it fell to a veteran Bengali politician to propose what is now seen as one of the fundamental texts of Pakistan, the Lahore Resolution. The resolution declared: 'the areas in which the Muslims are numerically in the majority, as in the north-western and eastern zones of India should be grouped to constitute "Independent States" in which the constituent units shall be autonomous and sovereign'. The resolution plainly indicated a desire for 'Independent States' and not one independent state. Some leading Bengali Muslims were highly conscious of the distinction. Speaking in Lahore, for example, the Bengali nationalist and future Pakistani prime minister, Husain Shaheed Suhrawardy, made it quite clear that: 'Each of the provinces in the Muslim majority areas should be accepted as a sovereign state and each province should be given the right to choose its future Constitution or enter into a commonwealth with a neighbouring province or provinces.'[5]

Those Bengali leaders who wanted two separate states had a problem. They could never control the Muslim League at the 'All India' level. Muslim activists from minority provinces in northern India, notably the United Provinces, had far more weight in the organisation. Their predominance, and the Bengali's relative weakness, had important consequences. At what turned out to be a crucial meeting of the India-wide Muslim League Legislators' Convention held in Delhi in April 1946, it was decided that the north-western and eastern zones referred to in the Lahore Resolution should form one country: a united Pakistan. In geographical terms the proposition seemed absurd but politically it made sense. A united Pakistan was not only in line with the two nation theory, it also countered British concerns about creating too many independent countries on the subcontinent. But some Bengali leaders were unhappy with the change. A senior Bengali Muslim League official, Abul Hashim, objected that the demand for a united Pakistan amounted to an amendment of the Lahore Resolution. He was ruled out of order. Even though it was not clear that the Delhi Convention had the right to amend the resolution,[6] the demand for a unified Pakistani state had been approved.

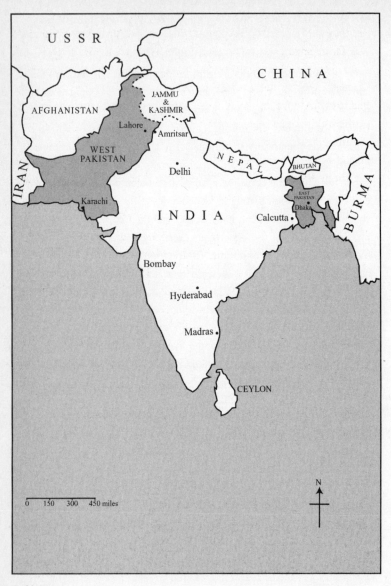

Pakistan, 1947

When Abul Hashim made his complaint, Jinnah, the lawyer, could see the problem clearly enough but his first attempt to get around it was feeble in the extreme. He suggested that the letter 's' after the word 'State' in the Lahore Resolution was a typographical error. When Liaquat Ali Khan produced the original minutes of the meeting Jinnah had to concede that he was wrong and that the word 'States' was indeed in the original text.[7] He then fobbed off Abul Hashim's objection by assuring the convention that the Lahore Resolution had not been amended. The resolution, he said, would be the document laid before the future Pakistani Constituent Assembly that, as a sovereign body, would take all final decisions.[8]

After the Delhi meeting, Jinnah took care to align himself with more amenable Bengali leaders such as the Dhaka-based, Urdu-speaking notable Khwaja Nazimuddin. Like many of his fellow Bengalis, Nazimuddin had voiced support for two separate Muslim countries. As late as April 1947 he said that: 'it is my considered opinion that an independent sovereign Bengal is in the best interest of its people'.[9] But Jinnah knew that, above all else, Nazimuddin was loyal and would follow the Quaid's leadership. And having made the decision to support a united Pakistan Nazimuddin never wavered. After Jinnah's death he held the two top jobs in Pakistani politics: first he became governor general and, later, the federal prime minister. In both posts he promoted the interests of the central government in Karachi rather than the provincial politicians in Dhaka.

Pakistan's founders had set themselves an enormous task. They had to govern two chunks of territory 1,000 miles apart. The eastern wing or East Pakistan was the more populous. When the first census was carried out in 1951, there were 42 million people living in the east and 34 million living in the west. Compared to West Pakistan, the east was linguistically homogeneous: both Hindus and Muslims in Bengal spoke Bangla and, according to the census, only 1 per cent spoke Urdu. The west, by contrast, was an ethnic cocktail and brought together Punjabis, Sindhis, Pukhtoons and the Baloch, as well as the newly arrived Urdu speakers.

In the euphoria that accompanied the creation of Pakistan the question of East Pakistan's place in the new state was put on hold, but not for long. The initial problem was that Pakistan's new rulers, many of whom had moved to Pakistan from the United Provinces, believed that if Pakistan

Languages spoken, 1951

Language	Percentage
Bangla	54.6
Punjabi	28.4
Urdu	7.2
Pukhto	7.1
Sindhi	5.8
English	1.8

Source: Keith Callard, *Pakistan: Political Study*, George
Allen & Unwin, Oxford, 1957, p. 181. The total adds up to
more than 100 per cent as some people declared more
than one language.

were ever to get its economy and armed forces in order there would
have to be a strong central government and just one national language:
Urdu. The leadership's concerns were not limited to East Pakistan. They
were also anxious about provincialism in Sindh, Balochistan and NWFP.
East Pakistan, though, plainly had the most fissiparous potential. Not only
was it a long way away but it was also considered an especially suspect
element in the new Muslim state because so many Hindus stayed there
after 1947.

In February 1948 Bengalis started articulating their concerns about
the language issue. A Hindu Bengali in the Constituent Assembly,
Dhirendra Nath Dutta, formally proposed that Bangla should be used
alongside Urdu, in Assembly sessions. Prime Minister Liaquat Ali Khan
rejected the idea out of hand declaring: 'It is necessary for a nation to
have one language and that language can only be Urdu and no other
language.'[10] To many East Pakistanis the statement, which was widely
publicised by the Dhaka newspapers, seemed uncompromising, arrogant
and unreasonable. A man who had never previously lived in the territory of Pakistan was insisting that his language, the language of just 7
per cent of the people, should become the national language.

By March the debate turned violent: a student demonstration in
Dhaka was baton-charged and some language activists were arrested.
The chief minister of East Pakistan, Nazimuddin, realised that the problem was getting out of hand and asked Jinnah to revive some enthusiasm for the Pakistan project by visiting Dhaka. In spite of the fact that

Jinnah himself spoke poor Urdu, he had long believed in the language's potential nation-building role. At a mass meeting in Dhaka he insisted that: 'the state language of Pakistan is going to be Urdu and no other language. Anyone who tries to mislead you is really an enemy of Pakistan.' Amazingly, the Quaid-e-Azam was shouted down. A group of students (rumour has it that Mujibur Rahman was among them) shouted 'No! No!' as the founder of Pakistan spoke. At the time Jinnah was treated as a living saint: such barracking was unheard of and should have alerted him to the seriousness of the problem. It did not. A session with the students after the meeting soon became a slanging match but Jinnah held firm and reasserted that Bangla had no place at the national level.[11]

Jinnah was not alone in failing to understand the depth of the discontent in East Pakistan. In January 1952 Nazimuddin told a public meeting in Dhaka that Jinnah had been right: for the sake of Pakistani unity, Urdu must be the official language of Pakistan, east and west. The fact that Nazimuddin could barely speak Bangla himself hardly helped to win popular support for his stance. It was a disastrous speech that provoked a general strike and, on 21 February 1952, riots, in response to which the police opened fire killing three students.[12] The Bangla language movement had its first martyrs. Eventually in May 1954 Nazimuddin's successor as prime minister, Muhammad Ali Bogra, announced that Bangla would be accepted as an official state language alongside Urdu. The demand had been granted – but too late.

The failure of both Jinnah and Nazimuddin to read the feelings of the Bengali people reflected a more general problem. The central government and the federal bureaucracy were located in West Pakistan. So too were all the military's main establishments. The fact that East Pakistan was so cut off helps explain why West Pakistani leaders never appreciated the intensity of feeling there. For the next twenty years senior figures in the federal government and the Pakistan army consistently viewed disturbances in East Pakistan as law and order, rather than political, issues. Bengali activists were dismissed as anti-Pakistan conspirators infiltrated by Hindus. At no point were they perceived as citizens with legitimate grievances.

When Nazimuddin made his disastrous speech he was both prime minister and leader of the Muslim League. In March 1954 the East Pakistani electorate punished him. A provincial election campaign was turned into a civil disobedience movement on the language issue and, just seven years after leading Pakistan to independence, the Muslim League was wiped out, winning just 10 of the 309 seats contested. Karachi no longer had a political base in East Pakistan. During the campaign the Muslim League leaders had repeatedly warned the electorate in East Pakistan that the future of the country was at stake. Apparently, the voters didn't care. As a result of the election, a new provincial administration, led by Fazlul Haq, the man who had proposed the Lahore Resolution fourteen years earlier, was sworn in. But his government was not to last. In May 1954 he caused havoc among the politicians and bureaucrats in Karachi by telling two foreign correspondents that he favoured the independence of East Pakistan.[13] At the time, the federal prime minister in Karachi was Chaudri Mohammed Ali (he held the job for just thirteen months), whose background as a Punjabi-speaking Mohajir and senior civil servant made him particularly unsympathetic to such unpatriotic sentiments. He launched a vituperative attack on Fazlul Haq describing him as 'a self-confessed traitor to Pakistan' and put him under house arrest.[14] Fazlul Haq's provincial government was dismissed and replaced by direct rule from Karachi.

As Fazlul Haq had made clear, the concerns of East Pakistan's political activists were not limited to the language issue. From the very outset, Bengalis complained that British colonialists had been replaced by West Pakistani colonialists. There was also a series of rows over constitutional issues. The task of writing a constitution threw up some genuinely difficult questions. The Objectives Resolution of March 1949, which laid down the framework of the new constitution, had opened with the observation that 'sovereignty over the entire Universe belongs to Allah Almighty alone and the authority which He has delegated to the State of Pakistan through its people for being exercised within the limits prescribed by Him is a sacred trust'.[15] It may have been in line with the two nation theory but, at a stroke, the formulation destroyed any faint hopes of co-opting East Pakistan's substantial Hindu community into the Pakistan project.

There was also the question of how the central and provincial government would divide power. The Constituent Assembly's first Interim Report of September 1950 gave the Central Legislature authority over a long list of subjects. The Awami League hit back with proposals that the central, federal government should have limited tax-raising powers and competence in just two policy areas: defence and foreign affairs. The provinces, it argued, should control everything else.

The most awkward constitutional question of all concerned East Pakistan's numerical representation in the proposed parliament. The Constituent Assembly at first ducked the issue altogether by failing to state clearly how many representatives each province would have. The Bengalis, who made up 55.4 per cent of Pakistan's population, took that to be an effective denial of their natural, democratic majority. With the Assembly unable to resolve the matter, further discussion was postponed. When the Assembly revisited the issue in 1954 it considered suggestions that the two houses of parliament should have parity. But now the Punjabis started to assert themselves, resisting any proposal that would have allowed East Pakistan's representatives to form alliances with the smaller provinces and thereby outvote Punjab. Again, the Constituent Assembly was deadlocked.

The matter was eventually resolved, at least temporarily, with the adoption of the 1956 Constitution. East and West Pakistan would be given an equal number of representatives (150 each) in a unicameral parliament. The Punjabis had been bought off by the imposition in 1955 of One Unit under which the four provinces of West Pakistan were amalgamated into one administrative structure that the Punjabis were confident they could dominate. By exploiting splits among the Bengali leadership, Chaudri Mohammed Ali was able to force the constitution through. But many Bengalis (notably supporters of the Awami League) saw it for what it was: a denial of their democratic majority.

By the time General Ayub Khan took over in 1958, Bengali opinion was more hostile to the notion of Pakistan than it had been in 1947. The existence of a military government made things worse. Previously, advocates of Bengali rights had at least been able to air their opinions quite freely. With the military in charge, that was no longer possible: political parties were banned. The army was even more prone than the bureaucrats to see Bengali activists as unpatriotic troublemakers. Indeed, the decision to mount a coup was in part motivated by concerns about East Pakistan. It was clear that any elections held under the 1956

Constitution would result in a clear victory in East Pakistan for the increasingly nationalist Awami League. With student activists in Dhaka still organising street protests, the military responded with arrests and detentions. Leading political players were interned. In January 1962 even former Prime Minister Suhrawardy, who had just been on a tour of East Pakistan, was arrested for anti-state activities. The Bengali students responded to his detention with riots that in turn led to army intervention and the arrest of Awami League leaders. Ayub's 1962 Constitution confirmed the trend, putting all key powers in the hands of the president. This was light years away from the type of solutions that had been discussed in the Constituent Assembly. It should have been no surprise when, in the presidential election of 1965, Ayub's worst results were in East Pakistan where 47 per cent of the electorate voted against him. Had the vote been held on the basis of universal suffrage, Ayub would almost certainly have suffered an even worse result.

The East Pakistanis' disillusionment with Ayub in part reflected the fact that they were poorly represented in the military, and consequently, had little say in his regime. At the time of independence they accounted for only 1 per cent of the members of Pakistan's three armed services and there were only 155 Bengali soldiers in the army.[16] The British military had always favoured recruiting Punjabis and Pukhtoons who they considered more warlike, and the imbalance that Pakistan inherited was not easy to correct. Ayub Khan did make efforts to recruit more East Pakistanis but came nowhere near to achieving a representative army. By 1963 Bengalis accounted for just 5 per cent of officers and 7 per cent of other ranks.[17]

It wasn't just a question of numbers. Ayub believed that the impossibility of defending East Pakistan's long borders meant that, in the words of his famous dictum, 'the defence of the East lay in the West'. Militarily he may have had a point; politically, the strategy was a disaster. It convinced the East Pakistanis that they were being kept dependent on West Pakistan. Similarly, the west's refusal to place major military bases in the east (it was proposed, for example, that the naval base should be moved from Karachi to Chittagong) may have been justifiable in terms of logistics and expense but it further alienated the Bengalis.

At a time of military rule, the composition of the army was especially important, but the national origins of senior civil servants told much the same story. In 1966 East Pakistani civil servants accounted for less than a quarter of the senior staff in the following ministries and departments: Finance, Defence (in which they held just 8.4 per cent of the jobs), Foreign Affairs, Health and Social Welfare, Agriculture, Home and Kashmir Affairs and Natural Resources.[18] The Bengali grievances, then, were numerous and in 1963 the Awami League elected a leader who could articulate them: Sheikh Mujibur Rahman. In 1966 he crystallised the Bengalis' demands into Six Points which together were to become the central issue in Pakistani politics for the next five years:

1) There should be a Federation of Pakistan on the basis of the Lahore Resolution.
2) Federal government should be limited to Defence and Foreign Affairs.
3) There should be two separate currencies for the two wings or measures to stop capital flight from East to West.
4) The centre should have no tax-raising powers.
5) Foreign exchange earnings of each wing should remain with each wing.
6) A militia or paramilitary force for East Pakistan should be set up.[19]

All these demands had been made before but the Six Points came to acquire symbolic status and won almost universal support in East Pakistan. And they were widely denounced by the west as a thinly veiled demand for secession.

That the Bengalis felt economically deprived was clear from the fact that three of the Six Points directly addressed economic issues. The Bengalis complained that Karachi, as the new capital, had better chances of attracting foreign investment and generating economic activity. Worse still, the Pakistani exchequer came to rely on the hard currency generated by East Pakistan's jute exports. Meanwhile, West Pakistani business concerns moved into the east, taking the place of Hindu entrepreneurs who had left at the time of independence. By 1970, six non-Bengali industrialists controlled over 40 per cent of all East Pakistan's manufacturing assets.[20]

The wealth gap between east and west grew throughout the 1950s. The government in Karachi was so short of resources that it was hardly in a position to begin a programme of subsidised development in the east. Nor was Ayub Khan indifferent to the economic situation in East Pakistan. Indeed, his 1962 Constitution required the removal of the disparity between east and west, but that objective was never given sufficient priority and Ayub failed to honour his pledge. In 1960 the per capita income in West Pakistan was 32 per cent higher than in the east. Although growth rates in the east did improve in the 1960s (the average for the decade was 4.2 per cent), there was a still faster growth rate of 6.2 per cent in the west. By the end of Ayub's period in office the gap between east and west had widened: per capita income in the west was 61 per cent higher than in the east.[21]

Relations between east and west deteriorated still further with the unmasking of the Agartala Conspiracy in December 1967. The plot was named after the Indian border town of Agartala where some Bengali nationalists were said to have made contact with Indian army officers. The conspiracy was uncovered when a plain-clothes security official overheard some men in the Chittagong Club discussing their plans to assassinate Ayub Khan on a PIA flight from Dhaka to Chittagong. Having killed Ayub, they intended to establish an independent state in East Pakistan. Over fifty Bengali civil servants, military personnel and politicians were accused of complicity and many of them put on trial. Ayub Khan then upped the ante by trying to implicate Mujibur Rahman in the conspiracy. He was put on public trial: a move that rapidly backfired. The more the Bengali public learnt about the conspirators, the more they admired them. Before this case, few in East Pakistan dared to discuss secession in public, but as the papers printed more and more details of the proceedings, debate about breaking away became a normal part of public discourse. Mujibur Rahman, meanwhile, secured his place as a political martyr and his support base became ever more solid. As backing for Ayub Khan in both East and West Pakistan slipped away, the atmosphere in Dhaka darkened. The army was frequently called out to restore law and order and the pro-Mujib protests became so intense that Ayub was forced to withdraw the Agartala Conspiracy case and release Mujib from prison. By the time Yahya Khan took over from Ayub in March 1969, there were almost continual protests in Dhaka.

At the end of the Ayub period there was an immense gulf between east and west. As we have seen, this happened first, and perhaps foremost, because Pakistan had set itself the very difficult task of maintaining national unity despite a lack of geographic contiguity. Shortly after partition, Mountbatten predicted that East Pakistan would break away within a quarter of a century. He was right, with one year to spare.[22] The Bengalis may have been Muslims but they had a distinct identity that West Pakistanis neither valued nor even recognised. Economic factors were also important. One West Pakistani who travelled to the east in 1970 recorded his impressions of the Dhaka suburbs:

> the women had hardly a patch of linen to preserve their modesty. The men were short and starved. Their ribs, under a thin layer of dark skin, could be counted from a moving car. The children were worse. Their bones and bellies were protruding. Whenever I stopped, beggars swarmed around me like flies. I concluded that the poor of Bengal are poorer than the poorest of West Pakistan.[23]

Some contemporary observers thought a profound crisis was inevitable. The UK deputy high commissioner in Dhaka, for example, took the view in June 1969 that East Pakistan was bound to break away. The martial law administration, he thought, would be forced by public disorder to hold elections in which Mujibur Rahman would emerge the clear winner. His government would demand a large degree of provincial autonomy that would lead to the imposition of martial law. This would be followed, he predicted, by a general uprising that the Pakistan army would not be able to control.[24] As we shall see, he wasn't far wrong.

Yahya inherited a difficult situation and he realised that to achieve a lasting constitutional settlement he would have to address the relationship between East and West Pakistan. At heart, Yahya believed that politicians could only be relied upon to break their word but he nevertheless accepted that he would have to negotiate with them. He also realised that it would be futile to try to create a pliant Bengali leadership with whom he could do business. Yahya understood that the most popular man in the east was Mujibur Rahman and, if any settlement were to work, Mujib would have to be on board. The crucial question for Yahya was whether Mujib could ever compromise on his Six Points.

Like many of his military colleagues, Yahya believed that the Six Points would leave the centre with so little authority that a united Pakistan could not survive. Throughout 1970 Yahya organised a number of meetings with Mujib and other politicians. Some of these encounters were face to face; others were conducted through intermediaries. Mujib did not hesitate to put forward his demands. He said he wanted elections to be held on a one-man one-vote basis that would reflect East Pakistan's numerical majority. He also wanted a clear statement on the division of powers between the centre and the provinces. If these demands were granted, he said, then his Six Points were not 'the Quran or the Bible'. And he insisted that his objective was autonomy and not secession.

Yahya reassured the Bengali leader that the army would accept any arrangements, including elections, that left Pakistan intact. And in March 1970 he announced a Legal Framework Order (LFO). Despite the misgivings of some members of the junta, the LFO stated that there would be elections to a unicameral National Assembly that would reflect East Pakistan's numerical superiority. As before, the Assembly would have 300 seats. Under the 1956 Constitution, however, both provinces had been given 150 seats each. Now East Pakistan would have 162 seats whilst West Pakistan would have just 138. The Assembly would be charged with drafting a new constitution within 120 days. The LFO made no stipulation about the size of the majority needed to pass the new constitution but stated that 'the National Assembly shall decide how a decision relating to the Constitution Bill is to be taken'.[25] For all intents and purposes that meant the constitution could be passed by a simple majority, which was exactly what Mujibur Rahman had been demanding. The constitution would set out the degree of regional autonomy for the two wings. Even if these arrangements left many fundamental questions unanswered, the LFO amounted to a major, and long overdue, concession by West Pakistan.

But while Yahya was trying to negotiate with Mujib in good faith, Pakistan's intelligence agencies remained suspicious. In late 1970 they hit gold. Having successfully bugged a meeting between Mujibur Rahman and his senior colleagues, they were able to play Yahya a devastating tape. On it Mujib was clearly heard to say: 'My aim is to establish Bangladesh: I will tear the LFO into pieces as soon as the elections are over. Who could challenge me once the elections are over?' One of Yahya's senior political advisers, G. W. Choudhury, was present when Yahya heard the tape:

> When Yahya listened to this 'political music' played by his intelligence services, he was bewildered. He could easily recognise Mujib's voice and the substance of his recorded talk. The next morning when I saw him he was still in a bewildered state; but he was never a serious administrator, so he soon recovered from his shock and told me: 'I shall fix Mujib if he betrays me.'[26]

It is difficult to assess Mujib's intentions at this time. He told some that he wanted to keep Pakistan united and others that he did not. It has been argued that Mujib was unable to resist the pressure of hardliners within the Awami League. Certainly that was the view of the Hamoodur Rehman Commission which, somewhat surprisingly, concluded that Mujibur Rahman was genuine when he said he did not want to break up Pakistan. In its report on the events of 1971, the Commission argued that:

> We must give full weight to the fact that before the elections he [Mujib] offered the Council Muslim League and the Jamaat-e-Islami a number of seats in East Pakistan which would have still permitted him to obtain the majority of the East Pakistan seats but not to have a clear majority in the whole house. Quite clearly his purpose was to be able to play the role of the leader of the largest single party without being under pressure for (*sic*) members of his own party to go through with the Six Point programme on the basis of an overall majority in the house. This fact clearly established that Sheikh Mujibur Rahman, at that time at least, had not decided on secession.[27]

When the election results were released, however, it became clear that such attempts to manage the outcome were futile. Pakistan's first ever national elections laid bare the yawning divide between east and west. Mujibur Rahman campaigned on the Six Points and won almost total victory. In the east his Awami League secured 160 out of the 162 directly elected constituencies – enough for an absolute majority in the National Assembly. It won no seats in the west. Zulfikar Ali Bhutto's Pakistan People's Party, meanwhile, gained 81 out of 138 seats in the west with a strong showing in Punjab and Sindh. It won no seats in the east. The clearest losers were the military which had always hoped that no single party would secure an absolute majority, thus allowing the generals to play a mediating role. The fact that the scale of the Awami League victory came as a shock to Yahya once more demonstrated the inability of West Pakistani leaders and officials to read Bengali opinion. Intelligence reports produced for the military had repeatedly predicted that the Awami League would win no more than 60 per cent of the votes in East Pakistan.[28]

Mujib was jubilant. Secure with his massive mandate, he declared that no one could stop him from framing a constitution on the basis of the Six Points. He could hardly say anything else. During the campaign he had repeatedly described the election as a referendum on the Six Points – and the result was unambiguous. In January 1971 the Awami League's successful election candidates made a pledge:

> In the name of Allah the Merciful the Almighty; in the name of the brave martyrs and fighters who heralded our initial victory by laying down their lives and undergoing the utmost hardship and repression; in the name of those peasants, workers, students, toiling masses and the people of this country; we, the newly elected members of the National and Provincial Assemblies, do hereby take oath that we shall remain whole-heartedly faithful to the people's mandate on the Six Points . . .[29]

Mujib's growing intransigence left Yahya dismayed. In January 1971 he went to Dhaka for talks with the Awami League leader. On the eve of his meeting with Mujib, Yahya once again revealed his remarkably casual attitude to high office. The Pakistani leader asked the Awami League to provide him with a copy of the Six Points. The East Pakistanis were understandably bewildered that Yahya seemed to be ignorant of the Six Points which had, after all, been at the centre of political discourse throughout his period in power. When the two men did meet, Mujib repeated his demand for the Six Points to be respected. Yahya implored Mujib to reach out to West Pakistan's politicians. He even went as far as saying that he had 'nothing against the Six Points programme but you will have to carry the West Pakistan leaders with you'.[30] Despite

1. The founder of Pakistan, Mohammed Ali Jinnah.

2. Partition. Muslim refugees flee Delhi in September 1947.

3. The founder of Bangladesh, Mujibur Rahman.

4. Bengali freedom fighters beat men suspected of collaborating with the Pakistani army, December 1971.

5. General and later Field Marshal Ayub Khan (*top and above right*),
Pakistan's first military ruler.

*I told him . . . since it was essential for him to be head and shoulders above
the others, it would be better if he elevated his own rank from that of a
General to that of a Field Marshal.*

—Zulfikar Ali Bhutto

6. The military ruler who led Pakistan to defeat in 1971, General Yayha Khan.

He starts with cognac for breakfast and continues drinking throughout the day; night often finding him in a sodden state.

—Zulfikar Ali Bhutto

7. Pakistan People's Party founder, Zulfikar Ali Bhutto.

He was the biggest dictator of Pakistan.

—General Musharraf

8. The military ruler who tried to Islamicise Pakistan, General Zia ul Haq.

Each minute, each hour and every day of your despotic rule is a living testimony of your hatred and enmity towards me.

—Zulfikar Ali Bhutto

9. General Zia's civilian successor, Nawaz Sharif.

Nawaz Sharif was driven by insecurity, paranoia and the politics of revenge.

—Benazir Bhutto

10. Pakistan's first female prime minister, Benazir Bhutto.

She has been prime minister twice and she has completely mismanaged and corrupted the country.

—General Musharraf

11. Pakistani nuclear scientist, A.Q. Khan.

12. Pakistanis in Lahore celebrate the country's first nuclear test in May 1998.

13. Pakistani children play on a replica Ghauri missile.

14. (*below*) Pakistani soldiers climb the gates of Pakistan Television headquarters during the coup that brought General Musharraf to power.

15. General Pervez Musharraf and his dogs Dot and Buddy in their first photo opportunity, October 1999.

General Musharraf is a military dictator. When he speaks, others jump to attention.If they don't, they are locked away.

—Benazir Bhutto

16. A car burns after an explosion during continuing political unrest in Karachi, March 2000.

17. Pakistani soldiers at a forward position on the Siachin glacier.

18. Pakistani troops pray during the Kargil conflict in Kashmir.

19. Pakistani troops in Kashmir fire artillery rounds across the line of control.

20. A young Talib, or religious student, learns the Quran in a Pakistani madrasa.

21. A member of Jaish-e-Mohammed in Peshawar calls for Jihad, October 2001.

22. Pro-Taliban, anti-US protestors demonstrate in Peshawar, September 2001.

that statement, there is little doubt that Yahya did think the Six Points would have to be amended if only to secure the support of his military colleagues for any future constitutional settlement. In the run-up to the elections, he had repeatedly told Mujibur Rahman that the Six Points would have to be modified. In response Mujib had repeatedly promised that he could compromise on them. Many of Yahya's colleagues had distrusted those assurances and now Yahya believed he should have listened to their advice: 'Mujib has let me down,' he said. 'Those who warned me against him were right. I was wrong in trusting this person.'[31] Publicly, though, he told reporters that: 'Sheikh Mujibur Rahman is going to be the future prime minster of the country.' Yahya, perhaps, hoped that the prospect of actually taking office might make Mujib realise that it would be worth his while showing greater flexibility.

Having made little progress in Dhaka, Yahya moved on to Larkana for talks (and a duck shoot) with Bhutto. Throughout the period when the LFO was under negotiation, Yahya had frequently asked for Bhutto's opinions on issues such as the Six Points, one-man, one-vote and the abolition of One Unit, but Bhutto had not wanted to commit himself and refused to declare his hand. After the elections, though, Bhutto could see things more clearly. Mujibur Rahman had won an overall majority and was in a position to prevent Bhutto becoming prime minister. Even though Bhutto had exceeded all expectations in the elections there was no getting around the fact that his PPP still had far fewer seats than the Awami League. With Yahya Khan still the military leader and Mujibur Rahman the prime minister in waiting, Bhutto had a problem.

The election results were a major blow but Bhutto refused to recognise the setback. 'No constitution', he proclaimed, 'could be framed, nor could any government at the centre be run without my party's co-operation.'[32] Plainly, this was not true. The new parliament could take decisions by a simple majority and the PPP did not have enough seats to veto anything. Despite those hard facts Bhutto insisted that the PPP was 'not prepared to occupy the opposition benches in the National Assembly'.

As he prepared to welcome Yahya to Larkana, Bhutto was determined to turn the election result to his favour. The two men's talks have long been very controversial. Some believe that Yahya and Bhutto reached a secret deal to work against Mujibur Rahman. This view has been most forcefully expressed by the man who subsequently ran West Pakistan's unsuccessful military campaign in East Pakistan, Lt. General Niazi:

> Bhutto was not prepared to accept the role of opposition leader in a united Pakistan: his endeavours were therefore directed at compromising Mujib's right to form the government, which would only be possible if East Pakistan gained independence. The final plan for the dismemberment of Pakistan was hatched between General Yahya and Bhutto at Larkana.[33]

Various conspiracy theorists have tried to prove much the same point but there is little hard evidence to back up their claims. Certainly the accusation seems unfair in respect of Yahya: though he arrived in Larkana deeply frustrated by Mujib's attitude, there is no reason to suggest that he was not still committed to a united Pakistan. Indeed, his subsequent use of military force to keep Pakistan united demonstrated his determination to keep the country together. For Bhutto, though, it was a different story. He was already thinking that Mujib was an obstacle to his ambitions. Shortly after the Larkana meeting Bhutto went to Dhaka to meet Mujib. Yahya had asked Bhutto to prevail upon the Bengali leader to be flexible about the Six Points but Bhutto had a different agenda. As one of the Awami League negotiators put it: 'He showed no interest in the basic constitutional issues. He spent all his time discussing his share of power and the allocation of portfolios.'[34] His attitude infuriated Mujib who felt that, once again, arrogant West Pakistan politicians were failing to take East Pakistan seriously. He had, after all, won the elections yet Bhutto was insisting that the PPP had a right to be in the government.

While determined to prevent it happening, Yahya knew that the break-up of Pakistan was now a distinct possibility.[35] He was also aware that some elements of the military leadership could never accept the Six Points.[36] Nevertheless, he had started a process and had little option but to see it through. He could only hope that Bhutto and Mujib could come up with a political compromise and, later, a constitution that would ensure the country's survival. Privately he made no secret of his frustration with Mujib and told fellow officers that he wanted 'to sort this bastard out'.[37] Whilst Yahya, Mujib and Bhutto acrimoniously negotiated in ever diminishing circles, one issue came to the fore: the date the National Assembly would be convened. Mujib wanted it to begin as soon as possible, suggesting mid-February. Bhutto, still uncertain that he could get into government, wanted it delayed until the end of March. Yahya split the difference and announced it would take place on 3 March.

It is at this point that Zulfikar Ali Bhutto made his most significant contribution to the dismemberment of Pakistan. Frustrated that the Awami League was offering him no guarantees about his future role, he told a mass rally in Lahore that the PPP would not attend the National Assembly's opening session. More than that, he declared that no other party from West Pakistan would attend it either. If any members of the Assembly did, Bhutto told a mass rally in Lahore, he would see to it that their 'legs will be broken'.

Bhutto had ended any possibility of resolving his differences with Mujib through constitutional means. He did attend more talks with both Yahya and Mujib but never made any significant concessions. Bhutto knew that some of Yahya's senior military colleagues increasingly favoured a military solution. They felt that they had given Yahya a relatively free hand to come up with a workable constitution and that he had botched the job. Bhutto could now see the way ahead. If Mujib stuck to the Six Points then the military would be left with only one democratically elected leader whom they could consider acceptable: Bhutto himself. Yahya's tragedy was that neither Bhutto nor Mujib had an interest in helping him find a compromise.

Yahya is often written off as a weak, lightweight drunk lacking the intellect and foresight to manage the national crisis he faced. It is only fair to point out, however, that up to this moment he had pursued a highly controversial but nonetheless fairly consistent course. With more realism than most of his military colleagues, he had understood that if it were to remain part of a united country, East Pakistan must be given major concessions. Elections had been held and East Pakistan's numerical majority was to be reflected in the new National Assembly. Yahya's mistake was that he played his most important cards – an East Pakistani majority in an Assembly with constitution-making powers – early. Worse, he got nothing in return. He believed that he had to make this concession if the elections were to have any credibility and he had a point. But after his overwhelming election victory Mujib was never going to make any concessions on the Six Points. The only hope would have been to blur the Six Points before setting out the terms of the Legal Framework Order and, in particular, the composition of the National Assembly – but, it must be said, it is far from clear how Yahya could have persuaded Mujib to give any public declaration to this effect.

As Yahya's talks with Mujib and Bhutto ground on, it became clear that the attitudes of the two politicians were hardening. Mujib now wanted an immediate end to martial law. Yahya and his negotiators increasingly got the impression that Mujib was not interested in taking up the position of Pakistan's duly elected prime minister and that his goal was only to govern an independent Bangladesh. Some thought was given to the idea of a loose federation with Mujib as prime minister in the east and Bhutto in the west. But Bhutto, probably aware that the military was preparing to strike, raised various procedural and legal issues and avoided any agreement.

With the talks in deadlock Yahya lost his nerve. He was not convinced the National Assembly meeting could work and, in true military fashion, fell back on the view that a 'whiff of grapeshot' might force the Awami League into line.[38] The military had first discussed the possibility of using force in February and now Yahya stepped up his military preparations. And two days before it was due to meet, he called off the National Assembly session. It was a catastrophic decision. Bhutto fully supported Yahya's move and confidently predicted that since the Awami League was a bourgeois party it would be quite incapable of launching a guerrilla struggle.[39] Yahya's military advisers on the ground in East Pakistan knew better and they repeatedly warned their chief that the reaction would be cataclysmic. They were right. Crowds armed with sticks surged on to the streets and enforced a total, nationwide strike. The final confrontation was rapidly approaching. Mujib was furious and threatened revenge. 'The Bengalis know how to shed blood,' he said.[40] And they did. There were strikes throughout East Pakistan and armed confrontations between protesters and troops. Denied their democratic rights inside Pakistan, the Bengali demands for full-blown independence became ever stronger. The Pakistani troops were overwhelmed. Students paraded through the streets waving Bangladeshi flags. The final push for independence had begun and Mujib was in control of events.

Fatally weakened, Yahya announced a new date, 25 March, for the Assembly meeting, making nonsense of his first postponement. No genuine move towards a compromise was possible in three extra weeks. The regime was on the run. By the time Yahya returned to Dhaka on 15 March, West Pakistan's authority in the east was steadily ebbing away. Shortly after, Mujib defied the martial law administration by proclaiming that he was taking over the administration of East Pakistan. It wasn't a declaration of independence but it came very close.

Civil War

At 8.00 p.m. on 26 March General Yahya addressed the rapidly disintegrating Pakistani nation. The political negotiations, he said, had failed. Denouncing Mujib as an obstinate, obdurate traitor, he declared that it was the duty of the armed forces to ensure the integrity, solidarity and security of the country. The party that had won the overwhelming backing of the East Pakistani people, the Awami League, was banned. 'I should have taken action against Sheikh Mujibur Rahman and his collaborators weeks ago,' declared Yahya. 'He and his party have defied the lawful authority for over three weeks. They have insulted Pakistan's flag and defiled the photograph of the Father of the Nation. They have tried to run a parallel government. They have created turmoil, terror and insecurity.'[41]

By the time he spoke, the Pakistan army had already moved into action. After the final breakdown of the talks with Mujib, Yahya had left Dhaka by plane. Operation SEARCHLIGHT began the moment he reached West Pakistani airspace. For weeks, West Pakistani troops in Dhaka had been too afraid to leave their barracks. Even to be seen in public risked violent attack from Bengali activists – some soldiers had been killed in the city in broad daylight. The troops wanted revenge and, in the words of the Hamoodur Rehman Commission, 'It was as if a ferocious animal having been kept chained and starved was suddenly let loose.'[42] At midnight, a commando unit raided Mujib's house and, after a brief fight, arrested the Awami League leader. The Pakistan army's next targets were any Bengalis with weapons.

While some soldiers from West Pakistan were trying to gather arms from their erstwhile colleagues, others headed for Dhaka University, long considered a hotbed of Bengali nationalism. At 2.00 a.m. soldiers arrived at two student hostels and met strong resistance but within a couple of hours the army had prevailed. It is impossible to say how many died – quite probably hundreds. By the morning, freshly-turned earth indicated that the West Pakistani troops had dug mass graves.[43]

Dhaka was, more or less, under control but outside the city it was a different story. With their obstinate refusal to understand East Pakistani opinion, the senior officers in West Pakistan predicted that the general population would remain largely neutral. It did not. The Bengali population stood full square behind their arrested leader, Mujibur Rahman. The West Pakistani troops responded to this defiance with furious aggression, raping, murdering and even massacring whole villages, women and children included. The man in charge of the campaign, General Tikka Khan, himself conceded that the West Pakistani troops killed as many as 30,000 people. Presumably, the true figure was far higher.

Given what was happening, it was not surprising that Bengalis in the Pakistani army decided to make a run for it. From all over East Pakistan, Bengali soldiers headed for India where they formed the rapidly emerging Bengali resistance army – the Mukti Bahini, or freedom fighters. The Hamoodur Rehman Commission reckoned that out of 17,000 army personnel of Bengali origin only 4,000 were successfully disarmed and that the rest made it to India.[44] The West Pakistani plans to take control of the radio stations also met with only partial success. In Chittagong, Bengali staff reacted to the army action by setting up their own Independent Bangladesh Radio station and broadcasting messages from Major Zia ur Rehman announcing the establishment of Bangladesh. For a week, there were fierce battles in the city. The West Pakistanis had to deploy both the navy and air force to attack what used to be Pakistani military establishments but what had become rebel positions. Whenever they travelled by road they were at risk of ambush. Some garrisons that came under rebel attack had to be evacuated by helicopter. The army also faced severe logistics and supply problems. Food supplies dried up and troops were deployed on hazardous missions to rural areas where they commandeered grain and other supplies from the civilian population.[45]

For all the difficulties it faced, though, the Pakistani army soon felt it was getting the upper hand. Even if they refused to acquiesce, the Bengalis suffered from a lack of arms and by May the army had managed to establish control of all the major towns. The countryside, however, remained a much more difficult proposition. And, as the Bengalis became better organised, the Pakistan army's problems mounted: 'From June onwards', Major General Shaukat Riza recalled, 'the Pakistan army was chasing ghosts. Every bush, every hut, every moving thing was suspect.'[46]

From their bases in India, the Mukti Bahini mounted hit-and-run attacks. Most were limited operations in which ten to fifteen men would slip across the border, strike at a defined target such as a bridge, and then move back to the safety of India. In some cases, though, groups of up to 250 men launched full-scale attacks on Pakistani military camps before melting away and beating a tactical retreat.

Most of these actions were in the border areas but there was also considerable rebel activity in Dhaka – supposedly the most secure place of all. The atmosphere there has been captured by Hasan Zaheer, a senior West Pakistani civil servant, who in June 1971 attended a dinner for a visiting mission from the International Bank for Reconstruction and Development and the International Monetary Fund. It was a difficult evening:

> While drinks were being served in the drawing-room of the Governor's House, sounds of bomb explosions, which did not seem to be very far off, were heard at regular intervals. This was while each one of us, the Pakistani officials, had got hold of one or two members of the mission and were arguing for our rehabilitation programmes and the bright future we envisaged for economic revival. By the time we had moved to the dining table, shooting had been added to the bomb explosions and the chatter of machine-gun fire almost drowned the polite conversation and both we and our guests found it hard to keep up. We avoided looking at each other and tried to finish the meal as

soon as possible. The incongruity of the situation was overwhelming: well-dressed people eating in a civilised manner off the finest china and sparkling silver and crystal under the sound and fury of death and destruction. No one knew the location of these happenings but they were obviously timed for the benefit of the World Bank officials. The dinner was over at around 10.00 p.m. and all of us departed in a cacophony of howling dogs, explosion of bombs and rapid firing of machine-guns.[47]

If senior civil servants were finding it difficult to hold a decent dinner party, the suffering of many others in East Pakistan was far more acute. The fighting grew ever more bitter. When killing Bengalis, the Pakistani soldiers used a euphemism: their victim, they used to say, 'was being sent to Bangladesh'. The following quotations are from Pakistani officers who gave evidence to the Hamoodur Commission Report:

There was a general feeling of hatred against Bengalis amongst the soldiers and officers including Generals. There were verbal instructions to eliminate Hindus. In Salda Nadi area about 500 persons were killed. When the army moved to clear the rural areas and small towns, it moved in a ruthless manner; destroying, burning, killing.

—Lt. Col. Mansoorul Haq

Many junior and other officers took the law into their own hands to deal with so-called miscreants. There have been cases of interrogation of miscreants which were far more severe in character than normal and in some cases blatantly in front of the public. The discipline of the Pakistani army, as was generally understood, had broken down.

—Brigadier Mian Taskeenudin

General Niazi visited my unit at Thakurgaon and Bogra. He asked us how many Hindus we had killed. In May, there was an order in writing to kill Hindus.

—Lt. Col. Aziz Ahmed Khan.[48]

Of course, the Pakistan army was not alone in committing atrocities. The Mukti Bahini also carried out acts of terrific violence, particularly against the Biharis who had moved from India to East Pakistan at the time of partition. Still loyal to Jinnah's vision of a united Muslim state on the subcontinent, the Biharis sided with the Pakistan army. There were many incidents of communal violence between them and the Bengalis. But the Mukti Bahini's main target was the Pakistan army itself. The Hamoodur Rehman Commission Report endorsed Pakistani claims that: 'Families of West Pakistani officers and other ranks serving in East Pakistan units were subjected to inhuman treatment, and a large number of West Pakistani officers were butchered by their Bengali colleagues.' [49] On General Niazi's account: 'In Bogra 15,000 persons were killed in cold blood. In Chittagong, thousands of men and women were bayoneted or raped. In Seraj Ganj women and children were locked in a hall and set on fire. The target of these brutalities were West Pakistanis . . .'[50]

Distracted by its effort to control the Bengali population, the Pakistani military command in Dhaka was perhaps insufficiently focussed on what was happening in India. While the Pakistani army believed that India was involved in instigating the Bengalis' belligerent attitude, few expected Delhi to intervene in East Pakistan directly. Once again, it was a faulty judgement. After Mujib had been arrested, most of the Awami League leadership had dressed in peasants' clothing and slipped away across the border. Delhi helped them set up a government-in-exile in Calcutta. As the civil war intensified, an increasing number of Bengalis – especially the Hindus – fled to India as well. According to the Indian government, over 8 million people (7 million of them Hindus) had become refugees by the end of August. The precise numbers are contested but there were certainly several million. The refugee movement had an important impact on world opinion and drew attention to the Pakistan army's repressive measures.

Pakistan's international problems were not restricted to India. The United States, having always supported the unity of Pakistan, now started making contingency plans for a possible break-up. Much has been written about the splits in the US administration at this time: Kissinger and Nixon, in the White House, were generally more sympathetic to General Yahya than the State Department.[51] In the event, the divisions in Washington didn't make much difference: with Congress and the press complaining about the repression in East Pakistan, decisive US military intervention to keep Pakistan together was never a realistic possibility. The Indians, meanwhile, were reaching out to new allies. The signing of the Treaty of Friendship and Co-operation with Moscow in August 1971 gave the Indians the crucial assurance they wanted. True, it wasn't a security guarantee but it did state that: 'in the event that any of the parties is attacked or threatened with attack, the High Contracting Parties will immediately start mutual consultation with a view to eliminating the threat and taking appropriate effective measures to ensure peace and security for the countries'.[52] It was an effective counter to Pakistan's hopes of receiving military support from China. In the event, Beijing never delivered as much as Yahya wanted. China did speak of its commitment to Pakistani unity but never came close to military intervention. And, if Pakistan was being outmanoeuvred at the regional level, things didn't look much brighter at the United Nations where opinion was increasingly swayed by press reports of atrocities in East Pakistan and of the suffering in the refugee camps.

It is not clear exactly when the Indian prime minister Indira Ghandi decided to go to war. Initially, Delhi believed that Operation SEARCH-LIGHT would be a short-lived affair, followed by a negotiated settlement in which the East Pakistanis would accept the unity of the country. But as the Pakistani army's campaign continued, and refugees flowed into India, opinion in Delhi hardened. By June, there was an emerging consensus that an independent Bangladesh was in India's interests and might even be worth fighting for. In July 1971, Lt. General Jagjit Singh Aurora was given the job of destroying the Pakistani forces in East Pakistan.[53] He was also given half a million men to complete the task.

International War

The first Indian attacks were limited to strikes on Pakistani forces followed by rapid withdrawals back to Indian territory. By 21 November, though, the Indians started digging in on East Pakistani soil. From the point of view of the military tacticians in Delhi, the timing could not have been better. The end of the monsoon meant that they would not be held up by torrential rain while the arrival of snow in the passes on the Chinese-Indian border limited Beijing's military options should it want to get involved.

Yahya responded to the Indian incursions by opening up the western front. He launched air attacks on nine airbases in north-west India on 3 December. The attacks were futile: due to faulty intelligence, not one Indian aircraft was destroyed. Yahya then ordered some limited ground offensives intended to draw the Indian forces in the west into the open. Throughout the war, though, Yahya never launched a full-blown offensive on the western front. That is not to say there wasn't some fierce fighting on the borders of West Pakistan: there was. The two armies clashed in Kashmir and in Sindh but these engagements were never on a big enough scale to affect the outcome of the war as a whole. On the many occasions when Yahya was urged to act more decisively in the west and commit more troops there, he always expressed reluctance to do so. Maybe he was afraid of defeat. For all the theorising, the defence of East Pakistan was to lie in the east.

After the Pakistani air strikes, Delhi could claim that Pakistan had dealt the first blow and India's full-scale invasion of the east, originally scheduled for 6 December, was brought forward. The Indian air force inflicted the first major damage by hitting Dhaka's military airport. Pakistan's squadron of Sabre fighter-jets were unable to take off and could play no part in the war: India enjoyed complete air superiority. It also had a significant manpower advantage, although its extent has been vigorously disputed. At one extreme Lt. General Niazi has claimed that, at most, he had 55,000 men under his command and that 'the ratio of troops between us and the Indians came to approximately one to ten'. The Hamoodur Rehman Commission report challenged these figures and estimated the Pakistani forces at between 73,000 and 93,000, while the Indians have suggested a one to eight ratio.[54] The numbers are complicated by the fact that the Indians could rely on the highly motivated Mukti Bahini (generally estimated at 100,000) whilst Niazi had far less effective support from various irregular forces, including some 'Mujahid Battalions' and madrasa students.[55] India also had a clear advantage in terms of military equipment. Indeed, the Pakistanis were short of many basic items such as land-mines. In some places, they had to create lines of defence with nothing more than sharpened bamboo sticks stuck in the ground.[56]

Lt. General Niazi never stood a chance. When the Hamoodur Rehman Commission questioned Yahya Khan and other senior generals, they freely conceded that, once India launched a full-scale invasion, defeat was inevitable.[57] Niazi was outnumbered, outgunned and operating in territory with a hostile population. Despite his hopeless situation, many Pakistanis have been strongly critical of his strategy in East Pakistan and have blamed him for the army's humiliation. The arguments about his record mainly concern his defensive strategy. Niazi repeatedly claimed that he would defend Dhaka to the 'last man, last bullet'. But rather than concentrate his forces there he spread them all along East Pakistan's 2,500-mile land border in small groups to hold up any Indian attack. Niazi said there was to be no withdrawal from these positions until 75 per cent casualties had been taken. One military historian described this as the most stupid order given during the whole war.[58] Under Niazi's plans, the surviving 25 per cent were then to regroup in over thirty strong points and fortresses that had been identified as crucial for the defence of East Pakistan. The fortresses were stocked with enough food and ammunition to hold out for a month.

Niazi's public relations officer Siddiq Salik recalls Niazi discussing his strategy with foreign correspondents in Dhaka shortly before the Indian attacks. Niazi said: 'My troops in the border outposts are like the extended fingers of an open hand. They will fight there as long as possible before they fold back to the fortresses to form a fist to bash the enemy's head.' Siddiq Salik went on to say: 'I was fascinated by the simile. But I recalled his latest decision prohibiting any withdrawals unless 75 per cent casualties had been sustained. When three out of four fingers are broken or wounded, is it possible to form a fist?'[59]

In his assessment of the military campaign, Lt. General Aurora's chief of staff, General Jacob, has written that:

Understandably this land with its huge rivers, swamps, mangroves and paddy fields and sparse roads and railways is very easy to defend. The very few bridges across the rivers add to the difficulties . . . Fortunately for us the Pakistanis had concentrated their troops in the towns. Had they chosen to defend approaches to the river crossing sites we would not have been able to cross the rivers and reach Dacca.[60]

Pakistani writers have generally used a different argument to criticise Niazi. In line with the findings of the Hamoodur Rehman Commission, they say that Niazi should have concentrated his forces in Dhaka. The capital of East Pakistan, they argue, was always India's ultimate objective and the fact that it was surrounded by rivers on three sides rendered it highly defensible. Had Niazi concentrated his forces there, the argument goes, he would have been able to hold up the Indians for longer. This reasoning is, however, unconvincing. The Indians would have been able to move through East Pakistan at will before besieging Dhaka. With a hostile population, and Indian air superiority, it is difficult to see how Niazi could have successfully defended the city. Furthermore, many of those who have criticised the fortress concept would have been the first to blame Niazi if he had let the Indians move through East Pakistan unopposed.

Niazi himself has rejected outright the argument that he should have concentrated his forces in Dhaka, but his book, *The Betrayal of Pakistan*, includes some plainly ridiculous claims. He suggests, for example, that: 'All the efforts of Yahya's junta and Bhutto's coterie were directed towards losing the war.'[61] There is no evidence whatsoever that Yahya wanted to lose the war though Niazi does have a point when he defends his fortress strategy. He believed he had to prevent the Indians, or the Mukti Bahini, from establishing control of a large chunk of territory. Niazi had good reason to fear that, given the chance, the Awami League would move its Bangladeshi government from Calcutta and establish a military base on East Pakistani soil.

It is significant that when Niazi submitted his plans to GHQ in Rawalpindi for approval, nobody objected to them.[62] He also has a point when he blames Yahya for not opening up the western front. If the long-standing strategy of 'the defence of the East lies in the West' meant anything, then he had every right to have expected that to have happened. Yet on 5 December Niazi received a message from Rawalpindi stating

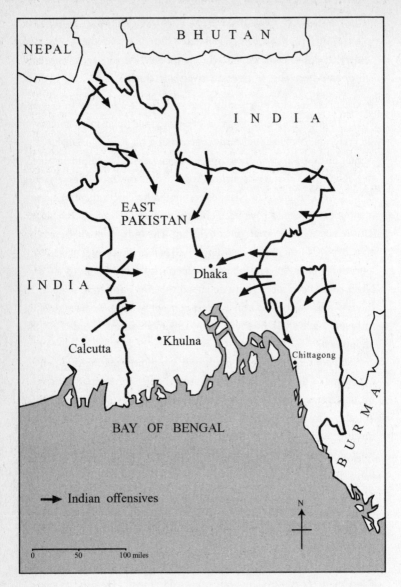

East Pakistan, 1971

that the Indian strategy was to take East Pakistan and then to concentrate its forces for an assault on the west.

Niazi was asked to hold out as long as possible so that Yahya had
time to rustle up some international support. Pakistan's plan had been
turned on its head. The defence of the west now lay in the east. With
Pakistan's strategists in disarray, Indira Gandhi, on 6 December, told the
Indian parliament that her government recognised Bangladesh as an
independent and sovereign state. She was confident of victory. General
Niazi, meanwhile, seemed sure of defeat. He sent the following message
to GHQ in Rawalpindi:

> . . . Indian air force causing maximum damage(.) have started using
> rockets and napalm against own defensive positions(.) internally rebels
> highly active, emboldened and causing maximum damage in all pos-
> sible ways including cutting of means of communication(.) this includ-
> ing destruction of roads/bridges/rail/ferries/boats etc.(.) local
> populations also against us(.) lack of communications making it
> difficult to reinforce or replenish or readjust positions . . . resorting to
> fortress/strong point basis(.) enemy will be involved though
> all methods including unorthodox action will fight it out to last man
> last round(.) request expedite actions vide your G-0235 of 5 Dec 1971[63]

Niazi was alarmed because the Indians were moving through East
Pakistan with extraordinary speed. Rather than engage the fortresses
one by one, they simply bypassed them. The fact that they were working closely with the Mukti Bahini, who knew the territory of East Pakistan well, helped the Indian forces find routes that the Pakistanis had
not anticipated.

Niazi was not helped by the fact that some of his men failed to put
up much resistance. In its assessment of the 1971 war, the Hamoodur
Rehman Commission bemoaned the performance of the Pakistan army,
saying that many of the fortresses gave up without even making a fight
of it: 'The only battle that was fought with any determination was in
the Hilli sector . . .' Elsewhere, the Commission found, some senior Pakistani officers in the fortresses fled their posts and abandoned their
troops as soon as the Indians came close.[64]

While some Pakistani officers could well be accused of cowardice others showed flamboyant bravery. At Jamalpur, near Dhaka, the Indian brigadier, Hardit Singh Kler, surrounded a Pakistani unit led by Lt. Colonel Ahmed Sultan. On 10 December the two officers exchanged letters. The first, written by the Indian brigadier, was taken across the front line by an elderly man who delivered it by hand.

To,
    The Commander Jamalpur Garrison

I am directed to inform you that your garrison has been cut off from all sides and you have no escape route available to you. One brigade with full compliment of artillery has already been built up and another will be striking by morning. In addition you have been given a foretaste of a small element of our air force with a lot more to come. The situation as far as you are concerned is hopeless. Your higher commanders have already ditched you.

I expect your reply before 6.30 p.m. today failing which I will be constrained to deliver the final blow for which purpose 40 sorties of MIGs have been allotted to me.

In this morning's action the prisoners captured by us have given your strength and dispositions, and are well looked after.

The treatment I expect to be given to the civil messenger should be according to a gentlemanly code of honour and no harm should come to him.

An immediate reply is solicited.

Brigadier HS Kler. Comd.

The reply was sent a few hours later:

Dear Brig,
    Hope this finds you in high spirits. Your letter asking us to surrender had been received. I want to tell you that the fighting you have seen so far is very little, in fact the fighting has not even started. So let us stop negotiating and start the fight.

40 sorties, I may point out, are inadequate. Ask for many more.

Your point about treating your messenger well was superfluous.

It shows how you under-estimate my boys. I hope he liked his tea.

Give my love to the Muktis. Let me see you with a sten in your hand next time instead of the pen you seem to have such mastery over,

Now get on and fight.

Yours sincerely

Commander Jamalpur Fortress.
(Lt. Colonel Ahmed Sultan)[65]

The next morning the fight did indeed begin when Lt. Colonel Sultan tried to break out of his garrison. Over 230 of his men were killed. They died in vain. When the Indian brigadier had written 'your higher commanders have already ditched you', he was absolutely right. The military and political leadership in Dhaka already knew that the war was lost. Fully two days before Lt. Colonel Sultan led his men to their deaths, the governor of East Pakistan, Dr A. M. Malik, had sent this message to General Yahya:

From Governor East Pakistan(.) A-4660 of 091800(.) for the President(.) military situation desperate . . . Enemy likely to be at the outskirts any day if no outside help forthcoming. Secretary general UN's representative in Dacca has proposed that Dacca city may be declared as an open city to save lives of civilians specially non-Bengalis(.) am favourably inclined to accept the offer(.) strongly recommend this be approved(.) Gen. Niazi does not agree as he considers that his orders are to fight to the last and it would amount to giving up Dacca(.) this action may result in massacre of whole army, WP police and all non-locals and loyal locals(.) there are no regular troops in reserve and once the enemy has crossed the Ganges or Meghna further resistance will be futile unless China or US intervenes today with massive air and ground support(.) once again urge you to consider immediate cease-fire and political settlement otherwise once Indian troops are free from east wing in a few days even west wing will be in jeopardy(.) understand local population has welcomed Indian army in captured areas and are providing maximum help to them(.) our troops are finding it impossible to withdraw and manoeuvre due to rebel activity(.) with this clear alignment sacrifice of West Pakistan is meaningless.

Five hours after sending his desperate message, the governor had Yahya's reply.

From President to Governor Repeated to Commander Eastern Command(.) your flash message A-4660 of 9 Dec. received and thoroughly understood(.) you have my permission to take decisions on your proposals to me(.) I have and am continuing to take all measures internationally but in view of our complete isolation from each other decision about East Pakistan I leave entirely to your good sense and judgement(.) I will approve of any decision you take and am instructing Gen. Niazi simultaneously to accept your decision and arrange things accordingly(.) whatever efforts you make in your decisions to save senseless destruction of the kind of civilians that you have mentioned in particular the safety of our armed forces, you may go ahead and ensure safety of our armed forces by all political means that you will have to adopt with our opponent.[66]

Pakistan's hopeless military situation on the ground was matched on the diplomatic front. The Indians' diplomatic position would have been far worse if Yahya had acted with greater speed and determination to isolate Delhi for what was, after all, a blatantly illegal invasion of a foreign country. Amazingly, Yahya failed to raise the Indian invasion of Pakistan formally at the UN Security Council. He probably feared that any ceasefire resolution would include a provision that he had to negotiate with the Awami League – something he was determined to avoid. But whatever the rationale, it was a significant blunder.

The Security Council did nevertheless discuss the situation in East Pakistan but successive resolutions were vetoed by either Russia or China. The Russians, backing India, wanted any resolution to include commitments for a transfer of power to the Awami League; the Chinese, backing Pakistan, did not. In his capacity of foreign minister, Zulfikar Ali Bhutto went to New York but was unable to affect the course of events. With Pakistan's unity on the verge of destruction and frustrated by the Russians'

Security Council vetoes, Bhutto decided to make the best of a bad job and strengthen his own political position back at home. On 15 December he told the Security Council that he would never address them again. As he ripped up some Security Council papers, he asked: 'Why should I waste my time here? I will go back to my country and fight.' It was the speech of a leader in waiting.

Despite the bleak communications emanating from Dhaka, Niazi has claimed that when the war came to a close Pakistan's position was not so bad:

> In fact when the time for an attack against Dhaka came, they [the Indians] were left with only four weak brigades. All the rest were fighting isolated battles against us and our well-stocked and well-prepared fortresses, and were having a tough time with heavy casualties. Aurora could not move his troops from these sectors to concentrate against Dhaka, his ultimate objective.[67]

Indian accounts of the war confirm many of Niazi's claims. General Jacob has described how he found himself in an increasingly awkward position. The Indian army chief, General Sam Manekshaw, had always made it clear that he did not consider Dhaka to be the primary objective for the Indian invaders. He argued that if the Indian forces took Chittagong and Khulna then Dhaka would automatically fall. His officers on the ground, however, wanted the big prize and struck straight for Dhaka. As international pressure for a ceasefire built up Manekshaw became ever more concerned that this focus on Dhaka was going to have disastrous consequences. He could foresee a ceasefire being imposed before India had taken any of East Pakistan's major towns.

'On 13 December', recalls General Jacob, 'we received a signal from Gen Manekshaw ordering us to immediately capture all the towns in Bangladesh that we had bypassed. All the towns were named with the exception of Dacca. These included Dinajpur, Rangpur, Sylhet, Maynamati Cantonment and also Khulna and Chittagong.' Jacob was dismayed:

> We had reached the outskirts of Dacca and to me it was imperative that we capture Dacca rather than waste our efforts in going back and

capturing those towns. Had we done so, our operations would have been bogged down. The only towns which we had been able to occupy were Jessore and Comilla from which the Pakistanis had withdrawn.[68]

General Jacob needed Pakistan to surrender as quickly as possible and he opted for some psychological warfare. He was greatly helped by the success of Indian intelligence operatives in intercepting messages between Dhaka and Rawalpindi, which indicated that morale in Dhaka was desperately low. Jacob then received another useful piece of intelligence: he was told that the East Pakistani governor had called a high-powered meeting in Government House on 14 December. Having looked up the location of the building on a tourist map Jacob ordered an air strike on it.

It was a masterful tactic. Niazi's public relations officer, Siddiq Salik, was at the receiving end and described what happened. The Indian bombs, he recalled,

> ripped the massive roof of the main hall. The Governor rushed to the air raid shelter and scribbled out his resignation. Almost all the inmates of this seat of power survived the raid. Except for some fish in a decorative glass case. They restlessly tossed on the hot rubble and breathed their last.[69]

Jacob's air raid had finished off not only the fish but also the West Pakistanis' will. The governor, his cabinet and some West Pakistani civil servants headed to the safety of the Hotel Intercontinental. The Red Cross, which had declared the hotel to be a neutral zone, refused to let them in unless they disassociated themselves from the Pakistani government. The terrified governor and his colleagues readily agreed.

On 14 December President Yahya sent Niazi this message:

> you have fought a heroic battle against overwhelming odds(.) the nation is proud of you and the world full of admiration(.) I have done all that is humanly possible to find an acceptable solution to the problem(.) you have now reached a stage when further resistance is no longer humanly possible nor will it serve any useful purpose(.) you should now take all necessary measures to stop the fighting

and preserve the lives of all armed forces personnel from West Pakistan . . .'[70]

That evening Niazi went to see Herbert Spivack, the US consul general in Dhaka, to send a message to the Indian army chief requesting a ceasefire. By 16 December negotiations were sufficiently advanced for General Jacob to go to Dhaka. It was a difficult assignment. Niazi was still hoping to sign a ceasefire document and not a surrender. As Jacob recalled: 'Colonel Khara read out the terms of surrender. There was dead silence in the room as tears streamed down Niazi's cheeks . . . I asked him whether the document was acceptable. He handed it back without comment. I took this as acceptance.'[71] To Niazi's dismay, Jacob then made it clear that his surrender would be in public.

Writing twenty-five years after the war Niazi claimed that he had never wanted to give up fighting but was forced to by Yahya. 'I had to swallow my pride', Niazi subsequently claimed, 'and make the supreme sacrifice of forfeiting reputation and honour, and the honour of my gallant troops, in the national interest.'[72] Niazi's account of his own defiance is, however, contradicted by a number of eyewitnesses who were in Dhaka during December 1971. One of Niazi's colleagues, General Rao Farman Ali, told the Hamoodur Rehman Commission that in fact Niazi's morale collapsed as early as 7 December. That day, Farman was present at a meeting between Niazi and the governor of East Pakistan, A. M. Malik, who had asked for a formal briefing on the progress of the military campaign. General Farman described what happened: 'The Governor had hardly said a few words when General Niazi started crying loudly. I had to send the bearer out. The Governor got up from his chair, patted him, and said a few consoling words.'[73] This was a decisive moment after which the governor actively and repeatedly urged Rawalpindi to agree to a ceasefire. Whilst agreeing with the governor's approach, Niazi was reluctant to put his own name to such requests and demanded that any messages discussing the possibility of a ceasefire be sent from the governor's house and not his own military headquarters.

Niazi's surrender seemed all the more craven because, before the Indian offensive, he had repeatedly boasted about how brave he was going to be. Amidst all the talk of fighting to the last man and last round he even claimed that, to reach Dhaka, the Indian tanks would have to roll over his chest. In the event his conduct fell well short of such claims.

The surrender ceremony took place at the Ramna Racecourse, the place where Mujibur Rahman had held some of his mass political rallies. To the fury of the Pakistanis, the most senior Indian officer present, Lt. General Aurora, brought his wife to witness the proceedings. Having met Aurora at the airport Niazi drove with him to the racecourse. The two men then sat down in front of a rickety wooden table. With Indian officers crowding all around him and hundreds of thousands of Bengalis looking on, Niazi signed East Pakistan away: 'As I signed the document with trembling hands', he later recalled, 'sorrow rose from my heart to my eyes, brimming them with unshed tears of despair and frustration.'

The document stated that: 'The Pakistan eastern command agree to surrender all Pakistani armed forces in Bangladesh to Lieutenant General Jagjit Singh Aurora General Officer Commanding in Chief of the Indian and Bangladesh forces in the Eastern Theatre. This surrender includes all Pakistan land, air and naval forces . . .'[74] With the paperwork out of the way Niazi stood up, took out his revolver and handed it over to his Indian counterpart.

Niazi has subsequently claimed that he only agreed to Jacob's demands because, again, he had been ordered to do so by President Yahya:

I never wanted, asked for or gave any indication for a ceasefire or surrender. My important signals ended with the assertion 'will fight to last man last round' . . . As a matter of fact Dhaka was so strongly held at this stage that it was impregnable and the Indians would have needed all their available troops to make an impression in it.[75]

It is a bold claim and an implausible one. Indeed, shortly after the surrender, Niazi himself told a different story. Siddiq Salik recounts Niazi's comments soon after the two men arrived in Calcutta as prisoners of war. Niazi freely conceded that there were too few troops in Dhaka and blamed Rawalpindi for failing to send more men.

'With what little you had in Dhaka', suggested Salik, 'you could have prolonged the war for a few days more.' 'What for?' asked Niazi:

> That would have resulted in further death and destruction. Dhaka's drains would have been choked. Corpses would have been piled up in the streets. Yet the end would have been the same. I will take 90,000 prisoners of war to West Pakistan rather than face 90,000 widows and half a million orphans there.[76]

When he eventually returned to West Pakistan, after twenty-eight months as a prisoner of war, Niazi was greeted as an incompetent coward who had brought shame on his nation. Pakistan's official enquiry into the 1971 war was especially damning.[77] It accused Niazi of serial womanising, venal corruption and total military incompetence. It recommended a court martial charging him, among other things, with failure to appreciate the imminence of all-out war with India; failing to concentrate his forces; relying on strong points and fortresses that couldn't lend each other mutual support; and failing to plan the defence of Dhaka. Finally the authors of the Commission's report concluded, somehow, that Yahya's communication of 14 December did not amount to an order to surrender:

> there was no order to surrender. But in view of the desperate picture painted by the Commander, Eastern Command, the higher authorities only gave him permission to surrender if he in his judgement thought it necessary. General Niazi could have disobeyed such an order if he thought he had the capability of defending Dhaka . . . if General Niazi had done so and lost his life in the process, he would have made history and would have been remembered by the coming generations as a great hero and martyr but the events show he had already lost the will to fight . . .[78]

It is an unfair assessment written by civilians who were never near the fighting, though defeated generals can expect little else. Few would claim that Niazi was either a saint or a brilliant general. But, surely, no one can believe that he ever had the remotest chance of defeating the Indian invaders or, indeed, that there was any point in leading his men to certain death so as to satisfy public opinion in West Pakistan. That such a high-powered committee should recommend such a futile course of action reflects the extent of Pakistan's humiliation. Twenty-four years after its creation, Pakistan was irreparably broken and its people distraught. For many of those who had witnessed the events of 1947 and who had had such high hopes of Pakistan, it was a devastating blow. Jinnah's Muslim nation no longer existed. Bangladesh was born.

6   The Bomb

If India builds the bomb, we will eat grass or leaves; even go
hungry, but we will get one of our own.

—Zulfikar Ali Bhutto, 1965[1]

Late in the evening of 27 May 1998, Pakistan's director general of
military operations in GHQ, Rawalpindi, made a series of urgent telephone calls. As well as contacting senior military colleagues he rang the
prime minister's Secretariat and the Foreign Office in Islamabad. His
message was extremely alarming. According to Saudi intelligence, he
said, Israeli fighter jets were moving from Chenai in India towards the
Pakistani border. He said the Israeli planes were tasked with destroying
Pakistan's nuclear capability. The director general of military operations
said Pakistan was just seven hours away from conducting its first ever
nuclear test – and the Israelis and Indians wanted to ensure that the test
would never take place.

Just two weeks before, on 11 and then 13 May, India had exploded
five nuclear devices under the desert at Pokaran in Rajasthan. Pakistan
was under huge international pressure not to follow suit. Whilst he
weighed his options, Prime Minister Nawaz Sharif asked his nuclear scientists to prepare for a test as a contingency. Delighted that decades of
research might at last bear fruit they told him they would be ready by
first light on 28 May.

The director general of military operations' phone calls had an immediate effect. Pakistan's chairman of the joint chiefs of staff, General
Jehangir Karamat, scrambled F-16 fighter planes and sent them to protect the test site in Balochistan. Mirage aircraft and ground-based air

defence units were tasked with preventing any attack on the Kahuta uranium enrichment plant just outside Islamabad. Pakistan also dispersed
its missile arsenal so as to preserve its nuclear capability in the event of
enemy attack. According to one of Pakistan's leading nuclear scientists,
A. Q. Khan, the military also decided to arm Pakistan's intermediate
range Ghauri missiles with nuclear warheads.[2] It is, however, far from
certain that Pakistan had the capability to mount a nuclear warhead on
a Ghauri at this time – the missile had been test-fired for the first time
just one month before. But armed or not, the Ghauris were moved out
of the Kahuta plant. Within minutes the Indians responded by rolling
out their own short-range Prithvi missiles. Pakistan and India had
started climbing the escalatory ladder with frightening speed.

Alerted by GHQ's phone call, Pakistan's Foreign Office swung into
action. By midnight all its most senior diplomats – and the foreign
minister himself – had gathered in the converted 1960s-style hotel in
which they worked. They contacted the Pakistani embassies in Beijing,
Tokyo, Moscow, many West European capitals and, of course, Washington, warning of the impending attack. They also communicated,
indirectly, with the Israeli ambassador in Washington. By 1.00 a.m. the
Indian high commissioner to Islamabad had been called from his bed and
summoned for a dressing down. Nawaz Sharif, backing up the Foreign
Office's efforts, personally called President Clinton in Washington and
Prime Minster Blair in London and told them that his intelligence reports
were clear: Israeli planes were on the way.

In New York, Pakistan's permanent representative to the United
Nations, Ahmed Kamal, received copies of the telegrams being sent
from Islamabad. He informed the UN secretary general, Kofi Annan, and
the Security Council about the threat. He then approached CNN and
offered himself for an interview. Within a couple of hours he was live
on air accusing Delhi of launching an attack. 'The world must understand that Pakistan is ready,' he said. 'The reaction would be massive
and dissuasive and that it would lead us into a situation which would
bode ill for peace and security not only in the region but beyond.'[3] Government spokesmen in Islamabad reinforced his message. Confusingly,
they claimed the Israeli planes were coming not from Chenai but from
Srinagar, the capital of Indian-controlled Kashmir.

The attack never happened. At the time Pakistan argued that its prompt diplomatic activity forced India and Israel to abandon the plan. Delhi said the whole story was a fabrication. As soon as they had received Pakistan's warnings, Western governments had started their own investigations. By the morning of 28 May they were able to assure the Pakistanis that no such attack was ever planned.

Some people within the Pakistani administration had also been sceptical about the possibility of an Israeli attack. Indeed, even some of those involved in the crisis management never really believed the Israeli planes were coming. They pointed out that if some F-16s were flying from Chenai to Kahuta, they would have to be refuelled three times – a process that would inevitably lead to their detection by Pakistani radar. But the dynamics of Pakistani politics are such that no one dared contradict the view from GHQ where many senior officers seemed convinced that the threat was real. For a civilian to challenge the military's assessment would open them up to the accusation of failing the country at a time of crisis. So, notwithstanding their doubts, senior officials and politicians acted on the basis that the threat was genuine. They knowingly responded to a non-existent threat. The inability of senior decision-makers to discuss the reality of the supposed danger openly raises serious questions about Pakistan's command and control capability. The most sobering comment was made by one of the most senior Pakistani officials involved in the events of that evening: 'Our radar stations were on high alert,' he said. 'If some Gulf State Prince had been travelling unannounced in a private jet towards Karachi that night, the results would have been cataclysmic.'

There were to be other moments of confusion. On 30 May Pakistan conducted its second round of nuclear tests. Shortly after 1.00 p.m., the foreign minister, Gohar Ayub Khan, announced that his country had successfully detonated two nuclear devices under the Chagai mountains in Balochistan. Within seconds, his statement was flashed around the world's international newsdesks. Then something strange happened. At 6.00 p.m. an official Pakistani spokesman issued a correction. The foreign minister had made a mistake. There had not been two detonations; there had been just one. The discrepancy was never explained but it did raise more questions about command and control. If Pakistan's own foreign minister did not know how many nuclear bombs had gone off then who did? Who was running Pakistan's nuclear programme?

There are various explanations for the events of 27 May 1998. Few now believe the threat of an Israeli attack was genuine. Some, however, believe it was a genuine mistake. Pakistan intelligence officials had been put on high alert ever since India's nuclear test. They were told to look out for any attempt to destroy Pakistan's nuclear facilities by methods such as an air strike, a helicopter raid or even a cruise missile attack. A Pakistani intelligence report from London straight after the Indian test said that ten Israeli planes had disappeared from an airfield in Israel. Ever distrustful of India and Israel's close defence relationship, the Pakistanis stepped up their surveillance of Indian airfields to see if the planes could be seen there. Pakistan has long considered the possibility of a joint Indian-Israeli strike. The former Pakistani army vice chief, General Retd. K. M. Arif, has said that in the mid-1980s he was made aware of possible Israeli attacks on three separate occasions.[4] The fact that the Israelis had used an air strike to destroy Iraq's Osirak nuclear plant just outside Baghdad in 1981 added to Islamabad's fears.

In reality, the Israelis never deployed any F-16s on 27 May. It is quite possible that some pro-test elements in Military Intelligence and the ISI were concerned that Prime Minster Nawaz Sharif, and for that matter the army leadership, might bow under the intense international pressure not to test and therefore decided to create a scare. To add credibility to the exercise they may have fed some of their information through contacts in Saudi intelligence. Many Western officials and a few Pakistanis involved in the events of 27 May believe this. Another piece of evidence suggesting that the Israeli scare was a deliberately planted, false alarm is that a pro-test Pakistani journalist wrote about Israel's plans to attack Kahuta as early as 21 May. How he could possibly have known about the Israeli 'attack' one week in advance of its happening is far from clear.[5]

The pro-test hawks had good reason to doubt the prime minister's intentions. Immediately after the Indian tests, there was a vigorous debate in Pakistan as to how Islamabad should respond. Many argued that Pakistan should answer India in kind. But a substantial body of opinion disagreed. On the evening of 12 May, after India had conducted its first test, the army chief Jehangir Karamat called the navy and air force chiefs for an informal discussion at his house. The navy chief, Admiral Fasih Bokhari, argued against testing on the grounds that, for once, Pakistan would be able to claim the moral high ground. He pointed out that Pakistan still had nuclear capability whether it tested or not and recommended waiting to see how the world reacted to India's move.

He was not alone in that view. When Sharif called a meeting of the Defence Committee of the Cabinet to discuss the issue, he arrived with the foreign minister, Sartaj Aziz, and one of his closest advisers, Chaudhry Nisar, who both urged restraint. Karamat took a middle course arguing that Pakistan should 'take it easy' and not make any precipitate decision. He said that Pakistan not only did not need to test but might also be able to benefit from not doing so. Sharif did not commit himself but others did. The minister for religious affairs, Raja Zafar ul Haq, told Karamat that if he did not approve a test the army rank and file would think they had a leader who lacked the courage to stand up to India. At the end of the meeting Sharif ordered that appropriate preparations should be put in place while he considered the matter further.[6]

Nawaz Sharif was giving serious consideration to not testing and it is noteworthy that his close confidantes wrote many of the press articles laying out the arguments for restraint. Take, for example, an article written by Mujeeb ur Rehman Shami who was one of the closest advisers to, and a speechwriter for, the prime minister at the time. On 13 May he wrote:

> it will not be a wise thing to give a tit for tat response to India's nuclear explosions. We must wait and see what international opinion does to India . . . to accede totally to the demands being made by the Pakistani Vajpayees [Atal Behari Vajpayee was the Indian Prime Minister who authorised the Indian tests] would be tantamount to providing India with an umbrella. If Pakistan joins battle with India immediately, this would distract world attention from India.[7]

Ever sensitive to signals being sent out in the national press, advocates of a Pakistani test complained that someone so close to the prime minister was promoting a policy of appeasement. But Mujeeb ur Rehman Shami carried on. As late as 26 May he wrote: 'If, as a last resort, we have to carry out a nuclear explosion then we will face whatever comes our way. But before this we must try to achieve our objectives without carrying out a nuclear explosion. This is only possible through active diplomacy.'[8] Another of the prime minster's inner circle, Altaf Hussain Quereshi, took a similar line. A long time supporter of Nawaz Sharif, he wrote:

> The greater interest of Pakistan lies in observing patience: we should not jump into the fire. Only political restraint and dignity will add to the difficulties of the Indian Government both at home and abroad. The tests have ruined India morally and its international status has been badly damaged. If the big powers want to stop Pakistan detonating its nuclear device we should do our homework and establish on what conditions we should agree with them. That way the nuclear option remains open to us whilst our economic and military strength continues to increase. We should play our cards skilfully and create an impression of our moral edge over India.[9]

But if there was to be no test then Pakistan wanted something in return. The prime minister laid out his terms. He asked for an end to US sanctions; the extension of International Monetary Fund (IMF) loans and security guarantees. President Clinton did try to meet some of these demands. US officials said that Pakistan's US $1.6 billion facility with the IMF could be trebled in size. They also offered to write off US $3 billion dollars' worth of bilateral debt. More importantly they said they were putting pressure on Japan to write off its bilateral debt that amounted to US $9 billion. On sanctions, President Clinton said that he would attempt to get them lifted but pointed out that the final decision rested with Congress. As for security guarantees, he could not even sound positive. Washington felt that any guarantee of Western military intervention in the event of an Indian attack on Pakistan would only encourage Islamabad to increase the level of the insurgency in Kashmir. Western diplomats in Islamabad tried to finesse the issue but there was no hiding the fact that substantive security guarantees would not be forthcoming. Clinton, however, did make an offer that he hoped Pakistan could not refuse. He sent General Antony Zinni of the US Central Command to meet Karamat and to offer him a huge conventional arms package in return for a no-test decision. Once again, however, there was always the risk that Congress could derail such a package and Clinton was in no position to make firm guarantees.

Taken as a whole, President Clinton's offer was substantial and could have resulted in a significant proportion of Pakistan's foreign debt being written off. But Nawaz Sharif was unimpressed. 'This is nothing,' he told a senior Finance Ministry official. 'If we test the whole world will give me money.' And if Sharif found the carrot unappetising, he was also unimpressed by the West's stick. The international response to India's tests was surprisingly muted. US sanctions were imposed but some European powers held back and no one really believed that the sanctions would be strong enough to make much impact in India. Sharif's foreign minister, Gohar Ayub Khan, and his finance minister, Sartaj Aziz, assured the prime minister that Pakistan could easily withstand a similar level of sanctions. Commenting on his decision to conduct the test, Prime Minister Sharif made no secret of the fact that this was a factor in his decision-making:

> The pressure was irresistible at home. It was mounting on the government every day, every hour. The world outside is not aware of the emotional feelings of the people of this region. I have been holding on and exercising the utmost restraint. But we were disappointed that the world community really failed to take a strong action against India.[10]

By the evening of 27 May Sharif had made up his mind. Karamat agreed. First, and perhaps foremost, he was reluctant to cause a rift between the army and the civilian government. India's increasingly bellicose statements about Kashmir also concerned him. The Indian home minister L. K. Advani had caused great anxiety in Islamabad when he said that India's tests had 'brought about a qualitatively new stage in Indo-Pakistani relations' and that India was 'resolved to deal firmly with Pakistan's hostile activities in Kashmir'.[11] But Karamat was not only guided by such matters of state. He had been stung by Raja Zafar ul Haq's suggestion that he lacked courage: no army chief, least of all a Punjabi one, likes to be called a coward.

And so, with Karamat and Sharif agreed, the scientists who had decamped to Balochistan put the final process in motion. As dawn broke over the Chagai mountains, Pakistan became the world's seventh acknowledged nuclear state.

History of the Programme

Many people have claimed to be the father of Pakistan's nuclear bomb. The struggle to take credit for the country's nuclear capability has lasted almost as long as the nuclear weapons programme itself. It is a story of personal rivalry and institutional division. On the one side was the Pakistan Atomic Energy Commission (PAEC) headed, during the crucial years, by its urbane chairman, Munir Ahmed Khan. And on the other was Abdul Qadeer Khan (no relation), whose talent for public relations means that he is popularly seen by Pakistanis as the man who gave their country the bomb. The Pakistani state has not hesitated to highlight A. Q. Khan's role: he is the most decorated citizen in the country. The official citation for one of his awards – the Hilal-i-Imtiaz – gives an impression of the almost cult status he enjoys in Pakistan:

The name of Dr Abdul Quadeer [sic] Khan will be inscribed in golden letters in the annals of the national history of Pakistan for his singular and monumental contribution in the field of nuclear science. Dr Khan has published more than 72 scientific research papers in the field of nuclear energy besides a well-known book on physical metallurgy.

In 1976, imbued with the supreme spirit of patriotism, he returned to Pakistan to serve his motherland and gave up a most lucrative job in the West. In the face of all sorts of threats he stoically remained steadfast in his resolve to work for the strength and solidarity of Pakistan.

His contribution in the field of nuclear physics has received national and international recognition by various agencies and organisations all over the world.

In recognition of his epoch-making contributions in the field of science, the President of the Islamic Republic of Pakistan has been pleased to confer on Dr Abdul Quadeer Khan, the award of Hilal-i-Imtiaz. 23 March 1989.[12]

A. Q. Khan's claim to be Pakistan's pre-eminent nuclear pioneer rests on the fact that, just six years after it was created, his Kahuta plant produced a vital bomb ingredient – enriched uranium. Dr Khan claims that the PAEC made just one contribution to the acquisition of the nuclear bomb – the production of uranium hexafluoride gas, a substance that is needed in the enrichment process. 'That's all they did,' he said. Indeed, he has gone so far as to claim that Munir Ahmed Khan was deliberately trying to undermine the programme and wanted to prevent Pakistan from acquiring nuclear capability because he had become imbued with the ideals of the UN's International Atomic Energy Agency where he had been on the Board of Governors for ten years. It is a remarkable claim and demonstrates the depth of the bitter rivalries within Pakistan's nuclear establishment.[13]

Given his long-running campaign to claim credit for all aspects of the weapons programme, A. Q. Khan was disturbed when, in June 1998, one of the PAEC officials who had conducted the nuclear tests, Samar Mubarakmand, returned from the deserts of Balochistan as a hero. A crowd of enthusiastic celebrants, who put garlands around his neck, fêted him at Islamabad airport. The international TV channels obtained the pictures and broadcast them. Within hours, A. Q. Khan's loyalists were ringing newsdesks complaining about the coverage. The real father of the bomb, they said, was A. Q. Khan. Suddenly the man who for decades had avoided Western journalists was available for on-the-record TV interviews in which he boasted about his role in the nuclear programme.

Samar Mubarakmand hit back and also started briefing the press. He said that building the bomb involved a chain with twenty-five separate links. The uranium had to be mined and refined. It had to be changed into uranium hexafluoride gas. Then there was the production of the warhead and the construction of the test site that had to be designed, built and monitored. A. Q. Khan, he argued, had provided one link in the chain – a golden link – but all twenty-five had been needed for success. To hit home his point, he added that while A. Q. Khan had indeed been at the test site in Balochistan on 28 May, he arrived only a few minutes before the tests and that the invitation for him to attend had been extended by the PAEC as a 'courtesy'. The PAEC he said (and not without a touch of condescension) thought he might like to 'see what a nuclear explosion looked like'.[14]

The controversies between A. Q. Khan and the PAEC continue but both sides do agree on one point: that the man who first got the programme underway was Zulfikar Ali Bhutto. It was Bhutto who, in 1965, made the famous remark that 'we will eat grass' to get the bomb. And, in 1969, he wrote that Pakistan had to obtain a nuclear bomb to match that of India:

> It will have to be assumed that a war waged against Pakistan is capable of becoming a total war. It would be dangerous to plan for less and our plans should therefore include nuclear deterrent ... If Pakistan restricts or suspends her nuclear programme, it will not only enable India to blackmail Pakistan with her nuclear advantage, but would impose a crippling limitation on the development of Pakistan's science and technology.[15]

Despite these statements of intent, Pakistan had still not yet seriously embarked on a weapons programme. By 1972, however, Zulfikar Ali Bhutto started taking more concrete steps. On 20 January he called a meeting of scientists in Multan. Beforehand he had contacted Munir Ahmed Khan, who was with the International Atomic Energy Agency (IAEA) in Vienna at the time, and asked him to prepare a report about the status of Pakistan's nuclear programme. Munir Ahmed Khan conducted a survey and concluded that the progress had been slight. Many at Multan agreed and the meeting was turbulent. Some of the younger scientists expressed frustration and complained that Pakistan was lagging in the nuclear field because the bureaucracy would never take any decisions. The nuclear programme, they said, lacked leadership. Bhutto responded in typical fashion. He drew on his ample stock of charisma to motivate the men in front of him. Pakistan, he said, had to guard against the possibility of India becoming nuclearised and he wanted 'fission in three years'. 'We can do it,' came back the enthusiastic response: 'you will have the bomb!'[16]

The fact that the Multan meeting took place in 1972 – two years ahead of India's first nuclear test – raises an interesting question. Pakistan has long argued that its programme was always entirely reactive to that of India and that had Delhi not pursued nuclear capability then neither would Pakistan have done so. Such an assessment is probably fair. By 1972, even if India had yet not tested, Bhutto was well aware that Delhi was trying to acquire nuclear weapons capability. And despite Bhutto's rhetoric at Multan the issue was only pursued with urgency after the Indian test of 1974. As A. Q. Khan has put it: '1974 was the turning point. It was then Bhutto got really serious.' [17]

Bhutto's problem was that Pakistan was nowhere near being able to build a bomb. The country's first, tentative step along the road to nuclearisation had been taken in the late 1950s with the establishment of the PAEC. Its programme was focussed on the peaceful use of nuclear technology and it immediately made plans to acquire an electricity-generating nuclear plant for Pakistan. But the process was painfully slow. Ten years after it was created, the PAEC had little to show for its efforts. There was just one very small research reactor that had been partly paid for by the United States under its Atoms For Peace programme.

In 1965 Pakistan's nuclear energy programme took a major step forward. The government reached an agreement with Canada to build a nuclear reactor outside Karachi. The Canadian plant became known by its acronym KANUPP (Karachi Nuclear Power Plant) and, by 1971, it was on stream. Since KANUPP produced not only electricity but also plutonium, which had potential military uses, the plant was put under international safeguards: to operate it Pakistan needed Canadian expertise, fuel and spare parts. [18] The dependence on Canadian co-operation proved to be critical. After the Indian test of 1974 international concerns about nuclear proliferation intensified. Pakistan complained bitterly that it should not be punished for India's test. But it was. Canada was worried that the safeguards on KANUPP were insufficient and it cut off all supplies of nuclear fuel to the plant.

With KANUPP's future in grave doubt, the PAEC focussed on France. Back in 1972, Pakistan had made a formal request to France for the procurement of a reprocessing plant. [19] The French government had been enthusiastic and a contract was signed. The IAEA gave its approval in February 1976 but, ultimately, the plant was never built. Despite the fact that, like KANUPP, the French plant would have been under international safeguards, the Americans feared that Pakistan could use the reprocessing plant to develop a nuclear weapon. The US concerns were so acute that the secretary of state, Henry Kissinger, personally visited Pakistan in an attempt to persuade Bhutto to cancel the deal. Bhutto insisted that Pakistan's nuclear plans were entirely peaceful. Kissinger, in turn, dismissed such assurances as an insult to American intelligence. Since Bhutto remained defiant, Kissinger tried his luck in Paris. Initially, the French insisted that their contract with Pakistan would be honoured but eventually, in 1977, President Giscard D'Estaing agreed to cancel it. A formal announcement was made in 1978. It was a huge blow to Pakistan which, once again, complained that the West was singling it out.

Given that the Canadian and French deals were always subject to international safeguards it was never clear exactly how Pakistan planned to use them for a weapons programme. Both plants would have produced plutonium but to have removed any of it from the site would have involved evading internationally administered monitoring systems. The cancellation of the French deal meant that even those hopes were dashed. Plutonium, however, is not the only substance that can be used for building a bomb. With the plutonium route closed for the foreseeable future Islamabad decided to go for the alternative: enriched uranium. And A. Q. Khan was just the man to make it.

Before he returned to Pakistan in March 1976, A. Q. Khan had been in Europe for fifteen years studying in Germany and Belgium. In 1973 he started work for the joint Dutch, German and British Urenco Consortium which had access to a uranium enrichment facility at the Almelo Ultracentrifuge Plant in Holland. There are two main recognised methods of enriching uranium to the levels necessary for a weapon: in a diffusion plant or by using ultracentrifuge technology. Almelo specialised in ultracentrifuge and, in 1974, A. Q. Khan wrote to Zulfikar Ali Bhutto saying that he not only had experience in uranium enrichment but would also be glad to return to Pakistan. His message provided Bhutto with hope that, despite the difficulties with Canada and France, the weapons programme could be resuscitated. In December of that year the two men met in Karachi and A. Q. Khan explained what he could do. On his return to Pakistan, A. Q. Khan spent a few unhappy months within the PAEC structure, before persuading Bhutto that he needed to work alone if he were to succeed in making weapons grade enriched uranium. The Kahuta laboratory was born.[20] And A. Q. Khan had no doubts about his mission. Throughout the 1980s he issued indignant statements insisting that Pakistan's programme was a peaceful one and had no military purpose. But after the 1998 tests he became more sanguine. 'I never had any doubts,' he said. 'I was building a bomb. We had to do it.'[21]

But how did he do it? Even Pakistani authors have said that, during 1975, A. Q. Khan plundered the Almelo facility to provide Pakistan with 'blueprints of the enrichment plant, design and literature relating to centrifuge technology and lists of suppliers, equipment and materials'.[22] In 1983 a Dutch court sentenced him, *in absentia*, to four years' imprisonment for attempting to obtain classified information. He was eventually cleared on appeal because of a technicality: he had not been properly served with a summons.[23] A. Q. Khan has always denied breaking any law and still strongly resents any suggestion that he was involved in espionage. Pressed on the point, he conceded that he was bound to pick up some knowledge at Almelo. 'As a technician I could understand how things there worked,' he said.[24] He has also said that the most useful knowledge he took away from Europe was not the technical data on ultracentrifuge techniques but information about European manufacturers in the nuclear sector. When Western governments tried to limit the supply of nuclear technology to Pakistan, A. Q. Khan was able to go directly to Western companies and make the purchases he wanted.[25]

And the Western governments did try. In 1975 the major powers had begun to co-ordinate their efforts. An international group was formed – the London Supplier's Group – which imposed an embargo on the supply of nuclear material and technology to any country which, like Pakistan, had not signed the Non-Proliferation Treaty.[26] In 1976 the US Congress had approved the Symington Amendment, which meant that US economic aid, credits and training grants could be blocked if Pakistan showed any sign of frustrating the US's non-proliferation objectives.[27] In April 1979 Washington did use the Symington Amendment to impose sanctions but later that year, on Christmas Day, something happened that effectively undermined the US non-proliferation efforts for the next decade: the Soviet invasion of Afghanistan. A new cold war frontline had been created and Washington could not defend it without

The five great powers look on as Pakistan and India force their way into the nuclear club.
The News, 30 May 1998.

Pakistan's help. President Carter lifted the Symington-related sanctions.[28] A new reality – the need for Pakistani support in combating the Soviets – meant non-proliferation became a secondary concern. By 1981 Pakistan and the US were discussing a US $3.2 billion aid package and the US secretary of state Alexander Haig told his Pakistani counterpart Agha Shahi 'we will not make your nuclear programme the centrepiece of our relations'.[29]

Even so, many export controls remained in place and Pakistan's procurement programme had to rely on extraordinary methods. The Pakistanis used fake front companies in Europe and the Far East. Some staff in the Pakistani embassies in France and Germany worked full-time on the procurement of nuclear supplies. Diplomatic bags were used to evade the prying eyes of Western customs officials.[30] Pakistani buyers regularly claimed that the items they had purchased were intended for civilian use when in fact they were destined for either the PAEC or Kahuta. It was a monumental – and costly – programme of clandestine activity and it worked.[31] However hard Western governments tried to stem the flow of nuclear technology, Pakistani buyers always seemed to be one step ahead.

Inevitably, Pakistan's buying spree attracted attention. By the late 1970s books were written about it[32] and there was even a TV documentary.[33]

The journalists and writers exposing Pakistan's nuclear programme hoped to put pressure on Western governments to step up their efforts to prevent nuclear proliferation. But what the journalists saw as a problem, Western companies considered an opportunity. A. Q. Khan has said that, as the publicity increased,

> . . . we received several letters and telexes. Many suppliers approached us with the details of machinery and with figures and numbers of instruments they had sold to Almelo. In the true sense of the word they begged us to purchase their goods. And for the first time the truth of the saying 'they would sell their mother for money' dawned on me. We purchased whatever we required.[34]

And Kahuta started making serious progress. By 1978, A. Q. Khan had enriched uranium to 3 per cent: the concentration needed for generating electricity. Moving to the next stage – 90 per cent – was a huge task. It involved creating thousands of intricately engineered, high-speed centrifuges connected by a complicated pattern of pipe work. As well as combating Western export controls, the scientists at Kahuta had to contend with earthquakes that knocked the centrifuges out of alignment.[35] But by 1982, just six years after he returned to Pakistan, A. Q. Khan had succeeded. He could produce enough highly enriched uranium for a bomb.[36]

After the withdrawal of the Soviets from Afghanistan in 1989, the Americans once again stepped up their non-proliferation efforts. The US Congress passed the Pressler and Glenn Amendments, which outlined far-reaching sanctions to prevent Pakistan obtaining nuclear capability. Both were used: in 1990 Pressler sanctions were imposed and after the 1998 tests, Glenn kicked into effect. But it was all too late. Pakistan was a nuclear state before Pressler and Glenn were even on the statute books.

Pakistan has often argued that the Western effort to deny it nuclear technology was discriminatory and that similar efforts were not made in relation to India. While it is fair to point out that Pakistan has indeed faced more international pressure over its nuclear programme, it is unreasonable to conclude that the West has simply been motivated by a desire to help India and harm Pakistan. Pakistan's programme was always likely to attract more international concern for two reasons. First,

India began to develop its technology far earlier – before an international non-proliferation regime was in place. Second, Pakistan relied on outside technology to a greater extent than India. Even A. Q. Khan has admitted that Pakistan could not have done it alone. In 1990 he told a Pakistani audience that:

> it was not possible for us to make each and every piece of equipment or component within the country. Attempts to do so would have killed the project in the initial stages. We devised a strategy by which we would go and buy everything we needed in the open market . . . .[37]

Having achieved the production of enriched uranium, Pakistan needed a warhead. It is on this point that the versions provided by A. Q. Khan and the PAEC clearly diverge.[38] Khan has said that he wrote to General Zia in 1982 saying that he had enriched uranium and now wanted to build a warhead. Zia apparently gave him the go-ahead and two years later the job was done. But, A. Q. Khan maintains, there was a twist to the tale: Zia's deputy, General G. M. Arif, 'stole' the papers and handed them on to the PAEC. Overnight, the PAEC was able to claim it could produce warheads – but using Kahuta's designs. A. Q. Khan says that the nuclear bombs that eventually went off in 1998 were all of his design.

The PAEC presents a very different story. It maintains that while A. Q. Khan had been given the task of enriching uranium, the PAEC was told to design the warhead back in 1974. The first cold tests took place in 1978 but the device was too big and had to be miniaturised. By 1983 the task was completed and the PAEC scientists were able to conduct a successful cold test on a usable design. But the PAEC was in for a shock. In 1984 it was told that Kahuta had also been working on a warhead and had also conducted a successful cold test. General Zia, perhaps afraid of penetration by foreign intelligence agencies, had embarked on a remarkably costly exercise – the creation of two warheads by two entirely separate parallel teams. The basic point of dispute is whether the PAEC tested before A. Q. Khan. The two sides present conflicting evidence but most neutral insiders believe the PAEC was the first to test.

So who is the father of the Pakistani bomb? Without A. Q. Khan Pakistan would probably still not have the bomb. The PAEC would, more likely than not, have remained wedded to the plutonium route and been frustrated by a whole barrage of international restrictions and monitoring regimes. But A. Q. Khan's claim that he and his Kahuta colleagues developed the nuclear bomb with virtually no help from other institutions does not stand up to close scrutiny. However great his personal contribution, the fact remains that building the bomb was a task that involved not just one but thousands of people.

Nuclear Doctrine

In August 1999 Delhi's Strategic Policy Advisory Board set out India's post-test nuclear doctrine. It described Indian intentions in the clearest possible terms. Even though ministers touted it as a discussion paper, few doubted that Delhi would act on its recommendations to develop an 'effective, credible nuclear deterrence and adequate retaliatory capability should deterrence fail'. This, the document said, would require a 'triad of aircraft, mobile land-based missiles and sea-based assets'.[39] There were also plans to develop effective early warning systems. Pakistan has not published any such document. The closest it came to doing so was in October 1999 when three veterans of Islamabad's foreign policy, Agha Shahi, Zulfiqar Ali Khan and Abdul Sattar, co-authored a newspaper article. In it they argued that nuclear weapons in South Asia do have deterrence value, that Pakistan does not need to match India's nuclear arsenal bomb for bomb and that Pakistan should not agree to no first use.[40]

General Musharraf has subsequently confirmed that approach saying that Pakistan does not plan to match India missile for missile; bomb for bomb. Indeed, he knows Islamabad cannot afford to do so. It is also clear that unlike India, which has to consider both Pakistan and China as potential enemies, Pakistan's nuclear weapons are all pointed at one country and one country alone: India. Because of its inferiority in conventional weapons Pakistan has always reserved the right to use nuclear weapons first. First use is the option of the weak and the possibility of a Pakistani first strike is its most effective method of deterring an Indian attack. There is, however, ambiguity about the point at which Islamabad would decide to go nuclear.[41] It is not certain, for example, how Pakistan would respond to an Indian offensive across the line of control in Kashmir. It is likely that the nuclear threshold would not be reached until a limited, or full-scale, invasion was mounted across the recognised international border.

Pakistani strategists point out that it is not simply a question of when they would cross the nuclear threshold. Before launching a nuclear attack Pakistan could just threaten to do so. It might also decide to back up that threat by conducting another nuclear test. There are many options. But while many in the West are calling for greater transparency about these issues so as to reduce the risk of accidental nuclear conflict, many in Islamabad argue that openness and clarity about its intentions would be counterproductive as it would weaken the deterrence effect of its nuclear arsenal and lead to greater instability.

Pakistan knows that in the event of a conflict, India would try to deny Islamabad the opportunity to launch a first strike: Pakistan must have the ability to launch a retaliatory, second strike. For Pakistan, then, a minimum credible deterrence requires a first- and second-strike capability. The absence of missile silos means that Pakistan's nuclear arsenal must be dispersed in so many locations that some weapons would survive an Indian first strike. According to Agha Shahi, mobility, dispersal, camouflage and deception can provide assurance of survival of at least a fraction of Pakistan's nuclear arsenal.[42] He is probably right. No Indian military commander is going to be able to tell the political leadership in Delhi that he can guarantee the destruction of Pakistan's nuclear capability in its entirety. Despite that, some Pakistani writers have suggested that Pakistan needs a submarine-based delivery system[43] but few believe the country could afford this.

The size of Pakistan's nuclear arsenal is constrained by a number of factors – not least the amount of fissile material produced in the country. According to the former army chief, General (Retd.) Aslam Beg, once it had built the bomb, Pakistan tried to create an arsenal around one third as large as that of India: 'India had fifty or sixty devices. We kept our stockpile in relation to that number.'[44] Many other sources confirm a similar ratio although the actual numbers vary considerably.[45] But in June 2000 reports emanating from the US gave a very different picture. Quoting unnamed US sources, the American TV network NBC reported that 'Pakistan's nuclear arsenal is vastly superior to that of India with up to five times the nuclear war heads, say US military and intelligence officials.'[46] The report said that the traditional understanding that Pakistan had around ten to fifteen nuclear weapons and India between twenty-five and a hundred should be reversed: it was Pakistan that had the larger number. It was also claimed that Pakistan 'appears far more capable than India of delivering nuclear payloads'. These views were backed up by comments from General Antony Zinni of the US Central Command. 'Don't assume that the Pakistani capability is inferior to the Indians,' he said. India, the Americans believed, 'has no nuclear-capable missiles and fewer aircraft capable of delivering a nuclear payload than Pakistan does'. The report, if accurate, may help to explain General Musharraf's repeated statements that Pakistan does not want to match India bomb for bomb. He is, perhaps, speaking from a position of strength.

Missiles

By 1983 or 1984 (depending whose version one believes), Pakistan had a serviceable nuclear bomb. The next task was to produce a missile to deliver it. Since 1947, Pakistan had relied on aircraft to fulfil this function although it didn't rule out the possibility of employing distinctly low-tech methods such as the bullock cart![47] Some Pakistani writers have suggested that Pakistan should continue to rely on aircraft to deliver nuclear weapons.[48] If India did agree to forgo missile development both sides would not only save money but also give each other a longer response time in the event of a nuclear conflict. Such arguments, however, stand no chance of prevailing. South Asia is already engaged in a missile race.

There are three Pakistani missile systems. First, there is the HATF programme. In February 1989 General Aslam Beg announced that two versions of the HATF had been successfully tested.[49] The most reliable version, built with Chinese co-operation, was HATF-1. First tested in April 1988, it was a relatively unsophisticated short range (just 80 kilometres) rocket which provided too few options for the military planners. HATF-2, tested at the same time, could travel 300 kilometres but it was unreliable, and efforts to generate a genuine intermediate range HATF-3 missile did not enjoy much success either.[50]

Recognising HATF's weakness, Pakistan decided that the system was incapable of carrying nuclear weapons and that it needed to acquire new, more reliable missiles. The PAEC asked China for help and received the Chinese M-11 missile. In Pakistan this was transformed into the Shaheen programme. The Shaheen-1 has a range of 500 kilometres and was first tested in 1999. Shaheen-2 has a range of 2,500 kilometres.

There is conflicting evidence about when Pakistan achieved the ability to put a nuclear warhead on a missile. Western experts believe the Shaheen became nuclear-capable in late 1999; by July 2000 PAEC sources were claiming that both the Shaheen-1 and Shaheen-2 were nuclear-capable. The Shaheen does seem set to become the mainstay of Pakistan's missile force but, as ever, A. Q. Khan has provided an alternative.

The development of missiles in Pakistan reflected the divisions that existed in the nuclear field. So while the PAEC looked to China, A. Q. Khan took a different route and approached North Korea. His Ghauri missiles are Pakistani-assembled versions of North Korea's Nodong missiles which have been supplied in parts by Pyongyang. In return, Pakistan sent money and rice to North Korea. The Ghauri-1 was test-fired in April 1998 when it was claimed that the missile could carry a warhead 1,500 kilometres.[51] Having acquired the basic technology, Kahuta characteristically made adaptations and improvements to the North Korean design. It devised, for example, a better guidance system – which was then shared with North Korea. The Ghauri-2 was meant to have a longer range – up to 2,000 kilometres – which would enable Pakistan to hit any target in India. However, the first test in April 1999 was a failure and the missile landed not in its intended spot but in Iran. Kahuta also has plans for a Ghauri-3 with a range of 3,000 kilometres.

Like Pakistan, India began its missile programme in earnest in the 1980s.[52] It has produced two nuclear-capable missiles: the Prithvi and the Agni. The former, based on Soviet designs, is a short-range weapon (150 kilometres) and was created with Pakistan in mind. The Prithvi-1 was first tested in February 1988 and went into production in 1994. According to Munir Ahmed Khan, it has already been deployed along the Pakistani border. Prithvi-2, which can reach 250 kilometres, was tested in 1996, and it is thought that a Prithvi-3 (350 kilometres) is now under development. The second missile system is the Agni which can take a bigger payload than the Prithvi and which has a much longer range of 1,500 to 2,500 kilometres. Agni-1 and Agni-2 were tested between 1989 and 1999 and India is currently working on an improved Agni-3 with a range estimated at between 3,500 and 5,000 kilometres. It is also, with Russian help, developing sea-based ballistic missiles which could be launched from submarines and which would have a range of 300 kilometres.[53]

The US has made efforts to control the proliferation of missile technology but seems to be having just as little success as it did with the bomb itself. Between 1991 and 1993, Washington imposed sanctions on Beijing on the grounds that M-11 technology had been transferred to Pakistan in breach of the Missile Technology Control Regime. But in the same way as the nuclear non-proliferation regime was undermined by the Soviet invasion of Afghanistan, different political considerations – in this case, the need to foster better relations with Beijing – came into play and the sanctions were dropped.

Command and Control

Given his role in creating Pakistan's nuclear device, and indeed his consistent defence of the value of nuclear weapons to Pakistan, it is surprising that one of the clearest possible warnings of the risk of an accidental nuclear detonation has come from none other than A. Q. Khan:

> . . . there is a real danger of nuclear war by accident due to technical failure or malfunctioning, or due to accidental detonation or launching of a nuclear weapon. Nuclear war can also be started by unauthorised action, human error or sheer madness. There is moreover, a great danger of a person or a group of persons responsible for launching nuclear weapons going insane and deciding to launch a nuclear attack on the enemy, eliciting immediate retaliation and a real holocaust.[54]

A former Pakistani foreign minister, Agha Shahi, has raised similar concerns:

Pakistan may well be confronted with a hair trigger alert situation. Neither country [India and Pakistan] has an effective early warning system against missile attack to detect intruding aircraft carrying nuclear devices. The flight time of their [India's] nuclear-armed short and medium range missiles is only three to less than ten minutes. Hence a 'launch-on-warning' system [launching missiles before incoming missiles arrive] that existed between the United States and the former Soviet Union – 25 minutes of warning time in the case of ICBMs [Inter Continental Ballistic Missile] and 15 minutes in that of their SLBMs [Submarine Launched Ballistic Missile] from deployed submarines – would elude Pakistan and India. The risk of nuclear strike by miscalculation or unauthorised use therefore cannot be but high, as the respective command and control systems cannot ensure real time instructions for alerting and launching nuclear forces.[55]

These warnings come from Pakistanis. Yet government officials and nuclear scientists in Islamabad tend to become indignant if Western officials or journalists express doubts about the efficacy of their command and control systems. To suggest that the systems might need improvement is to invite an accusation of racism.[56] 'Are you saying', the argument runs, 'that only white Europeans and Americans are capable of looking after nuclear devices? Are you claiming that Pakistani (or for that matter Indian) scientists and strategists are less capable or less responsible than their counterparts in the five declared nuclear states?' For all such rhetoric, there are serious issues at stake.

There are three routes to a nuclear holocaust in South Asia. First, either India or Pakistan might take a deliberate decision to use nuclear weapons. Second, the two countries might blunder into an accidental nuclear war. Finally, there is the possibility that the nuclear arsenal in either country could be the subject of unauthorised use.

In assessing the likelihood of a deliberately executed nuclear conflict the crucial issue is whose finger is on the button. In April 1999 – before the coup – a number of press reports stated that the chairman of the joint chiefs of staff was to be the strategic commander of the nuclear forces but that the final decision to use the bomb would be the prime minister's, acting on the basis of consultations with the National Command

Authority.[57] The release of this information may have been intended to soothe Western fears about the role of the military. In the context of Pakistani politics, however, while there would doubtless be a search for consensus, few in the army, and for that matter, few outside of it, believe that any civilian prime minister would be able to face down the military chief on such a crucial question at a time of crisis. Furthermore, it is difficult to imagine any Pakistani officer accepting an order to use the bomb from the prime minister without first clearing the instruction with the army chief.

Senior Pakistani officers are tight-lipped about their command and control structure but some say that the system is based on a dual key arrangement with one key under military control and the second under civilian control. If this is true then the prime minister and army chief would have to agree on the need to use nuclear weapons. Such a procedure, of course, makes little sense during periods of military rule in Pakistan. Presumably the army chief would be solely responsible for taking the final decision. When, for example, General Musharraf assumed power on 12 October 1999, he became chief executive (the equivalent of a civilian prime minister) and remained as chairman of the joint chiefs of staff and chief of army staff. He subsequently added the position of president. There was no one who could veto his decision.

Apart from the initial years under Zulfikar Ali Bhutto, the army has always enjoyed more control over the nuclear programme than civilians. Senior Pakistani analysts accept this. The deputy head of a government-sponsored think tank, the Islamabad Policy Research Institute, for example, has said: 'It's always been a military programme. If it came to it, the civilian Prime Minister would have to do as he's told by the military.'[58] Similarly, a veteran of Pakistan's nuclear programme, the former foreign minister Agha Shahi, has written: 'Control over Pakistan's nuclear capability has always remained with the military.'[59]

Washington seems to share that assessment. In the summer of 1998 the US responded to the Africa embassy bombings by launching cruise missile attacks on some militant training camps in Afghanistan. The fact that the missiles flew over Pakistani airspace raised the clear possibility that Islamabad could misinterpret the attack as the start of an Indian offensive. Consequently, General Antony Zinni arrived in Islamabad hours before the attack began. As the cruise missiles flew overhead, he gave assurances that the missiles were American and that Pakistan was not the target. During those crucial hours, he sat not with the Pakistani prime minster Nawaz Sharif, but rather with the country's most senior military officer at the time, General Karamat. Washington was in no doubt as to whose finger needed to be restrained.

Benazir Bhutto has famously complained that when she was prime minister she wasn't even allowed to visit a nuclear facility. Senior military officers who were serving at that time have insisted that had she wanted to go to any site she could have done so but that she had never asked. They have also pointed out that civilians have taken some of the key decisions relating to the programme. Zulfikar Ali Bhutto got the programme under way. As prime minister, his daughter Benazir decided to continue with it and, in 1998, it was Nawaz Sharif who opted for the nuclear tests.[60] But all these decisions were in line with the military's wishes. The real question is: would the military have ever accepted decisions that they didn't agree with? Few believe they would have done so.

While the ultimate decision, then, is likely to lie with the army chief, there is one body that might act to restrain him: the National Command Authority (NCA). The establishment of the organisation was announced in February 2000 and in May of that year officials spoke publicly about the 'inaugural, first meeting of the NCA'.[61] The body, it was stated, would include civilian members, and the foreign minister (a post always held by a civilian) would not only sit on the NCA by right but also act as its deputy chairman.[62]

For all the talk of a 'new' body holding its 'inaugural' meeting, the NCA had in fact existed, without any official acknowledgement, for a quarter of a century: it was set up in 1975 by Zulfikar Ali Bhutto to oversee the creation of Pakistan's bomb.[63] After the 1998 tests the military ordered a review of the NCA and completely overhauled the body. The military's pre-eminent role in nuclear policy was institutionalised: six of the nine places on the NCA were given to military officers. The NCA was given control of all aspects of Pakistan's nuclear programme including the Kahuta plant. It was also given authority over a new body, the Strategic Plans Division, which was established in the military's Joint

Services Headquarters and put in charge of managing the command and control system. It is responsible not only for ensuring that a nuclear weapon can be used when so ordered by the proper authority, but also for creating a system that will prevent unauthorised or accidental use.

Both Western and Pakistani officials have said that Pakistan's command and control system is more reliable than that of India but there is little published evidence to back up the claim. Proponents of the view, however, point to the role of the military in controlling the nuclear programme in Pakistan, which, they argue, has led to its incorporation into the country's overall defence forces in a way that has not happened in India. Without having more information about the arrangements put in place by the Strategic Plans Division however, it is impossible to reach a definitive conclusion.

There are good reasons for believing that a nuclear South Asia poses new, genuine threats that did not exist during the cold war. India and Pakistan have a disputed border, a history of armed conflict (even after the 1998 tests), and no early warning systems.[64] The case of the non-existent Israeli 'attack' cited at the start of this chapter demonstrates that, at best, false intelligence or, at worst, deliberate misinformation have already been fed into the decision-making process at a time of nuclear crisis.

There are many stories about moments when, during the cold war, the United States and the Soviet Union nearly launched nuclear missiles on the basis of false intelligence. Reliable information on these near-disasters is scarce: the governments in Washington and Moscow have never wanted to advertise their intelligence failures. Nevertheless, it is clear that some serious lapses in command and control did occur. A US early warning system, for example, once mistook a flock of geese and, on another occasion, the moon, for incoming Soviet missiles.[65]

In South Asia the risks are greater. As we have seen, Pakistan's nuclear decision-makers might have just three minutes to respond to an incoming attack. That time-scale puts pressure on both India and Pakistan to have operationally capable weapons ready to fire at all times. The extent to which this has already taken place is unclear. India's nuclear doctrine envisages 'assured capability to shift from peacetime deployment to fully employable forces in the shortest time . . .'[66] Pakistani scientists have said that they do not keep fully assembled nuclear weapons in times of peace. Asked whether it would take 'days or hours' to render the bombs operationally deployable, one senior Pakistani scientist replied: 'Less than that. Minutes.'[67] Having both sides ready to fire in such a short period of time evidently enhances the risk of a misinterpretation of the other side's intentions leading to a deliberate but unnecessary nuclear detonation. There is little indication that Pakistan and India are ready to agree on non-weaponisation but such an agreement could clearly enhance nuclear safety. Agha Shahi has estimated that if nuclear weapons were not deployed in forward positions then the warning time would increase from three minutes to between seven and ten minutes.[68]

An accidental detonation of a nuclear device cannot be ruled out but what, finally, of unauthorised use? The fact that Pakistan could suffer a devastating surprise attack opens up the possibility of the military chief, the civilian prime minister or both, being killed or rendered incommunicado before any decision on retaliation could be taken. In the event of such decapitation, who would have the authority to launch a retaliatory strike? Pakistani officials say the Strategic Plans Division has drawn up contingency plans but that they will not be announced publicly. There are two possibilities. The fall-back authority could follow the traditional pattern and rest with the longest standing service chief (army, navy or air force) who is formally considered the next most senior officer after the chairman of the joint chiefs of staff. Alternatively, the chain of command could be restricted to the army, in which case, the authority would presumably be passed on to the longest serving corps commander. There is a similar lack of clarity in India. The August 1999 Indian nuclear doctrine stated that 'The authority to release nuclear weapons for use reside in the person of the Prime Minister of India, or the designated successor(s).'[69] Again, the identity of the 'designated successor(s)' is not revealed.

Even if the Strategic Plans Division has laid down contingency plans, there is no escaping a tension between protecting a nuclear arsenal against a first strike and ensuring that it is sufficiently tightly controlled to prevent unauthorised use. A policy of dispersing the nuclear arsenal in a time of crisis is bound to weaken command and control and put weapons in the hands of relatively junior officers. PAEC sources insist that all Pakistan's nuclear weapons have codes without which the warheads cannot be armed. In the case of airborne missiles, for example, those codes would not be given to an aircraft crew until the plane was outside Pakistani airspace. But, as some Pakistani analysts have acknowledged, the command and control structure has to take into account the possibility that an Indian first strike would disable at least some elements of the nuclear leadership. Consequently, not only the authority to launch an attack but also the technical know-how of doing so must be passed down the chain of command. That plainly increases the possibility of unauthorised use.[70]

Yet, for all these dangers, many Pakistanis are remarkably relaxed about command and control issues. Senior figures in Pakistan, such as the retired army chief Aslam Beg, have argued that the risks are exaggerated:

> The Presidents of Russia and America carry a black box and are in a constant state of alert: that is not the case with us. We don't need that kind of elaborate command and control system and state of readiness. In our context we have a period of tension and confrontation; a period of conventional forces deployment. At that stage there may be a need to activate the National Command Authority. But that comes at the last stage.

> And in any case, he said: 'I don't think India would be stupid enough to take advantage by attacking facilities without any reason, just to damage our programme.' It is a breathtakingly casual assessment.[71]

Does South Asia's Deterrence Work?

While many in the West deplored the 1998 nuclear tests and spoke of growing regional instability, the majority of Pakistanis and Indians said they felt more secure because of their nuclear capability. They see their weapons as a deterrent that will prevent nuclear attack and probably a conventional war as well. Those who want to establish that the nuclear weapon has been a deterrent point to three Indo-Pakistani disputes: Exercise BRASSTACKS in 1987, the Kashmir crisis of 1990 and Kargil in 1999.

In 1987 India began some ambitious, large-scale military exercises. Islamabad noticed the development and asked the Indian military for reassurances. They were not forthcoming. The Indian prime minister, Rajiv Gandhi, did tell his Pakistani counterpart, Mohammed Khan Junejo, that the exercises were only for training purposes but Pakistani suspicions were increased when they noticed the Indians creating arms and fuel dumps in forward positions. Pakistan's intelligence agencies warned the military leadership in Rawalpindi that Exercise BRASSTACKS could be transformed into Operation BRASSTACKS and advised the deployment of armoured formations in the border areas. The Pakistan army agreed. Having noticed that deployment, India, with unrelenting inevitability, started planning its response. Rajiv Gandhi even discussed a pre-emptive ground attack on Pakistan, including a strike on its nuclear facilities, to forestall any moves Islamabad might be planning. Eventually, the two countries managed to open direct communication and to de-escalate the crisis.[72]

According to India's official report into the Kargil war, Pakistan did use a nuclear threat during BRASSTACKS: 'In 1987 Pakistan conveyed a nuclear threat to India at the time of Operation BRASSTACKS. This was officially communicated by Pakistan's minister of state for foreign affairs Zain Noorani, to the Indian ambassador in Islamabad.'[73] Pakistani officials have always denied this. General K. M. Arif, who was the vice chief of the Pakistan army throughout the BRASSTACKS episode, has said that nuclear weapons never came into play during the crisis. 'There was no operational deployment of nuclear weapons,' he said.[74] But he also argues that since both sides knew about each other's nuclear capability there was added pressure to defuse the crisis. Some Indian sources take a similar view. In the crucial meeting when Rajiv Gandhi was considering a possible Indian pre-emptive strike, an adviser from the Ministry of Defence argued: 'India and Pakistan have already fought their last war, and there is too much to lose in contemplating another one.'[75] Although some of the evidence is contradictory, it is reasonable to conclude that nuclear weapons did have some deterrence value.

In 1990 another crisis emerged with both India and Pakistan stepping up the rhetoric, and the level of military activity, in Kashmir. By this time the insurgency in Kashmir was well underway and the Indians were trying to suppress it. There was intense artillery shelling over the line of control and the Indians continued to pour troops into Kashmir. It has been argued that the two countries came close to nuclear war at this time. The US became convinced that during the crisis the PAEC was ordered to assemble at least one nuclear weapon. The US also believes that nuclear-armed F-16s were deployed in the South of Pakistan. The US assumed these moves were linked to the situation in Kashmir. According to General (Retd.) Aslam Beg, though, there was another aspect to the situation. Pakistani intelligence agents had reported that Israeli planes would take off from Israel, refuel in India and then strike Kahuta. India was to provide the co-ordinates. Pakistan sent a message to Delhi. It was blunt in the extreme: 'If Israel hits us, you shall be held responsible and Bombay will cease to exist.'[76]

The one point these accounts agree on is that Washington had detected a move up the nuclear escalatory ladder. The US deputy national security adviser, Robert Gates, was dispatched to Islamabad. He urged restraint, revealed the US information about the nuclear weapons and threatened sanctions. He told Islamabad that the US had carried out extensive war-gaming exercises and that, in every one of them, Pakistan lost. He then went to India and said Pakistan had been persuaded to reduce the level of the insurgency in Kashmir by closing down militant training camps. The crisis passed. But afterwards a US official described it as: 'the most dangerous nuclear situation we have ever faced . . . it may be as close as we've got to a nuclear exchange'.[77]

Since there is no definitive evidence that nuclear weapons were deployed in 1990 it is difficult to assess the deterrence effect they might have had. But, once again, they were certainly in the background and all the decision-makers on both sides were well aware of each other's capability. As he looked back on 1990, General (Retd.) Mirza Aslam Beg said: 'The fear of retaliation lessens the likelihood of war between India and Pakistan. I can assure you that if there were no such fear we would have probably gone to war in 1990.'[78] It is only fair to point out that many in Pakistan's military establishment believe that both Beg and the US have grossly exaggerated the extent of the crisis in 1990. One explanation that helps reconcile some of these differing perceptions is that

Pakistan had for some years been working on modifications to the F-16 with a view to making them capable of carrying nuclear weapons. In 1990 it succeeded. Having noticed this development, the US misinterpreted it and mistakenly saw it as a deliberate threat linked to the deteriorating situation in Kashmir.

In 1999, in the midst of the Kargil crisis, Kashmir was once again causing international concern. Pakistani troops had crossed the line of control and were occupying territory on the Indian side. The Indians, humiliated by the failure to spot the incoming troops and embarrassed by their difficulties in removing them, considered the possibility of a full-scale invasion across the international border. Another option was to cross the line of control elsewhere in Kashmir and hold it until negotiations returned the situation to the *status quo ante*. In the event, India relied on international diplomatic pressure to force a Pakistani withdrawal. This restraint won Delhi much international praise. Again, the nuclear issue was in the background. In the midst of the crisis, the religious affairs minister and leader of the Pakistani Senate, Raja Zafar ul Haq, openly threatened the use of nuclear weapons. Even if this was a wild bluff, his statement had to be taken seriously: throughout the crisis he had attended all the meetings of Pakistan's Defence Committee of the Cabinet. On 30 June he told his fellow senators, 'We made it [the nuclear weapon] for what? It is not something sacrosanct to be kept in an arsenal even if your own throat is cut by someone. It is our duty and right to defend ourselves with all the military might at our disposal.' Four days later, India responded in kind. Brajesh Mishra, a senior adviser to Prime Minister Vajpayee, said: 'we will not be the first to use nuclear weapons. But if some lunatic tries to do something against us, we are prepared . . .'[79] Again, it is difficult to claim that the nuclear issue did not play some role in the two sides' decision-making processes.

Many of those involved in the Kargil affair insist there was no nuclear element to the crisis and certainly no nuclear deployment. But it is interesting to note that nuclear considerations were very much in the mind of the Pakistani prime minister, Nawaz Sharif. In the third week of June, with the Kargil crisis at its height, he told a Pakistani columnist of his fear that the conflict could lead to a nuclear war. He said that since the West was against Pakistan, India could be given high technology defence equipment that could disable Pakistan's electronic weapons systems and radar. He said that the conflict could lead to the complete destruction of both countries but that if it came to a matter of national survival he would have to use the bomb.[80] And in his account of the Kargil conflict, the former special assistant to the US president, Bruce Riedel, has recorded how the Americans believed that the Pakistan military was preparing nuclear tipped missiles – possibly without even telling the civilian leadership.[81] Speaking after the Pakistani withdrawal from Kargil, Pakistan's foreign minister Sartaj Aziz told the Senate: 'It was our nuclear deterrence that kept India at bay.'[82] For its part, the Indian leadership calculated that not extending the war to the international borders not only carried diplomatic benefits but also reduced the risk of the nuclear factor coming into play. Again, it seems that the very existence of the nuclear arsenal did have a deterrence effect.

Pakistan: A Proliferator?

Pakistani officials have repeatedly said that their non-proliferation record is 'impeccable'.[83] To emphasise its credentials (and in response to US pressure), Pakistan amended an existing law to tighten control further over the export of nuclear technology in March 1999. The revised law required the PAEC to approve any export of 'nuclear substances, radioactive material . . . equipment used for the production, use or application of nuclear energy, including generation of electricity'.[84]

The new law, however, could not conceal the fact that, for all the claims about having an impeccable record, Pakistan had already shared some of its nuclear secrets – with China. Little has been published about the extent of Sino-Pakistani nuclear co-operation[85] and the issue is so sensitive that Pakistani officials – normally prone to leak plenty of information – clam up when asked about it. Western officials, however, believe that the two sides have extended their diplomatic and political relationship into close collaboration in the nuclear field. Some have suggested that China and Pakistan have even shared nuclear tests. They believe that some of the Chinese tests in the mid-1990s were in fact of

Pakistani devices. All these claims have regularly been denied in Pakistan, though interestingly, Zahid Malik, who had very close access to A. Q. Khan, stopped short of an outright dismissal of the possibility of Pakistani tests in China. He wrote: 'some agencies have mentioned Lop Nor in the Province of Sinkiang in the People's Republic of China. Without debating the truth of these news items and rumours, it can definitely be said that Pakistan has made at least successful simulation experiments in the laboratory . . .'[86] But even if Pakistan and China have enjoyed close nuclear co-operation, any accusations of proliferation should be aimed at China. Since China's programme pre-dated that of Pakistan, any Sino-Pakistani links would have been for Pakistan's, rather than China's, benefit.

If Pakistan becomes a proliferator the most likely beneficiaries would be Saudi Arabia, the Gulf States and North Korea. Some Indian authors and many Western journalists have raised fears that a Pakistani bomb would be made available to other Muslim countries. Such fears were particularly acute when Pakistan was just starting its programme. Evidence emerged that Zulfikar Ali Bhutto had approached Libya and Saudi Arabia for funds to finance the project. It was assumed that any such financing would be followed by demands to share the fruits of the research.[87] Some Indian strategists have even gone so far as to suggest that a Pakistani bomb might in itself encourage Muslim countries to abandon the idea of the nation state and to form a religious union:

> A nuclear armed Islamic state may vitalise the psychological links among Islamic countries though this in turn might lead to an erosion of loyalty to their own country of origin and residence. In other words while strengthening Islamic solidarity around the world, reliance on a common nuclear strategy based on an Islamic bomb could weaken the unity and cohesion of national societies. At the same time the possibility of fissile material from Pakistan sources being passed on to groups like the PLO should seriously be considered.[88]

In Pakistan such claims are (justifiably) denounced as hostile propaganda. Nonetheless, in 1999, there were indications of Saudi interest in Pakistan's nuclear programme. In August of that year the Saudi crown prince and defence minister, Sultan Bin Abdul Aziz, visited the Kahuta plant amid tight security and great secrecy.[89] Pakistani spokesmen, anxious that their non-proliferation credentials were being undermined, vehemently denied the visit even took place. It is still far from clear what the Saudi defence minister was doing. He might have been interested in some of the weapons (nuclear or conventional) produced at Kahuta but more likely than not he was just indulging in a piece of political tourism.

He was not the only foreign official interested in Kahuta. In May 2000 an Urdu-language Pakistani newspaper reported that the minister of information from the United Arab Emirates, Shaykh Abdullah Bin Zayid Al Nahyyan, had also visited the plant. The prince reportedly asked A. Q. Khan what help Pakistan could give him in the nuclear field. Khan replied that he could not present the UAE with 'a bomb on a platter' but said that he could help train UAE manpower.[90] One US ambassador to Islamabad, Bill Milam, has confirmed that some Gulf States have expressed interest in buying a bomb but he has also said that there is no evidence to suggest that Pakistan was willing to sell.[91] And while it is true that Pakistan and North Korea have worked together closely on the Ghauri missile, there is no evidence to back up claims that Pakistan and North Korea are also co-operating in the nuclear field.

Indeed, Islamabad has an interest in holding on to its nuclear knowledge and remaining one of only eight nuclear powers. There is a risk, however, that proliferation could occur without government authorisation. The US has indicated that this is in fact happening. In June 2001 the US deputy secretary of state Richard Armitage voiced concerns about 'people who were employed in the [Pakistani] nuclear agency and have retired'. He suggested that such people were already working in North Korea.[92] Pakistani officials may also feel tempted. With a foreign debt of nearly US $40 billion and a growing population, the country has a desperate need for foreign currency. Ever since the 1998 tests everyone has known that it is in possession of a highly marketable asset: its nuclear know-how. If the economy continues to fail, the temptation to sell nuclear technology could become irresistible.

Pakistan matters. The country's proven nuclear capability means that its stability concerns not only those who live there but also the international community as a whole. The fears of many in the West are encapsulated in a single, potent phrase: 'the Islamic bomb'. It was first coined by a Pakistani, Zulfikar Ali Bhutto, but many Pakistanis now react adversely to its use. They point out that no one talks of the US or Russia having 'the Christian bomb' or India possessing 'the Hindu bomb'.

The controversial American historian Samuel Huntingdon has written about the risks of conflict between the world's major civilisations, including the Islamic world and the West. He has argued that the differences between Islam and the West are both centuries old and bitter. He has claimed that while: 'Muslim states have had a high propensity to resort to violence in international crises,' the West simultaneously has an increasing tendency to worry about, and to make military plans to counter, the 'Islamic threat'.[93] Huntingdon quotes Bhutto in defence of his theory that a clash of civilisations is a real possibility. As he sat in his prison cell awaiting execution, Bhutto wrote his memoirs and recalled his decision to build the bomb: 'We know that Israel and South Africa have full nuclear capability. The Christian, Jewish and Hindu civilisations have this capability. The Communist powers also possess it. Only the Islamic civilisation was without it, but that position was about to change.'[94]

Many Islamic radicals have embraced Huntingdon's thesis. The leader of Lashkar-e-Toiba, for example, Hafiz Mohammed Seed, has said: 'We believe in the clash of civilisations and our Jihad will continue until Islam becomes the dominant religion.'[95] Reluctant to keep such intellectual company, however, many liberals in the West and in Pakistan have rejected Huntingdon's views. His sweeping statements about the world's leading civilisations, they complain, ignore the competing political traditions within them. And civilisation loyalties, they argue, play less of a role in determining political behaviour than old-fashioned national interest.

The 11 September attacks on New York and Washington gave Huntingdon's ideas a new lease of life. While President Bush talked of launching a 'crusade', senior figures in the Islamic world warned that Huntingdon's prediction of a clash between Islam and the West was not so outlandish after all. The British prime minister Tony Blair may have insisted that the bombing of Afghanistan was not part of an attack on Islam, but other Western leaders seemed to see things differently. The Italian prime minister Silvio Berlusconi, for example, offered the view that Christian culture was intrinsically superior to that of the Islamic world. 'We must be aware of the superiority of our civilisation', he said, 'a system that has guaranteed well-being, respect for human rights and, in contrast with Islamic countries, respect for religious and political rights.'[96]

Many Muslims' response to the events on and after 11 September was also guided by civilisational loyalties. When the bombing campaign against Afghanistan began, the sympathy many Muslims had felt for the victims in the United States was outweighed by their concern for the Afghan people. Throughout Pakistan people spoke of their sense of outrage that their Muslim brothers in Afghanistan were being attacked by the United States. Of course, many Christians in the West shared these feelings. Nonetheless it is indisputable that most Westerners responded differently to the events on and after 11 September to most people in the Islamic world. One litmus test was the attitude people took towards Osama Bin Laden. When President Bush and Prime Minister Blair asserted that Bin Laden was responsible for the 11 September attacks, most people in the West were inclined to believe them. Among Muslims (whether or not they were living in the West), an overwhelming majority argued that since he was sitting in a cave in Afghanistan, Bin Laden was in no position to organise the attacks on the World Trade Center and the Pentagon. Western leaders, they demanded, should provide some evidence to back up their claims.

That religious, cultural and civilisational affiliations did play a significant role in determining people's reactions to the attacks on the United States and Afghanistan should have come as no surprise. The same factors had affected people's reactions to the Pakistani nuclear tests in May 1998. In the West most people responded with concern and anxiety. In the Muslim world, by contrast, there was rejoicing, and even signatories of the Comprehensive Test Ban Treaty, such as Saudi Arabia, congratulated Pakistan for showing that the Muslim world was capable of matching the West's scientific achievements. Ironically, some of the most enthusiastic supporters of the Pakistani tests came from the very madrasas who have consistently rejected modern science.

None of this proves that a military clash between the West and the Islamic world is inevitable. It does, however, suggest that should a radical Islamic government ever gain control of a nuclear device the implications would be serious. Many Muslims would hope that, at last, they had a means of putting pressure on the West to stop what they perceive to be the continued exploitation of developing countries in general and the Islamic world in particular. And many in the West would fear that the Islamic radicals' possession of the bomb would at best destabilise the existing international security regime and at worst be used against the West in an irrational burst of bitterness. The prejudices on both sides are deep. And in the context of nuclear doctrine, perceptions are everything.

7 Democracy

We have had sham democracy.

—General Musharraf, October 1999

Democracy has few supporters in Pakistan. The army has been in power for nearly half the country's existence and it is commonplace for senior officers to complain wistfully that the politicians are too incompetent and too corrupt to govern. 'The Western type of parliamentary democracy', Ayub Khan once wrote, 'could not be imposed on the people of Pakistan.'[1] Many civilians have shared his jaundiced view. The feudal landlords, the bureaucrats, the intelligence agencies and the judiciary have all shown a reluctance to accept, never mind promote, the rule of law. Pakistan's urbane, sophisticated elite and the country's Islamic radicals do not agree about much. But on the issue of democracy they can find common ground. 'It's a good thing', said Lashkar-e-Toiba's spokesman Abdullah Muntazeer speaking of Musharraf's 1999 coup, 'the parliament was un-Islamic and he's got rid of it.'[2]

There have been three periods of civilian rule in Pakistan. The first, between 1947 and 1958, began with independence and ended when the chief of army staff, Lt. General Ayub Khan, mounted the country's first military coup. The second, between 1971 and 1977, belonged to Zulfikar Ali Bhutto. The third, dominated by Bhutto's daughter, Benazir, and her rival, Nawaz Sharif, started after General Zia's death in a plane crash and came to an end when Musharraf took over. Many Pakistanis explain the failure of democracy to take root by bemoaning the poor quality of their elected leaders. In reality, there are more fundamental reasons for the fact that no civilian leader in the country's entire history has ever completed his or her term in office.

1947–1958

Mohammed Ali Jinnah wanted Pakistan to be a constitutional, parliamentary democracy informed by Muslim values. Many Pakistanis believe that, had he lived longer, Jinnah would have been able to transform his vision into reality. Yet, for all his ideals, Jinnah never behaved democratically. From the moment of independence he effortlessly assumed control of all the key levers of power in Pakistan. He was not only the governor general but also the president of the Muslim League and the head of the Constituent Assembly. As the founder of the nation, Jinnah had such massive personal authority that few dared to challenge him and, even if they did, a momentary scowl was enough to silence his most determined opponent. Arguably, the new country, lacking any political institutions, needed a strong leader. But even Jinnah's most ardent supporters concede that the concentration of power in his hands set an unfortunate precedent.[3] When Jinnah died, thirteen months after Pakistan was born, there was no one capable of filling the vacuum he left behind.

Pakistan's first generation of politicians were inexperienced men faced with truly daunting challenges. As well as being confronted by fundamental national issues such as the demand for provincial rights, the status of the Urdu language and the role of Islam in the new state, they had to deal with the millions of Muslim refugees who arrived in Pakistan at a time when an economy barely existed. It was perhaps inevitable that power inexorably slipped into the hands of the only people capable of delivering any semblance of governance: Pakistan's small cadre of highly educated civil servants. As Jinnah's aide-de-camp, Ata Rabbani wrote:

> . . . our senior politicians had little experience of the running of a government for they had spent most of their lives criticising governments in power. Now saddled with the responsibility they took the easy way

out. Instead of applying themselves to the task and working hard to learn the ropes they relied on the advice of senior bureaucrats.[4]

Masters of the new nation, the bureaucrats had little interest in organising elections, and political developments following Jinnah's death can only be described as chaotic. There were no fewer than seven prime ministers in ten years. Liaquat Ali Khan (50 months in office) was assassinated. His successors, Khwaja Nazimuddin (17 months); Mohammed Ali Bogra (29 months); Chaudri Mohammed Ali (13 months); Shaheed Suhrawardy (13 months); I. I. Chundrigar (2 months); and Firoz Khan Noon (11 months), all became victims of palace intrigues. Out of the seven only two, Liaquat Ali Khan and Suhrawardy, could have claimed to have had any substantial popular support. Throughout the 1950s two archetypal bureaucrats, Ghulam Mohammed and Iskander Mirza, brazenly abused their powers as head of state to make or break governments. In April 1953 Ghulam Mohammed set an unfortunate precedent when, citing the government's failure to resolve 'the difficulties facing the country', he dismissed Khwaja Nazimuddin and installed Bogra in his place. When Bogra responded by trying to limit the governor general's power, Ghulam Mohammed simply dismissed him too. And so it went on.

As the politicians and bureaucrats bickered and quarrelled, the military became increasingly involved in political decisions. This was partly a result of the civilians' failure to govern effectively: the military was frequently called upon to fulfil functions that should have been performed by the police. Indeed, the army soon became the only organisation capable of keeping order on the streets and in 1953 the relative competence of the military and the civilians became plain for all to see. In February law and order in Lahore started to deteriorate when some Islamic-based parties demanded that the Ahmedis be declared non-Muslims. Within a matter of days, a frenzied anti-Ahmedi campaign spread throughout Punjab. By March the civilian government had to admit that it had lost control of events and it asked the army to take over Lahore. The martial law administrator in the city, General Azam Khan, soon managed to restore calm. But he did not restrict himself to the Ahmedi question. Before he relinquished his martial law powers he undertook a number of other initiatives including a highly popular 'Cleaner Lahore Campaign'. In the

Heads of state, 1947–present

Name	Title	Dates
Mohammed Ali Jinnah	governor general	Aug 1947–Sept 1948
Khwaja Nazimuddin	governor general	Sept 1948–Oct 1951
Ghulam Mohammed	governor general	Oct 1951–Aug 1955
Iskander Mirza	governor general/ president	Aug 1955–Oct 1958
Mohammed Ayub Khan	chief martial law administrator/president	Oct 1958–Mar 1969
Mohammed Yayha Khan	chief martial law administrator/president	Mar 1969–Dec 1971
Zulfikar Ali Bhutto	chief martial law administrator/president	Dec 1971–Aug 1973
Chaudhry Fazal Elahi	president	Aug 1973–Sept 1978
Mohammed Zia ul Haq	chief martial law administrator/president	July 1977–Aug 1988
Ghulam Ishaq Khan	president	Aug 1988–July 1993
Wasim Sajjad	acting president	July 1993–Nov 1993
Farooq Leghari	president	Nov 1993–Dec 1997
Rafiq Tarar	president	Dec 1997–June 2001
Pervez Musharraf	president	June 2001–

Chief executives, 1947–present

Name	Title	Dates
Liaquat Ali Khan	prime minister	Aug 1947–Oct 1951
Khwaja Nazimuddin	prime minister	Oct 1951–Apr 1953
Mohammed Ali Bogra	prime minister	Apr 1953–Aug 1955
Chaudhri Mohammed Ali	prime minister	Aug 1955–Sept 1956
H. S. Suhrawardy	prime minister	Sept 1956–Oct 1957
I. I. Chundrigar	prime minister	Oct 1957–Dec 1957
Firoz Khan Noon	prime minister	Dec 1957–Oct 1958
Zulfikar Ali Bhutto	prime minister	Aug 1973–July 1977
Mohammed Khan Junejo	prime minister	Mar 1985–May 1988
Benazir Bhutto	prime minister	Aug 1988–Aug 1990
Ghulam Mustafa Jatoi	caretaker PM	Aug 1990–Oct 1990
Nawaz Sharif	prime minister	Oct 1990–Apr 1993
Balkh Sher Mazari	caretaker PM	Apr 1993–May 1993
Nawaz Sharif	prime minister	May 1993–July 1993
Moeen Quereshi	caretaker PM	July 1993–Oct 1993
Benazir Bhutto	prime minister	Oct 1993–Nov 1996
Meraj Khalid	caretaker PM	Nov 1996–Feb 1997
Nawaz Sharif	prime minister	Feb 1997–Oct 1999
Pervez Musharraf	chief executive	Oct 1999–

eyes of many, martial law in Lahore proved that while the civilian politicians consistently failed to provide effective government, the military could deliver. By asking the army to manage a political crisis the civilians had undermined their own authority. When Ayub Khan took over in 1958 few were surprised, and many were relieved, that the failed democratic experiment was over.

Zulfikar Ali Bhutto

In 1963 Zulfikar Ali Bhutto met President J. F. Kennedy in Washington. After a day of talks Kennedy looked at Bhutto and said: 'If you were American you would be in my cabinet.' 'Be careful Mr President,' Bhutto replied, 'If I were American you would be in my cabinet'.[5] Bhutto was a deeply ambitious man whose undoubted abilities were matched by his massive ego. Had he been operating in the American environment he might have fulfilled his potential. But in Pakistan, with no checks on his executive power, he ran amok. His choice of role model said it all. Bhutto's bookshelves were filled with biographies of Napoleon Bonaparte, a man who rose to power by appealing to the people above the heads of the ruling establishment and who invited personal disaster because he overreached himself. The parallels between Bhutto and his hero are striking.

The radical programme put forward by Bhutto's Pakistan People's Party (PPP) in the 1970 elections inspired many Pakistanis. But its heady mix of socialist and Islamic idealism was an illusion. Even before the elections it was clear to PPP insiders that the party was little more than a vehicle for Bhutto's personal ambitions. His control of the party was absolute and he demanded complete loyalty from even the most senior party officials. By the time Bhutto had come to power, those who dared to disagree with him found they were not only removed from their party positions but, in many cases, thrown into prison as well.[6] Bhutto had little difficulty in replacing them with sycophants who could be relied upon to do his bidding. Having dealt with the party, Bhutto moved on to the civil service. Arguing that he wanted to make the bureaucracy more responsive to the wishes of the government,[7] he swept away legal provisions that gave civil servants job security. The consequent politicisation of the civil service has remained one of Bhutto's most damaging legacies.

Like his predecessors (and his successors) Bhutto resisted demands for greater provincial autonomy. But the force with which he did so was unique. Within months of taking over, he provoked a fierce clash between Islamabad and the provinces. When the provincial government in Balochistan insisted on its right to take local decisions, Bhutto brushed it aside and installed a PPP administration. He then deployed the army, ordering it to open fire on any 'miscreants' who continued to resist the authority of the Pakistani state. It was the start of a four-year campaign in which 80,000 troops were deployed in Balochistan. The army's presence there served clear notice to all Pakistan's provinces – those who challenged Zulfikar Ali Bhutto would pay the price.

While Bhutto relied on the army to assert his authority in the provinces, he simultaneously undermined it by creating a new paramilitary outfit, the Federal Security Force (FSF). It was widely seen as Bhutto's personal army and the generals in Rawalpindi bitterly resented it. That Bhutto used the FSF to scare his opponents is beyond dispute, but establishing the extent of the force's excesses is difficult. Certainly, at the time, many Pakistanis believed that the organisation was routinely carrying out murders, and leading independent historians have concluded that the FSF was involved in several incidents in which Bhutto's political enemies were harassed and even killed.[8]

Bhutto's regime consistently relied on heavy-handed tactics. When, in 1972, he decreed that the state should nationalise plants in the iron and steel, chemical, cement and energy sectors there was inevitably bitter resentment among those who lost their property. Characteristically, Bhutto met their opposition with brute force. Leading industrialists were imprisoned or asked to surrender their passports.[9] Opposition politicians met the same fate. The memoirs of a former Pakistani air chief, Asghar Khan, give a flavour of Bhutto's authoritarian tendencies.[10] When, after his retirement, Asghar Khan went into politics and opposed Bhutto's government, the FSF responded with characteristic force. Virtually every time Asghar Khan tried to organise a political rally he faced violent mobs who, together with the local police, would try to prevent the meeting from taking place. On some occasions Asghar Khan and his party workers were fired on and one party worker was killed in such an incident. Asghar Khan himself received death threats and was repeatedly arrested. The treatment meted out to him revealed not only Bhutto's intolerance but also his insecurity: at no stage did the former air chief enjoy significant levels of popular support and he never posed a serious political threat to the government.

Bhutto's downfall came after the 1977 elections. Despite his being the favourite to win, the election was rigged in Bhutto's favour. Many methods were used to influence the result. Local government officials managed to remove some opposition candidates' names from the ballot paper by citing various technical breaches of the election law. In constituencies where there was a contest, the police and FSF routinely disrupted opposition campaign rallies. While such tactics were not unexpected, the rigging of the actual result did cause surprise and widespread anger. Independent analysts have pointed out that while 63 per cent of the electorate had voted in Pakistan's first national elections of 1970 (for which there had been considerable public enthusiasm), the 1977 turnout of 80 per cent was implausibly high.[11] The extent of the rigging remains uncertain but it is clear that Bhutto, or his supporters, not only tried to influence the result but also, to a considerable extent, succeeded.

The aftermath of the 1977 elections brought out the worst in Zulfikar Ali Bhutto. Anti-government protestors who were demanding a new poll were shot dead and opposition politicians arrested. As the public protests grew out of control, Bhutto tried to shore up his increasingly vulnerable position by reaching out to the Islamic parties, decreeing that drink, gambling and nightclubs would be banned. It was a futile effort. The public pressure on Bhutto to step down became so overwhelming that he was forced to call in the army to keep control of the major cities. But the army sided with the protestors and General Zia ul Haq took over.

The execution of Bhutto at 2 a.m. in the morning of 4 April 1979 on a charge of attempted murder has been described as the final blow to democracy in Pakistan. In truth democracy was already in serious trouble before Zia decided that the only way to neutralise his most formidable political opponent was to have him killed. Like many other politicians in postcolonial countries, Zulfikar Ali Bhutto wanted to govern for life. As a young man he never doubted that he would become

Pakistan's leader and once he had fulfilled his destiny he did not believe that anyone else in the country was able to match him. His failure to hang on to power is one of the clearest indications of just how difficult it is to manage Pakistan. The nationalists in the provinces, the pro-democracy campaigners and, most importantly, the army were strong enough to frustrate Bhutto's ambitions.

The Return of the Civilians

On 17 August 1988 General Zia's Hercules C-130 plummeted to the ground shortly after taking off from Bahawalpur airport. Remarkably little is known about the crash. The Pakistani investigation produced little information of any value but concluded that Zia was probably the victim of sabotage. According to Sardar Muhammad Chaudhry, who at the time was the head of Special Branch in Lahore, the enquiry established just one significant point: the plane's debris was spread over a very restricted area. That suggested that the Hercules had neither exploded in the air nor been hit by a missile. The investigators wondered whether the crew had been debilitated by nerve gas.[12] One rumour about the crash which refuses to die down, is that a box of mangoes, loaded on to the plane at the last moment, was in fact packed with explosives but there is no evidence to substantiate the story.

Zia's death ushered in the third period of democratic rule in Pakistan and many in the country had high hopes that they were embarking on a new era. There was to be no shortage of elections in the post-Zia period: the people were called upon to vote in 1988, 1990, 1993 and 1997. But it is surely significant that the turn-out figures of those elections steadily declined from 50 per cent in 1988 to 45 per cent in 1990 and to 40 per cent in 1993. The official figure for 1997 was 35 per cent although the true figure was probably closer to 26 per cent. By 1999 disillusionment with democracy had become so deep that General Musharraf's coup was welcomed as a blessed relief.

Most Pakistanis believe that the post-Zia politicians have been self seeking, corrupt and unprincipled. They have a point. Two leaders, Benazir Bhutto and Nawaz Sharif, dominated the 1990s. There were important differences between them. As the daughter of Zulfikar Ali Bhutto and heir to a large estate in Sindh, Benazir Bhutto had her roots in the traditional feudal system. Nawaz Sharif, by contrast, was from a self-made industrial family that had steadily accumulated massive wealth ever since 1947. By the end of the twentieth century, Nawaz Sharif and his family owned the biggest industrial empire in the country. There were other dissimilarities. Bhutto, bitter about her father's execution, was always afraid of and hostile to the army. Sharif, who had served as General Zia's chief minister in Punjab, was closer to the military establishment. And while Bhutto was educated in the West and well aware of secular liberal ideas, Sharif was, as his image-makers put it, 'made in Pakistan' and far more sympathetic to the religious parties. As prime minister he made a point of paying his respects to Zia's memory by visiting his grave on anniversaries of his death. It is also worth remembering that the rivalry between the Sharifs and the Bhuttos had a history. In 1972 the Sharif family's factory, the Ittefaq Foundry, was nationalised by Zulfikar Ali Bhutto. It was a bitter blow to the Sharifs and they have never forgotten it.

There were also dissimilarities in the way the two leaders governed. While both encouraged state-owned radio and television stations to broadcast blatant pro-government propaganda, Benazir Bhutto was generally more tolerant of press criticism than Sharif. She also showed more interest in human rights issues and never attacked the non-governmental organisations in the way that Sharif did. On religious matters, Bhutto clearly had a more modernist outlook than Sharif but, like her father, she was always willing to pander to the religious lobby for short-term political advantage.

For all these differences, however, the similarities of the Sharif and Bhutto administrations are striking. Neither pushed through any significant reforms. In national policy terms, their most important shared characteristic was their ability to run up huge levels of foreign debt. By the time General Musharraf took over in 1999, Pakistan owed foreign creditors over US $25 billion and debt servicing had become the largest component of the annual budget. Most of this had been incurred in the 1990s. Between 1947 and 1970 Pakistan ran up a modest foreign debt of just US $3 billion dollars and the country was widely cited as one

of the developing world's best users of foreign loans.[13] By the time
General Zia was killed in 1988 that foreign debt had increased substantially – to US $13 billion dollars.[14] General Zia and, to a lesser extent,
Zulfikar Ali Bhutto may have been profligate but their appetite for foreign loans was dwarfed by that of Nawaz Sharif and Benazir Bhutto.

Between 1988 and 1999 Pakistan borrowed, and failed to repay, US
$13 billion.[15] Of course, nobody knows how much of that money was
stolen but Pakistan has remarkably little to show for it. Major spending
projects in the 1990s included the Lahore–Islamabad motorway and the
opulent Prime Ministerial Secretariat in Islamabad. A substantial amount
was also spent on Nawaz Sharif's 'Yellow Cab' scheme in which tens of
thousands of taxis were distributed to towns and villages throughout
the country. Theoretically, the beneficiaries were meant to pay back the
cost of the taxis but few have ever done so. Taken together, these
projects cost around US $3 billion. That leaves US $10 billion unac-
counted for. Some of that money went towards the provision of
electricity and irrigation projects but few can claim that the democratic
governments used their foreign loans with even a modicum of prudence.
Indeed, these figures do not reveal the full extent of their profligacy. In
1998, after the Sharif government froze all the foreign currency bank
accounts in the country, it transpired that the democratic governments
had spent several billion dollars of foreign exchange that had been lying
in personal bank accounts in the domestic banking sector.

Both Nawaz Sharif and Benazir Bhutto face corruption cases in
Pakistan's courts. Both claim that their trials are politically motivated
and, in a sense, they are right. Pakistani governments have always used
selective accountability to target and discredit political opponents. Nevertheless, many Pakistanis believe that, whatever the motivation for their
trials, both Bhutto and Sharif are indeed guilty of corruption. They
point out that despite all the rhetoric about improving the lot of the
poor, both lived in considerable luxury. Sharif's opulent estate at Raiwind near Lahore and Benazir Bhutto's ancestral home in Larkana in
Sindh both boast private zoos. Both prime ministers also accumulated
valuable foreign properties. The extent of the Sharif family's foreign
holdings has never been clear, though Nawaz Sharif was embarrassed
throughout his second term in office by the revelation that he owned

some undeclared, luxury flats on London's Park Lane. The deeds of the properties were in the name of offshore companies based in the British Virgin Islands but Sharif never denied that he possessed them. Indeed, it would have been difficult for him to do so. His son, Hasan Sharif, was living in one of the flats while he studied at the London School of Economics and freely admitted that he did not have to pay any rent for his accommodation. While the Sharifs aspired to the glamour of Park Lane, Bhutto's husband, Asif Zardari, remained true to his rural roots and opted for a country estate in the UK. The Pakistani press generally refers to his nine-bedroomed house with 350 acres of land as 'Surrey Palace'. Both Zardari and Bhutto have denied buying the house. In August 2001, however, the British authorities handed over various artefacts from the house to the Pakistani High Commission. The objects included plates and antiques bearing inscriptions stating that they had been presented to Asif Zardari and Benazir Bhutto.[16]

That the Sharifs and the Bhuttos are multi-millionaires is beyond dispute. The methods used to acquire their wealth are far less apparent. The Sharifs made most of their money in the 1980s and 1990s. After his business was nationalised, Nawaz Sharif's father, Mohammed Sharif, realised that to protect his interests he would need political as well as financial muscle. Once Zulfikar Ali Bhutto had been removed from power in 1977 the possibilities opened up. Mohammed Sharif told his youngest son, Nawaz, (who showed no interest in, or much aptitude for, business) to join the Zia administration. In June 1979 the Sharifs were rewarded for their services to the Zia regime by having their company denationalised and handed back to them. From that moment the Sharif family fortunes soared.

Many of the Sharifs' assets were acquired through bank loans. As early as 1991 the Pakistani press was printing detailed stories alleging that senior politicians were pressurising banks into giving them multi-million-dollar bank loans.[17] Eventually, in 1998, Nawaz Sharif acknowledged that he did have many outstanding loans and vowed to pay back everything he owed. In a televised address to the nation in June 1998, he said that the Ittefaq group of companies would offer its assets to the banks so that all the loans could be recovered.[18] The credibility of the pledge was hardly helped by another promise he made in the same speech. He said that his family would contribute to his government's austerity campaign by eating only one meal a day. Aware of their prime minister's penchant for earthy Punjabi food, most Pakistanis remained sceptical.

They were right to be so. While the Sharif family did surrender over thirty-three industrial units to the state, subsequent investigations established that most of them were inoperative and worthless. Pakistani press reports revealed that the value of the units given up by the Sharifs would not cover the amount owed to the banks. The precise size of the debt remains contested but when General Musharraf's military regime published a list of major loan defaulters in November 2001 it put the total amount owed by politicians and businessmen at 211 billion rupees (over US $3 billion) and the Sharifs' liability at over 3 billion rupees (US $50 million).[19] The Pakistani press generally quotes figures of two or three times that amount.[20] The situation is complicated by internal disputes within the Sharif family, various members of which have taken each other to court because it is not clear which branches of the family own which parts of the empire. Consequently, when Nawaz Sharif announced that he would pay off his loans, it was far from obvious which debts were his direct responsibility and which fell to his relatives.[21]

Despite being an extremely rich man, Nawaz Sharif showed little enthusiasm for paying tax. According to his 1996 nomination form for the National Assembly elections, he paid under US $10 in income tax between 1994 and 1996.[22] Sharif's supporters argued that this was entirely legal and pointed out that in the same period he had paid nearly US $60,000 in wealth tax. Nevertheless the sums were remarkably small for a man whose family controlled assets worth hundreds of millions, if not billions, of dollars.

Benazir Bhutto and Asif Zardari are also accused of using their political power for personal gain. The most serious charges against them concern kickbacks. In Benazir Bhutto's first term, Zardari was widely known as Mr 10 Per Cent. By the second term Zardari, like the Pakistani people, was suffering from the effects of inflation: he had become known as Mr 20 Per Cent. The couple still face a number of cases in the Pakistani courts. The first to reach some sort of conclusion was the SGS Cotecna case. It concerned a Swiss-based company that, in 1994, was hired by Benazir Bhutto's government (in which Zardari was a minister) to improve the system for collecting customs duties on imports. Determined to discredit his most popular political opponent, Nawaz Sharif ordered his second government to investigate the SGS Cotecna case. His enquiry concluded that Bhutto and her husband had been paid millions of dollars' worth of bribes as kickbacks for awarding the contract. Some of the most damning evidence came from a Geneva magistrate Daniel Devaud. He said he had found Swiss bank accounts in the name of offshore Virgin Islands companies, which were in fact controlled by Asif Zardari. Furthermore, he said that Benazir Bhutto had used money from one of the accounts to buy a diamond necklace worth US $175,000. Devaud charged Zardari with money laundering and formally recommended that the Pakistani authorities should indict Benazir Bhutto as well. He then froze accounts containing US $13 million dollars and seized the necklace, which he found in a Swiss safe deposit box.

In 1999 the Lahore High Court, hearing the SGS Cotecna case convicted Bhutto and Zardari of corruption, fined them US $8 million dollars and sentenced them to five years in prison. But in March 2001 the conviction was overturned because a British newspaper, the *Sunday Times*, printed transcripts of some audiotapes, which suggested that the outcome of the trial was fixed.[23] The source of the tapes was Abdul Rahim, a senior official in the Intelligence Bureau, who claimed that he had been ordered to tap the phone of Abdul Qayoom, the judge hearing the case. The tapes suggested that Qayoom had come under heavy pressure from senior officials in the Sharif administration. In one passage, recorded two days before he gave his verdict, the judge was heard discussing the outcome of the case with Sharif's most senior anti-corruption investigator Senator Saif ur Rehman:

Justice Qayoom: 'Now you tell me what punishment do you want me to give her?'

Saif ur Rehman: 'Whatever you have been told by him.'

Justice Qayoom: 'How much?'

Saif ur Rehman: 'Not less than seven years.'

Justice Qayoom: 'No, not seven. Let us make it five years. You can
  ask him. Seven is the maximum punishment and nobody awards
  maximum.'
Saif ur Rehman: 'I will ask and tell you.'

According to Abdul Rahim, the Intelligence Bureau then recorded a
second conversation that took place after Saif ur Rehman had discussed
the matter with Nawaz Sharif:

Saif ur Rehman: 'When I enquired about five or seven he said I should
  ask you why you would not like to give them the full dose.'
Justice Qayoom: 'It is not like this. You know it is never done like
  this by anybody. It would look odd.'
Saif ur Rehman: 'OK if you think five. But whatever he said I have
  told you.'

When the tapes were published Justice Qayoom issued a statement
saying he believed they were 'doctored'.[24] His credibility, however, was
severely undermined by the revelation that, in 1998, Nawaz Sharif
had given explicit orders that Qayoom and his wife be provided with
diplomatic passports despite the fact that, technically, High Court judges
did not qualify for them. Musharraf's military regime accepted the
quashing of the verdict but indicated that it still wanted to pursue
the case and would start another trial afresh.[25] Both Nawaz Sharif and
Benazir Bhutto have, of course, consistently denied the corruption
charges they face.

It is, perhaps, only fair to point out that neither Bhutto nor Sharif
governed in easy circumstances. Having enjoyed a decade of unre-
strained power under Zia ul Haq, the army and the civil service resented
the democratic governments. Aitzaz Ahsan, the interior minister in
Benazir Bhutto's first administration, has related how the senior bureaucrats in his ministry exhibited their disdain for the Pakistani public.
Whenever Ahsan had constituents visit him in his office he noticed that,
as soon as the meeting was over and the guests had departed, the three
most senior civil servants working under him developed a habit of
spraying his room and the corridors with air freshener.

The Pakistani establishment had other, more serious methods of
displaying their dislike for the politicians. In the first place successive

presidents were able to use General Zia's notorious Eighth Amendment, which allowed the head of state to dismiss a sitting government. The amendment was employed to remove two of Benazir Bhutto's governments and one of Nawaz Sharif's. Throughout the 1990s the judiciary consistently failed to stand up to these displays of executive power. Indeed, Pakistan's judiciary has never provided a strong defence of civilian rule. In 1955, following the decision of governor general Ghulam Mohammed to dissolve the Constituent Assembly and remove the government of Mohammed Ali Bogra, the Supreme Court declared: 'That which otherwise is not lawful, necessity makes lawful.'[26] The doctrine of necessity has been used on many subsequent occasions to justify the removal of various governments retrospectively. Generals Ayub Khan, Yayha and Zia all browbeat the courts into validating their coups. In 1999 General Musharraf followed their example. Having been bullied into declaring an oath of loyalty to his regime, the Supreme Court judges once again validated an illegal assumption of power and, as in the past, they relied on the doctrine of necessity.

Many entrenched interests, then, have contributed to the failure of democracy in Pakistan. But the army remains the single most significant obstacle to the survival of elected governments. Throughout Benazir Bhutto's first administration the chief of army staff, General Aslam Beg, repeatedly sought credit for his decision that following Zia's death, the civilians would be 'allowed' to rule again. The implication was that the politicians should have been grateful for the military's generosity. Bhutto never showed any willingness to challenge this utterly undemocratic and presumptuous attitude.[27] Given that the army had executed her father, it was perhaps understandable that she decided, in her own words, 'to give them whatever they wanted'.[28] Asked in one news conference whether she intended to cut the defence budget she replied, 'Not unless we want the army to take over again'.[29] Bhutto's foreign affairs adviser, Iqbal Akhund, who witnessed her government operate at first hand, concluded that: 'On Afghanistan, Kashmir and India, the government was faced with very complex and thorny issues, but the decision-making in all of these had been taken over by the army and the intelligence agencies in Zia's time and there, in the ultimate analysis, it remained.'[30] It is a fair assessment and Bhutto was neither sufficiently confident nor strong enough to take the generals on.

Sharif, particularly during his second administration, showed greater determination to establish control over the military. Indeed, from the moment he was re-elected in 1997, he concentrated on making his political position impregnable. He began by undermining the parliamentarians by forcing through a Constitutional Amendment that required all members of the National Assembly to vote according to party lines. He then bullied the press by arresting journalists who wrote against him and by ordering tax investigations into those editors who continued to print critical articles. He also tackled the judiciary. When the Supreme Court tried to hear a case in which he was a defendant, Sharif's supporters ransacked the building and terrified the judges into backing down. He moved on to tackle the presidency and forced Farooq Leghari to resign. By 1998 the only significant power centre that remained untouched was the army. And when the chief of army staff, General Jehangir Karamat, voiced concern about the government's performance, he was also forced to step down. But in confronting the army, Sharif had gone a step too far and eventually Karamat's successor, General Pervez Musharraf, responded in the traditional manner. He forced Sharif out of office at gunpoint.

The Intelligence Agencies

The civil service, the judiciary, the politicians and the army have all played their part in undermining Pakistani democracy. But so, too, have Pakistan's many intelligence agencies. The two most important civilian intelligence agencies are the Intelligence Bureau (IB) and the Special Branch of the police, both of which are answerable to the prime minister. Of the two, the IB is the better financed and more powerful. Officially, it is responsible for counter-intelligence but in reality it spends most of its time monitoring and disrupting the activities of the political opponents of the government of the day. There are also two military agencies. Military Intelligence or, as it is more usually known, MI, is almost entirely focussed on internal army matters. Run by a major general, it is formally charged with gathering information that the armed forces might require to wage war. In practice the MI is the ears and eyes of the army chief who uses it to gauge morale within the armed forces and to ensure that discipline is maintained.

All three of these organisations are dwarfed by Pakistan's premier agency, the Inter Services Intelligence (ISI). Often described as a state within the state, the ISI is headed by a lieutenant general and its senior positions are filled by officers who are seconded to the organisation for two to three years before being transferred back to the army. When it was founded the ISI reported directly to the three service chiefs.[31] Theoretically that has now changed and the ISI is answerable to the prime minister. In recent years, however, most director generals of the ISI have usually felt that their first loyalty is to their fellow generals and, in practice, have worked for the chief of army staff.

When the ISI was created in 1948 there was a reasonably clear distinction between its role and that of the IB. While the IB looked after domestic issues, the ISI focussed on external threats to security. In practice, that meant that the ISI concentrated on India. Since then, the ISI has broadened its remit and it is now responsible for monitoring internal and external threats to the security of the state. The first major opportunity for the ISI to extend its area of competence came with the 1971 war in East Pakistan. Since General Yayha's regime did not trust the Bengali IB officers, he relied on the ISI to generate intelligence in East Pakistan. After the war, Zulfikar Ali Bhutto substantially increased the ISI's funding.[32] He wanted to bolster the organisation for two reasons. First, he sought more information on regional and international politics so that he could better formulate his foreign policy. Second, he wanted the ISI to spy on his political opponents. In the run-up to the 1977 elections, the agency was asked to produce assessments of the likely results and to bug the phones of some of Bhutto's opponents.[33] After Bhutto's removal from power, General Zia did not hesitate to use the organisation to harass Bhutto's own party, the PPP.

Indeed, the Zia years were the ISI's heyday. The organisation took over management of the anti-Soviet campaign in Afghanistan and was given responsibility for distributing the billions of dollars pumped into the struggle by the US. The American funding, and the Mujahideen's success in forcing a Soviet withdrawal, transformed the ISI into one of the best financed and most powerful of all Pakistan's state institutions. It has been a significant force in the land ever since.

The Soviet retreat from Afghanistan gave the ISI huge confidence and in 1990 it turned its attention to domestic politics. Still loyal to Zia's agenda, the agency actively conspired to prevent Benazir Bhutto from being re-elected to prime ministerial office. A former director general of the ISI, Lt. General (Retd.) Azad Durrani, has recorded in a Supreme Court affidavit that he was instructed by Zia's successor as chief of army staff, General Aslam Beg, to provide 'logistic support' to the disbursement of funds to Benazir Bhutto's opponents in the Islami Jamhoori Ittehad coalition led by Nawaz Sharif. According to Durrani, the ISI opened some cover bank accounts in Karachi, Rawalpindi and Quetta and deposited money into them. The sums were not small. One account in Karachi was credited with over two million dollars and smaller amounts were then transferred to other accounts on the instruction of the chief of army staff and the election cell in the presidency. The recipients of the money included Nawaz Sharif (US $58,000), the Jamaat-e-Islami (US $83,000) and a whole series of anti-PPP politicians based in Sindh.[34]

When this activity came to light General Aslam Beg brazenly told the Supreme Court that: 'It would be in the fitness of things that further proceedings on this matter are dropped.' As to the substance of the allegations, he did not deny that the ISI had been involved in disbursing the funds. Rather, he argued that such activity was quite normal, proper and lawful: 'A full account was maintained of all the payments made by the DG ISI and no amount was misappropriated or misused.'[35]

The ISI's undemocratic tendencies are not restricted to its interference in the electoral process. The organisation also played a major role in creating the Taliban movement. When the Taliban leader, Mullah Mohammed Omar, took the city of Kandahar in 1994 his Taliban forces were joined by Pakistani fighters. Many were religious students of the madrasas in Balochistan and NWFP who went to Afghanistan with the support of the ISI. It is also quite possible that the ISI not only organised the deployment of some regular Pakistani troops to support the Taliban's offensive but also paid off the Taliban's opponents in Kandahar to ensure the city fell without much of a fight.[36] By the time the Taliban took Kabul in 1996, the ISI was making little secret of its involvement in installing a new Afghan government. According to one reliable eyewitness in the city, a senior ISI officer was openly performing basic command and control functions on behalf of the Taliban.[37]

The ISI has also become deeply involved in Kashmir. From the very start the Kashmiri insurgency was encouraged and, to some extent, organised by the ISI. The agency has become close to many of the militant groups that fight in Kashmir and there are also deep links between the ISI and the militant organisations active within Pakistan itself. Indeed, the ISI has helped to create much of the Islamic militancy that General Musharraf is now trying to combat and the extent to which he has control of the more radical elements of the ISI remains unclear.

Many Western authors portray the ISI as an organisation that is completely out of control and pursuing its own policies. But it should not be forgotten that the agency's efforts to back the Taliban and to foster the Kashmiri insurgency were state-approved. In neither case was the ISI proceeding without the sanction of the military and political leadership. For all the dire predictions about the agency acting as a major obstacle to Musharraf's reform programme, it is quite possible that the ISI will continue to execute government policy albeit with considerable misgivings. The fact that many of the ISI's senior officers do not work in the organisation on a permanent basis, but are seconded from the army, clearly works in Musharraf's favour and limits the growth of an institutional 'ISI view'. That is not to deny that some in the ISI are reluctant to change. In the first few weeks after 11 September, for example, there were credible reports that the ISI was continuing to supply the Taliban with weapons despite Musharraf's decision to abandon Mullah Omar.[38] Similarly, many ISI officers had misgivings about General Musharraf's decision in early 2002 to arrest Islamic radicals who had been active in Kashmir. It could hardly be otherwise. Just months before, the ISI had been supplying and training the very same people. But there is no indication to date that the ISI is running a concerted or successful campaign to overturn Musharraf's policies.

Feudalism

As they contemplate the failure of democracy in their country, many Pakistanis are apt to blame the major landowners. The 'feudals', as they are known, are routinely denounced as pretentious, self-interested, unprincipled, reactionary hypocrites who constitute a huge obstacle to social and democratic development. The Pakistani historian and political scientist Iftikhar H. Malik, for example, argues that having been given land and power by the British, the feudals have managed to hang on to both ever since by using a combination of cunning and brute force. 'A new generation of aristocrats', Malik writes, 'with degrees from privileged Western universities have seen to it that their near monopoly of national politics and the economy remains unchallenged. In lieu of political support to a regime, whether military or quasi-democratic, feudalists exact favours through ministerial positions, loans and property allocations.'[39] Malik argues that in periods of both military and civilian rule the feudals have been the power behind the throne.

It is certainly true that many major landholders in Pakistan have not only remained close to the seat of power but also continued to command extraordinary degrees of loyalty in their own localities. One story about a leading Sindhi feudal, Pir Pagaro, helps demonstrate the remarkable authority that some feudals enjoy. When Pakistan's military ruler Ayub Khan visited the pir in the 1960s, he advised the field marshal to walk one step behind him. Otherwise, he warned, my followers may think you consider yourself equal to me and they could harm you. It was not an idle comment. His devotees would have been quite capable of mounting a frenzied attack on any one who challenged the pir's supremacy.

Throughout Pakistan the rural elite carries out a number of functions that would, in most other countries, be seen as the responsibility of the courts, police or other administrative bodies. Take, for example, Nawab Bugti. Each day tribesmen arrive at his fort in Dera Bugti and ask him to resolve various legal issues. Should a Bugti tribesman, for example, want to get divorced, all he has to do is sit before the nawab and throw a stone on the ground three times saying the words 'I divorce her. I divorce her. I divorce her'. Given that the whole procedure takes a few minutes and does not cost anything, it is hardly surprising that the slow, expensive and notoriously corrupt civil courts in Balochistan rarely hear any divorce cases.

The nawab is even able to order trials by fire. Anyone forced to undergo this ordeal has to wash his feet in the blood of a goat and then walk seven paces along some burning embers. If his feet blister the nawab declares him to be guilty. The nawab only orders a trial by fire if he feels he cannot decide which party to a dispute is telling the truth. Despite being a highly educated man, the nawab insists that the trials by fire (they happen about once a month) never fail to identify the guilty and exonerate the innocent. While feudal landowners in Punjab and Sindh would, for the most part, no longer be strong enough to order trials by fire, the fact remains that they are widely respected in their own areas and do settle local disputes without reference to the courts. Many feudal leaders order punishments – such as a physical beating – for those they consider guilty of a crime.

Defining the feudals with any precision isn't easy and the issue has given rise to an academic debate in Pakistan. By most accounts the 'classic' feudals are the major landowners in southern Punjab and Sindh. There is also widespread agreement that many of these grandees derive their power not only by virtue of the sheer size of their estates but also by claiming spiritual powers. As well as distinguishing between economic and religious sources of feudal authority, some analysts differentiate between the feudal leaders of Sindh and Punjab and the tribal leaders who hold sway in Balochistan and, to a lesser extent, NWFP. They point out that the tribal leaders do not have unquestioned title over all their tribe's lands and, unlike the feudals, cannot be certain that their power will be passed down to their sons.

For some analysts, however, such distinctions are largely irrelevant. S. Akbar Zaidi, for example, maintains that the mode of production in most of today's agricultural sector is no longer feudal but capitalist. He argues that Britain's imperial government in Delhi introduced a number of reforms such as the recognition of private property and the establishment of agricultural commodity markets, and that, as a result, 'capitalist agriculture has been the leading trend and it is not possible to label Pakistan or Pakistani agriculture today as feudal'.[40] Such arguments, however, miss the point. When Pakistanis complain about the feudals they are protesting about the undoubted fact that the rural elite is able to ignore the state institutions and use religion, their landholdings and the tribal system to wield huge amounts of power.

Nevertheless, those who insist on a strict definition of feudalism do make one important point. Many of those described as feudals in reality have quite small landholdings and enjoy very limited authority in their home area. Take the case of Ghulam Mustafa Khar, one of the founders of the Pakistan People's Party, a close political ally of Zulfikar Ali Bhutto and, at one stage, his chief minister of Punjab. Khar's conduct has often been described as typically feudal and one of his wives, Tehmina Durrani, wrote a book about him entitled *My Feudal Lord*.[41] She recounts how Khar, in his personal as well as his political life, was a violent tyrant. For many, he provides a clear example of everything that is wrong with feudalism. But Khar was never a major landowner. Even if his family was powerful in his hometown of Muzaffargarh, he never enjoyed the same loyalty or adoration as some of the major religious landowners in Sindh. The source of Khar's power was initially his close relationship with Zulfikar Ali Bhutto and, in later years, his status as a national political leader. Khar, in short, behaved like the worst kind of feudal lord even if he was little more than a Punjabi farmer.

For all the definitional difficulties, it is indisputable that successive Pakistani parliaments have been filled with landowners and tribal leaders who have not hesitated to use their power to protect their own interests. Despite considerable pressure from the IMF, for example, no Pakistani government has ever been able to impose a tax on agriculture. It is also beyond dispute that some feudal landowners have held on to their authority by blocking the government's attempts to foster social and economic development in their areas. In his memoirs, Lt. General (Retd.) Attiqur Rahman recalled a visit he made to the nawab of Dir, a major landowner in NWFP:

> When the government sent him an educationalist to offer all help and provide schools the Nawab said nothing. He changed the subject and said they would go for a duck shoot the next morning. This was in the middle of winter and it can be very cold in the early mornings.

The Nawab shot a duck and told his followers to collect it, at which about thirty jumped into the water. The Nawab then turned to the educationalist and said: 'If I educated my people, not one of these men would have gone into the water to fetch the duck.'[42]

While the nawab of Dir never aspired to much more than having a ready supply of people to fetch his dead ducks, many other feudals have participated in national politics. Amir Mohammed Khan, the nawab of Kalabagh, provides a good example. At the age of fourteen, he became the undisputed master of his family's estate in a remote part of southern Punjab. Like many feudals, he was initially doubtful about the creation of Pakistan.[43] But once he realised that Pakistan was going to happen he sought to protect his interests first by joining the Muslim League and then by becoming one of its major financial contributors. By the time of independence he had ingratiated himself with the new ruling establishment and in the early 1950s he was able to secure seats in both the Punjab and West Pakistan Assemblies. When military rule was imposed in 1958, the nawab of Kalabagh was well placed: Ayub Khan was a regular guest at his partridge shoots. Within months, he was a federal minister and in 1965 he became the governor of West Pakistan. The nawab was a feudal and he ruled like one. His orders were delivered verbally and all civil servants and police officers in Punjab were told that they owed their loyalties not to the Pakistani state but to the nawab alone. Even his defenders, such as his military secretary Jahan Dad Khan, concede that the nawab could never outgrow his feudal origins:

He had inherited his full share of the negative traits of feudalism which included commitment to the maintenance of the status quo and an authoritarian outlook. He strongly believed in breeding, family background and the caste system . . . he resisted every change which posed a threat to his interests as a feudal landlord.[44]

Although he had good relations with many feudals, Ayub Khan did recognise that they were a brake on social and political development. In his memoirs, he recorded that in 1958 in West Pakistan 'more than 50 per cent of the available land in the Punjab, a little less than 50 per cent in NWFP and over 80 per cent in Sindh was in the possession of a few thousand absentee landlords.'[45] In 1959 he announced a land reform programme under which no one would be allowed more than 500 acres of irrigated land or 1,000 acres of unirrigated land. Ayub subsequently claimed that this policy had far-reaching effects: 'The disappearance of the class of absentee landlords, who exercised great political influence under the previous land-holding system, marked the beginning of a new era in West Pakistan.'[46]

In reality, however, Ayub's land reforms never worked. In the first place, his limits of 500 and 1,000 acres were not stringently enforced. The feudals managed to get around the law, for example, by transferring ownership to close relatives and even farm workers. In some cases, illiterate peasants were told to put their thumbprint on a piece of paper. Technically the land now belonged to them but since they were illiterate they did not even know it. The feudals also made liberal use of an exemption that allowed them to hold on to hunting grounds and orchards in excess of the stipulated limits.

Recognising that Ayub's efforts had been thwarted, Zulfikar Ali Bhutto made his own attempt to introduce land reform in 1972. He reduced the ceilings to 150 acres of irrigated and 300 acres of non-irrigated land. The land would be taken, he said, without compensation and handed to landless peasants without payment. Although Bhutto did close down some of the loopholes that undermined Ayub's programme, others remained in place. It was still possible, for example, for landowners to transfer ownership to relatives and, for all Bhutto's rhetoric, the amount of land handed over to the government was insignificant.

Neither Ayub Khan nor Bhutto was serious about land reform. Only a small percentage of the country's cultivable land was taken from the feudals. But even if the major landowners have shown great resilience, a number of election results suggest that while they enjoy great authority in their local areas they are not always able to persuade people to vote for them. The feudals' electoral difficulties began in 1970 when Zulfikar Ali Bhutto's campaign slogan of 'Bread, Clothing, and Shelter' gave him a resounding victory in Punjab and Sindh. Many feudal landowners lost their seats. Those who were defeated included representatives of major families such as the Chandios, Khuhros and Legharis. These results were not a one-off. In 1988 more feudal leaders such as Pir Pagaro, Mohammed Khan Junejo and Ghulam Mustafa Jatoi also lost their seats. The nawab of Kalabagh's sons have experienced similar difficulties. As all these men now know, party affiliation has become an ever more important determinant of voting behaviour.

It would be wrong, however, to conclude that the feudals are a spent force. There are still some areas in the more remote parts of Punjab and Sindh where a feudal landowner can stand as an independent candidate, with no party affiliation, and win. But perhaps more importantly, the feudals' uncanny ability to adjust to the various political dispensations in Pakistan means that they are seldom far removed from the seat of power for long. This enduring trait in their conduct was apparent even before partition. Many landowners, such as the nawab of Kalabagh, spent several years opposing the creation of Pakistan. They feared that the division of Punjab would leave them with property on both sides of the new border and force them to abandon some of their lands. But as soon as they realised that Mohammed Ali Jinnah's appeal to the Muslim masses had resonated, they adjusted their positions, joined his Muslim League and promptly rose to high positions in the party. Their success can be gauged by the fact that, following independence, major landowners were given the chief ministerships in Punjab, Sindh and NWFP. (At that stage Balochistan did not have a chief minister.)

Many of the feudals defeated in 1970 performed a similar manoeuvre, deciding that if they could not beat the PPP they would join it. By the time of the next elections in 1977 many had become PPP candidates. As Andrew Wilder has put it: 'The PPP's slate of 1977 election candidates read like a Who's Who of Punjab's rural elite.' And having penetrated the party, the feudals did not hesitate to influence PPP policy so as to protect their interests. By 1977 Bhutto had dropped his anti-feudal rhetoric and instead issued a manifesto, which made the implausible claim that there was no need for more land reform as the PPP's policies had already 'brought an end to feudalism in Pakistan'.[47] By 1985, after Bhutto had been hanged, the feudals had switched sides once again. In the partyless elections of that year they had a field day. Rural notables secured over three-quarters of the 875 national and provincial level positions at stake in the elections.[48]

Take, as an example, the pir of Ranipur, Abdul Qadir Shah. The pir is both a religious leader and major landowner in the Khaipur district of Sindh. In 1970 he opposed the PPP and lost. In 1977 he stood for the PPP. Under General Zia, with the PPP at its lowest ebb, he abandoned the party and stood in the 1985 non-party elections. In 1988, after Zia's death, he patched up his differences with Benazir Bhutto and became a PPP candidate once again.[49]

The feudals employ other strategies to remain in powerful positions. Many have married their children to senior figures in the army or bureaucracy. Both sides gain from the arrangement: the civil servant or army officer wins some of the social respectability associated with land-ownership; the feudals gain access to corridors of power. Another tactic is for close relatives to join different political parties and contest elections against each other. Whoever wins the election, the family will have someone in the National Assembly. In the 1988 elections, for example, the Makhdooms of Rahim Yar Khan put up two candidates for Nawaz Sharif's IJI and one for Benazir Bhutto's PPP. Similarly the shahs of Nawabshah covered their options by having two candidates for the IJI and another two for the PPP.

The feudals, of course, deploy many arguments to justify their pre-eminent position. 'People have lost faith in the police, the judiciary and the parliament', Benazir Bhutto's first cousin Mumtaz Bhutto once said; 'we are doing the job that the administration should be doing.'[50] The feudals also argue, with some justification, that their critics make far too many sweeping generalisations about them. The Sindhi landowner Abdul Ghaffar Jatoi, for example, has complained about 'city-bound pseudo-intellectuals and armchair experts sitting hundreds of miles away from the countryside offering utopian solutions to the complex and deep-rooted problems of the country dwellers'.[51]

Jatoi also argues that a more equitable distribution of land would do little to improve agricultural productivity. Experience in East Asia and beyond suggests he is wrong. If Pakistani farmers cannot get loans to buy the tools they require to cultivate small plots of land, then the state should provide them with what they lack. If Pakistan is to enjoy higher economic growth and social development then it needs a middle class. Although the feudals might not like to admit it, there can be little doubt that Pakistan would benefit if people were able to rise to the top of the system on the basis of merit rather than because of land titles handed out by the British decades ago. Those who believe that the feudals are overrated argue that they have less authority than they used to and that the trend is against them. Increased labour mobility and the (albeit woefully slow) processes of spreading education and providing micro-credit are undermining the feudals' power bases. For all that, men like Pir Pagaro, Nawab Bugti and many others are still able to lock up people in private prisons, dispense justice without reference to the courts and own bonded labourers. There are few countries, and no successful ones, where local landlords wield such power.

General Musharraf's regime, like virtually all its predecessors, stated its concern about the feudals. In February 2000 it announced plans to carry out a massive land reform programme to remove what one official described as 'centuries old feudalism'.[52] In October 2000 it issued a report 'Decentralisation and the Devolution of Power' that called for rapid land redistribution so as to empower landless peasants. 'This is being done', the report said, 'to stop the rural elite from dictating their terms and conditions and getting their own candidates elected . . . These power holders have traditionally controlled and even subverted the electoral process at the national and provincial levels.'[53] As in so many other policy areas the rhetoric was impressive but there is little indication that Musharraf is serious about implementing land reform. To do so would involve a major confrontation with some of Pakistan's most astute politicians. The events of 11 September further reduced the chances of Musharraf tackling the feudal issue. With Islamic extremists clearly defined as the enemy Musharraf knows that he cannot afford to jeopardise the feudals' support. Since the feudals are more committed than most Pakistanis to the maintenance of the status quo Musharraf is well aware that they can be relied upon to back up and support his campaign against the forces of radical Islam.

8   The Army

> Throughout the whole world, yes throughout the world, no
> armed force is so irrevocably devoted to Islam as the Pakistani
> armed forces.
>
> — Editorial in the armed forces' weekly journal *Hilal*, 1996.[1]

> The story of Pakistan is the story of ambitious and adventurist
> generals denying the people their rights.
>
> — Former air force chief, Mohammad Asghar Khan, 1983

Soldiers of Allah?

Brigadier Nusrat Sial, the commander of Pakistan's 62nd Infantry Brigade, was sitting in his office in Skardu when the news came through. 'Allah-o-Akbar!', a young officer yelled down the line. 'We've shot down two Indian jets.'[2] It was in the midst of the Kargil campaign and just two days earlier, on 25 May 1999, the Indian prime minister had authorised the use of air power to help to repel Pakistani troops who had crossed the line of control. The brigadier could not surpress his delight and within hours was escorting a group of international journalists to see the wreckage of one of the planes, an Indian MiG-27. Scraps of twisted metal lay all around the steep mountainside where it had hit the ground. The brigadier smiled broadly as he surveyed the scene and contemplated Pakistan's success in shooting down the plane. He then dilated on a subject close to his heart: Islam. 'I have seen something of the world,' he said. 'I spent two years in Germany and do you know the fastest growing religion there? It is Islam. Yes, even Germany could become an Islamic state. And the United States too.'[3] The more the brigadier spoke, the more it became clear that his whole world-view was defined by Islam. He may have been a soldier but he considered himself to be serving a divine purpose.

If the Pakistan army can be characterised as an Islamic army then the implications are profound. Should there ever be an Islamic-based challenge to Pakistan's existing system of government the attitude of the army would probably be decisive. A modernist army leadership, sure of its orders being obeyed, could prevent the Islamic radicals from grasping power. An ambivalent or divided military leadership, unsure of the willingness of its men to do battle with the Islamists, might take a different attitude. So, if an Islamic revolution ever did get underway, what would the army do?

Had that question been asked in 1947 there would have been no doubt as to the answer. At that time Pakistan did not have an Islamic army: it had an army with an overwhelming majority of Muslims. Brought up in the British system, Pakistan's leading officers were more interested in modern military theory than theology. Their attitudes were put to the test. In a report on partition-related violence in Lahore, Field Marshal Sir Claude Auchinleck described how the nascent Pakistani army performed when communal riots seemed likely to sweep the city:

> There is very strong evidence that the police are taking little notice of their officers (all the remaining European officers left yesterday) and that they have actually joined hands with the rioters in certain instances. But for the presence of the army there would by now be a complete holocaust in the city. Local Muslim leaders are trying to persuade the Muslim soldiers to follow the bad example of the police – so far without success.[4]

The army faced a not dissimilar challenge during the 1953 anti-Ahmedi riots in Lahore. When the army intervened there was not the slightest suggestion that it would side with the extremists. Officers involved in the operation saw their mission as the restoration of law and order and the suppression of the Islamic leaders' destabilising campaign.

A story told by Major General (Retd.) Shahid Hamid further illustrates the attitudes of senior officers during this period. In 1950 the General was given command of a brigade stationed on the Afghan border and he decided to hold regular open meetings with his men. In one of these sessions an army mullah stood up to ask a question:

> He came to stand at the head of the queue expecting me to give him preference above the troops. I did not like this and made him wait

his turn. He said that he wanted me to issue an order that the troops should attend all the five prayers in the mosque. Thereupon I repeated his request on the loudspeaker and added that the orders on the subject already existed from the Holiest of the Holiest and required no further directive. Later I told the centre commander to get rid of him as he was a potential troublemaker.[5]

Such actions would probably have won the approval of Mohammed Ali Jinnah. In the run-up to the transfer of power he fought hard to persuade the British that their cherished India Army should be dismantled. Eventually he succeeded in securing agreement for a separate, Pakistani, army but there is no reason to believe that he ever envisaged an Islamic army. In the few months he had to effect the development of the military forces in Pakistan, Jinnah concentrated not on the army's religious sentiment but its professionalism. Indeed, the first two commanders-in-chief, General Sir Frank Messervy and General Sir Douglas Gracey, were British Christians. Speaking to officers at the Staff College in Quetta in February 1948, Jinnah characteristically laid emphasis on national rather than religious concerns. 'Every officer and soldier', he said, 'no matter what the race or community to which he belongs, is working as a true Pakistani.'[6]

Like Jinnah, Pakistan's first commander-in-chief, Ayub Khan, was no religious zealot. On the contrary, Sandhurst-educated and strongly pro-American, he consistently downplayed the role of Islam in the Pakistani state. The views of Jinnah and Ayub reflected those of the vast bulk of the officer corps at the time. They wanted, above all else, to create an effective modern military machine that could match the Indian armed forces. They took as their role models not the Muslim commanders of times past but rather the American generals who had stormed to victory in the Second World War.

The first Pakistani army chief to play on religion was General Zia ul Haq. His Islamisation campaign affected Pakistani society as a whole but he made an especial effort to reform the military and to create a more puritanical, devout army. He made it clear that the alcohol ban imposed during the last days of Zulfikar Ali Bhutto's government was to apply in officers' messes where, previously, alcohol had flowed very freely. Greater emphasis was laid on organising prayer times and religious fasts for army personnel. He also allowed some religious groups to operate in the army with relative freedom. In particular, Zia encouraged the largest Islamic organisation in Pakistan, the Tablighi Jamaat, to become active within the army and he became the first army chief to attend the Tablighis' massive annual conventions in Raiwind near Lahore.[7] While the Tablighis were known to hold some extreme opinions, it should also be said that they were not generally regarded as a potential source of instability. The organisation had always advocated 'Jihad through conscience' rather than 'Jihad through the sword' and promoted a policy of non-intervention in politics.

Zia also wanted religion to be integrated into the syllabus of the Staff College and he encouraged the study of Islam's teaching regarding the conduct of war. All the Quranic passages relevant to war were printed and distributed in military circles. One article published in Pakistan's Defence Journal in 1979 was typical of the debate that Zia encouraged. It argued that the Muslim laws of war contained more extensive humanitarian provisions than the Geneva Convention. The Quran and subsequent Islamic teaching, the article argued, required Pakistani soldiers to refrain from committing excess cruelty; to respect the sanctity of non-combatants; to refrain from taking hostages (unless for the purpose of freeing Muslims); and so on.[8] Similarly, Zia supported the publication in 1979 of Brigadier S. K. Malik's *Quranic Concept of War*. Starting from the premise that 'As a perfect divine document, the Holy Quran has given a comprehensive treatment to its concept of war', the brigadier went on to apply Quranic principles to modern military strategy. In a signed forward to the publication, General Zia wrote:

> This book brings out with simplicity, clarity and precision the Quranic philosophy on the application of military force within the context of the totality that is JEHAD. The professional soldier in a Muslim army, pursuing the goals of a Muslim state, CANNOT become 'professional' if in all his activities he does not take on 'the colour of Allah'.[9]

General Zia also took religion into account when making senior military appointments. In 1982 Cecil Chaudhry, one of Pakistan's leading fighter pilots, who had been decorated for his bravery in the 1965 war, was up for promotion. The Air Board approved his appointment as a staff officer, a post of such seniority that it had to be approved by the president, General Zia. But he rejected the Air Board's recommendation. 'No reason was given', Chaudhry later recalled, 'but I attribute it to my being a non-Muslim. Before the Zia era a Christian did make it to the number two post in the Air Force. But after Zia took over no non-Muslim was able to make it even to Group Captain. It was the same in the army.'[10]

Zia's ideas left a deep mark on the army and seven years after his death some senior officers tried to build on his legacy. On the morning of 26 September 1995 Brigadier Mustansir Billah was driving from Pakistan's tribal areas when he was stopped at a police checkpoint. Inside his car the police found a cache of recently purchased kalashnikovs and rocket launchers. The brigadier, eager to get away, tried to pull rank and called GHQ in Rawalpindi, demanding help to get his car released. His pleas fell on deaf ears. The brigadier had just walked into a trap.

The police who made the discovery had been tipped off and, far from helping Billah, the officers at GHQ ordered his immediate arrest. The brigadier had purchased the weapons for a coup attempt. The leader of the plot was a major general, Zahir ul Islam Abbasi, who had first tasted popular acclaim in 1988 when he was serving as Pakistan's military attaché in Delhi. In the course of his work he had acquired some sensitive security documents from an Indian contact. When Indian intelligence agents found out, they beat him up and threw him out of the country. He returned to Pakistan a national hero. Seven years later, the ambitious major general, disenchanted by the failure of Zia's successors to press on with Islamic reform, decided to take matters into his own hands.

When Abbasi and his co-conspirators were later put on trial it emerged that he had planned to storm the GHQ during a corp commanders meeting, kill the participants, arrest other prominent personalities and impose Sharia or Islamic law. In an earlier version of the plot the general had considered the possibility of killing some generals when they were playing golf. Eventually, however, he settled on the corps commanders meeting because all the military leadership would be in the same place at the same time. He planned to have a staff car lead a bus-load of thirty Harakat ul Ansar militants dressed in commando uniforms into the military headquarters. Once inside the perimeter they would storm the building and establish control. Abassi had hoped to proclaim himself not only as the chief of the army staff but also the leader of the faithful or Amirul Momineen.[11]

The major general's intended address to the nation left no doubt as to the kind of administration he had had in mind: 'We are thankful to Almighty Allah and, with complete confidence, after declaring Pakistan a Sunni state, we announce the enforcement of the complete Islamic system.' The draft speech also announced bans on films, music, interest payments, contraception and photographs of women, and stated that Islamic scholars would be invested with the power to take any decisions they considered necessary.[12]

In army circles Abbasi had long been known as a religiously minded man, not least because he had established a Quranic study group in the officers' mess. Even if most senior officers viewed the intensity of Abassi's religious views with some misgivings they did not want to create an incident by limiting his activities. Nor did they consider him a serious threat. He was known to have links with Tablighi Jamaat but ever since the Zia period that was seen as quite acceptable.

Had the army delved deeper, however, they would have discovered that the general was also associated with other religious groups. The investigation that followed his arrest revealed that he had established close links with many religious leaders who openly called for Islamic revolution. Not only did Abbasi invite these clerics to preach to his troops, he also frequently attended political meetings in their homes. In these meetings the general, together with Brigadier Billah, openly advocated an Islamic-inspired military take-over. Once the general was arrested, it turned out he was well-known to all the major Islamic-based parties in Pakistan. Jamaat-e-Islami and the SSP both rallied to his defence saying he was a man known for his 'love of Islam' and 'patriotism'.[13]

The Abbasi coup attempt can be read in two ways. It can be argued that it demonstrated the weakness of Islamic forces in the army. Neither General Abbasi nor any of his fellow plotters occupied key positions. All had been passed over for promotion and none had any direct command over any troops.[14] That may have been, in part, because they were known to hold strong religious views. It was surely significant that in his planned coup the general was going to rely on Harakat ul-Ansar militants rather than disaffected troops. Furthermore, Abbasi's desire to kill all the corps commanders indicates that he was far from impressed by his colleagues' religious credentials. And the fact that the coup was thwarted showed that discipline within the Pakistan army remained strong enough to withstand internal Islamic-based challenges.

On the other hand, there are good reasons for believing that Abbasi was not representing an isolated bunch of fanatics. After his arrest, Islamic elements in the army, far from being cowed into submission, were emboldened. The appointment of a new, modernist army chief, General Jehangir Karamat, brought matters to a head. Embittered by the failure of Abassi's coup attempt and frustrated by Karamat's appointment, Islamists sought to project their views in *Hilal*, a weekly magazine produced by the army and distributed to all soldiers. In January 1996 the journal published an article which first of all caricatured the suspected attitudes of the new army chief. Under the headline: 'Expulsion of Islam from Pakistan Armed Forces' *Hilal* claimed that:

An order had been received that:
  a) Armed forces of Pakistan should be secularised;
  b) Armed forces of Pakistan should be reorganised along the lines of certain countries of the Middle East and Africa;
  c) All officers possessed of Islamic thought and action should be scrupulously weeded out of the armed forces;
  d) Promotion of bearded officers already shortlisted must be stopped. No bearded officer or *jawan* [regular soldier] should be seen in the armed forces in the future.

Having described this implausible 'order' the *Hilal* article went on to denounce it:

By Allah's grace no other official, semi-official or non-official institution of Pakistan has been so attached and devoted to Islam in thought and action as the armed forces of Pakistan. Throughout the world, yes throughout the world no armed forces is so irrevocably committed to Islam as the Pakistani armed forces.[15]

Hilal was a magazine with official status: it would have been quite impossible for the magazine's editor to publish such material without senior support. Despite Karamat's attempts to moderate the views being expressed in the journal, the articles kept on coming. In March 1996, for example, *Hilal* ran an item that described the proper role of the 'The Soldiers of Allah'. It was clear to all those who read *Hilal* that while some elements of the army remained as modernist as ever, others had the passion and the confidence to advance a radical Islamist agenda.

The Pakistani army, obsessed with secrecy, has always refused to disclose any figures about its recruitment patterns or, indeed, the attitudes of its men. Western defence attachés in Islamabad are so short of information on the subject of Islam and the army that they are reduced to conducting 'beard counts' at annual ceremonies inducting new officers into the army. For some years now the beard count has been steady at 15 per cent. They also rely on anecdotal evidence. Two stories related by Colonel (Retd.) Brian Cloughley, an author (and former defence attaché in Islamabad) who has had considerable access to the Pakistan military, help reveal the attitudes of some in the army:

> During an exercise I crawled 100 metres to a dug-in artillery observation post where a young officer showed me a laser range-finder with which I busied myself. After congratulating him on this device I was treated to an exposition on how, in fact, there is no need for advanced technology providing one believes in Allah. On another occasion I was informed gravely by a junior officer that the beard of one of his soldiers (the luxuriance and shade of which had attracted my admiration) had turned red of its own accord because of the piety displayed during his Haj. His commanding officer buried his head in his hands, but made no comment.[16]

In his classic account of the Pakistan army, the American academic Stephen Cohen has identified three generations of officers.[17] First, he argues, there was the British generation. When Pakistan's army was established, its men were all products of Britain's India Army. Many of its officers had served in the Second World War and in some cases had been trained at Sandhurst. The British had selected most of these men because they came from loyal westernised families and, for the most part, did not hold strong religious views.

Impoverished by the Second World War, however, Britain was in no position to provide the type of aid that the young Pakistan army so badly needed. Ayub Khan instead looked to the United States for support and thereby spawned, according to Cohen, the American generation of Pakistani officers. Many Pakistani military personnel officers went to the US for training and their US counterparts came to live in Pakistan. In general terms, these men had modernist, even secular, attitudes and the leading figures had distinctly un-Islamic lifestyles. In its examination of the causes of the 1971 defeat the Hamoodur Rehman Commission came to the view that, in the run-up to the war, 'a considerable number of senior Army officers had not only indulged in large-scale acquisition of lands and houses and other commercial activities but had also adopted highly immoral and licentious ways of life which seriously affected their professional capabilities'. The report went on to accuse the most senior officer in East Pakistan, General Niazi, of having relations with two prostitutes, adding that 'he came to acquire a stinking reputation owing to his association with women of bad repute and his nocturnal visits to places also frequented by several junior officers under his command'.[18]

If some officers serving in East Pakistan were living it up, then so, too, were their military superiors. General Yayha, even when he was chief of army staff, regularly drank himself into a stupor. A senior Pakistani police officer, Sardar Muhammad Chaudhry, has described the atmosphere in the army high command when Yayha was in charge. As the Special Branch Superintendent of police in Rawalpindi he was responsible for President Yayha's security. When he first saw President House (known to his policemen as 'the whore house') he was surprised to find that it was filled with prostitutes, pimps and drunks. Yayha's staff and friends were endlessly covering up for the president's excesses. On one occasion:

> The Shahinshah of Iran, on a state visit, was getting late for his departure but the President would not come out of his bedroom. A very serious protocol problem had arisen but nobody could enter his bedroom. General Ishaq, Military Secretary to the President, requested Rani (one of Yayha's lovers) to go in and bring him out. When she entered the room, she claims she found the most famous female singer

of the country performing oral sex on Yayha. Even Rani found it abhorring. She helped the President dress and brought him out.

Chaudhry even considered Yayha's activities a security risk: 'The armed guards intensely resented such behaviour by the head of a Muslim state. I was afraid they could harm him in a fit of frenzy.' [19]

After the 1971 defeat in Bangladesh, the rakish American generation was totally discredited and came to be replaced by the third generation of officers identified by Cohen: the Pakistani generation (or, as he later described it, the Zia generation). Writing in 1998, Stephen Cohen rejected the view that these men were driven by radical Islamic ideals. Zia, he pointed out, would have opposed the Abassi coup:

> The idea of a coup followed by the Islamic transformation of Pakistan was *not* one that Zia subscribed to, nor were his close associates cut from this cloth . . . Even the officers who pushed Zia into his own coup were not 'Islamic' types – in that sense Zia, his colleagues and the Zia experience did not promote a 'Zia Generation'. [20]

Many Pakistani liberals do not accept this. Those who believe that the army is becoming increasingly Islamic argue that ever since the 1960s and especially after the defeat of 1971, the army has been forced to recruit a different type of soldier. The shortage of jobs in the civilian sector and the diminished prestige of the army meant that a military career became less attractive to the elite and more attractive to people from lower middle class, urban families. As a result, the army became more representative of Pakistani society as a whole. As one retired officer has put it: 'These young men were basically conservative in their views, hostile to western ideas and far more receptive to religious ideas.' [21] It is a fair point, although there is also reason to believe that the recruitment of a new generation of lower middle class soldiers may not be as significant a factor as some believe. While there is no denying that many new recruits are religiously minded it is also true that a military career has given many in this group new aspirations. Far from being a force for revolutionary upheaval, many in the lower ranks of the army are deeply conservative and hostile to radical ideas that could derail their attempts to climb the social and economic ladder.

One compelling reason for believing that the rank and file of the army is becoming increasingly radical is the ever closer relationship between the military and various Islamic militant groups or Jihadis. This should not be seen as a one-way street. While India's propaganda machine inevitably concentrates on the role of the Pakistan army in aiding various militant groups there is another, more insidious, aspect of the issue. Pakistani soldiers are bound to be affected by their experience of working and fighting with Jihadis. Caught up by the romance of the Mujahideen's struggle, some Pakistani soldiers have come to admire their civilian militant counterparts.

Throughout the 1980s Pakistani soldiers became used to fighting alongside the Mujahideen in Afghanistan. Similarly, in Kashmir, army regulars and civilian Islamic militants have co-operated closely. During the Kargil campaign, for example, just as it had before the 1965 war, the army provided support to the Jihadis. At least one of the militant groups, Tehrik-e-Jihad, fought in Kashmir using army maps and on the basis of briefings from military officers. As the relationship between the army and the militant organisations has grown closer, mutual trust has been established to the point where some officers use militants to carry out limited operations on the line of control. In the past, regular soldiers would have carried out such activities. The officers say that the tactic works because Indian soldiers are more frightened of the militants than regular Pakistani troops.

The radical Islamist sentiment of some former Pakistani soldiers is plain for all to see in the Tanzeemul Ikhwan movement. Based in a madrasa 90 miles from Islamabad, the organisation is made up of retired Pakistan army personnel. The supreme leader of Tanzeemul Ikhwan, Mohammed Akram Awan, campaigns for radical Islamic reform within Pakistan itself. 'We can extend Jihad beyond our boundaries', he once said, 'only after we have achieved our objective at home'.[22] Awan, who claims to have support from numerous serving officers, has dozens of retired officers and hundreds of former soldiers at his command. In December 2000 he openly threatened to storm Islamabad so as to bring about an Islamic revolution.

The Zia era, the Abbasi coup attempt and the subsequent *Hilal* articles indicate that the question of Islam's role in the army should be taken seriously. But discussing this subject is a hazardous exercise. Many Pakistani officers become highly defensive whenever it is raised. They accuse Pakistani liberals and Western observers alike of harbouring anti-Islamic prejudices that distort reality and exaggerate the importance of Islam in the army. Captain (Retd.) Ayaz Amir, for example, writing in 1995, dismissed claims that the nature of the officer corps was changing: 'There has been little difference between the drinking and club-going General of old and his more outwardly pious successors. The continuities of the Pakistan army accordingly are stronger than its discontinuities.' He went on to argue that the army 'has never been a breeding ground of radical ideas', and that the idea of revolution, whatever its motivation, was anathema to most officers.[23] Speaking in 2001, another retired officer made a similar point:

If five per cent of the population could be described as extremist, then in the army they will number only three per cent. The recruitment policies weed them out. And the more senior you get, the more difficult it is for an extremist to survive. At the top of the army only a tiny percentage could be described as having strong religious views.

Furthermore, this retired officer argued, if Zia did have a religious impact, then it did not last: 'Under Zia many in the officer corps tried to join the ranks of the religious in search of advancement. After his departure most reverted to a more secular way of life.'[24]

So, which side of the debate has the upper hand? What would the Pakistan army do if some elements in Pakistani society tried to mount an Islamic revolution? Clearly, some in the army would support such a move and, probably, a far greater number would oppose it. But it is worth considering one final point. Whenever a Pakistan *jawan* or officer is asked whether he would fire on Pakistani civilians his answer is emphatic: such a scenario is dismissed as totally inconceivable. Those in the army who favour Islamic revolution may be in the minority but that may not matter. If it were ever faced with mass Islam-inspired street protests in Pakistan, the army leadership could find itself facing an awkward dilemma. An order to fire on such a crowd could well be disobeyed by some of the men. Such an outcome, creating conditions in which the army might be split, would be viewed as catastrophic by the army which has always considered the maintenance of unity as being one of its highest priorities. And in those circumstances it would not be surprising if the army stood aloof and let events take their course.

The Fighting Army

From the day of its creation Pakistan's army has struggled to keep up with its Indian counterpart. Most of the arms production facilities and training centres established under British rule were located on land that became part of India. To a large extent, this was a matter of chance, but the Indians also took deliberate steps to ensure that the Pakistan army was weak and ill-equipped. In the run-up to partition, it was agreed that India should receive about two-thirds of the ammunition, weapons and other stores left behind by the British. The rest was meant to go to Pakistan, and plans were drawn up to move 160 train-loads of military equipment from southern India to Pakistan. India, however, reneged on the deal and the trains never arrived.

Faced with an acute military imbalance, Pakistan's first politicians made defence expenditure their top priority. Between 1947 and 1959 up to 73 per cent of Pakistan's total government spending was devoted to defence. The average for the period was 60 per cent. By the 1960s the

A Pakistani civilian sweats with worry as he contemplates the army's capacity for spending scarce resources. *The Muslim*, 28 May 1991.

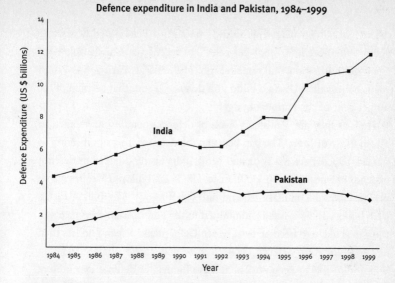

Defence expenditure in India and Pakistan, 1984–1999

Source: Figures for 1984–1986 from *World Military Expenditures and Arms Transfers 1995*, US Arms Control and Disarmament Agency, Washington 1996. Figures for 1987–1997 from *World Military Expenditures and Arms Transfers 1997*, US Arms Control and Disarmament Agency, Washington 1998. Figures for 1998 and 1999 from US State Department, *Annual Report on Military Expenditures*, 1998 and 1999. Available on www.state.gov/www/global/arms/98_amiextoc.html and www.state.gov/www/global/arms/99_amiextoc.html. All figures rounded to one decimal point.

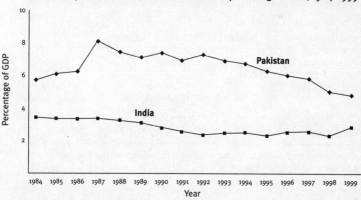

Defence expenditure in India and Pakistan as a percentage of GDP, 1984–1999

Source: Figures for 1984–1986 from *World Military Expenditures and Arms Transfers 1995*, US Arms Control and Disarmament Agency, Washington 1996. Figures for 1987–1997 from *World Military Expenditures and Arms Transfers 1997*, US Arms Control and Disarmament Agency, Washington 1998. Figures for 1998 and 1999 from US State Department, *Annual Report on Military Expenditures*, 1998 and 1999. Available on www.state.gov/www/global/arms/98_amiextoc.html and www.state.gov/www/global/arms/99_amiextoc.html. All figures rounded to one decimal point.

figure had fallen to between 46 per cent and 61 per cent with an average for the decade of 48.7 per cent.[25] In recent years, the levels have
again diminished but still remain high. In the fiscal year 1998 Pakistan
spent no less than US $3.2 billion on defence, a sum that accounted for
29 per cent of the national budget.[26]

High as they are, Pakistan's levels of defence spending have failed to
match those of India. The gap between the two widened significantly in
the late 1990s. Between 1992 and 1999, India nearly doubled its defence
expenditure from US $6.3 billion to US $12.2 billion. Over the same
period Pakistan's military expenditure fell from US $3.5 billion to US
$2.8 billion. India is totally committed to the South Asian arms race and
the gap is likely to become even wider. Delhi plans to spend no less than
US $95 billion on defence between 2001 and 2016.[27] Plainly, Pakistan
will not be able to keep up. The relative figures for defence expenditure
as a percentage of gross domestic product reveal the extent of Pakistan's
difficulty. Even after its huge boost to military expenditure in the late
1990s, by 1999 India was allocating just 3 per cent of its GDP to defence.
To achieve its far lower level of absolute spending Pakistan had to
allocate 4.5 per cent of its GDP. The different absolute spending levels
are reflected not only in the number of men in the two countries' armed
forces but also in the amount of military hardware available to those men.

Comparison of men and hardware in India and Pakistan

	Pakistan	India
Armed forces personnel	612,000	1,303,000
Tanks	4,570	6,204
Submarines	10	16
Combat aircraft	353	747

Source: *The Military Balance, 2000–2001*, International Institute of Strategic Studies,
Oxford University Press, London, 2000.

That India has always managed to maintain its conventional military
lead over Pakistan has never been in doubt. The hard numbers, however, do not tell the whole story. Factors such as the quality of leadership and the levels of training are also important, as are strategic
considerations. Although some of Ayub Khan's advisers did harbour

dreams of a drive for Delhi in 1965, no Pakistani army chief has ever given serious thought to the conquest of India. While Pakistan wants to maintain the capability to go on the offensive in Kashmir, the main purpose of its military is to deter or counter an Indian attack over the international borders. This defensive objective requires fewer resources than any offensive goals. Pakistan also hopes that its nuclear arsenal will make up for its conventional inferiority. Pakistan's military makes regular assessments of its strength compared to that of India. The resulting documents are, of course, classified but Pakistanis who are familiar with these assessments say that, in broad terms, the Pakistani army remains capable of absorbing an Indian attack. Some Pakistani officers, however, are concerned that this capability could be threatened in the not too distant future because of the increasing gap in the two countries' absolute military expenditures.

Bad Strategy

There is no doubt that, compared to India, Pakistan's army has a resource problem. But many of its difficulties can be attributed to another factor: bad strategy. The army's most humiliating defeat came in 1971. And, with the exception of the Rann of Kutch campaign (a relatively minor affair), the Pakistani army has consistently failed to achieve its military objectives. This is not the place to attempt a comprehensive military history of Pakistan but it is worth expanding on one point: Pakistan's record in developing military strategy is atrocious.

It would perhaps be unfair to refer to the conflict of 1947 and 1948 in support of this contention. The Pakistan army, after all, barely existed at the time and some of its problems were a result of the reluctance of its British commander to deploy men. By 1965, however, the Pakistan army had managed to equip itself and its main problems were self-inflicted. First, despite being the initiators of the conflict, the army was unprepared. As Major General S. Shahid Hamid has recorded: 'The army was not trained or ready for the offensive; some 25 per cent of the men were on leave.'[28] Secondly, the army was overconfident. During the Rann of Kutch campaign in early 1965, the Pakistani forces were generally considered to have acquitted themselves well. Ayub Khan apparently drew the conclusion that all his efforts to train the army and to secure good, modern equipment had paid off. As one senior Pakistani officer wrote:

> The success of arms in the Rann of Kutch skirmish and the subsequent settlement of the dispute appears to have had a profound affect on Ayub . . . It was in the euphoric aftermath of the short-lived conflict in the salt marsh that Ayub's senior advisors [sic] found a sudden change in his thinking on the Kashmir issue.[29]

Ayub Khan should have known better. The fighting in the Rann was localised and on a small scale. It was clearly a mistake to think that victory there would mean victory in Kashmir.

Thirdly, and crucially, the Pakistani leadership thought the fighting could be restricted to Kashmir. It was an absurd assumption. When the Indians came under serious pressure they did not hesitate to extend the fight to the international borders. Fourthly, Ayub Khan miscalculated the international reaction to the fighting. His stated aim was to bring India to the conference table to discuss Kashmir. During the conflict he repeatedly called for US support. It should, however, have been clear to Ayub that ever since the 1962 Sino-Indian war, Washington, fearful of Chinese expansion, was never going to abandon its relationship with India for the sake of Pakistan. Pakistan had started a war that it was in no position to win.

Much the same can be said of 1971. The loss of East Pakistan was the subject of a major government enquiry in Pakistan. The Hamoodur Rehman Commission's findings could scarcely have been more critical of the military's performance. Perhaps the most damning criticism of the military high command in 1971 is the way in which it drifted toward a war without contemplating the consequences. The Hamoodur Rehman Commission was especially unforgiving on this point: 'It is remarkable that, even in the critical months after March 1971, when war was clearly a probability, if not an imminent certainty, the question seems to have bothered the general staff very little. It does not appear that even the chief of staff, much less the commander-in-chief, ever showed any interest in this all important question.'[30]

It was like 1965 all over again and many of these problems re-emerged during the Kargil campaign of 1999. Speaking after the campaign a former director of the ISI, Lt. General (Retd.) Durrani, made this comment on Pakistan's performance: 'Tactically', he said 'it was a brilliant operation. But we had not set our strategic priorities and failed in the diplomatic and political preparations to back it up.'[31] It is a correct assessment. In operational terms, the Kargil campaign was one of the most successful ever mounted by the Pakistan army. The infiltration of Indian-held territory was executed without any serious setback. Admittedly, Kargil was a relatively small-scale affair: the number of Pakistani troops who crossed the line never exceeded 2,000. Nevertheless, the military could claim for once that they had lived up to their own high opinion of themselves.

But, at a strategic level, Kargil also revealed that Pakistan had failed to learn from its previous mistakes. Just as in 1965 and 1971, the generals did not think through the consequences of their actions. The high levels of distrust between the political and military elites hampered the planning process. The failure to factor in the diplomatic and international consequences of Kargil is partly explained by the military's reluctance to consult fully all the relevant civilian officials. The military was afraid of leaks but its desire for secrecy was so great that it undermined the quality of the decision-making process.

Another consistent weakness in Pakistani strategy has been the Pakistan high command's heavy reliance on volunteer fighters. It has tried to fight its battles by proxy. This practice began in 1947, when tribal forces from NWFP marched into Kashmir. Even if one accepts the Pakistani argument that they did so in part on their own initiative, there is no doubt that the army was soon working with the tribals and, by 1948, Pakistani army officers in Kashmir were co-ordinating their military actions with them. The relationship between regular and irregular Pakistani forces in Kashmir has remained close ever since. In 1965 Ayub Khan hoped that Kashmir could be secured by Operation GIBRALTAR, in which armed militants would cross into Indian-held Kashmir and instigate a general revolt. Since 1988 Pakistan's military establishment has employed similar tactics. Its support for the insurgency has demonstrated a continuing faith in militant groups. And, in

Kargil too, the military high command used irregular troops together with civilian volunteers.

Pakistani strategists seem to believe that the element of deniability afforded by the use of irregular forces works to Pakistan's advantage. In reality, the use of irregulars has proved counterproductive. In 1947, just as during the Kargil campaign fifty-two years later, Pakistani spokesmen had to perform an impossible balancing act. On the one hand, they wanted to justify the tribals or militants in their battle against the Indians. On the other, they had to issue unconvincing statements insisting that the Pakistan government had no connections with the irregulars – especially when they committed human rights atrocities. The duplicity required to advance these two positions has fooled nobody and has only undermined Pakistan's diplomatic standing. Perhaps more importantly from Pakistan's point of view, the tactic has consistently failed in military terms. The gains secured by irregular forces in Kashmir have consistently fallen short of the hopes invested in them. Pakistan's repeated reliance on irregular forces in Kashmir reflects a basic lack of confidence. The Indians have never suffered from this problem. Ever since 1947, if the leadership in Delhi thought there was a national objective that had to be secured, it showed no hesitation in using the army to do it. The invasions of Junagadh, Hyderabad and East Pakistan all prove the point.

No assessment of the Pakistani armed forces' military performance would be complete without consideration of the most hostile of all its battlegrounds: the Siachin Glacier. Ever since 1984 the Pakistani and Indian armies have fought on the highest battlefield on earth. Some of the forward posts are located at a bone-chilling 20,000 feet above sea level. Temperatures on Siachin drop to minus 50 degrees Celsius and blizzards can exceed 100 miles per hour. Before the troops can fire a gun they have to thaw it on a kerosene stove. The air is so thin and the winds so violent that the artillery shells which the two sides lob at each other follow unpredictable trajectories. In some places, the opposing troops are just 1,000 feet away from each other but the extreme cold, the crevasses and the avalanches claim more lives than any fighting.

However brave the men who fight on Siachin may be, there is no escaping the fact that they are engaged in a futile and outrageously expensive battle. While there are no reliable figures, it is conservatively estimated that both sides commit more than half a million US dollars to the conflict each day. What is Pakistan hoping to achieve by this lavish use of scarce resources? When General Musharraf was asked, he gave the following reply: 'We have the upper hand here. It costs the Indians more to fight on Siachin than us. It's all about the degree of difficulty we can create for the other side.'[32] Factually, the general was quite correct. But for Pakistan to think that it can reduce India to bankruptcy is clearly absurd. Morally, it is difficult to see how either India or Pakistan can justify expending so many lives and so much money on such a useless conflict.

A Political Army

The Pakistan army has repeatedly shown a greater willingness to grasp power than to give it up. None of the first three army chiefs to rule Pakistan – Ayub Khan, Yayha Khan and Zia ul Haq – gave up power voluntarily. There is no reason to believe that General Musharraf will act differently. After taking over, the first task of any military ruler is to address the nation on radio and television. It has happened in Pakistan four times and on each occasion the coup leaders have summoned as much sincerity as they could muster and have delivered carbon copy speeches.

> This is a drastic and extreme step taken with great reluctance but with the deepest conviction that there was no alternative to it except the disintegration and complete ruination of the country.
>
> —Ayub Khan, 8 October 1958

> The armed forces could not remain idle spectators of this state of near anarchy. They have to do their duty and save the country from utter disaster.
>
> —Yayha Khan, 26 March 1969

> I was obliged to step in to fill the vacuum created by the political leaders.
>
> —Zia ul Haq, 5 July 1977

I wish to inform you that the armed forces have moved in as a last resort to prevent any further destabilisation.

—Pervez Musharraf, 13 October 1999

The four addresses have other passages in common. Ayub Khan pledged: 'Our ultimate aim is to restore democracy.' His successor Yayha insisted: 'I have no ambition other than the creation of conditions conducive to the establishment of a constitutional government.' Ironically, the least democratically-minded of the lot, Zia ul Haq, gave the clearest assurance of all: 'My sole aim is to organise free and fair elections which would be held in October this year.' Most recently, Pervez Musharraf has claimed that: 'The armed forces have no intention to stay in charge any longer than is absolutely necessary to pave the way for true democracy to flourish in Pakistan.'

A few days after the 1999 coup, Musharraf's spokesman, Brigadier Rashid Quereshi, insisted that while: 'Others may have tried to hang on to power, we will not. We will make history.'[33] Musharraf agreed. 'All I can say', he assured a television interviewer in January 2000, 'is that I am not going to perpetuate myself . . . I can't give any certificate on it but my word of honour. I will not perpetuate myself.'[34] Later in 2000 Musharraf went a stage further and said he would respect a Supreme Court judgement that stated he should remain in office for just three years. In June 2001, however, Musharraf performed a complete U-turn. Following the examples of Ayub, Yayha and Zia, he made himself president. And in May 2002 he held a referendum that allowed him to remain in power for a further five years.

Pakistan's military leaders have had other traits in common. All of them have placed great emphasis on devising arrangements for the better governance of the country. Ayub Khan was particularly enthusiastic about constitutional reform. During a sleepless night in a London hotel in 1954 (four years before he took over), he set down his political views on paper. The document he produced, entitled 'A Short Appreciation of Present and Future Problems of Pakistan',[35] was filled with the kind of mess-room 'common sense' that has characterised the thinking of all Pakistan's military rulers.

Ayub started from the premise that Pakistan wasn't ready for a Westminster style democracy and needed some form of controlled or guided democracy. The system he devised was called Basic Democracies and it was introduced on the first anniversary of his coup. At the lowest, district level there were constituencies of approximately 1,000 people, which each elected a representative or Basic Democrat. These Basic Democrats would then elect some of their number to participate in the next tier of government. In all there were five tiers (although this was later reduced to four). At the higher levels, however, the elected representatives were joined by appointed civil servants. Ever the paternalist, Ayub Khan believed that while the Basic Democrats might be able to articulate the people's wishes and needs, only bureaucrats would be capable of devising and implementing policies to address those needs.

By January 1960, 80,000 Basic Democrats had been elected and the next month Ayub Khan held a referendum to ask them whether they had confidence in his leadership. Since all the representatives owed their positions to Ayub Khan there was never any doubt about the result. An overwhelming majority voted for the military leader and three days later he was sworn in as president. Ayub insisted the result gave his regime democratic legitimacy but few were convinced. The vast majority of the traditional politicians rejected the Basic Democracies scheme as nothing more than a device to prop up Ayub Khan.

The field marshal apparently never realised that he was attempting the impossible. He wanted to combine an authoritarian system, in which he made all the decisions, with a democratic process. The two goals were incompatible. Ayub Khan's political naïveté was fully exposed when the Basic Democrats were called upon to elect a National Assembly in 1962. During the run-up to the vote, Ayub refused to allow political parties to operate insisting that independent individuals should be elected on merit. As soon as the National Assembly started functioning, however, its members inevitably began to organise themselves into factions and, within weeks, Ayub Khan was forced to back down and sanction the functioning of political parties. By December the irreconcilable tensions between democracy and military rule were plain for all to see. Completely abandoning all he had previously stood for, Ayub Khan himself became a party leader, accepting the presidency of a faction of the Muslim League. The man who took over to rid Pakistan of scheming politicians had joined their ranks.

When he was in power, the Western press lavished praise on Ayub referring to him as the 'Asian de Gaulle'. In retrospect, such plaudits seem far too complimentary. Ayub Khan cannot be faulted for boldness: he tried to create a new type of political system in Pakistan. The fact remains, however, that he failed.

No one has ever described Ayub's successor, General Yayha Khan, as an Asian de Gaulle. A more typical assessment was made by one of his colleagues, Lt. General Jahan Dad Khan:

> It is generally felt that his highest ceiling was a divisional commander. His rise beyond that level was disastrous for the country and also unfair to the General who was a happy-go-lucky person without the stamina or the intellectual discipline to undertake the rigours of a higher appointment. It was unfortunate for Pakistan that Ayub decided first to appoint Yayha as the Army C-in-C and then hand over power to him.[36]

For all his detractors, however, Yayha Khan's constitutional reform programme was in many respects far more convincing than Ayub's. Within twenty-four hours of taking over, Yayha Khan had promised 'the smooth transfer of power to the representatives of the people elected freely and impartially on the basis of adult franchise'.[37] For a military leader to make such a pledge was not unusual but Yayha actually meant it.

The 1970 elections are widely accepted to have been the fairest that have ever occurred in Pakistan. During the campaign Yayha allowed the political parties to operate freely and encouraged the political leaders to broadcast their views on national radio and television. The campaign was fought on genuine issues. In East Pakistan the electorate was effectively asked to give its verdict on Mujibur Rehman's Six Point programme for regional autonomy. In West Pakistan Zulfikar Ali Bhutto's Pakistan People's Party battled against the Islamic-based parties. True, it was never clear how or when Yayha would step down and it is also indisputable that, once the elections results became known, Yayha proved incapable of controlling events. Nevertheless, it would be churlish to ignore the fact that, for the first time since 1947,

Pakistan had a leader who not only was genuinely committed to free and fair elections but also actually delivered them.

General Zia ul Haq, by contrast, was never sincere about restoring democracy. Whenever pressure for some form of democratic representation became irresistible, Zia consistently gave as little as he could, as late as he could. Arguing that Western style democracy was un-Islamic, he announced, in 1981, the creation of the Majlis-e-Shoora. Zia himself chose all the members of this body and although he described it as a legislature, it was no such thing. It had only advisory powers, Zia made the laws. The Majlis convinced nobody and, by 1984, Zia realised he would have to give more concessions to the politicians. Before doing so he wanted to make his own position impregnable and he consequently put the following, utterly fatuous, question to the Pakistani electorate in a referendum:

> Whether the people of Pakistan endorse the process initiated by General Muhammad Zia ul Haq, the President of Pakistan, for bringing the laws of Pakistan in conformity with the injunctions of Islam as laid down in the Holy Quran and Sunnah of the Holy Prophet PBUH [peace be upon him] and for the preservation of the ideology of Pakistan, for the continuation and consolidation of that process and for the smooth and orderly transfer of power to the elected representatives of the people?[38]

Despite a low turn-out Zia declared that, since most people had answered in the affirmative, he would be the president for the next five years. National elections on a non-party basis followed in February 1985. The new parliament enjoyed more powers than the Majlis-e-Shoora and Zia's hand-picked prime minister, Mohammed Khan Junejo, did try to assert his independence. As a result, he was sacked shortly before Zia died. General Zia's main objective was always to hang on to power. His 'parliaments' were nothing more than fronts and they were dismantled as soon as the general was killed.

Eleven years after Zia's death Pakistan had another military ruler: General Pervez Musharraf. He has said he wants to create a more stable political system by giving the army a permanent role in decision-making but there is little reason to believe that he will prove any more capable of establishing durable political institutions than his predecessors. His idea of a National Security Council on which the politicians and senior officers work together is doomed to fail. Like Ayub Khan before him, Musharraf is unwilling to accept that trying to create a hybrid of military and democratic government cannot and will not work. Politicians elected during a period of military rule face a choice: they can either co-operate with the army, thereby losing all their credibility, or they can insist that the generals should restore democracy thereby forcing a political crisis.

General Musharraf has shown some awareness of these potential difficulties. Realising that Ayub Khan's attempt to hold non-party elections did not work, Musharraf accepted from the outset that the political parties would have to be allowed to take part in any vote for a new National Assembly and Senate. But if the parties were to participate, Musharraf wanted to be sure that he could control them. In January 2002 he announced a series of measures that were touted as electoral reforms but which, in reality, were nothing more than mechanisms through which the military hoped to manage the new parliament.

First, Musharraf declared that the two most popular politicians in the country, Nawaz Sharif and Benazir Bhutto, would not be allowed to participate in the electoral process. The army next decreed that the National Assembly would include twenty-five appointed technocrats and sixty appointed women. At a stroke it had ensured there would be a significant voting block of military-appointed National Assembly members. The army hoped that if neither the PPP nor the Muslim League won a landslide then the eighty-five appointees could hold the balance of power. The army employed some other timeworn tactics. It announced, for example, that many constituency boundaries would have to be redrawn. Again, this amounted to nothing more than a lever, which would allow the military to influence the result. But perhaps more important than all these control mechanisms, Musharraf knew that if any member of a new parliament tried to challenge the military's right to rule, the army could always open up a corruption case against him or her. For obvious reasons, many Pakistani politicians live in fear of having their financial affairs investigated – and Musharraf's army has not hesitated to use threats of probes to bully the politicians into line.

As Musharraf contemplated the possibility of working with a newly elected National Assembly, then, he had some reason to believe that he could manage the situation. But he still had one concern. By constitutional tradition, the Pakistani president is elected by the membership of the National Assembly and Senate. And even if the elections were heavily manipulated, Musharraf could not rule out the possibility that a majority of the politicians would fail to vote for him. The only solution, he concluded, was to avoid the need for a parliamentary vote by holding a referendum in which he would ask the Pakistani people for five more years in power. The referendum, he hoped, would finally neutralise the argument that, as a coup leader, he lacked legitimacy.

In seeking a popular mandate Musharraf was following the example of General Zia ul Haq. But Zia's referendum had backfired: while he had claimed a turn-out of 80 per cent, most observers put the true figure at between 5 and 10 per cent. Musharraf faced much the same problem. After his April 2002 referendum, his claims were, characteristically, more modest than Zia's. The Electoral Commission said 71 per cent had turned out to vote but, again, the true figure was generally reckoned to be far lower and estimated at 25 per cent. The fact that the voters did not even have to be on the electoral register to participate in the referendum hardly helped to convince people that Musharraf had won fairly. Indeed, the army's efforts to ensure a high turn-out by, for example, threatening to sack government employees who did not vote undermined the very purpose of the exercise. Musharraf's referendum victory will help him in his tussles with politicians but it will not provide him with the degree of legitimacy he craves. For his first three years in office Musharraf has governed virtually unchallenged. He will never enjoy such freedom of action again.

Civil-Military Relations

It is often said that Pakistan has been ruled by the military for nearly half the country's existence. That is a serious underestimate: even in times of civilian rule, the military has interfered in foreign and domestic policy and intervened in the political process. The peculiar circumstances of Pakistan's creation has meant that the army has had a large degree of influence from the outset. During the country's first decade, the politicians and senior military officers did not have a particularly adversarial relationship and there was a sense in which both groups believed they were working together to get Pakistan established. After Ayub took over that changed. His coup not only led officers to believe that they had a right to be involved in the country's governance but also made all future civilian leaders nervous that they, too, could be thrown out of office.

Should any prime minister, for example, try to strike a deal on Kashmir without the army's approval he or she could not expect to survive in office. Similarly, any serious attempt to pursue nuclear disarmament in Pakistan would certainly result in a coup. A leading scholar of the Pakistani army, Hasan-Askari Rizvi, has identified five other areas in which he believes the army will not tolerate civilian interference. They are weapons procurement and related foreign policy issues; internal military personnel decisions; cuts in defence expenditure; and any moves to curtail the perks associated with high military office. Rizvi also argues that the military would tolerate a government only if it proved capable of delivering social and political stability.[39] In fact, the military considers any issue of 'strategic national importance' to be within its domain.

The first civilian leader to suffer as a result of the army's post-Ayub confidence was Zulfikar Ali Bhutto, who was always alive to the risk of a coup. He appointed Zia ul Haq as chief of army staff precisely because he thought he would be pliant and controllable. It was, of course, a monumental misjudgement but the 1977 coup cannot be explained by Zia's personal ambition alone. Throughout Bhutto's period in power there was a lack of stability in civil-military relations. The difficulty of establishing a sustainable working relationship between the military and the civilian politicians re-emerged after Zia's death. During the campaign that followed her father's hanging, Benazir Bhutto launched vitriolic attacks on the Zia regime but when she became prime minister she adopted a much more conciliatory position. It was a futile effort. Zia's successor, General Mirza Aslam Beg, with the connivance of President Ghulam Ishaq Khan, played an active political role. The two men, and their successors, repeatedly used their powers under the Eighth Constitutional Amendment to dismiss a sitting government. In 1990, 1993 and 1996 the army influenced and fully supported presidential decisions to remove civilian governments. As long as the Eighth Amendment was in place, democratically elected leaders knew that their fate depended on the army leadership.

When Sharif came into office for the second time he was determined to cut the army down to size and overturned the Eighth Amendment: no longer could an army chief, working through the president, use constitutional means to remove a government. The army, however, still believed it had the right to be involved in the governance of the country. In April 1999 Musharraf spoke at a seminar in Karachi and compared Pakistan to a boat full of trained soldiers waiting for the enemy. Their boat, Musharraf said, had started to develop holes: 'So what should these trained soldiers do? Should they keep on waiting for the enemy ship and let their own boat sink? Or should they try and plug the leakage?'[40] Six months later he plugged the leak and once again established that the Pakistan army is not only a military machine but also a political organisation.

The army is also a major player in the Pakistani economy.[41] Taken together, the military's enterprises account for nearly 3 per cent of Pakistan's gross national product. The military has five major business groups. The biggest – in fact it is the biggest conglomerate in the country – is the Fauji Foundation. It has assets worth nearly US $2 billion, which include sugar mills, chemical plants and fertiliser factories. In the energy sector it owns a gas company and power plants. As well as generating funds, the Fauji Foundation runs its own welfare programmes and owns over 800 educational institutions and more than 100 hospitals.

The second largest military business is the Army Welfare Trust (AWT). While the Ministry of Defence runs the Fauji Foundation, the AWT is answerable to the adjutant general of the Pakistan army who is based in GHQ. Its assets, worth nearly one billion US dollars, include one of Pakistan's biggest financial institutions, the Askari Bank. Its also owns farms, real estate businesses, sugar mills and plants which produce petrochemicals, pharmaceuticals and shoes. Unlike the Fauji Foundation, the AWT does not run any charitable projects: all its profits are sent to GHQ.

About half of the income generated by the AWT is used to pay army pensions. The remaining three military businesses, which are all run from GHQ, are the Frontier Works Organisation (FWO), the National Logistics Cell and the Special Communications Organisation. The FWO is a road construction company which, since 1966, has undertaken projects worth around half a billion US dollars. It has a subsidiary business sending mine clearers around the world – an activity that, during the 1990s, earned around US $10 million a year. The Special Communications Organisation is responsible for supplying telecommunications services to the people of Pakistani-held Kashmir. The National Logistics Cell, which employs serving army officers, is a transport company, with a fleet of over 2,000 vehicles. It has also been involved in road and bridge construction and, for some reason, the control of locusts and other pests.

One of the reasons that the army's economic units are so successful is that they are in a good position to lobby for tax exemptions and subsidies. By managing to register itself as a charity, for example, the Fauji Foundation has avoided paying tax on its income. The military's enterprises also benefit from the fact that Pakistani consumers favour organisations which have army backing because they believe they will never be allowed to go bankrupt. The extent of the military's economic interests is significant. Its direct interest in the performance of the Pakistani economy provides another motive for its involvement in the political process.

Pakistan's army enjoys a better reputation than it deserves. Both on the field of battle and in periods of military rule its record has been far from glorious. If Pakistan is, as many Pakistanis believe, a failed state, then the army must take its fair share of the blame. As well as governing the country for nearly half its existence it has consumed a disproportionate amount of government expenditure. No Pakistani military officer can credibly argue that the army has played a positive role in the country's political development. And it is arguable that the army's performance has been more damaging to Pakistan in times of civilian rather than military rule. Under military regimes, Pakistan has at least achieved a level of stability. No civilian government has been able to operate free of army interference.

The Pakistani public, though, tends to direct its invective and vitriol at the country's civilian leaders. With good reason, the politicians are routinely denounced as corrupt, self-interested and incompetent. There is a genuine belief that while the civilian institutions have become tarnished, the army retains some glitter. Even politicians share this perception. Ever since 1947 the military has frequently been called upon to carry out tasks which the politicians have felt unable to manage themselves. But the keenest advocates of the view that the army is a cut above the rest of Pakistani society are its own officers. They have a genuine pride in their institution which they believe to be the only major organisation in the country that works. And yet, whenever the army has been in government, the generals have found Pakistan's problems less easy to resolve than they imagined.

In 1976 a Pakistani Lt. General, M. Attiqur Rahman, wrote a devastating critique of the Pakistani army. His book, *Our Defence Cause*, lifted the veil from an institution that had hitherto conducted its business behind a tight wall of secrecy. His complaints were legion. Under Ayub Khan's period of military rule, he argued, army officers had been exposed to opportunities for making money. Many had become corrupt. If fellow officers learnt of their corruption, however, it went unpunished for fear that the morale of the army would suffer. Rahman was also unimpressed by the criteria for promoting senior officers. In some cases, he wrote, officers' careers were advanced on the basis of nepotism or regional affiliation. There was also a tendency to favour 'yes men' who would not rock the boat. Rather than raising genuine problems, junior officers soon learnt that they were better off writing positive reports that reflected well on the army high command. In the prevailing atmosphere of smug self-satisfaction, discipline slackened and too much time was spent on staging ceremonial events to impress the public. Attiqur Rahman described how military setbacks would inevitably be followed by attempts to restore damaged reputations. He even claimed that after the 1965 war some officers went as far as altering records by fraudulently writing orders that they should have issued during the conflict. Attiqur Rahman made his criticisms a quarter of a century ago but many of them remain valid.

None of Pakistan's military rulers has left office in happy circumstances. After the 1965 presidential elections, Ayub Khan became increasingly unpopular and isolated. By early 1968 he was also sick and exhausted. A year later his administration ended amid a wave of popular protest and rancour. This reduced the field marshal to crisis management in the face of an increasingly active opposition. However bold his vision, Ayub Khan had failed to realise his dreams. When Yayha Khan took over and imposed martial law, Ayub was harsh about his own achievements. Shortly before he stepped down he remarked to a group of ministers: 'I am sorry we have come to this pass. We are a very difficult country structurally. Perhaps I pushed it too hard into the modern age. We were not ready for reforms. Quite frankly I have failed. I must admit that clearly.'[42]

By the time he was forced out of office, the loss of East Pakistan meant that Yayha Khan was even more thoroughly discredited than Ayub. But of all Pakistan's military rulers, it is General Zia who left the most damaging legacy. Most of Zia's major policy initiatives went wrong. Pakistan's political development was retarded by his fear that if he ever handed power back to the civilians the PPP would avenge Bhutto's death. His Islamicisation campaign never enjoyed much popular support and gave rise to one of Pakistan's most debilitating scourges: sectarian violence. His support of the Afghan Mujahideen may have pleased Washington but the impact on Pakistan was disastrous. Millions of Afghan refugees settled in Pakistan; drugs and guns became ever more widely available.

Pakistan's fourth military ruler, General Musharraf, may be a more benign leader but so far he has failed to do much better. It was perhaps understandable that in his address to the nation after the 1999 coup Musharraf concluded with the thought that 'we have reached rock bottom'. Sadly, as we shall now see, despite all his bold pronouncements, he has failed to convince many that he will prove any more capable than his military predecessors of leading the country to a higher level.

9   The Day of Reckoning

Pakistan has come to stay and no power on earth can destroy it.

—Mohammed Ali Jinnah, 1948

Violence and terrorism have been going on for years and we are weary and sick of this Kalashnikov culture . . . The day of reckoning has come.

—General Pervez Musharraf, 12 January 2002

There are good reasons for believing that General Musharraf understands the depth of the crisis Pakistan faces. In his first major speech after the 1999 coup, he said:

Fifty two years ago we started with a beacon of hope and today that beacon is no more and we stand in darkness. There is despondency and hopelessness surrounding us with no light visible anywhere around. The slide down has been gradual but has rapidly accelerated in the last many years.

Having made this bleak assessment, he outlined what he thought was needed to rescue Pakistan. He promised to eliminate corruption, give people access to speedy justice, depoliticise the state institutions, devolve power from the centre and restore democracy.

Three years after his coup, Musharraf had proved unwilling or unable to fulfil these pledges. The anti-corruption drive had disappeared without trace, the courts remained as slow as ever, Musharraf's military regime turned out to be as political as any of its civilian predecessors, the centre remained all-powerful and as for the restoration of democracy, Musharraf organised a referendum that allowed him to rule until the year 2007.

General Musharraf has never stopped making promises. In January 2002, he argued that Islamic militants had been allowed to flout the

authority of the central government for too long. He declared he was
going to confront them. 'The day of reckoning,' he said, had come. 'Do
we want Pakistan to become a theocratic state? Do we believe that religious education alone is enough for governance or do we want Pakistan
to emerge as a progressive and dynamic Islamic welfare state? The
verdict of the masses is in favour of a progressive Islamic State.' Complaining that the religious extremists had created a 'state within a state',
he vowed that the writ of the government would be established. The
very fact that he dared to say such a thing sent waves of relief across
the whole of Pakistan. But most Pakistanis tempered their hopes with
a large dose of cynicism. While they desperately wanted Musharraf to
succeed they wearily recalled that Pakistani leaders have always been
good on rhetoric and poor on implementation.

There are some reasons for believing that Musharraf can buck the
trend. In the first place, he does at least have an agenda. Throughout
the 1990s Pakistan was led by politicians who never had a comprehensive reform programme. Neither Nawaz Sharif nor Benazir Bhutto even
tried to dismantle Zia's legacy. Musharraf, by contrast, does have a vision
of where Pakistan should be going. He wants a modernist, liberal
Pakistan in which there is religious tolerance and respect for the law.
There is another significant difference between Musharraf and his
immediate predecessors. Since 11 September Musharraf has had the luxury of considerable international support. The most obvious benefit of
his decision to join the US-led coalition against Afghanistan was the
flow of funds from the multilateral financial institutions to Pakistan.
Partly because of their profligacy, but also because of the economic
sanctions imposed on Pakistan as a result of its nuclear programme, the
civilian governments of the 1990s were distracted by repeated financial
crises. In 1998, during Nawaz Sharif's second administration, the situation had become so acute that Pakistan was on the verge of bankruptcy
and almost unable to meet its foreign debt repayments. Shortly after 11
September 2001 Musharraf could boast that he had 5 billion US dollars
in the reserves.

Musharraf has another great advantage that the civilian leaders did
not enjoy: he does not have the army breathing down his neck. Civilian governments have failed in Pakistan for a number of reasons. The

civilian leaders have been corrupt. The civil service has proved incompetent. But the army's willingness to intervene in policy decisions and remove elected politicians from power has also been a significant factor. Musharraf does not have to worry about such interference. While the possibility of an internal army putsch can never be ruled out, the history of the Pakistan army suggests that its discipline is strong enough to withstand a challenge from within. Barring assassination, Musharraf will govern Pakistan for as long as he likes.

Furthermore, Musharraf's military status allows him to do things that no civilian leader would ever risk attempting. Take, for example, his policy towards India. In July 2001 Musharraf went to the Indian city of Agra to meet the Indian prime minister, Atal Behari Vajpayee. On the first day of his trip, Musharraf visited the Mahatma Gandhi memorial in Delhi. Gandhi has long been reviled in Pakistan as a man who tried to prevent the country's creation and, before Musharraf, no Pakistani leader had seriously considered going to the site. Any prime minister who might have gone there would, without doubt, have been accused of a sell-out. But when Musharraf paid his respects to Gandhi's memory, the Pakistani people accepted the move as a gesture that might help pave the way for better relations between India and Pakistan.

Neither Benazir Bhutto nor Nawaz Sharif was allowed to formulate her or his own policies regarding India. During her first administration Benazir Bhutto had wanted to go to India to meet Rajiv Gandhi but the military establishment was so strongly opposed to the idea that she abandoned the trip. It was much the same story ten years later when, in February 1999, Nawaz Sharif invited Vajpayee to Lahore. In doing so, he faced opposition not only from the Islamic radicals but also from the army. Jamaat-e-Islami displayed its displeasure by organising thousands of activists to rampage through the streets of Lahore during Vajpayee's visit. The protest turned into a riot. One policeman was killed, hundreds of protestors were injured and, as the security forces tried to clear the streets, clouds of tear gas floated over the historic Lahore Fort where the two prime ministers were trying to eat their dinner. General Musharraf (who at the time was chief of army staff) was not much more helpful than Jamaat. In a pointed gesture of ill-will, he and his senior colleagues undermined Sharif's diplomatic effort by refusing to go to the Wagah border point to welcome Vajpayee to Pakistan. They maintained that it would have been unacceptable for Pakistan's military leaders to be seen shaking the hand of the prime minister of an enemy state.

It is impossible to avoid the conclusion that the military stand a much better chance of delivering radical change in Pakistan than the civilians. That is true in part because the Pakistani people are more likely to accept change coming from the military. But it is also the case because successive military leaderships have treated civilian governments with distrust and have limited their freedom of action. It is difficult, for example, to imagine any civilian government being able to strike a deal with India over Kashmir. The Pakistani people, and the army, would surely denounce any such settlement as a betrayal. According to conventional wisdom even a military leader could not expect to survive if he made a significant compromise on Kashmir. The army, it is argued, has invested so much in the Kashmir dispute that it would simply remove any army chief who was seen as giving in to India. That analysis may be correct – and we will never know for sure until someone, maybe Musharraf, tries it. But it is also worth considering the possibility that, if he did want to make a compromise on Kashmir, Musharraf might just get away with it.

The conventional wisdom, after all, used to hold that it would also be impossible for any Pakistani leader to survive a showdown with the Islamic radicals. Although the radicals are by no means a spent force, Musharraf has gone some way towards dispelling that myth. Certainly, his January 2002 speech, in which he announced a whole series of measures designed to control the activities of the radicals, produced barely a whisper of protest. This was especially notable given that his speech did have an important bearing on the Kashmir dispute. When Musharraf banned Lashkar-e-Toiba and Jaish-e-Mohammed, he dealt a severe blow to the Kashmir insurgency. Even so, there was little reaction to his move. Although many in the army and the ISI are reluctant to admit it, outside of Punjab there is little interest in the Kashmir dispute. Admittedly, the army is Punjabi-dominated and that may prove decisive. But after a decade in which the insurgency has contributed to Pakistan's underdevelopment, and brought so much suffering in Kashmir itself, many Pakistanis want a settlement. Should Musharraf ever persuade India to accept a face-saving formula, such as autonomy with joint sovereignty for the Kashmir Valley, he might find that most Pakistanis are ready to support him.

These, then, are some of the reasons for thinking that Musharraf could succeed in implementing his policies. There is, however, an even stronger case for believing that he will fail.

Pakistan's state institutions are so weak that no Pakistani leader has ever been able to get his or her ideas enacted. The result has been a prolonged, deep economic and social crisis. Each month the newspapers in Pakistan carry reports of men and women who have committed suicide because of their failure to feed their families. The corrupt go free, hardly anyone pays tax and few can expect to receive justice from the courts. There are too few schools and there is no social welfare system. The United Nations' Human Development Report tells the story. Pakistan's GDP per capita is ranked 123 out of 162 countries. Its human development ranking (which takes into account such factors as leading a long life, being knowledgeable and being able to enjoy a decent standard of living) is even worse. To take just two examples of Pakistan's dire social indicators, 25 per cent of children are born with low birth weight and 55 per cent of adults are illiterate.[1]

Social indicators in Pakistan, 1999

	Millions	*Percentage of population*
Population	137.6	100
People not expected to survive to age forty	27	20
People without access to adequate sanitation facilities	54	39
People without access to essential drugs	48	35
Undernourished people	27	20
Adult illiteracy rate	–	55(a)
Infants with low birth-weight	–	25(b)

(a) Percentage of population aged over 14
(b) Percentage of infants
Source: United Nations Development Programme, *Human Development Report 2001*, Oxford University Press, New York, 2001, passim.

Can Musharraf turn this round? The early indications are that he is trying but not succeeding. Take, as an example, the issue of tax reform. Fewer than 1 per cent of Pakistanis pay tax. An official report commissioned by General Musharraf found that:

Tax receipts are insufficient to pay even for debt service and defence and there is hardly any net foreign assistance for development. Simultaneously there is a crisis of confidence between the taxpayer and the government. If taxes relative to GDP do not increase significantly, without new levies, Pakistan cannot be governed effectively, essential public services cannot be delivered and high inflation cannot be avoided. The reform of tax administration is the single most important economic task for the government.[2]

It is not difficult to work out why Pakistan has such a dire tax collection rate. Since 1947 no one has served a prison sentence for income tax evasion. Pakistan's tax-raising body, the Central Board of Revenue, frequently announces crackdowns on evaders, but the threats of stern action and declarations of 'final' deadlines make no difference. Few Pakistanis believe that the state institutions are strong enough to force them to pay tax. And even when taxpayers do pay their share, there is little guarantee that the money will end up in the state's coffers. In 2001 a former senior World Bank official claimed that almost 50 per cent of the money paid by Pakistani taxpayers went straight into the pockets of tax officials.[3]

Tax revenues in Pakistan as a percentage of GDP, 1992–1993

Tax	World average	Pakistan 1992–1993
Direct taxes	7.26	2.71
Income tax	5.11	2.58
Wealth and property tax	0.45	0.13
Social security taxes	1.30	–
Indirect taxes (domestic)	5.21	4.33
Sales, turnover, VAT	2.46	1.74
Excises	2.07	2.59

Source: S. Akbar Zaidi, *Issues in Pakistan's Economy*, Oxford University Press, Karachi, 2000, p. 211.

In May 2000, shortly after he took over, General Musharraf announced that improving the tax collection system was one of his main priorities. He focussed on a tax which he thought would be relatively easy to raise: a General Sales Tax or GST. It was by no means a new idea. The IMF had long championed the GST. Initially, General Musharraf showed considerable determination to make people register for GST. When the country's traders went on strike to oppose the tax, the general stood firm. After the strike collapsed, small businessmen in all Pakistan's major cities reluctantly participated in a National Survey and filled out forms giving key data about their businesses.

In the event, though, the traders had little to fear. In 2001 an official from the Central Board of Revenue admitted that most of the survey forms gathered by the government had not been processed and consequently had 'not yielded a single penny'.[4] By April 2001 – one year after the general's stand-off with the traders – there were still only 62,000 registered sales tax payers in all of Pakistan.[5] The National Survey data had been collected but the whole initiative got bogged down in Pakistan's notoriously lethargic bureaucracy. In January 2002 the finance minister, Shaukat Aziz, said that the National Survey had yielded data that meant there were another half a million 'potential taxpayers'.[6] Even if those potential taxpayers were transformed into actual ones, only 1.5 per cent of the population would be registered taxpayers. Meanwhile tax collectors remained so hopelessly underpaid that even senior government officials conceded that they had little choice but to supplement their income through corrupt practice. It was hardly surprising that for all Musharraf's efforts, the IMF was once again complaining that Pakistan's rate of tax collection was hopelessly inadequate.[7]

General Musharraf has been similarly unsuccessful in implementing his social policies. Take, as just one example, his attempt to eliminate bonded labour, a phenomenon that again reveals the weakness of the Pakistani state. Successive governments have vowed that they will eliminate the scourge: they have all failed to do so. Bonded labour remains a pernicious feature of many rural communities, especially on the farms of southern Sindh and in the brick kilns of Punjab. The system is built on debt. Typically a landlord or brick kiln owner will extend a small loan to a labourer who, for example, needs some money to cover the cost of a daughter's marriage. The loan, however, will carry an exorbitant rate of interest. The factory owner or landlord then requires the labourer, his wife and all his children to work for him so that they can earn money to pay off the debt. But the family's combined income never covers the interest rate payments. The family ends up trapped, sometimes for several years.

Since 1992 there has been legislation making it illegal to extend a loan with the purpose of forcing someone into bonded labour, but the law has never been consistently enforced. Although the courts do free hundreds of victims each year, there are many more who are still being kept as virtual slaves. On some estimates there are over 50,000 bonded labourers in Pakistan.[8] In southern Sindh landlords sometimes buy and sell their labourers. A male labourer would generally fetch around 50,000 rupees (US $100).[9] Often the bonded labourers' living conditions are truly terrible. Those who try to escape from the place of their employment are captured and have to work in chains and fetters.

True to form, the Musharraf administration came up with a 'Plan of Action' to deal with bonded labour. It proposed training the children of freed bonded labourers, establishing micro-financing schemes and creating 'vigilance committees' in rural areas. The policy declaration sounded fine but, as ever, there was little change on the ground. Two years after Musharraf took over power, human rights activists were reporting that bonded labour was just as prevalent as before. Even under a military government, no landlord or factory owner feared imprisonment for exploiting bonded labourers.

General Musharraf's anti-corruption drive has also failed. Straight after his coup, Musharraf stated that the elimination of corruption was one of his top priorities, but even at the outset there were indications that he would compromise on this commitment if it were politically expedient to do so. The judiciary managed to secure an undertaking that, in return for its retrospective validation of Musharraf's coup, judges would not be investigated for corruption. Mindful of the need for positive press coverage, the military also let it be known that journalists would not be investigated. And by 2002 the regime's commitment to anti-corruption had disappeared without trace as was amply demonstrated by the case of Mansur ul Haq.

Admiral Mansur ul Haq was chief of the navy between 1994 and 1997. Shortly after he took up his post there were rumours that he was taking kickbacks on defence contracts. The civilian government of the time, (probably wishing to conceal its own involvement in the scandal), accepted the view of the other service chiefs that formally charging the admiral would undermine the prestige of the armed forces.[10] After Musharraf's coup the authorities said they were determined to pursue the case and, by May 2001, had gathered sufficient evidence to secure Mansur ul Haq's extradition from the United States so that he could face charges in the Pakistani courts. But by the end of the year, the military's commitment to the anti-corruption drive had weakened. The National Accountability Bureau struck a deal with Mansur ul Haq in which he secured his freedom by promising to pay back US $7.5 million to the state. No one in authority even attempted to explain why, if he admitted misappropriating the money, the admiral did not remain in gaol. As one Pakistani journalist pointed out, the amount Mansur ul Haq promised to return was the equivalent of 1,270 years of an Admiral's salary or twice the annual salary bill for the navy's entire personnel.[11]

The admiral's case was part of a pattern. By the start of 2002 several politicians also found that their corruption cases had been dropped. The military attempted to excuse itself on the grounds that finding solid evidence of white-collar crime is extremely difficult and time-consuming but the real reason for the softened approach was that the army saw corruption cases as useful levers with which they could control politicians. If politicians transgress the line of 'acceptable' criticism of the military they can expect to have their corruption cases revived. Equally, if politicians accommodate themselves with the military regime they can expect to have their cases dropped. For short-term political gains Musharraf had abandoned one of the strategic objectives of his regime.

It is not only the elite who benefit from the state's failure to apply the law. An astonishing 60 per cent of Pakistani electricity is stolen. Yet, if anyone is found to have tampered with his or her electricity meter, or to have set up an illegal supply line, the only punishment he or she will receive is a request to pay some of the money owed. If General Musharraf is serious about reforming Pakistani society he will have to overturn the culture of impunity. He shows little sign of doing so.

Other Musharraf initiatives have also run into the sand. His plans to de-weaponise Pakistani society have inevitably encountered the problem that no one wants to give up serviceable weapons. Unwilling to face the genuine difficulties of implementing the policy, army officers instead resorted to buying useless old firearms so that the newspapers could publish pictures hailing the success of the government's programme. The army has never acknowledged its military shortcomings and it is equally unwilling to admit to its political failures.

It remains to be seen whether Musharraf's attempt to reverse the Zia legacy will bear any fruit. After 11 September General Musharraf found the courage to say that the Islamic radicals did not represent mainstream Pakistani opinion. Many Pakistanis welcomed his remarks with enthusiasm. Yet Musharraf's decision to speak out against the radicals did not mean that they had disappeared. And some of the measures which were intended to tackle radical Islam were doomed from the outset. Musharraf's plan, for example, to get the madrasas to broaden their syllabi to include English and science was never realistic. Since the military regime (like its predecessors) was unable to recruit enough teachers to work in Pakistan's mainstream schools, it was hardly likely that they would be able to find teachers to fill new posts in the madrasas.

General Musharraf's regime has another problem. It faces a fundamental contradiction. A man who assumed power illegally, and whose legitimacy depends on military force, has argued that he alone can restore democracy to the country. Musharraf's tolerance of press criticism and his modernist ideas have given him credibility. In many ways Musharraf *is* set on a cause diametrically opposed to that of General Zia. Yet there is also a striking similarity between the two men. Neither was prepared to give up the primacy of the army.

What the generals find more difficult to accept is that Pakistan's military governments have been just as incompetent as their civilian counterparts. If General Musharraf is to transform his vision of Pakistani society into a reality he will need great reserves of political will, and a more effective bureaucracy. He has neither. And while he still believes that the Pakistan army is the solution to the country's problems, he shows no sign of accepting that, in fact, it is part of the problem.

Notes

Introduction

1   Strictly speaking, Pakistan's eastern wing should be referred to as East Bengal until 1956 when it was renamed East Pakistan. For the sake of clarity, however, I shall use the term East Pakistan throughout the text. Similarly, I shall refer to the western wing as West Pakistan.

Chapter 1

1   'Pakistan as Ground Zero', *asiaweek.com*, 28 September 2001 and interviews conducted by the author.
2   Interview with Pakistan's finance minister, Shaukat Aziz, January 2002.
3   Interview with Mohammed Ali, October 2001.
4   Andrew R. Wilder, *The Pakistani Voter: Electoral Politics and Voting Behaviour in the Punjab*, Oxford University Press, Karachi, 1999, p. 170.
5   Ibid., passim.
6   Khalid Rahman *et al.* (eds), *Jama'at-e-Islami and National and International Politics*, volume 2, Bookmakers, Islamabad, 1999, p. xviii.
7   There are many ways to spell Maududi's name. I am using the spelling preferred by Jamaat-e-Islami.
8   General Musharraf's address is available on www.pak.gov.pk/public/president-address-19-09-01.htm.
9   Interview with Sami ul Haq, July 1999.
10 Rahimullah Yusufzai, 'Islamic Jirga sets TV and VCRs on Fire in Mardan', *The News*, 19 February 2001, p. 10.
11 Richard Kurin, 'A View from the Countryside', pp. 115–27, in Anita M. Weiss (ed.), *Islamic Reassertion in Pakistan*, Vanguard, Lahore, 1987.

12   Afzal Iqbal, *The Islamisation of Pakistan*, Vanguard, Lahore, 1986, p. 25.

13   Akbar S. Ahmed, *Jinnah, Pakistan and Islamic Identity: The Search for Saladin*, Rout-
      ledge, London, 1997. p. 175.

14   Hamid Khan, *Constitutional and Political History of Pakistan*, Oxford University
      Press, Oxford, 2001, p. 100.

15   Ibid., p. 92.

16   Mohammad Ayub Khan, *Friends Not Masters: A Political Autobiography*, Oxford
      University Press, Karachi, 1967, p. 209.

17   Ibid., p. 203.

18   Ibid., p. 106.

19   Hamid Ali, *Martial Law Orders & Regulations*, The Ideal Publishers, Karachi,
      1980, Martial Law Order, No. 5, subsection 1(6).

20   Weiss, (ed.), *Islamic Reassertion*, p. 11.

21   Interview with General Pervez Musharraf, November, 1999.

22   Address to the nation by General Pervez Musharraf, 17 October 1999. Avail-
      able on www.pak.gov.pk/public/president-address-19-09-01.htm

23   'Blasphemy Law: Old FIR procedure restored', *Dawn*, 16 May 2000, available
      on www.dawn.com/2000/05/17/top4.htm.

24   Zaffar Abbas, 'Man on a Mission?', *Herald*, July 2001, p. 34.

25   Azhar Abbas, 'Tentacles of Hatred', *Herald*, September 2001, p. 62.

26   Ibid., p. 62.

27   Interviews with senior Pakistani officials, July–August 1999.

28   'Musharraf Wants At Least 5 Years', *The News*, 21 January 2002.

29   See *Guardian*, 9 October 2001.

30   *2001 Report on Foreign Terrorist Organizations*, available on www.state.gov/s/ct/
      rls/rpt/fto/2001/5258.htm

31   Craig Baxter and Charles H. Kennedy (eds), *Pakistan 2000*, Oxford University
      Press, Karachi, 2000, p. 157.

32   Rory McCarthy and Richard Norton-Taylor, 'Alliance Closes on Key City',
      Guardian, 9 November 2001.

33   'Twelve Dead in Attack on Indian Parliament', *Guardian*, 13 December 2001.

34   'Inside Jihad', *Newsline*, February 2001, p. 32.

35   See 'Musharraf speech highlights', http://news.bbc.co.uk/hi/english/world/
      south_asia/newsid_1757000/1757251.stm.

36   A. H. Nayyar, 'Madrasa Education', pp. 215–50, in Pervez Hoodbhoy (ed.), *Edu-
      cation and the State: Fifty Years of Pakistan*, Oxford University Press, Karachi, 1998,
      p. 226.

37   Musa Khan Jalalzai, *Sectarianism in Pakistan*, A. H. Publishers, Lahore, 1992,
      p. 287.

38   General Musharraf, television interview with CNN, 30 September 2001.

39   Baxter and Kennedy, (eds) *Pakistan 2000*, p. 185.

40   Jessica Stern, 'Pakistan's Jihad Culture', *Foreign Affairs*, November/December
      2000, available on www.foreignaffairs.org/issues/001/stern.html.

41   'Action Plan for Deeni Madaris Today', *The Nation*, 3 December 2001, p. 1.

Chapter 2

This account of the coup is largely based on my own eyewitness observations and contemporaneous interviews. It also draws from the transcript of all the (sometimes conflicting) evidence given in the trial of Nawaz Sharif. The full verdict reached by Judge Rehmat Hussain Jaffri can be found on the Pakistani government website: http://pak.gov.pk/public/govt/reports/vtext.htm. The site contains the judge's (accurate) summary of the evidence he heard.

1 Azhar Abbas, 'The Creeping Coup', *Herald*, May 1998, p. 28.
2 Interview with Admiral (Retd.) Fasih Bokhari, July 2001.
3 Interview with Mushahid Hussain, July 2001.
4 In October 2001 Musharraf said: 'This project was designed by the former Prime Minister and ex-director general of the Inter Services Intelligence and I had no knowledge till I took over as Chief Executive. This project could not have met with success so we shelved it.' See 'Attacks to be short, targeted, says Musharraf', *The News*, 9 October 2001, p. 8.
5 *Reuters*, 20th September 2000.
6 Interview with US embassy officials, 21 September 2000.
7 Brigadier Javed Iqbal revealed the prime minister's fears in his evidence at Sharif's trial. Other close advisers have, privately, confirmed this account of Sharif's state of mind.
8 'We have made it clear to the Taliban that this [the existence of the camps] is not acceptable to us,' Sharif said. *The News*, 8 October 1999, p. 1.
9 'Events', *Pakistani Defence News Bulletin*, 1–15 October 1999.
10 Brigadier Javed Iqbal who was also in the car gave an account of this conversation at Nawaz Sharif's trial.
11 This and all subsequent quotations involving air traffic control are taken from the transcript of the tapes recorded in the tower at the time. The court that tried Nawaz Sharif never heard the tapes but the news magazine *Herald* obtained them. A full transcript can be found on www.dawn.com/herald/pk805/index.htm.
12 Eyewitness account from *The Nation*, 13 October 1999.
13 'Events', *Pakistan Defence News Bulletin*, 1–15 October 1999.
14 His account, which follows, was published by the Associated Press of Pakistan, 11 November 2000.
15 *Newsline*, November 1999, pp. 25–6.
16 Ibid.
17 Full text available on http://news.bbc.co.uk/hi/english/world/monitoring/newsid_473000/473175.stm.

Chapter 3

Throughout this chapter I shall use the word Kashmir to refer to the State of Jammu and Kashmir. I shall make it clear when I am referring to the more limited area of the Vale of Kashmir or Kashmir Valley.

1   Chaudri Muhammad Ali, *The Emergence of Pakistan*, Research Society of Pakistan, Lahore, 10th impresion, 1998, p. 297.

2   Karan Singh, *Autobiography*, Oxford University Press, Delhi, 1994, p. 31.

3   Larry Collins and Dominique Lapierre, *Freedom at Midnight*, Harper Collins, London, 1997, p. 191.

4   Patrick French, *Liberty or Death: India's Journey to Independence and Division*, Harper Collins, London, 1997, p. 373.

5   Alastair Lamb, *Kashmir: A Disputed Legacy 1846–1990*, Oxford University Press, Oxford, 1992, p. 88.

6   Sumantra Bose, *The Challenge in Kashmir: Democracy, Self-Determination and a Just Peace*, Sage, New Delhi, 1997, p. 24.

7   Singh, *Autobiography*, p. 20.

8   Collins and Lapierre, *Freedom at Midnight*, p. 257.

9   Ali, *Emergence of Pakistan*, p. 286.

10 Prem Shankar Jha, *Kashmir 1947: Rival Versions of History*, Oxford University Press, Delhi, 1998, p. 38.

11 He also had to demarcate the new boundary in Bengal.

12 Ali, *Emergence of Pakistan*, p. 202.

13 Christopher Beaumont, interview with BBC Radio 4, in the programme *Document: A Judge Remembers*, 22 September 1994. Provided by Andrew Whitehead.

14 See, for example, Jha, *Kashmir 1947*, pp. 74–82.

15 Ali, *Emergence of Pakistan*, p. 216.

16 Lamb, *Kashmir*, p. 111.

17 Collins and Lapierre, *Freedom at Midnight*, p. 355.

18 His testimony is reproduced in Jha, *Kashmir 1947*, p. 143.

19 Lamb, *Kashmir*, p. 110.

20 Singh, *Autobiography*, p. 80.

21 Akbar S. Ahmed, *Jinnah, Pakistan and Islamic Identity: The Search for Saladin*, Routledge, London, 1997, p. 116.

22 Hasan Zaheer, *The Rawalpindi Conspiracy 1951*, Oxford University Press, Karachi, 1998, p. 63.

23 Victoria Schofield, *Kashmir in Conflict: India, Pakistan and the Unfinished Conflict*, I. B. Tauris, London, 2000, p. 46.

24 Ijaz Hussain, *Kashmir Dispute: An International Law Perspective*, Quaid-i-Azam University, Rawalpindi, 1998, p. 112.

25 Schofield, *Kashmir in Conflict*, p. 51.

26 Singh, *Autobiography*, p. 57.

27 Sherbaz Khan Mazari, *A Journey to Disillusionment*, Oxford University Press, Karachi, 2000, pp. 11 and 12.

28 Jha, *Kashmir 1947*, pp. 133–8.

29 This is now accepted by historians from both sides of the debate. See ibid., pp. 133–8.

30 Lamb, *Kashmir*, p. 135.

31 Jha, *Kashmir 1947*, p. 62.

32 Stanley Wolpert, *Jinnah of Pakistan*, Oxford University Press, New York, 1984, p. 13.

33   Schofield, *Kashmir in Conflict*, p. 63.

34   Zaheer, *Rawalpindi*, p. 149.

35   Chaudri, *Emergence of Pakistan*, p. 299.

36   Zaheer, *Rawalpindi*, pp. 55 and 56.

37   Ali, *Emergence of Pakistan*, p. 305.

38   Lamb, *Kashmir*, p. 189.

39   Mohammad Ayub Khan, *Friends Not Masters: A Political Autobiography*, Oxford University Press, Karachi, 1967, p. 242.

40   Roedad Khan (ed.), *The American Papers: Secret and Confidential. India–Pakistan Bangladesh–Documents, 1965–1973*, Oxford University Press, Karachi, 1999, p. 82.

41   Stanley Wolpert, *Zulfi Bhutto of Pakistan: His Life and Times*, Oxford University Press, New York, 1993, p. 78.

42   Major General (Retd.) Shaukat Riza, *The Pakistan Army War 1965*, Services Book Club, Lahore, 1984, p. 19.

43   Ibid., p. 82.

44   Wolpert, *Zulfi Bhutto*, p. 88.

45   Brigadier (Retd.) Z. A. Khan, *The Way it Was*, Ahbab, Karachi, 1998, pp. 155 and 156.

46   Wolpert, *Zulfi Bhutto*, 1993, p. 90.

47   Brian Cloughley, *A History of the Pakistan Army: Wars and Insurrections*, Oxford University Press, Karachi, 2000, pp. 70 and 71.

48   Khan (ed.), *American Papers*, p. 35.

49   Riza, *Pakistan Army War*, p. 192.

50   Lamb, *Kashmir*, p. 267.

51   Schofield, *Kashmir in Conflict*, p. 118.

52   Hussain, *Kashmir Dispute*, p. 157. Some Pakistani versions of the Simla Agreement – strangely, including the one given in Ijaz Hussain's index, omit this part of the text.

53   Lamb, *Kashmir*, p. 307.

54   Interview with JKLF leader Amanullah Khan, 12 October 2001.

55   'Alliance Closes on Key City', *Guardian*, 9 November 2001.

56   US Department of State, *Country Reports on Human Rights Practices*, 1996–2000, available on www.state.gov/www/global/human_rights/hrp_reports_mainhp.html.

57   US Department of State, *Country Report on Human Rights Practices*, 1998, available on www.usis.usemb.se/human/human1998/india.html.

58   Bose, *The Challenge in Kashmir*, p. 71.

59   'Karnal Sher Revives Spirit of Martyrdom', *The News*, 18 July 1999.

60   See www.rediff.com/news/1999/jul/16akd1.htm.

61   'Enemy Mounting Pressure', *Dawn*, 4 October 2001.

62   See, for example, Ikram Sehgal's 'The Wages of Truth', *The Nation*, 14 August 1999 and Ayaz Amir's 'Islamabad Diary', *Dawn*, 2 July 1999.

63   *Executive Summary of the Kargil Review Committee Report*, p. 4. Available on http://alfa.nic.in/rs/general/25indi1.htm.

64   Syed Ali Dayan Hasan, 'Double Jeopardy', *Herald*, July 2000, p. 26.

65   Interview with a cabinet minister, who wishes to remain anonymous, December 1999.

66   Rajeev Sharma, *Pak Proxy War: A Story of ISI, Bin Laden and Kargil*, Kaveri Books, Delhi, 1999, p. 9.

67   Interview with Niaz Naik, January 2000.

68   Sharma, *Pak Proxy War*, p. 30.

69   Major General Y Bahl, (ed.), *Kargil Blunder: Pakistan's Plight, India's Victory*, Manas Publications, Delhi, 2000. See chapter 11 by Air Commodore (Retd.) N. B. Singh, p. 162.

70   M. K. Akbar, *Kargil: Cross Border Terrorism*, Mittal Publications, Delhi, 1999, p. 179.

71   Yadav, interview with *Hindustan Times*, 17 August 1999.

72   For an account of the fighting see the Indian press on 5 July – for example, *Indian Express*, 5 July 1999.

73   See www.idsa-india.org.

74   Cloughley, *A History of the Pakistan Army*, p. 388.

75   Interview with Brigadier (Retd.) Shaukat Qadir, November 2001.

76   Hasan, 'Double Jeopardy', p. 36.

77   Sharma, *Pak Proxy War*, p. 49.

78   Ibid. p. 24.

79   Interviews with two participants of the meeting, October 2001.

80   Interviews with eyewitnesses who wish to remain anonymous, March 2001.

81   Schofield, *Kashmir in Conflict*, p. 236.

82   Bose, *The Challenge in Kashmir*, p. 92.

Chapter 4

1   The quotation comes from an interview Altaf Hussain gave to the *Herald* in October 2000. The numbers are somewhat wayward but his point is nonetheless clear. His description of partition as a great mistake was first made in his speech at Acton Hall London, 17 September 2000.

2   The quotation about Nawab Akbar Bugti's Baloch, Muslim and Pakistani background, made in an interview with the author in March 1999, is similar to a remark made by the prominent Pukhtoon leader, Wali Khan, for which see Victoria Schofield, (ed.) *Old Roads and New Highways: Fifty Years of Pakistan*, Oxford University Press, Karachi, 1997, chapter by Akbar S. Ahmed, p. 141.

3   Strictly, all those who moved to Pakistan at the time of partition can be described as Mohajirs – the word means refugee.

4   Quoted in Akbar S Ahmed, *Jinnah, Pakistan and Islamic Identity: The Search for Saladin*, Routledge, London, 1997, p. 236.

5   These are the opening words of Ayub Khan's memorandum entitled 'A Short Appreciation of the Present and Future Problems of Pakistan', written on 4 October 1954. It is reproduced in full in Hasan-Askari Rizvi, *The Military and Politics in Pakistan: 1947–1986*, Progressive Publishers, Lahore, 1987 p. 265.

6   Rizvi, *Military and Politics*, p. 283.

7   Quoted in Selig S. Harrison, *In Afghanistan's Shadow: Baluch Nationalism and Soviet Temptations*, Carnegie Endowment for International Peace, New York, 1981, p. 156.

8   Ibid., pp. 150 and 151.

9   Mohammad Ayub Khan, *Friends Not Masters: A Political Autobiography*, Oxford University Press, Karachi, 1967, p. 93.

10 Andrew R. Wilder, *The Pakistani Voter: Electoral Politics and Voting Behaviour in the Punjab*, Oxford University Press, Karachi, 1990, p. 59.

11 Tariq Rahman, *Language and Politics in Pakistan*, Oxford University Press, Karachi, 1996, p. 111.

12 G. M. Syed, *A Case for Sindu Desh*, Sorath Publication, Bombay, 1985, p. 11.

13 Feroz Ahmed, *Ethnicity and Politics in Pakistan*, Oxford University Press, Karachi, 1999, p. 110.

14 Rahman, *Language and Politics*, p. 114.

15 Syed, *A Case for Sindu Desh* pp. 4, 5 and 38.

16 Tahir Amin, *Ethno-National Movements of Pakistan*, Institute of Policy Studies, Islamabad, 1993, p. 75.

17 Anita M. Weiss, and S. Zulfiqar Gilani (eds), *Power and Civil Society in Pakistan*, Oxford University Press, Karachi, 2001, p. 200.

18 Akbar S. Ahmed, 'Tribes, Regional Pressures and Nationhood', pp. 139–55 in Schofield (ed.) *Old Roads and New Highways*, p. 147.

19 *Herald*, September 1987, p. 131.

20 *Dawn*. See front page stories in editions from 8 to 17 July 1972.

21 Syed, *A Case for Sindu Desh* p. 77.

22 Ian Talbot, *Pakistan: A Modern History*, Vanguard Books, Lahore, 1999, p. 254.

23 See Seyyed Vali Reza Nasr, 'State Society and the Crisis of National Identity', pp. 103–30 in Rasul Bakhsh Rais (ed.), *State Society and Democratic Change in Pakistan*, Oxford University Press, Karachi 1997, p. 122.

24 Roedad Khan, *Pakistan: A Dream Gone Sour*, Oxford University Press, Karachi, 1998, pp. 89–90.

25 Ahmed, *Ethnicity and Politics*, p. 123.

26 *Herald*, September 1987, p. 130.

27 Altaf Hussain has himself given the date of March 1984 for the founding of the MQM although the party could not be formally registered until January 1986 after General Zia lifted martial law. See his interview in the *Herald*, September 1997, p. 32.

28 This account of 14 December 1986 is drawn from contemporaneous accounts in the Pakistani press. The fullest is in the *Herald*, January 1987, pp. 38–52 and p. 60.

29 Rahman, *Language and Politics*, pp. 121 and 130.

30 *Herald*, March 1987, p. 30.

31 *Herald*, September 1997, p. 32.

32 *Herald Annual*, January 1993, pp. 129 and 130.

33 *Herald*, November 1989, p. 51.

34 Amnesty International, *Pakistan: Human Rights in Karachi*, ASA 33/01/96, February 1996.

35 At the time of writing he is still there.

36 *Herald Annual*, January 1996, p. 54.

37 *Herald*, August 1995, p. 25.

38   'Karachi Resurgent' – a *Herald* hand-out, June 2000. The *Herald* obtained its figures from the Sindh Home Department.

39   *The News*, 22 May 1999, p. 1.

40   Mian Ata Rabbani, *I was the Quaid's ADC*, Oxford University Press, Karachi, 1996, p. 150.

41   See, for example, Lt. Colonel Syed Iqbal Ahmad, *Balochistan: Its Strategic Importance*, Royal Book Company, Karachi, 1992.

42   For Z. A. Bhutto's account of this affair see Roedad Khan, (ed.), *The American Papers: Secret and Confidential. India–Pakistan–Bangladesh Documents, 1965–1973*, Oxford University Press, Karachi, 1999, p. 888.

43   Harrison, *In Afghanistan's Shadow*, p. 3. Ian Talbot also estimates the Pakistani force at 80,000. Talbot, *Pakistan*, p. 224.

44   Harrison, *In Afghanistan's Shadow*, p. 38.

45   Brian Cloughley, *A History of the Pakistan Army: Wars and Insurrections*, Oxford University Press, Karachi, 2000, p. 361.

46   Talbot, *Pakistan*, p. 226.

47   *Herald*, December 2000.

48   Sometimes also referred to as Pushtunistan or Pukhtunistan.

49   Quoted in Rizvi, *Military and Politics*, p. 40.

50   Lawrence Ziring, *Pakistan in the Twentieth Century: A Political History*, Oxford University Press, Karachi, 1998, p. 86.

51   Ainslie T. Embree, *Pakistan's Western Borderlands*, Vikas, Delhi, 1985, p. 24.

52   Quoted in Harrison, *In Afghanistan's Shadow*, p. 144. The Oxus River marks Afghanistan's northern border with the then Soviet Union (now Tajikistan). Attock is a town on the Indus River 65 miles west of Islamabad.

53   Amin, *Ethno-National Movements*, p. 100.

54   Ibid., pp. 82 and 175.

55   Rahman, *Language and Politics*, p. 178. Most of this account of the Seraikis is drawn from this source.

56   Tariq Ali, *Can Pakistan Survive? The Death of a State*, Penguin, London, 1983, p. 150.

57   Tariq Rahman, 'Centre of Power Struggle', *Dawn*, 30 June 2000, p. 31.

58   *Gallup Poll*, April 2000 and May 1985, Gallup Pakistan, Islamabad.

Chapter 5

1   *Hamoodur Rehman Commission Report*, part IV, chapter XII, para. 16, *Dawn*, 24 January 2001, p. 23. The Commission was set up by Zulfikar Ali Bhutto to investigate the events of 1971, and in particular, why the Pakistani army surrendered. The Commission's report came in two stages. The main report was finished by July 1972 but not published until 2000. The supplementary report, which relies on evidence from some of the key Pakistani participants like General Niazi, was completed in 1974 and also published in 2000. For both, see successive copies of *Dawn* from 8 January to 1 February 2001 inclusive. A version of the full report is also available at www.dawn.com/report/hrc.

2   Interview with eyewitness, June 2001.

3   Maj. General Shaukat Riza, *The Pakistan Army 1966–1971*, Army Education Press, Lahore, 1990, p. 83.

4   Richard Sisson and Leo E. Rose, *War and Secession: Pakistan, India and the Creation of Bangladesh*, Oxford University Press, Karachi, 1990, p. 57.

5   K. K. Aziz, *The Making of Pakistan: A Study in Nationalism*, Sang-e-Meel Publications, Lahore, 1998, p. 56.

6   K. K. Aziz, for example, argues that under the All India Muslim League Constitution, the All India Muslim League Legislators' Convention had no such right. Any amendment could only be made by a full session of the All India Muslim League itself. See K. K. Aziz, *The Murder of History: A Critique of History Textbooks Used in Pakistan*, Vanguard, Lahore, 1993, p. 147.

7   Anwar Dil and Afia Dil, *Bengali Language Movement to Bangladesh*, Ferozons, Lahore, 2000, p. 62.

8   Hasan Zaheer, *The Separation of East Pakistan, The Rise and Realization of Bengali Muslim Nationalism*, Oxford University Press, Karachi, 1995, p. 10.

9   Dil and Dil, *Bengali Language Movement*, p. 68.

10 Ibid., p. 82.

11 Ibid., p. 82.

12 For an account of the riots see Lawrence Ziring, *Pakistan in the Twentieth Century: A Political History*, Oxford University Press, Karachi, 1998, p. 130.

13 Dil and Dil, *Bengali Language Movement*, p. 92.

14 Zaheer, *The Separation of East Pakistan*, p. 35.

15 It is quoted in full in Riza, *Pakistan Army 1966–1971*, p. 215.

16 This figure and those that follow have been collated by Hasan-Askari Rizvi. See Hasan-Askari Rizvi, *The Military and Politics in Pakistan: 1947–1986*, Progressive Publishers, Lahore, 1987, p. 137 passim.

17 Sisson and Rose, *War and Secession*, p. 10.

18 Riza, *Pakistan Army 1966–1971*, pp. 32 and 33.

19 This is a summary. A full version can be found in the *Hamoodur Rehman Commission Report*, part I, chapter V, para. 18, *Dawn*, 10 January 2001, p. 24. In subsequent years there were revised versions of the Six Points but the essential demands always remained the same.

20 Zaheer, *The Separation of East Pakistan*, p. 144.

21 G. W. Choudhury, *The Last Days of United Pakistan*, Oxford University Press, Karachi, 1993, p. 15.

22 Larry Collins and Dominique Lapierre, *Freedom at Midnight*, HarperCollins, London, 1997, p. 159.

23 Siddiq Salik, *Witness to Surrender*, Oxford University Press, Karachi, 1977, p. 3.

24 Roedad Khan, (ed.), *The American Papers: Secret and Confidential. India–Pakistan–Bangladesh Documents, 1965–1973*, Oxford University Press, Karachi, 1999, p. 274.

25 Herbert Feldman, *The End and the Beginning. Pakistan 1969–1971*, Oxford University Press, Karachi, 1976, p. 67.

26 Choudhury, *The Last Days*, p. 85.

27 *Hamoodur Rehman Commission Report*, part I, chapter VI, para. 96, *Dawn*, 13 January 2001, p. 21.

28 *Hamoodur Rehman Commission Report*, part I, chapter VI, para. 26, *Dawn*, 11 January 2001, p. 22.

29 Salik, *Witness to Surrender*, p. 32.

30 Zaheer, *The Separation of East Pakistan*, p. 134. See also Sisson and Rose, *War and Secession*, p. 63.

31 Choudhury, *The Last Days*, p. 149.

32 Choudhury, *The Last Days*, p. 146.

33 Lt. General A. A. K. Niazi, *The Betrayal of East Pakistan*, Oxford Pakistan Paperbacks, Karachi, 1999, pp. xxiv and xxv.

34 Salik, *Witness to Surrender*, p. 36.

35 Khan, (ed.), *American Papers*, p. 466.

36 Ziring, *Pakistan*, p. 334.

37 Sisson and Rose, *War and Secession*, p. 81.

38 Zaheer, *The Separation of East Pakistan*, p. 41.

39 Sisson and Rose, *War and Secession*, p. 85.

40 Khan, (ed.), *American Papers*, p. 497.

41 *Dawn*, 27 March 1971, p. 1.

42 *Hamoodur Rehman Commission Report*, part VI, chapter VI, para. 81, *Dawn*, 13 January 2001, p. 22.

43 Salik, *Witness to Surrender*, p. 76.

44 *Hamoodur Rehman Commission Report*, part I, chapter VI, para. 11, *Dawn*, 19 January 2001, p. 21.

45 *Hamoodur Rehman Commission Report*, supplement, part V, chapter I, para. 11, *Dawn*, 6 February 2001, p. 15.

46 Riza, *Pakistan Army 1966–1971*, p. 103.

47 Zaheer, *The Separation of East Pakistan*, p. 201.

48 *Hamoodur Rehman Commission Report*, supplement, part V, chapter II, paras. 12–17, *Dawn*, 6 February 2001, p. 16.

49 *Hamoodur Rehman Commission Report*, supplement, part V, chapter II, paras. 2–6, *Dawn*, 6 February 2001, p. 16.

50 Niazi, *Betrayal*, p. 42.

51 See, for example, Henry Kissinger, *The White House Years*, London, Weidenfeld and Nicolson and Michael Joseph, 1979, passim and Zaheer, *The Separation of East Pakistan*, pp. 237–73.

52 Rizvi, *Military and Politics*, p. 190.

53 Cloughley, *A History of the Pakistan Army*, p. 183.

54 For the various estimates see Niazi, *Betrayal*, p. 112; *Hamoodur Rehman Commission Report*, part I, chapter II, para. 1, *Dawn*, 8 January 2001, p. 15; and Lt. General J. F. R. Jacob, *Surrender at Dacca: Birth of a Nation*, Manohar Publishers, Delhi, 1997, p. 157.

55 Niazi, *Betrayal*, p. 78.

56 Ibid., p. 85.

57 See, for example, *Hamoodur Rehman Commission Report*, part IV, chapter IV, para. 22, *Dawn* 18 January 2001, p. 21.

58 Cloughley, *A History of the Pakistan Army*, p. 208.

59 Salik, *Witness to Surrender*, p. 128.

60   Jacob, *Surrender at Dacca*, p. 56.

61   Niazi, *Betrayal*, p. xxv.

62   Ibid., pp. 198 and 200.

63   *Hamoodur Rehman Commission Report*, supplement, part IV, chapter II, para. 8, *Dawn*, 4 February 2001, p. 24.

64   *Hamoodur Rehman Commission Report*, supplement, part V, chapter III, para. 7, *Dawn*, 7 February 2001, p. 23.

65   The letters are reproduced in Riza, *Pakistan Army 1966–1971*, p. 160–1.

66   *Hamoodur Rehman Commission Report*, supplement, part IV, chapter II, paras. 19–20, *Dawn*, 4 February 2001, p. 24.

67   Niazi, *Betrayal*, p. 211.

68   Jacob, *Surrender at Dacca*, p. 129.

69   Salik, *Witness to Surrender*, p. 206.

70   *Hamoodur Rehman Commission Report*, supplement, part IV, chapter II, para. 38, *Dawn*, 5 February 2001, p. 17.

71   Jacob, *Surrender at Dacca*, p. 142.

72   Niazi, *Betrayal*, p. 235.

73   *Hamoodur Rehman Commission Report*, supplement, part IV, chapter II, para. 11, *Dawn*, 4 February 2001, p. 24.

74   Full text in Jacob, *Surrender at Dacca*, p. 176.

75   Niazi, *Betrayal*, pp. 194 and 211.

76   Salik, *Witness to Surrender*, p. 213.

77   *Hamoodur Rehman Commission Report* (supplement). There are references to Niazi throughout the supplement.

78   *Hamoodur Rehman Commission Report*, part V, chapter IV, para. 33, *Dawn*, 8 February 2001, p. 8.

Chapter 6

Many of those who know about Pakistan's nuclear weapons programme are unable to speak about it openly. Both in Pakistan and in the West many interviewees requested anonymity. Unless otherwise stated in subsequent footnotes, this chapter relies on interviews with these Western and Pakistani officials conducted between April 1998 and February 2001.

1   As so often with famous quotations, there is some uncertainty as to the actual words used by Z. A. Bhutto in 1965. The version given here has appeared many times in Pakistani literature. George Perkovich, however, has found a contemporaneous account, in the *Manchester Guardian*, which reported Bhutto saying that if India built the bomb, 'then we should have to eat grass and get one, or buy one of our own'. George Perkovich, *India's Nuclear Bomb: The Impact on Global Proliferation*, University of California Press, 1999, p. 108.

2   Interview given by A. Q. Khan to *Al-Akbar*, 13 July 1998. Khan subsequently said that while he had given an interview to the newspaper he had not made any remark about the Ghauris being armed with nuclear warheads.

3   See www.cnn.com/transcripts, 7 May 1998.

4   Interview with General (Retd.) K. M. Arif, July 2000.

5   See Dr Zafar Iqbal Cheema, 'How to Respond?', *The News*, 21 May 1998, p. 6.

6   Interview with a participant at the Defence Committee of the Cabinet meeting, July 2001.

7   *Jang*, 13 May 1998.

8   Ibid., 26 May 1998.

9   Ibid., 28 May 1998.

10   *Time*, 8 June 1998.

11   Craig Baxter and Charles H. Kennedy (eds), *Pakistan 2000*, Oxford University Press, Karachi, 2000 p. 120.

12   The citation is quoted in S. Shabbir Hussain and Mujahid Kamran (eds), *Dr A. Q. Khan on Science and Education*, Sang-e-Meel Publication, Lahore, 1997, that also reproduced the (longer) citation of the 1989 Nishan-e-Imtiaz award.

13   Interview with A. Q. Khan, July 2000.

14   BBC news, 3–4 June, 1998.

15   Zulfikar Ali Bhutto, *The Myth of Independence*, Classic, Lahore, 1995, p. 153.

16   An account of the Multan meeting can be found in Shahid ur Rehman, *Long Road to Chagai: Untold Story of Pakistan's Nuclear Quest*, Print Wise Publication, Islamabad, 1999, pp. 16–19. Also see Zahid Malik, *Dr A. Q. Khan and The Islamic Bomb*, Hurmat Publication, Islamabad, 1992, p. 128.

17   Interview with A. Q. Khan, July 2000.

18   Munir Ahmed Khan, 'Nuclearisation of South Asia and its Regional and Global Implications', *Regional Studies*, autumn 1998, Institute for Regional Studies, Islamabad, p. 7. The article has histories of both the Indian and Pakistani nuclear programmes.

19   Malik, *Dr A. Q. Khan*, p. 185.

20   When it was founded, the laboratory went under the name of Aviation Development Workshop. In July 1976 it was renamed the Engineering Research Laboratory. Then, in May 1981, after a visit by General Zia, it was given its current name of Khan Research Laboratory. Many refer to the plant as Kahuta – the name of a nearby village. Interview with A. Q. Khan, July 2000.

21   Ibid.

22   Rehman, *Long Road*, p. 51. The charge is also made in Steve Weissman and Herbert Krosney, *The Islamic Bomb: The Nuclear Threat to Israel and the Middle East*, Times Books, New York, 1983, 2nd edition.

23   Simon Henderson, 'Pakistani Scientist Cleared', *Khaleesh Times*, 19 July 1986. See also 'Court Quashed Nuclear Spying Conviction', *Gulf News*, 29 March 1985.

24   Interview with A. Q. Khan, July 2000.

25   Hussain and Kamran (eds), *A. Q. Khan*, p. 117.

26   Khan, 'Nuclearisation', p. 15. See also Jorn Gjelstad and Olav Njolstad (eds), *Nuclear Rivalry and International Order*, Sage Publications, 1996, p. 163.

27   The details of the sanctions imposed on Pakistan are based on interviews in June 2000 with officials from the Pakistani Foreign Office and the US Embassy in Islamabad.

28   Perkovich, *India's Nuclear Bomb*, p. 221.

29 Interview with Agha Shahi, July 2000.

30 Malik, *Dr A. Q. Khan*, p. 76.

31 It is documented in great detail in Weissman and Krosney (eds), *Islamic Bomb*, passim.

32 For example, ibid.

33 'Project 706 – The Islamic Bomb' was broadcast by the BBC's *Panorama* programme in 1980.

34 Quoted in Malik, *Dr A. Q. Khan*, p. 83.

35 Letter from the former Pakistani president Ghulam Ishaq Khan to Zahid Malik, editor of the *Pakistani Observer* and author of *Dr A. Q. Khan*.

36 Interivew with A. Q. Khan, July 2000.

37 Speech to the Pakistan Institute of National Affairs, 9 September 1990, quoted in Hussain and Kamran (eds), *Dr. A. Q. Khan*, p. 117.

38 Interview with A. Q. Khan and former PAEC official, July 2000.

39 Kamal Matinuddin, *The Nuclearisation of South Asia*, Oxford University Press, Karachi, 2002, pp. 340–4.

40 'Responding to India's Nuclear Doctrine' *Dawn*, 5 October 1999.

41 Agha Shahi, address to seminar organised by Islamabad Council of World Affairs and Institute of Strategic Studies held in Islamabad, February 2000.

42 Ibid.

43 Anon., 'Nuclear South Asia: Opportunities and Challenges for Pakistan', *Air War College Journal*, 1999, pp. 19–37, p. 29.

44 Interview with General (Retd.) Mirza Aslam Beg, July 2000.

45 See E. A. S. Bokhari, 'India–Pakistan: The Nuclear Option', *Defence Journal*, March 1998, 2:3, pp. 49–52, p. 51; Shahi, address to seminar, Islamabad, February 2000.

46 'Pakistan nukes outstrip India's, officials say', www.msnbc.com.news, 6 June 2000.

47 Shahi, address to seminar, Islamabad, February 2000.

48 See, for example, Syed Akhtar Ali, 'Towards a Safe and Stable Nuclear Environment in South Asia: Options, Choices and Constraints for Pakistan', *National Development and Security*, 'Special on Nuclear', 8:2, November 1999, pp. 1–26, p. 8, published by the Foundation for Research on International Environment, National Development and Security, Rawalpindi, Pakistan.

49 Leonard S. Spector with Jacqueline Smith, *Nuclear Ambitions: The Spread of Nuclear Weapons 1989–1990*, Farda Publishing Company, Karachi, 1990, pp. 102 and 103.

50 Carnegie Endowment for International Peace, 'Non-Proliferation', fact sheet, 15 April 1999. Western officials have confirmed this assessment of the intermediate range HATF.

51 Ibid.

52 Khan, 'Nuclearisation', p. 9. For an account of Pakistan's and India's missile programmes, see also anon., 'Nuclear South Asia'.

53 Khan, 'Nuclearisation', p. 9. Also see Carnegie Endowment for International Peace, 'Non-Proliferation, fact sheet, 15 April 1999.

54 Quoted in Hussain and Kamran (eds), *Dr A. Q. Khan*, p. 28. A. Q. Khan has

confirmed that he wrote this address but since West European countries were denying visas to him at the time, it was delivered by somebody else who read it out in his name.

55 Shahi, address to seminar, Islamabad, February 2000.

56 See, for example, Ashok Kapur, 'Western Biases', *Bulletin of the Atomic Sciences*, 51:1, January/February 1995, passim. Available on www.bullatomsci.org/issues/1995/jf95/jf95Kapur.html.

57 See, for example, *The News*, 10 April 1999 and 'Pakistan Expected to Announce Nuclear Command Authority Soon', *Press Trust of India (PTI)*, 11 April 1999. See also *Khabrain*, 13 May 1999.

58 Interview with Brigadier (Retd.) Shaukat Qadir, vice president, Islamabad Policy Research Institute, July 2000.

59 Shahi, address to seminar, Islamabad, February 2000.

60 Interview with General (Retd.) Mirza Aslam Beg, July 2000.

61 *Pakistan Observer*, 27 May 2000, p. 1 and *The Nation*, 27 May 2000, p. 1.

62 *Radio Pakistan*, 4 February, 2000.

63 Interview with General (Retd.) Mirza Aslam Beg, July 2000.

64 See Steven Erlanger, 'India's Arms Race Isn't Safe Like the Cold War', *New York Times*, 12 July 1998.

65 Shaun Gregory, 'Nuclear Command and Control in South Asia', *Strategic Issues*, 3, March 2000 entitled 'The Nuclear Debate', published by The Institute of Strategic Studies, Islamabad, p. 77.

66 Matinuddin, *Nuclearisation*, passim.

67 Interview with Pakistani scientist, July 2000.

68 Shahi, address to seminar, Islamabad, February 2000.

69 Matinuddin, *Nuclearisation*, passim.

70 Interview with Brigadier (Retd.) Shaukat Qadir of the Islamabad Policy Research Institute, July 2000.

71 Interview with General (Retd.) Mirza Aslam Beg, June 2000.

72 This account of BRASSTACKS is partly based on an interview in July 2000 with General (Retd.) K. M. Arif who was at the time vice chief of the Pakistan army. There is a much fuller account of the BRASSTACKS episode in Perkovich, *India's Nuclear Bomb*, p. 280.

73 *Executive Summary of the Kargil Review Committee Report*, section 111, The Nuclear Factor. Available on http://alfa.nic.in/rs/general/25indi1.htm.

74 Interview with General (Retd.) K. M. Arif, July 2000.

75 Perkovich, *India's Nuclear Bomb*, p. 280.

76 Interview with General (Retd.) Mirza Aslam Beg, July 2000.

77 Perkovich, *India's Nuclear Bomb*, p. 309.

78 Quoted in ibid., p. 312.

79 For coverage of these two comments see *PTI*, 30 June and 4 July.

80 The columnist was Naseem Zehra who made a typewritten record of Nawaz Sharif's remarks immediately after their conversation.

81 Bruce Riedel, 'American Diplomacy and the 1999 Kargil Summit at Blair House', University of Pennsylvania, available on www.sas.upenn.edu/casi.

82 *Reuters*, 14 August 1999.

83 This was stated by Foreign Office spokesman Tariq Altaf in numerous press briefings during 1999.

84 *Associated Press*, 14 March 1999.

85 There are some references in Spector with Smith, *Nuclear Ambitions*, p. 93. There are also references in Perkovich, *India's Nuclear Bomb*.

86 Malik, *Dr A. Q. Khan*, p. 256.

87 For details on the Libyan connection see Weissman and Krosney, *Islamic Bomb*, pp. 53–65.

88 Major Gen. D. K. Palit and P. K. S. Namboodiri, *Pakistan's Islamic Bomb*, Vikas Publishing House, New Delhi, 1979, p. 21.

89 See contemporary coverage on www.arabicnews.com. Pakistan's Foreign Office denial of his visit was distributed in an official press release on 6 August 1999.

90 'UAE Minister Visiting Pakistan', *Pakistan*, 26 May 1999, pp. 9 and 10.

91 Interview with ambassador Bill Milam, July 2000.

92 *Reuters*, 1 June 2001.

93 Samuel P. Huntingdon, *The Clash of Civilisations and the Remaking of World Order*, Viking, India, 1996, p. 210 and p. 258.

94 Zulfikar Ali Bhutto, *If I Am Assassinated*, Classic, Lahore, 1979, pp. 137 and 138.

95 'Inside Jihad', *Newsline*, February 2001, p. 22.

96 www.bbc.co.uk/hi/english/world/europe/newsid_1569000/1569068.stm.

Chapter 7

1   Mohammad Ayub Khan, *Friends Not Masters: A Political Autobiography*, Oxford University Press, Karachi, 1967, p. 208.

2   Interview with Abdullah Muntazeer, 13 October 1999.

3   See, for example, Akbar S. Ahmed, *Jinnah, Pakistan and Islamic Identity: The Search for Saladin*, Routledge, London, 1997, p. 133.

4   Mian Ata Rabbani, *I Was the Quaid's ADC*, Oxford University Press, Karachi, 1996, p. 142.

5   Stanley Wolpert, *Zulfi Bhutto of Pakistan: His Life and Times*, Oxford University Press, New York, 1993, p. 76.

6   Lawrence Ziring, *Pakistan in the Twentieth Century: A Political History*, Oxford University Press, Karachi, 1998, p. 380.

7   Lt. General Jahan Dad Khan, *Pakistan: Leadership Challenges*, Oxford University Press, Karachi, 1999. p. 51.

8   Ziring, *Pakistan*, p. 381 and Ian Talbot, *Pakistan: A Modern History*, Vanguard Books, Lahore, 1999, p. 219.

9   Shahid ur Rehman, *Who Owns Pakistan?*, Mr Books, Islamabad, 1998, p. 15.

10 Mohammad Asghar Khan, *Generals in Politics: Pakistan 1958–1982*, Vikas, Delhi, 1983, passim.

11 Andrew R. Wilder, *The Pakistani Voter: Electoral Politics and Voting Behaviour in the Punjab*, Oxford University Press, Karachi, 1990, p. 26.

12 Sardar Muhammad Chaudhry, *The Ultimate Crime: Eyewitness to Power Games*, Quami Publishers, Lahore, 1999, p. 393.

13 Mohammad Uzair, 'Foreign Aid and Indebtedness in Pakistan', pp. 367–73 in Mehrunnisa Ali (ed.), *Readings in Pakistan Foreign Policy 1971–1998*, Oxford University Press, Karachi, 2001, p. 369.

14 *Economic Survey 2000–2001*, government of Pakistan, published by the Economic Advisers Wing, Finance Division, Islamabad, See table 9.3.

15 Ibid.

16 'Benazir Bought Surrey Palace out of Kickbacks', *The News*, 1 September 2001.

17 See, for example, Zahid Hussain, 'The Great Loan Scandal', *Newsline*, September 1991.

18 *Dawn*, 13 June 1998.

19 'Nawaz Sharif Tops Defaulters List', *Associated Press*, 14 November 1999.

20 See, for example, Amir Mir, 'The Great Repayment Scandal', *Newsline*, October 1998.

21 See Amir Mir, 'Slipping Through the Net', *Herald*, August 1988, p. 34.

22 Nawaz Sharif's nomination paper for the National Assembly elections 1996.

23 *Sunday Times*, 4 February 2001.

24 'Justice, Lies and Audio Tapes', *Newsline*, March 2001, pp. 32–7.

25 'Benazir Zardari Ordered to Appear in Court on Sept 7', *The Nation*, 11 August 2001.

26 Rafi Raza (ed.), *Pakistan in Perspective 1947–1997*, Oxford University Press, Karachi, 1997, p. 8.

27 Iqbal Akhund, *Trial and Error: The Advent and Eclipse of Benazir Bhutto*, Oxford University Press, Karachi, 2000, p. 118.

28 Interview with Benazir Bhutto, summer 1999.

29 Akhund, *Trial and Error*, p. 119.

30 Ibid., p. xiii.

31 Major General S. Shahid Hamid, *Early Years of Pakistan*, Ferozons, Lahore, 1993, p. 67.

32 Abbas Nazir, 'The Inside Story', *Herald Annual*, 1991, p. 29.

33 Wolpert, *Zulfi Bhutto*, p. 279.

34 Lt. General Durrani's affidavit to the Supreme Court.

35 Reply to Supreme Court by Mirza Mohammed Aslam Beg.

36 Illyas Khan, 'The ISI–Taliban Nexus', *Herald*, November 2001, p. 22.

37 Ibid., p. 24.

38 Interviews with NWFP officials, October 2001.

39 Iftikhar H. Malik, *State and Civil Society in Pakistan*, Macmillan, Basingstoke, 1997, pp 81–93.

40 S. Akbar Zaidi, *Issues in Pakistan's Economy*, Oxford University Press, Karachi, 1999, p. 18.

41 Tehmina Durrani, *My Feudal Lord*, Corgi, London, 1994.

42 M. Attiqur Rahman, *Back to the Pavilion*, Ardeshir Cowasjee, Karachi, 1989, p. 142.

43 Anita M. Weiss and S. Zulfiqar Gilani (eds), *Power and Civil Society in Pakistan*, Oxford University Press, Karachi, 2001, p. 126.

44 Khan, *Pakistan: Leadership Challenges*, p. 82.

45 Mohammad Ayub Khan, *Friends Not Masters: A Political Autobiography*, Oxford University Press, Karachi, 1967, pp. 86 and 87.

46   Ibid., p. 90.

47   Wilder, *Pakistani Voter*, p. 77.

48   Zahid Hussain, 'House of Feudals', *Herald*, April 1985, p. 41.

49   *Herald Election Special*, 1988, p. 109.

50   *Far Eastern Economic Review*, 20 May 1999.

51   *Dawn*, 11 May 2000.

52   'System of Absentee Landlords to be Abolished', *Dawn*, 21 February 2000.

53   'Provinces Asked to Expedite Land Reform', *Dawn*, 26 October 2000.

Chapter 8

1   Quoted in Brigadier (Retd.) Abdul Rahman Siddiqi, 'Army and Islam: An
     Appraisal', *Defence Journal*, 21, May–June 1996, 3–11, p. 5.

2   Jason Burke, 'India Walks into Kashmir Trap', *Observer* 30 May 1999.

3   Interview with Brigadier Nusrat Sial, May 1999.

4   Quoted in Major General S. Shahid Hamid, *Early Years of Pakistan*, Ferozons,
     Lahore, 1993, p. 212.

5   Ibid., p. 30.

6   Stephen Cohen, *The Pakistan Army*, Oxford University Press, Karachi, 1998, p. 89.

7   Anita M. Weiss and S. Zulfiqar Gilani, (eds), *Power and Civil Society in Pakistan*,
     Oxford University Press, Karachi, 2001, p. 207.

8   Dr Marcel A. Boisard, 'Islamic Conduct of Hostilities and the Protection of the
     Victims of Armed Conflicts', *Defence Journal*, 5: 1–2, January–February 1979,
     9–19, p. 18.

9   Brigadier S. K. Malik, *The Quranic Concept of War*, Wajidalis, Lahore, 1979,
     p. xi.

10   Interview with Cecil Chaudhry, May 2001.

11   See 'Maj. Gen. Abbasi's Intended Address to the Nation', *Defence Journal*, 21,
     May–June, 1996, pp. 53–4.

12   *The Frontier Post*, 15 March 1996.

13   Zaffar Abbas, 'Defenders of the Faith', *Herald*, November 1995, p. 34.

14   Zaffar Abbas, 'The Coup That Wasn't', *Herald*, November 1995, p. 28.

15   A discussion of the *Hilal* article can be found in Siddiqi, 'Army and Islam',
     passim.

16   Brian Cloughley, *A History of the Pakistan Army: Wars and Insurrections*. Oxford
     University Press, Karachi, 2000, p. 361.

17   Cohen, *The Pakistan Army*, pp. 55–74.

18   *Hamoodur Rehman Commission Report*, supplement, part V, chapter I, para. 15,
     Dawn, 6 February 2001, p. 16. General Niazi, it should be said, denied the
     accusations.

19   Sardar Muhammad Chaudhry, *The Ultimate Crime: Eyewitness to Power Games*,
     Qaumi Publishers, Lahore, 1997, p. 97.

20   Cohen, *The Pakistan Army*, pp. 169 and 170, italics in original.

21   Quoted in Talat Aslam, 'The Changing Face of the Army', *Herald*, July 1989,
     p. 8.

22　Zahid Hussain, 'Jihad Begins at Home', *Newsline*, February 2001, p. 23.

23　Captain (Retd.) Ayaz Amir, 'Soldiering On', *Herald*, November, 1995, p. 37.

24　Interview with Brigadier (Retd.) Shaukat Qadir, February 2001.

25　Hasan-Askari Rizvi, *The Military and Politics in Pakistan: 1947–1986*, Progressive Publishers, Lahore, 1987, pp. 44, 45, 124 and 125.

26　US State Department, *Annual Report on Military Expenditures*, 1998, available on www.state.gov/www/global/arms/98_amiextoc.html.

27　Jonathon Marcus, 'India and Pakistan: The Military Balance', http:// news.bbc.co.uk, 4 July 2001.

28　Hamid, *Early Years*, p. 177.

29　Lt. General Jahan Dad Khan, *Pakistan: Leadership Challenges*, Oxford University Press, Karachi, 1999, p. 51.

30　*Hamoodur Rehman Commission Report*, part IV, chapter 5, para. 2, *Dawn*, 18 January 2001, p. 21.

31　'Retired Pak Generals Criticise Kargil Manoeuvre', available on www.rediff. com/news/1999/jul/18pakgen.htm.

32　Interview with General Musharraf on the Siachin Glacier, February 1998.

33　Interview with Brigadier Rashid Quereshi, October 1999.

34　Star TV interview with General Musharraf, 28 January 2000.

35　See Mohammad Ayub Khan, *Friends Not Masters: A political Autobiography*, Oxford University Press, Karachi, 1967, pp. 186–91.

36　Khan, *Pakistan: Leadership Challenges*, p. 126.

37　G. W. Choudhury, *The Last Days of United Pakistan*, Oxford University Press, Karachi, 1993, p. 48.

38　Hamid Khan, *Constitutional and Political History of Pakistan*, Oxford University Press, Oxford, 2001, p. 660.

39　Hasan-Askari Rizvi, 'Civil Military Relations in Pakistan', *Herald*, May 1999, p. 40.

40　Azhar Abbas, 'The Creeping Coup', *Herald*, May 1998, p. 30.

41　The following material on the army's economic interests is based on interviews with senior retired officers who wish to remain anonymous.

42　Roedad Khan, *Pakistan: A Dream Gone Sour*, Oxford University Press, Karachi, 1998, p. 43, quoting Altaf Gauhar, *Ayub Khan: Pakistan's First Military Ruler*, Sang-e-Meel Publications, Lahore, 1994, p. 479.

Chapter 9

1　United Nations Development Programme, *Human Development Report 2001*, Oxford University Press, New York, 2001, passim.

2　Reform of Tax Administration in Pakistan, *Report of the Task Force on Reform of Tax Administration*. 24 April 2001, p. 2.

3　Raising Tax Revenues, *Dawn*, 9 August 2001.

4　Shaukat Announces Tax Survey, *The News*, 5 August 2001.

5　*Report of the Task Force on Reform of Tax Administration*, p. 91.

6　Interview with Shaukat Aziz, January 2002.

7   *The News*, 28 August 2001.

8   'Bonded Labour Rife in Sindh', *The Nation*, 11 January 1999.

9   Qurat ul Sadozai, 'Bonded Labour', *Frontier Post*, 22 May 2000.

10 *The Friday Times*, Lahore, 27 April–3 May 2001.

11 'NAB agrees to free Mansur ul Haq for Rs 457.5 million', *The News*, 1 January 2002.

Bibliography

Journals and Reports

2001 Report on Foreign Terrorist Organizations, US Department of State, available on www.state.gov/s/ct/rls/rpt/fto/2001/5258.htm.

Abbasi, Major General Zahir ul Islam, 'Maj. Gen. Abbasi's Intended Address to the Nation', *Defence Journal* 21, May–June 1996, 53–4.

Ali, Syed Akhtar, 'Towards a Safe and Stable Nuclear Environment in South Asia: Options, Choices and Constraints for Pakistan', *National Development and Security*, 'Special on Nuclear', 8:2, November 1999, 1–26, published by the Foundation for Research on International Environment, National Development and Security, Rawalpindi, Pakistan.

Amnesty International, *Pakistan: Human Rights in Karachi*, ASA 33/01/96, February 1996.

Annual Report on Military Expenditures, US State Department, 1998 and 1999, available on www.state.gov.

Anon., 'Nuclear South Asia: Opportunities and Challenges for Pakistan', *Air War College Journal*, 1999, 19–37.

Boisard, Dr Marcel A., 'Islamic Conduct of Hostilities and the Protection of the Victims of Armed Conflicts', *Defence Journal*, 5:1–2, January–February 1979, 9–19.

Bokhari, E. A. S., 'India–Pakistan: The Nuclear Option', *Defence Journal* 2:3, March 1998, 49–52.

Carnegi Endowment for International Peace, 'Non-Proliferation', fact sheet, 15 April 1999.

Country Report on Human Rights Practices, 1998, US Department of State, available on www.usis.usemb.se/human/human1998/india.html.

Country Reports on Human Rights Practices, 1995–2000, US Department of State, available on www.state.gov/www/global/human_rights/hrp_reports_mainhp.html.

Economic Survey 2000–2001, government of Pakistan, published by the Economic Advisers Wing, Finance Division, Islamabad.

'Events', *Pakistan Defence News Bulletin*, 1–15 October 1999.

Executive Summary of the Kargil Review Committee Report, available on http://alfa.nic.in/rs/general/25indi1.htm.

Gallup Poll, May 1985 and April 2000, Gallup Pakistan, Islamabad.

Gregory, Shaun, 'Nuclear Command and Control in South Asia', *Strategic Issues* 3:, March 2000, entitled 'The Nuclear Debate', published by The Institute of Strategic Studies, Islamabad.

Hamoodur Rehman Commission Report, Dawn, 8 January–1 February 2001. A version of the report is also available on www.dawn.com/report/hrc.

Jaffri, Judge Rehmat Hussain, verdict on the trial of Nawaz Sharif, SPL. Case No. 385/1999, available on http://pak.gov.pk/public/govt/reports/vtext/htm.

Human Rights Commission of Pakistan, *State of Human Rights in 1997*, Lahore, 1998.

——, *State of Human Rights in 1998*, Lahore, 1999.

Kapur, Ashok, 'Western Biases', *Bulletin of the Atomic Sciences* 51:1, January/February 1995, available on www.bullatomsci.org/issues/1995/jf95/jf95/Kapur.html.

Khan, Munir Ahmed, 'Nuclearisation of South Asia and its Regional and Global Implications', *Institute of Regional Studies*, Islamabad, 1998.

Musharraf, Pervez, *Address to the Nation, 12 October 1999*, available on http://news.bbc.co.uk/hi/english/world/monitoring/newsid_473000/473175.stm.

——, *Address to the Nation, 17 October 1999*, available on www.pak.gov.pk/public/president-address-19-09-01.htm.

——, '12 January 2002, Speech Highlights', available on http://news.bbc.co.uk/hi/english/world/south_asia/newsid_1757000/1757251.stm.

Reform of Tax Administration in Pakistan, *Report on the Task Forces on Reform of Tax Administration*, 21 April 2001.

Siddiqi, Brigadier (Retd.) Abdul Rahman, 'Army and Islam: An Appraisal', *Defence Journal* 21, May–June 1996, 3–11.

United Nations Development Programme, *Human Development Report 2001*, Oxford University Press, New York, 2001.

World Military Expenditures and Arms Transfers 1995–1997, US Arms Control and Disarmament Agency, Washington, 1996–1998, available on www.state.gov/www/global/arms/98_amiextoc.html and www.state.gov/www/global/arms/99_amiextoc.html.

Zaman, Muhammad Qasim, 'Sectarianism in Pakistan: The Radicalisation of Shi'-e- and Sunni Identities', *Modern Asian Studies* 32: 3, 1998, 689–716.

Books

Ahmad, Lt. Colonel Syed Iqbal, *Balochistan: Its Strategic Importance*, Royal Book Company, Karachi, 1992.

Ahmed, Akbar S., *Jinnah, Pakistan and Islamic Identity: The Search for Saladin*, Routledge, London, 1997.

——, 'Tribes, Regional Pressures, and Nationhood', pp. 139–55 in Victoria Schofield (ed.), *Old Roads and New Highways: Fifty Years of Pakistan*, Oxford University Press, Karachi, 1997.

Ahmed, Feroz, *Ethnicity and Politics in Pakistan*, Oxford University Press, Karachi, 1999.

Akbar, M. K., *Kargil: Cross Border Terrorism,* Mittal Publications, Delhi, 1999.

Akhund, Iqbal *Trial and Error: The Advent and Eclipse of Benazir Bhutto*, Oxford University Press, Karachi, 2000.

Ali, Chaudri Muhammad, *The Emergence of Pakistan*, Research Society of Pakistan, Lahore, 10th impression, 1998.

Ali, Hamid, *Martial Law Orders and Regulations*, The Ideal Publishers, Karachi, 1980.

Ali, Tariq, *Can Pakistan Survive? The Death of a State*, Penguin, Harmondsworth, 1983.

Amin, Tahir, *Ethno-National Movements of Pakistan*, Institute of Policy Studies, Islamabad, 1993.

Aziz, K. K., *The Murder of History: A Critique of History Textbooks Used in Pakistan*, Vanguard, Lahore, 1993.

——, *The Making of Pakistan: A Study in Nationalism*, Sang-e-Meel Publications, Lahore, 1998.

Bahl, Major General Y. (ed.), *Kargil Blunder: Pakistan's Plight, India's Victory*, Manas Publications, Delhi, 2000.

Baxter, Craig and Kennedy, Charles H. (eds), *Pakistan 2000*, Oxford University Press, Karachi.

Bose, Sumantra, *The Challenge in Kashmir: Democracy, Self-Determination and a Just Peace*, Sage, New Delhi, 1997.

Bhutto, Zulfikar Ali, *The Myth of Independence*, Classic, Lahore, 1995.

——, *If I am Assassinated . . .*, Classic, Lahore, n.d.

Callard, Keith, *Pakistan: A Political Study*, George Allen & Unwin, Oxford, 1957.

Chaudhry, Sardar Muhammad, *The Ultimate Crime: Eyewitness to Power Games*, Qaumi Publishers, Lahore, 1999.

Choudhury, G. W., *The Last Days of United Pakistan*, Oxford University Press, Karachi, 1993.

Cloughley, Brian, *A History of the Pakistan Army: Wars and Insurrections*, Oxford University Press, Karachi, 2000.

Cohen, Stephen, *The Pakistan Army*, Oxford University Press, Karachi, 1998.

Collins, Larry and Lapierre, Dominique, *Freedom at Midnight*, HarperCollins, London, 1997.

Dil, Anwar and Dil, Afia, *Bengali Language Movement to Bangladesh*, Ferozons, Lahore, 2000.

Duncan, Emma, *Breaking the Curfew: A Political Journey through Pakistan*, Arrow, London, 1989.

Durrani, Tehmina, *My Feudal Lord*, Corgi, London, 1994.

Embree, Ainslie T., *Pakistan's Western Borderlands*, Vikas, Delhi, 1985.

Feldman, Herbert, *The End and the Beginning, Pakistan 1969–1971*, Oxford University Press, Karachi, 1976.

French, Patrick, *Liberty or Death: India's Journey to Independence and Division*, HarperCollins, London, 1997.

Gjelstad, Jorn and Njolstad, Olav (eds), *Nuclear Rivalry and International Order*, Sage, London, 1996.

Hamid, Major General S. Shahid, *Early Years of Pakistan*, Ferozons, Lahore, 1993.

Harrison, Selig S., *In Afghanistan's Shadow: Baluch Nationalism and Soviet Temptations*, Carnegie Endowment for International Peace, New York, 1981.

Hoodbhoy, Pervez, (ed.), *Education and the State: Fifty Years of Pakistan*, Oxford University Press, Karachi, 1998.

Huntingdon, Samuel P., *The Clash of Civilisations and the Remaking of World Order*, Viking, India, 1996.

Hussain, Ijaz, *Kashmir Dispute: An International Law Perspective*, Quaid i Azam University, Rawalpindi, 1998.

Hussain, S. Shabbir and Kamran, Mujahid (eds), *Dr A. Q. Khan on Science and Education*, Sang-e-Meel Publications, Lahore, 1997.

Iqbal, Afzal, *The Islamisation of Pakistan*, Vanguard, Lahore, 1986.

Jacob, Lt. General J. F. R., *Surrender at Dacca: Birth of a Nation*, Manohar Publishers, Delhi, 1997.

Jalalzai, Musa Khan, *Sectarianism in Pakistan*, A. H. Publishers, Lahore, 1992.

Jha, Prem Shankar, *Kashmir 1947*, Oxford India Paperbacks, OUP, Delhi, 1998.

Khan, Hamid, *Constitutional and Political History of Pakistan*, Oxford University Press, Oxford, 2001.

Khan, Lt. General Jahan Dad, *Pakistan: Leadership Challenges*, Oxford University Press, Karachi, 1999.

Khan, Mohammad, Asghar, *Generals in Politics: Pakistan 1958–1982*, Vikas, Delhi, 1983.

Khan, Mohammad Ayub, *Friends Not Masters: A Political Autobiography*, Oxford University Press, Karachi, 1967.

Khan, Roedad, *Pakistan: A Dream Gone Sour*, Oxford University Press, Karachi, 1998.

—— (ed.), *The American Papers: Secret and Confidential. India–Pakistan–Bangladesh Documents, 1965–1973*, Oxford University Press, Karachi, 1999.

Khan, Brigadier (Retd.) Z. A., *The Way it Was*, Ahbab, Karachi, 1998.

Kissinger, Henry, *The White House Years*, Weidenfeld and Nicolson and Michael Joseph, London, 1979.

Kurin, Richard, 'A View from the Countryside', pp. 115–27 in Anita M. Weiss (ed.), *Islamic Reassertion in Pakistan*, Vanguard, Lahore, 1987.

Lamb, Alistair, *Kashmir: A Disputed Legacy 1846–1990*, Oxford University Press, Karachi, 1992.

Lamb, Christina, *Waiting for Allah: Pakistan's Struggle for Democracy*, Viking, Delhi, 1991.

Malik, Iftikhar H., *State and Civil Society in Pakistan*, Macmillan, Basingstoke, 1997.

Malik, Brigadier S. K., *The Quranic Concept of War*, Wajidalis, Lahore, 1979.

Malik, Zahid, *Dr A. Q. Khan and The Islamic Bomb*, Hurmat Publications, Islamabad, 1992.

Matinuddin, Kamal, *The Nuclearisation of South Asia*, Oxford University Press, Karachi, 2002.

Mazari, Sherbaz Khan, *A Journey to Disillusionment*, Oxford University Press, Karachi, 2000.

The Military Balance, 2000–2001, International Institute of Strategic Studies, Oxford University Press, London, 2000.

Nasr, Seyyed Vali Reza, 'State Society and the Crisis of National Identity', pp. 103–30 in Rasul Bakhsh Rais (ed.), *State Society and Democratic Change in Pakistan*, Oxford University Press, Karachi, 1997.

Nayyar, A. H., 'Madrasa Education', pp. 215–50 in Pervez Hoodbhoy (ed.), *Education and the State: Fifty Years of Pakistan*, Oxford University Press, Karachi, 1998.

Niazi, Lt. General A. A. K., *The Betrayal of East Pakistan*, Oxford Pakistan Paperbacks, Karachi, 1999.

Palit, Major General D. K. and Namboodiri, P. K. S., *Pakistan's Islamic Bomb*, Vikas, Delhi, 1979.

Perkovich, George, *India's Nuclear Bomb: The Impact on Global Proliferation*, University of California Press, 1999.

Rabbani, Mian Ata, *I Was the Quaid's ADC*, Oxford University Press, Karachi, 1996.

Rahman, Khalid et al. (eds), *Jama'at-e-Islami and National and International Politics*, volume 2, Bookmakers, Islamabad, 1999.

Rahman, Lt. General M. Attiqur, *Our Defence Cause*, White Lion Publishers, London, 1976.

——, *Back to the Pavilion*, Ardeshir Cowasjee, Karachi, 1989.

Rahman, Tariq, *Language and Politics in Pakistan,* Oxford University Press, Karachi, 1996.

Rais, Rasul Bakhsh (ed.) *State Society and Democratic Change in Pakistan*, Oxford University Press, Karachi, 1997.

Raza, Rafi (ed.), *Pakistan in Perspective 1947–1997,* Oxford University Press, Karachi, 1997.

Rehman, Shahid ur, *Who Owns Pakistan?*, Mr Books, Islamabad, 1998.

——, *Long Road to Chagai: Untold Story of Pakistan's Nuclear Quest*, Print Wise Publications, Islamabad, 1999.

Riza, Major General (Retd.) Shaukat, *The Pakistan Army War 1965*, Services Book Club, Lahore, 1984.

——, *The Pakistan Army 1966–1971*, Army Education Press, Lahore, 1990.

Rizvi, Hasan-Askari, *The Military and Politics in Pakistan: 1947–1986*, Progressive Publishers, Lahore, 1987.

Salik, Siddiq, *Witness to Surrender*, Oxford University Press, Karachi, 1977.

Schofield, Victoria, *Kashmir in Conflict: India, Pakistan and the Unfinished Conflict*, I. B. Tauris, London, 2000.

—— (ed.), *Old Roads and New Highways: Fifty Years of Pakistan,* Oxford University Press, Karachi, 1997.

Sharma, Rajeev, *Pak Proxy War: A Story of ISI, Bin Laden and Kargil*, Kaveri Books, Delhi, 1999.

Singh, Karan, *Autobiography*, Oxford India Paperbacks, Oxford University Press, Delhi, 1994.

Sisson, Richard and Rose, Leo E., *War and Secession: Pakistan, India and the*

Creation of Bangladesh, Oxford University Press, Karachi, 1990.

Spector, Leonard S. with Smith, Jacqueline, *Nuclear Ambitions: The Spread of Nuclear Weapons 1989–1990,* Farda Publishing Company, Karachi, 1992.

Syed G. M., *A Case for Sindu Desh,* Sorath Publication, Bombay, 1985.

Talbot, Ian, *Pakistan: A Modern History,* Vanguard Books, Lahore, 1999.

Uzair, Mohammad, 'Foreign Aid and Indebtedness in Pakistan', pp. 367–73 in Mehrunnisa Ali (ed.), *Readings in Pakistan Foreign Policy 1971–1998,* Oxford University Press, Karachi, 2001.

Weiss, Anita M. (ed.), *Islamic Reassertion in Pakistan,* Vanguard, Lahore, 1987.

—— and Gilani, S. Zulfiqar (eds), *Power and Civil Society in Pakistan,* Oxford University Press, Karachi, 2001.

Weissman, Steve and Krosney, Herbert, *The Islamic Bomb: The Nuclear Threat to Israel and the Middle East,* Times Books, New York, 1983, 2nd edition.

Wilder, Andrew R., *The Pakistani Voter: Electoral Politics and Voting Behaviour in the Punjab,* Oxford University Press, Karachi, 1999.

Wolpert, Stanley, *Jinnah of Pakistan,* Oxford University Press, New York, 1984.

——, *Zulfi Bhutto of Pakistan: His Life and Times,* Oxford University Press, New York, 1993.

Zaheer, Hasan, *The Separation of East Pakistan: The Rise and Realization of Bengali Muslim Nationalism,* Oxford University Press, Karachi, 1995.

——, *The Rawalpindi Conspiracy 1951,* Oxford University Press, Karachi, 1998.

Zaidi, S. Akbar, *Issues in Pakistan's Economy,* Oxford University Press, Karachi, 2000.

Ziring, Lawrence, *Pakistan in the Twentieth Century: A Political History,* Oxford University Press, Karachi, 1998.

Index

OTHER YEARLING BOOKS YOU WILL ENJOY:

ONE OF THE THIRD GRADE THONKERS, *Phyllis Reynolds Naylor*
NIGHT CRY, *Phyllis Reynolds Naylor*
WITCH'S SISTER, *Phyllis Reynolds Naylor*
WITCH WATER, *Phyllis Reynolds Naylor*
THE WITCH HERSELF, *Phyllis Reynolds Naylor*
THE AGONY OF ALICE, *Phyllis Reynolds Naylor*
HOW TO EAT FRIED WORMS, *Thomas Rockwell*
HOW TO FIGHT A GIRL, *Thomas Rockwell*
CHOCOLATE FEVER, *Robert Kimmel Smith*
THE WAR WITH GRANDPA, *Robert Kimmel Smith*

YEARLING BOOKS/YOUNG YEARLINGS/YEARLING CLASSICS are
designed especially to entertain and enlighten young people.
Patricia Reilly Giff, consultant to this series, received her bache-
lor's degree from Marymount College and a master's degree in
history from St. John's University. She holds a Professional
Diploma in Reading and a Doctorate of Humane Letters from
Hofstra

many

reader